EGYPT
in England

Chris Elliott

EGYPT

in England

Chris Elliott

ENGLISH HERITAGE

Published by English Heritage, The Engine House, Fire Fly Avenue, Swindon SN2 2EH
www.english-heritage.org.uk
English Heritage is the Government's lead body for the historic environment.

The views expressed in this book are those of the author and not necessarily those of English Heritage.

First published 2012

ISBN 978 1 84802 088 7

Product code 51617

British Library Cataloguing in Publication data
A CIP catalogue record for this book is available from the British Library.

For more information about English Heritage Archive, contact Archives Research Services, The Engine House, Fire Fly Avenue, Swindon SN2 2EH; telephone (01793) 414600.

Brought to publication by René Rodgers and Jess Ward, Publishing, English Heritage.

Typeset in Gill Sans Light 9.5pt

Edited by Susan Kelleher
Indexed by Ann Hudson
Hieroglyphic typesetting by Mark Rudolph
Illustrations by Judith Dobie
Page layout by Andrea Rollinson, Ledgard Jepson Ltd

Printed in UK by Butler Tanner and Dennis.

Frontispiece
A riot of coloured stucco and Coade stone, the façade of the Egyptian House in Penzance, originally created to house a geological museum and specimen shop, shows Egyptian style architecture in England at its most exuberant. Elements of an Ancient Egyptian temple entrance are mixed with Classical decorations and geometric glazing bars, with the royal arms of William IV above, and the whole creation topped off with a most un-Egyptian eagle on a pile of rocks.
[DP114986]

Contents

For Sally, for everything; for Jack and Suzy, who have waited a long time to see this; and also for the Excellent Scribe, Vivien Raisman, who taught me to hear what the Ancient Egyptians had to say.

Introduction

It is a long way from Egypt to England and a long time since the reigns of the pharaohs, but the influence of Ancient Egypt on British culture has been both longer lasting and more widespread than perhaps most people realise. Our alphabet itself was inherited from the Romans and by them from the Greeks, but the model for the Greek alphabet was likely to have been one used by the Phoenicians and other cultures in the Middle East, which borrowed and adapted its characters from Ancient Egyptian hieroglyphs. Christianity was born outside Egypt but the Bible as we know it took shape in Alexandria, and for millions of Christians Egypt was the land of oppression for the Israelites but also of refuge for the Holy Family. In the Anglo-Saxon ship burial at Sutton Hoo were found bronze bowls known as 'Coptic bowls', probably imported from Alexandria, and from the Middle Ages onwards pilgrims sought out sites in Egypt connected with the Holy Family and Saints Mark and Catherine. Whether or not the Black Land of the Ancient Egyptians, Kemet, actually gave its name through Arabic to the philosophy and practice of alchemy, this became widely believed, and only enhanced an ancient reputation of Egypt as a land of esoteric wisdom. Cargoes of mummies were brought back to England by traders to be ground into medicine by apothecaries (Fig 1), and Renaissance scholars sought to penetrate the mysteries behind the teachings attributed to the 'Thrice-Great Hermes', Hermes Trismegistus, identified with the Egyptian god Thoth and thought by them to be a contemporary of Moses.

As the Renaissance gave way to the Enlightenment, a handful of travellers began to bring back more accurate accounts of the remains of Ancient Egypt, and the French invasion of 1798 opened the country and its history to the world again. The Egyptian style was the height of fashion in Regency England and Napoleonic France (Fig 2), and in 1805 the French Egyptologist Vivant Denon conceived a great Sèvres dinner service modelled on the temples of Ancient Egypt. By 1818, however, when the service originally intended for the Empress Josephine was given by Louis XVIII to the Duke of Wellington, there was concern that it might no longer be fashionable.

Fig 1
Mummification was practised in Egypt until Roman times, when this mummy was produced, and in Europe powdered mummy was believed for hundreds of years to have almost miraculous medical properties.
[© Trustees of the British Museum]

Even when the Egyptian style became, as it were, 'so last dynasty' for the furniture and interiors of the rich, the general public still craved things Egyptian. The middle and professional classes in particular could afford to patronise panoramas showing the ruins of Karnak or a voyage along the Nile (Fig 3), and increasing numbers of them could afford to go there themselves, thanks to the pioneers of mass tourism, Messrs Cook and Messrs Gaze. Public unrollings of mummies took place in London and in provincial towns and cities, and great collections of Egyptian antiquities were acquired by public museums.

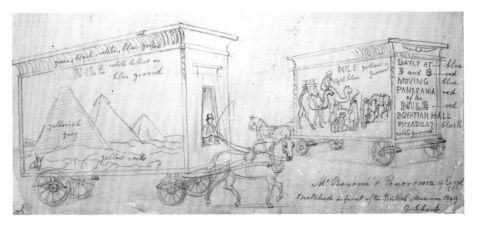

Buildings and monuments in the Egyptian style were features of the new city cemeteries in particular. Between 1832 and 1847 eight joint stock cemetery companies were set up, seven of them in London, and two of the new garden cemeteries created by them, Highgate and Abney Park, had Egyptian-style buildings. Others, particularly Kensal Green, had elaborate monuments modelled on pharaonic architecture. Although a comparatively rare style, they continued to be built into the early 20th century, with the Illingworth mausoleum in Bradford being erected in 1907 and the Gordon mausoleum in Putney Vale in 1910.

Long after the Hermetic scholars of the Renaissance, Egypt still represented wisdom and mystery for both Freemasons and occultists, and the public were (and for that matter still are) obligingly receptive to journalistic suggestions of ancient curses. In the 20th century the discovery of the almost intact tomb of Tutankhamun gave the world some of its most iconic images of Ancient Egypt, and later its first example of the museum exhibition as cultural blockbuster when a selection of its treasures visited London.

The most obvious and enduring sign of our fascination with Ancient Egypt is the buildings and monuments that it has inspired, and this book examines Ancient Egypt as a cultural theme in British society through its use in buildings and interiors. You can no longer buy powdered mummy from the apothecary, or wonder whether it was a component of the Mummy Brown oil paint which bore its name, but the instantly recognisable forms of Egyptian architecture can still be seen around England.

When Alexander the Great's general Ptolemy and his descendants ruled Egypt, they not only built temples in the style of the pharaohs but moved their statues, sphinxes and obelisks to their new capital on the coast at Alexandria. The Romans, who succeeded them, adopted Egypt's gods and goddesses, and continued to build and decorate temples in Egypt itself. They also spread the Egyptian style throughout the Roman Empire, importing and imitating Egyptian architecture and ornament. They decorated their homes with mosaics of Egypt and Egyptian artefacts. Emperors brought obelisks to Rome, and sphinxes and statues to the city and to sites such as Hadrian's villa at Tivoli. Centuries later, when these were unearthed again, they were to inspire the imagination of popes, priests, scholars and artists. Through the legacy of the Classical world, Europe became aware of the simple forms and pure powerful geometry of the obelisk and pyramid, and of the hybrid sphinx. Some elements of Egyptian temples were present in Roman architecture, but it was the rediscovery of Ancient Egypt in the early 19th century that was most responsible for introducing architects to the distinctive elements of sloping, or battered, walls and entrance pylons, overhanging cavetto cornices, rounded-edge mouldings, and columns inspired by lotus and papyrus plants and palm trees.

Of all the elements of Ancient Egyptian architecture only the obelisk has really become established outdoors in England – but they usually appear singly, rather than in pairs flanking a temple entrance as they would have been in Ancient Egypt. They also, apart from two genuine exceptions, the Bankes Obelisk at Kingston Lacy and Cleopatra's Needle on the Victoria Embankment, have no hieroglyphic inscriptions, unlike the obelisks of Ancient Egypt. Despite several ambitious designs for huge pyramidal monuments, the few pyramids that were built were relatively modest private funerary memorials or garden architecture. But just as the architecture of medieval cathedrals was borrowed for railway stations, cemeteries and public libraries, so the Egyptian style, almost exclusively confined in its own culture to religious and funerary buildings, has lent itself to some unlikely applications. Among those that survive are not only cemetery buildings and monuments, and two religious buildings (a church and a synagogue), but also mills and factories, shops, pumping stations, private residences, a former museum and library, offices, a Masonic temple, a cinema and even a garden.

An exotic import, the Egyptian style has been seen both positively and negatively. To its supporters, it was massive, clean, and imposing, and could be a reminder of a civilisation that prefigured or prophesied Christianity, which they believed inspired the architecture of Greece and which to the enlightened symbolised moral principles and virtues, even occult wisdom. Some saw it as evocative of the decline and fall of a great civilisation, and a sort of memento mori reminding us that one day our civilisation too might be one with Ancient Egypt, and known only by its remains. To those who opposed it, it was not only unsuited to the climate and landscape of England, but was the architecture of a pagan culture obsessed with death, associated with pharaonic tyranny, and having no place in a Christian and increasingly democratic society. More than 2,000 years separate the building of the Great Pyramid from the construction of the Temple of Horus at Edfu; however, because almost as much time again had passed before the rediscovery of Ancient Egypt by Europe in the 19th century, its architecture was often seen as representative of a single ancient and unchanging culture, rather than the product of a complex and evolving one. The pyramid, in particular, has symbolised a monumental endurance which transcends cultures, and inspired the possibly apocryphal Arab saying that, 'Men fear Time, but Time fears the Pyramids.'

For over 200 years we have been constructing buildings and monuments in England inspired by Ancient Egypt, and though there have never been many, the process still continues. The buildings and interiors covered in this book have been selected because there is still something there that can be seen, and in most cases they are accessible to the public. The aim of the book is not simply to tell their story, but to inspire its readers to visit them. They represent a remarkable range of forms and functions, and are located as far north as Lancashire, as far south as Sussex, as far east as Norfolk, and as far west as Cornwall. Each says something about how we view the civilisation of the pharaohs, and is also the outward and visible sign of how their influence has reached down to us over the centuries as part of the rich mix that makes our culture what it is today. There is, in that sense, a little bit of Egypt in all of us.

How to use this book

Egypt in England is divided into two parts. The first, 'Understanding Egypt in England', is a series of seven topic essays giving the background to the sites described in the rest of the book. The second, 'Finding Egypt in England', describes sites throughout the country where surviving architecture and interiors inspired by Ancient Egypt can be found.

It can be read cover to cover but is really intended to allow readers to follow their own path. The topic essays can be read first to prepare for later site visits, the sites can be visited first and the topic essays used later to put them into context, or individual themes pursued, such as cemeteries or Freemasonry, using both sections. The topic essays in Understanding Egypt in England have cross-references to key sites, where more detail can be found on specific aspects of a particular subject. Finding Egypt in England is split into eight sections, each covering a geographic region. At the start of each section you will find an overview of the sites in that region and then the sites are listed alphabetically. No information has been included on opening times, prices etc where these apply, or on public transport links, as these are liable to change, and are better checked online before any visit. A note at the end of each site entry indicates where applicable whether it is open to the public.

Egypt in England was conceived as an 'accessible academic' title, that is one which can be read by a lay audience, but which has enough depth to be useful to academics in a range of subject areas. Such a beast runs the risk of being a hybrid that satisfies no one, and some compromises have had to be made. For the sake of readability, full citations have not been given, but selected references have been included. The bibliography is a list of works consulted during research for the book, including those cited in the text, allowing access to primary and secondary sources, but it can also be used as a guide to further reading on broad topics such as Ancient Egyptian architecture and deities. Even those with a background in architectural history may not be familiar with the terms used to describe Ancient Egyptian buildings, and for those who do not know their architrave from their entablature, the architectural glossary can be consulted in moments of crisis. The glossary of gods and goddesses does the same for those Ancient Egyptian deities mentioned in the text. Finally, the index is there to allow the text to be searched for specific references.

A note on prices and measurements

It is notoriously difficult to make comparisons between prices in different eras. Not only have wages and prices changed, but the relative values of many things have been drastically altered by mass production. For simplicity, I have used the Bank of England's price comparison tables to give some idea of what given prices would be worth in today's terms. This is not perfect, but at least has the virtue of being consistent.

I have used imperial rather than metric measurements for sites that were built before metrification and this conversion table will help readers unfamiliar with imperial units:

1 ft   = 304.8mm
1 yard = 0.914m
1 mile = 1.6km
1 acre = 0.4 hectares

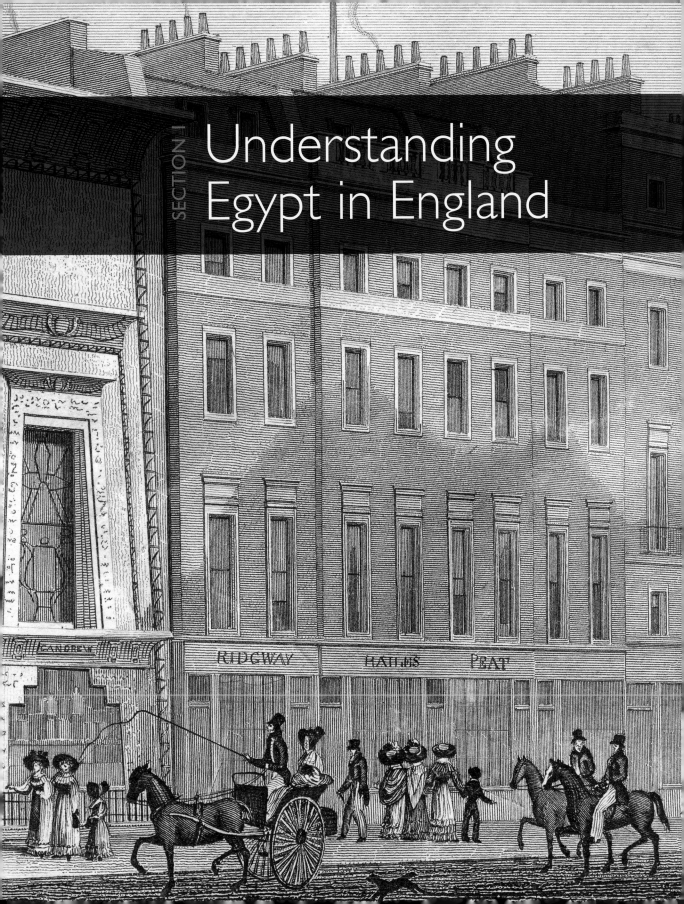

Understanding Egypt in England

Architecture: Imhotep in England

For centuries, while the civilisation of Ancient Egypt faded into obscurity, its scripts a mystery and much of the country itself largely inaccessible to European travellers, its most enduring legacy was its architecture – but an architecture that had been transplanted into other lands. Its obelisks stood as trophies in the cities of the Roman Empire, and Egyptian religion, particularly the worship of the goddess Isis (Fig 4), had spread throughout the Roman world, and with it went the distinctive imagery and symbols of the various deities. Even at the edges of the empire, in London, there was a temple of Isis. Wealthy Roman citizens decorated their houses and villas with Egyptian murals and mosaics, and adorned them with Egyptian artefacts. Much of this was lost and buried with the fall of the Roman Empire, until the rediscovery of Classical civilisation in the Renaissance, and even the great obelisks, with their by then meaningless inscriptions, fell and were buried. And yet, more than 2,000 years after the last native Egyptian pharaoh, we find cemeteries, cinemas, houses and even a DIY supermarket being built in the Ancient Egyptian style in a land more than 2,000 miles from Egypt. It has been a long and far from straightforward journey to England for this distinctive and exotic architecture, which stubbornly survived the death of the civilisation that produced it and has gone on to inspire new buildings to this day.

Fig 4
Isis showing the hieroglyph which names her on her head, and carrying an *ankh*, the hieroglyph for life.

Ancient Egypt – the legacy of Imhotep

What many people think of as Ancient Egyptian architecture is really its religious and funerary buildings. These were built of stone and have survived, as have the rock-cut tombs of the social elite, while domestic buildings, even those of royalty and the rich, were constructed of mud brick. Far less is left of them and many early Egyptologists paid them little attention. The Step Pyramid of Djoser (Fig 5) built around 4,600 years ago, was the first major architectural construction in stone – its design and the invention of building in dressed stone itself credited to Imhotep, vizier to the pharaoh Djoser.[1]

Fig 5
The Step Pyramid at
Saqqara, built around
2650 BC for the pharaoh
Djoser, and the first
large-scale building in
stone in Egypt. Centuries
later its architect, Imhotep,
was deified, and credited
as the inventor of both
architecture and medicine.
[© Chris Elliott]

The complex of ritual structures around the Step Pyramid is also important because they
reproduced in stone features of earlier architecture in natural materials, such as roofing
made from split palm trunks.[2] Archaic structures had been made from reeds, reed matting,
mud and palm trunks, with sides which sloped inwards, flat roofs and small window openings.
Bundles of reeds or other plant stems were tied together to provide reinforcement where
necessary. Even when the use of stone for building was developed further, and the size of
rooms no longer reproduced the dimensions of the original archaic structures as they had
in the Step Pyramid complex, many elements of these archaic forms were still preserved
right up until Greek and Roman times. Temples continued to have flat roofs and sloping,
or battered, walls and entrance pylons. The walls were decorated with mouldings that
mimicked bound plant stems and topped with overhanging concave mouldings which would
originally have been the ends of plant stems falling forward.[3] Columns, originally made of
bundled reeds or palm fronds lashed together, continued to have plant forms even when
made entirely of stone – some representing archaic original structures and some with
more symbolic significance. As well as columns representing bundled papyrus stems, there
were forms with capitals representing papyrus in bud and in flower, palm branches lashed
together, the closed flower of the lotus and elaborate composite capitals combining different
plant forms, which may have represented floral offerings. Some columns had simple square
sections, and there were also polygonal forms, which may have influenced Greek architecture
and are sometimes referred to as Proto-Doric. There were also columns with engaged
statues representing Osiris, or the pharaoh as Osiris, and ones whose four-sided capitals
were decorated with images of the cow-eared goddess Hathor.[4]

The architecture of temples and tombs was not only highly conservative, but highly symbolic. Stone was used because of its permanence, and although there were some changes over time and as existing temples were rebuilt and extended, the classic form of the Egyptian temple represented a microcosm of the Egyptian cosmos. It normally faced east and west, the directions of the rising and setting sun, and the various sections of it followed one another along this line. From the New Kingdom onwards, their entrances were composed of a rectangular pylon of twin towers with battered or sloping sides and an entrance between them. The shape of this entrance echoed the shape of a hieroglyph representing the sun rising between mountains, and because of the orientation of most temples would have actually framed the sun at certain times. Beyond the entrance pylon there were two courtyards with columns, an outer peristyle and an inner hypostyle court. From the latter the floor level rose through a series of rooms to an inner sanctuary. The sanctuary, as the highest point, represented the primal mound of creation, the *sep tepy* or 'First Time'. The hypostyle court, with densely clustered rows of columns, symbolised the marshes and papyrus swamps surrounding the mound, and as the temple went back towards the sanctuary light open areas were replaced with smaller and darker areas reflecting the increasingly sacred nature of the space. The walls, inside and out, were covered with relief carvings and hieroglyphic texts, and these changed as well, with depictions of the pharaoh smiting the enemies of Egypt on the outer public areas and ones showing his interaction with the gods on the interior, private, areas. Flanking the entrances between the towers of pylons in larger temples were twin obelisks carved with dedicatory texts glorifying the pharaoh and his devotion to the gods, and in niches on the pylons were wooden flagpoles with cloth streamers hanging from them which symbolised divine protection (Fig 6). On processional ways up to and between temples, particularly those of Karnak and Luxor, were avenues of sphinxes representing the divine power of the pharaoh, sometimes human-headed, sometimes with the heads of rams or hawks, linking them to the gods Amun and Horus (Fig 7). Inside the temples, ceilings were decorated with stars and zodiacal designs to represent the heavens and outside the whole temple was surrounded by massive mud-brick walls, whose courses undulated

Fig 6
A 19th-century artist's reconstruction of part of an Ancient Egyptian temple showing the flagpoles and streamers which used to decorate their pylons.
[Courtesy of Museum Books]

to mimic the waters surrounding the primal mound and which created a sacred precinct separate from the secular outside world.

Ancestor worship was a key part of Ancient Egyptian religion and the most iconic of Egyptian buildings, the pyramids, were built as royal tombs. After the great era of pyramid building in the reigns of the early pharaohs, from the 3rd to the 5th Dynasty (around 2686 BC until 2181 BC), which produced the Pyramids of Giza (Fig 8), they continued to be built, although on a reduced scale and with inferior construction techniques, until the 17th Dynasty which ended around 1570 BC. The so-called Pyramid Texts carved into the walls of chambers in 5th- and 6th-Dynasty pyramids are the earliest known religious writings. From the first two reigns of the 17th Dynasty, royal burials were made in rock-cut tombs in the Valley of the Kings at Thebes until the seat of power shifted north to the Delta – although small brick pyramids continued to be used as part of private tombs, and small, steeply sloped pyramids were revived for royal burials by Nubian rulers in the 25th Dynasty nearly 1,000 years later. Like temples, which included mortuary temples dedicated to the cult of the deified dead ruler, the architecture of tombs was heavily symbolic. The royal tombs of the Valley of the Kings were lined with religious scenes and texts designed to ensure the successful and continued resurrection of the dead monarch. Pyramids and obelisks both had solar symbolism and obelisks in particular were topped with sheets of electrum, a naturally occurring alloy of gold and silver, to emphasise this. Until the decipherment of hieroglyphs, the texts carved on and in Ancient Egyptian buildings, which provided valuable information on their religious function, could not be read. When the forms of pyramids and obelisks were revived centuries later, they were therefore largely divorced from their symbolic function and their original role in Ancient Egyptian society.

Fig 7
Cult images of the gods were worshipped in temples. This modern representation of one of the few to survive shows Horus in hawk form, with a crown of twin feathers, and a protective cobra.

Fig 8
From Roman times to our own, travellers to Egypt have been fascinated by the Great Pyramid of Khufu at Giza, better known by the Greek form of his name as Cheops. The pyramid is shown here during the former annual flooding of the Nile. [AL0178/024/01]

During its long history, Ancient Egypt was invaded and conquered on a number of occasions, particularly in its latter stages when it was ruled by dynasties of Libyan and Nubian origin, and invaded twice by the Assyrians, before becoming part of the Persian empire. Despite this, its religion and architecture survived, preserving their classic forms, and before the Persian invasion there had been a revival, under the native Saite dynasty, of art forms from hundreds of years before in the Old and Middle Kingdoms.[5] In 332 BC Alexander the Great conquered Egypt and founded the city of Alexandria. After his death when his empire was divided between his generals, one of them, Ptolemy, became ruler of Egypt and founded the dynasty that bore his name for around three hundred years, until the conquest of Egypt by the Romans. Although they were of Macedonian Greek origin and had their capital in the new city of Alexandria, the Ptolemies observed the forms of Egyptian kingship to help legitimise their rule, and supported the native religion and its temples.

Many of the best preserved temples in Upper Egypt, such as Dendera, Esna, Edfu, Kom Ombo and Philae, although constructed on established sites of worship, were largely built in the Graeco-Roman period.[6] On them, Ptolemaic rulers (and later Roman) were depicted as pharaohs, carrying out the traditional rituals of Egyptian kingship. The design of temples evolved, with certain elements such as screen walls and decorated composite capitals being used more frequently, and becoming typical of temples of this era.[7] Large numbers of new hieroglyphs were introduced into inscriptions, as well as cryptic or sportive writings, which added to their complexity, and reflected the degree to which the script was now confined to religious and monumental use.[8] Elsewhere, particularly in Alexandria, Greek and Egyptian cultures influenced each other, with the creation of the hybrid deity Serapis and the introduction of new architectural forms and practices. These included the erection of obelisks singly, rather than in pairs, a practice continued by the Romans, and the introduction of the curved segmental pediment,[9] which was later used by the Romans in temples associated with the worship of Egyptian deities, particularly Isis.

In 30 BC, after the defeat and death of Anthony and Cleopatra, Egypt became a Roman province. Under the first two emperors to rule it, Augustus and Tiberius, new temples were built, and existing ones added to and decorated, and they and the emperors who succeeded them were depicted on the temples, like the Ptolemies, as Egyptian pharaohs. Although later Roman emperors including Claudius, Trajan and Hadrian continued to add to and decorate temples, new building in the traditional Egyptian style declined and had ceased by the mid 3rd century AD.[10] Both native Egyptian rulers and the Ptolemies had moved monuments to new sites within Egypt, and this process continued under Augustus, but he and his successors began to send monuments, particularly obelisks, abroad and especially to Rome.[11] There, genuine Egyptian obelisks were supplemented by others completed in Rome, two of which had hieroglyphic inscriptions added.[12] Several obelisks were situated in or near the great temple of Isis in Rome, the Iseum Campense, whose architecture, like that of other temples devoted to the cults of Egyptian deities, seems to have been perceived by the Romans as Egyptian without using the elements normally associated with Egyptian temples except in decorative features. In particular, the segmental pediment, introduced by the Ptolemies, seems to have been associated with the goddess Isis.[13] The popularity of Egyptian cults in the Roman empire owed much to their support by a number of emperors, including Caligula, Vespasian, Titus, Domitian and Hadrian, whose villa complex at Tivoli (the Villa Adriana) had an area evoking the Egyptian port of Canopus and its temple of Isis and Serapis.[14]

For those Romans that could afford them, genuine Egyptian antiquities were probably preferred, but copies of them, of varying quality and faithfulness to their originals, were also made by Roman craftsmen, or by Egyptian craftsmen working outside Egypt, and original works such as mosaics of Nile scenes were created to evoke an Egyptian setting.[15]

From the granaries of Joseph to the obelisks of the popes

Because of its biblical connections, which included its role as a refuge for the Holy Family and the tradition that the pyramids were built to serve as the granaries of Joseph, Ancient Egypt was still important to Europe during the Middle Ages. Information in a limited number of texts from the Classical and Arabic world was supplemented by the accounts of travellers, traders and pilgrims who had actually visited the country, and occasionally described its monuments.[16] There was a tradition, given authority by the Bible, of Egypt as a land of magicians and occult wisdom, and in the 15th century this underwent a powerful revival after the discovery and translation of a medieval version of 5th-century Graeco-Roman texts on hieroglyphs, the *Hieroglyphica*, often referred to as Horapollo, after its author, a 5th-century scholar living in Alexandria. The texts' original authorship was attributed to the legendary figure of Hermes Trismegistus, believed to be a pagan Egyptian contemporary with Moses himself, and their allegorical and mystical explanations of hieroglyphs were to provide much of the inspiration for the so-called Hermetic tradition. Around the same time as the Horapollo text another manuscript was translated (and later presented to Pope Martin V), containing the writings of the Classical author Ammianus Marcellinus. Scholars became aware that the sacred writings of the Egyptians that Marcellinus referred to were the hieroglyphs on the obelisks of Rome, and that these in turn had come from Egypt. By the beginning of the 15th century, under the Medici popes, Ancient Egyptian lions and sphinxes were being re-erected in Rome and there were plans to do the same with at least one obelisk. Egyptian themes and imagery, albeit often with a Classical influence, were used in decorating papal and private residences. It was not until the end of the 16th century, under Pope Sixtus V, that obelisks began to be excavated, restored, and re-erected – but then they were highly visible, being set up at important locations in the city (Fig 9). However, although this created

Fig 9
Moving the St Peter's or Vatican obelisk in Rome in 1586 from its former site in the Vatican circus to its present site in front of the Basilica of St Peter. This was done at the command of Pope Sixtus V, in whose pontificate several other obelisks were excavated and re-erected.
[© Trustees of the British Museum]

renewed interest in their hieroglyphic texts, the allegorical and mystical interpretation of them by the Hermetic tradition persisted and was to prove a serious impediment to their interpretation for hundreds of years.

Into the Enlightenment – the rediscovery of Egypt

Throughout the 17th and 18th centuries the use of Egyptianising forms continued. As they were unearthed again the genuine Egyptian objects and statuary, and their Roman copies which had been prized by wealthy Romans, were acquired by those Romans' modern counterparts. As early as the end of the 15th century, the site of the Emperor Hadrian's villa at Tivoli, which had many Egyptianising features, had been identified, and from the mid-16th century it had been dug in search of statuary, mosaics and other treasures. In 1740 a now famous statue of the Emperor Hadrian's lover Antinous in Egyptian dress was found there and when restored it became a model for Neoclassical sculpture. Other statues from the villa were also widely copied. European travellers were beginning to explore Egypt, and were bringing back not just the first accurate accounts of the surviving ancient monuments, but also Ancient Egyptian artefacts. Among these travellers were the English mathematician John Greaves, who drew the first accurate cross section of the Great Pyramid, and William Lethieullier and his nephew Pitt Lethieullier, who donated some of the first items in the British Museum's Egyptian collection, including its first mummies.

Although awareness of Ancient Egypt had persisted, however tenuously, throughout the Middle Ages and then with greater strength through the Renaissance and Enlightenment, its culture was seldom experienced directly, but rather through the legacy of the Classical Graeco-Roman world. In England, so-called Egyptian Halls were built in the 18th century, and examples can be found in the Mansion House and St Mary Woolnoth in London, and in the Assembly Rooms at York, but these were inspired by a work on architecture by the Roman author Vitruvius and despite their name have no recognisable Egyptian features.[17] Lord Burlington[18], who designed one of them, the Assembly Rooms at York, also built Chiswick House, whose use of sphinxes and obelisks has been seen as a reference to the Hermetic tradition, and also as linked to Freemasonry, which was influenced by Hermetic philosophy (Fig 10 and see p 65). Sphinxes of this period, however, often confused the main Egyptian form, male and with the royal '*nemes*' headcloth, and the winged female Greek form. Obelisks too were different from their Egyptian originals; despite the fact that the form had become well established in monumental architecture, obelisks in England were without the inscriptions that distinguished their Egyptian originals, and

Fig 10
One of the sphinxes set up near the entrance of Chiswick House. They have been interpreted as its symbolic guardians. Although the sphinx is female, rather than male, it lacks the wings often found on Greek sphinxes, and has an Egyptian headdress. This confusion of types may reflect an inability at the time it was made to distinguish between genuine Egyptian antiquities and Roman copies of them, which were not always accurate.
[DP043047]

were usually erected singly rather than in pairs as was the rule in Ancient Egypt. They were also erected in the Roman fashion on pedestals rather than as the Egyptians did, on low bases.

The first Ancient Egyptian interior in Britain was probably the Billiard Room in Cairness House in Aberdeenshire,[19] originally designed in 1789 for Charles Gordon by James Playfair.[20] It was decorated with hieroglyphs (albeit inaccurate and purely decorative) on the door case, chimneypiece and a frieze. However it was not built until 1793, after Playfair had visited Rome, and then to a revised design suggesting that he had been influenced by what he saw there. The *Caffè degli Inglesi* or 'English Café' in Rome, which as its name suggests was popular with English travellers on the Grand Tour, had been decorated in the Egyptian style by the artist and designer Giovanni Battista Piranesi, and probably inspired Playfair. The wealthy connoisseur Thomas Hope, however, had not only gone to Rome, but actually visited Egypt, first on his extensive Grand Tour which lasted over seven years from 1777 to 1785, and then again in 1797, and brought back a number of antiquities. Hope coined the phrase 'interior decoration' and explicitly set out to influence the taste of the upper sections of society. He remodelled the interior of his house in London at Duchess Street to reflect his views on contemporary design, and the rooms included one in the Egyptian style and a chimneypiece in another room, on which were displayed a number of antiquities, including some from Ancient Egypt. Although many of the architectural elements were still firmly rooted in the Neoclassical tradition, the design of the room, particularly ornaments copied from temples in Thebes and at Dendera, still owed much to his personal experience of Ancient Egyptian monuments.

Then, in 1798, everything changed. Napoleon invaded Egypt with a force that included the 167-strong Commission on the Sciences and Arts, a contingent which as well as civil engineers, surveyors and cartographers, quite remarkably also included artists, scholars and scientists. The Commission was charged with exploring and recording the country, including its ancient remains. Although the expedition ended in military failure, by 1802 the first material from it was being published by Dominique Vivant Denon, one of the Commission's members, in the form of his *Voyages dans la Basse et la Haute Égypte* (*Travels in Upper and Lower Egypt*). Denon's book was not the first such publication. The Dane Frederik Norden had written an account of his Egyptian travels in French in 1755, with an English translation two years later (Fig 11), and in 1792 a volume of 165 engravings taken from his drawings made on the spot was published at a fairly modest price of 2½ guineas. This included depictions of pyramids, obelisks and temples, with

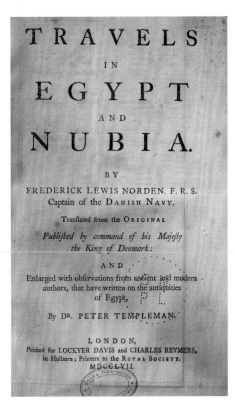

TRAVELS
IN
EGYPT
AND
NUBIA.

BY
FREDERICK LEWIS NORDEN. F. R. S.
Captain of the DANISH NAVY.

Tranſlated from the ORIGINAL

Publiſhed by command of his Majeſty
the King of Denmark:

AND

Enlarged with obſervations from ancient and modern
authors, that have written on the antiquities
of Egypt,

By DR. PETER TEMPLEMAN.

LONDON,
Printed for LOCKYER DAVIS and CHARLES REYMERS,
in Holborn; Printers to the ROYAL SOCIETY.
MDCCLVII.

Fig 11
An early (1757) English translation of a work by the Danish naval captain Frederik Norden, who was sent to explore Egypt by Christian VI in 1738. Norden stayed in Egypt for a year, travelling beyond Aswan, and his book was one of the first detailed and accurate modern accounts of the remains of Ancient Egypt. He was later attached to the Royal Navy, and became a member of the first Egyptian Society while living in London. [Courtesy of Museum Books]

plans and cross sections. Denon's work, however, came at a time when Egypt was becoming increasingly important in the struggles between the European powers as the Ottoman Empire weakened, and it benefited from the widespread public interest in Ancient Egypt inspired by the recent military campaigns in Egypt. The official account of the Commission's work, the *Description de L'Égypte*, did not begin to emerge until 1809 and it took until 1828 for publication of its 24 volumes to be completed. Not only that, but they were huge, in 'elephant folio' size, 28in high and nearly 2ft wide. Denon's work, by contrast, the full version of which had numerous plates showing Ancient Egyptian antiquities including surviving buildings, was quickly available in much more manageable folio size and later reissued in a number of other reduced formats. An English translation was available by 1802, with the folio edition costing 21 guineas, but an unabridged pocket-sized version was also on sale with full-sized maps, but only a few of the illustrations, at 10s or 14s for a coloured version. The translator's preface made clear that the aim of this reduced format edition was to make it 'attainable by all classes', and Denon's dedication to Napoleon said that his association with the Egyptian expedition meant that 'all Europe … will receive my Work with eagerness and interest'. For Denon, Egyptian architecture not only withstood comparison with Classical works but was the inspiration for them:

> [It] has become the basis of all that is the subject of admiration in modern structures, and of what we have considered as exclusively belonging to Architecture, the three Greek orders, Doric, Ionic, and Corinthian. Hence we should be cautious of entertaining the false idea, which is so absurdly prevalent, that the Egyptian architecture is the infancy of this art; it should rather be considered as the paragon of excellence.[21]

The temple of Hathor at Dendera held a special place in Denon's affection for Egyptian architecture, and he wrote that:

> Dendira (Tintyris) taught me that it was not in the Doric, Ionic, and Corinthian orders alone, that the beauties of architecture were evident: wherever a harmony of parts exists, there beauty is perceptible … I had the presentiment that I should meet with nothing finer in Egypt; and after having made twenty journies [sic] to Dendira I found my opinion confirmed.[22]

His opinion had been shared by the earlier French traveller and naturalist Charles Sonnini de Manoncourt, who travelled in Egypt between 1777 and 1780, but whose account of his travels, similarly called *Voyages dans la Haute et Basse Égypte* (*Travels in Upper and Lower Egypt*), was only published in 1799, three years before Denon's work. Sonnini noted in his preface that the 'singular figures discovered in the temple of Isis at Dendera, will attract particular attention', and went on to describe the temple as 'one of the most beautiful monuments of Ancient Egypt' and 'one of the most striking edifices on which antiquity has endeavoured to impress the seal of immortality'.[23]

Denon illustrated his work with 141 plates and maps. Some of these were landscapes illustrating temples like that of Hathor at Dendera (Fig 12), but there were also plans and elevations, illustrations of architectural elements, hieroglyphs, Ancient Egyptian antiquities, scenes in contemporary Egypt, and portraits of the Egyptians that Denon encountered. There is a noticeable difference between the contemporary scenes and portraits, and

Vue géométrale du Portique du Temple de Tentyris.

those depicting Ancient Egyptian material. Denon was an able artist and draughtsman who accomplished astonishing things in difficult and frequently dangerous conditions, often under great pressure of time, but he was unfamiliar with the conventions of Ancient Egyptian art and his hieroglyphic calligraphy and copying of reliefs and decorations often 'Classicised' them, which in turn would have influenced those using his book as a source of designs. He illustrated 24 column capitals in two plates, but without their shafts, and other plates showed a collection of 110 hieroglyphs taken from various temples and a variety of repeating designs taken from temple friezes. The illustration of so many elements out of context made it easy for subsequent designers to use them in ways that were not archaeologically accurate.

Regency Egyptomania – the pharaonic and the Picturesque

The influence of Denon's work was soon felt. The earliest architecture which we know to have been inspired by it was at Stowe in Buckinghamshire, where the Egyptian Hall, a small area under the north portico linking to a carriage porch under the main entrance stairs was created in 1803 (see p 211). Not long after, Walsh Porter, a connoisseur, collector and *arbiter elegantiae* (judge of taste) of his day, who was also an intimate of the Prince Regent, acquired Craven Cottage, a two-storey rustic building in Fulham, and in 1806 commissioned an extensive remodelling of it with a central reception room based on illustrations from Denon's book. The first commercial building in the Egyptian style in London was the offices of the *Courier* newspaper, built around 1804 with Egyptian detailing on the ground floor, but the best known was the Egyptian Hall in Piccadilly, built in 1811–12 (Fig 13).

The Egyptian Hall, built to house the London Museum of William Bullock, was the first major public building in England to have an exterior in the Egyptian style. It was designed by Peter Frederick Robinson,[24] who had advised the Prince Regent on furnishings for the Royal Pavilion at Brighton. Like Thomas Hopper, the surveyor who had remodelled Craven Cottage, Robinson was also inspired by Denon's book, and specifically by illustrations of the Temple of Hathor at Dendera,[25] but unlike Hopper and others before him, he did not restrict the

Fig 12
An illustration of the Temple of Hathor at Dendera from Denon's influential work *Voyages dans la Basse et la Haute Égypte (Travels in Upper and Lower Egypt)* showing the unusual designs on the cornice that were to be a recurring theme in architectural use of the Egyptian style in England. [With permission of the Warden and Scholars of New College, Oxford]

use of the Egyptian style to interior decorative elements. Although inspired by the Temple of Hathor, the Egyptian Hall was not an archaeologically correct recreation of it, but included the key elements of the surviving stone-built architecture of Ancient Egypt which came to define the Egyptian style when it was revived. These were the cavetto cornice, the use of battered sides and the pylon form, the half-round or torus moulding on pylons, columns modelled on the papyrus, lotus, or palm, the winged solar disc above entrances and the use of hieroglyphs. The *Courier* office had the cavetto cornice and palmiform columns, and the Egyptian Hall had all of them apart from battered sides, although the illusion of these was created by the use of the pylon form. These key elements tended to work best on the exterior of larger buildings, particularly public ones, but only a few were built in such an uncompromisingly Egyptian style. Far more common was the incorporation of a few fashionably Egyptian elements into buildings. These elements included columns, capitals on columns (often bud capitals), pilasters, cornices, battered window openings and door cases. In interiors, the Egyptian style was mostly confined to entrance halls, reception rooms, libraries and other such areas, and to elements such as friezes and fireplaces (Fig 14). The influence of wealthy connoisseurs like Thomas Hope and Walsh Porter helped

to make the Egyptian style hugely fashionable for a while, and despite the continuing war with Revolutionary France, there was still a strong continental influence on British taste. The Prince Regent, who was advised by Porter and commissioned a number of pieces with Egyptian decoration, including an expensive and elaborate silver-gilt table service, was a confirmed Francophile in matters of taste if not politics.

Use of the Egyptian style in the early 19th century can also be seen as part of a general use of exotic styles inspired by the aesthetic concept of the Picturesque, which became popular after the publication in the late 18th century of a number of books by the Revd William Gilpin, a talented amateur artist, clergyman and progressive educationalist, and which was influential in the development of the Romantic movement. The term 'picturesque' was originally used to mean that something was in the style of a painting, and although Gilpin concentrated on landscape and scenery, he believed that the composition of a landscape was an important element in its attractiveness and that buildings, particularly ruined ones, could enhance this. Another concept popular at this time was that of the 'sublime', and in Picturesque landscapes this was often thought to be emphasised by a low viewpoint, rather than when scenes and buildings were viewed from above. Piranesi (see p 48), who was an important early exponent of the Egyptian style, was also influential in the development of the idea of the 'sublime'. To Gilpin, the function of buildings forming part of a scene was unimportant compared to their aesthetic qualities, but in 1805 the artist and architect Joseph Gandy[26] attempted to combine the Picturesque and the practical.

Gandy, who worked closely with Sir John Soane[27] as a draughtsman between 1798 and 1809, produced *The Rural Architect,* a book of designs for cottages, lodges, farmyards, a mill, inn, entrance gates, and even a rural institute or what would now be termed an agricultural college. Unlike the detailed architectural fantasies for which Gandy is probably now best known, with their strong sense of the Sublime, the designs in *The Rural Architect* were intended as practical buildings, and were the sort of structures which might be built by a wealthy and progressive landowner on their model estate, designed to combine aesthetic appeal with practicality. Two of the designs, for a 'dwelling' and a 'double cottage', were described as Picturesque. The designs also included two entrance lodges, with accommodation for gatekeepers or labourers and their families, in an Egyptian style – one in the form of two flanking pyramids, the other 'after the model of the Egyptian entrances to their temples', of pylon form flanked by stubby plain obelisks. Although few of Gandy's designs were ever built, and he was a commercial failure, the buildings of *The Rural Architect* show how the concept of the Picturesque could lend itself to exotic styles in general and the Egyptian style in particular.

The Royal Pavilion in Brighton was ultimately built in an Indian style but in 1808 Humphry Repton,[28] who unsuccessfully submitted designs for its remodelling, had considered the Egyptian style for it, ultimately deciding against it as 'too cumbrous for the character of a villa'. Peter Robinson, who was involved with its interiors, went on to design the Egyptian Hall in Piccadilly. While the Egyptian style might be considered unsuitable for a residential villa, even one as grand as the Royal Pavilion, it was adopted for the Civil and Military Library in Devonport, Plymouth, designed in 1823 in the Egyptian style by the architect John Foulston[29] (see p 229.). The library was one of a group of public buildings in the Greek, Egyptian and Oriental style, a combination explicitly designed by Foulston to create 'a picturesque effect'.

Although such a grouping followed the principles of Gilpin and others by being intended to create an aesthetic impression, Foulston recognised the disadvantage that it also tended, in his own words, to create buildings 'which neither emulate the character, or serve the purposes' of the originals which inspired them.[30] To be fair, there was little alternative in the case of Egyptian-style buildings. It was not until 1822 that Jean François Champollion published his famous *Lettre à Monsieur Dacier* setting out the principles of the hieroglyphic script, and two years later his *Précis du Système Hiéroglyphique*. Even then it was to be years before enough was known from the hieroglyphic texts which were an integral part of temples and tombs to allow their function to be properly understood, and such knowledge was the province of the emerging discipline of Egyptology rather than the profession of architecture.

By the time the Egyptian Hall was built, the first volumes of the massive *Description de L'Égypte* had begun to appear, containing the work of the other scholars and artists who had accompanied the Napoleonic expedition, and more Egyptianising buildings followed. At around the same time that Foulston had designed the Civil and Military Library in Plymouth, a stucco façade with Egyptian features was incorporated into a shop built in Hertford, at Fore Street (see p 248). Although examples were still not numerous, the use of the Egyptian style for public and commercial buildings was now established, and several more followed. In 1835 the Egyptian House in Penzance was built as a museum, and shared many features with the Egyptian Hall and Foulston's library, including distinctive glazing bars in the windows (see p 231). These shared features suggest a common influence, and perhaps the involvement in the design of more than one of these buildings of either Robinson, Foulston or George Wightwick,[31] Foulston's partner.

Mill, mausoleum and monument – the Victorian era

In 1838, only three years after the building of the Egyptian House, a radically different version of the Egyptian style was adopted for a new single-storey flax mill begun in Leeds for John Marshall and Company. The civil engineer James Combe was responsible for the mill itself, but the artist David Roberts, who had travelled to Egypt and the Holy Land between August 1838 and July 1839, was called in to advise on the Egyptian façade. Although now best known for his paintings, Roberts, whose celebrated views of Egypt and its antiquities were to appear as lithographs between 1842 and 1849 and were to be highly influential in the popular perception of Ancient Egypt, had experience of working with architects. He in turn involved the artist and sculptor Joseph Bonomi Jnr, who had architectural training, and who had already spent nine years in Egypt working with various expeditions and the leading Egyptologists of his day. The result was an impressive building based on actual temples, particularly that of Horus at Edfu, and much more archaeologically accurate than the buildings of Robinson and Foulston, and the Egyptian House at Penzance. Even the beam engines in Marshall's Mill were given Egyptian-style decoration (see p 270). Use of the Egyptian style for industrial structures or what we would now describe as civil engineering has been rare, although an initial design by I K Brunel in 1831 for the Clifton Suspension Bridge featured pylons surmounted by sphinxes and decorated with hieroglyphs, and one proposed design for a railway terminus is known.[32] After the construction of Marshall's Mill (now known as Temple Mill), use of the Egyptian style for such industrial buildings almost ceased for the best part of a century, apart from occasional small and fairly plain examples such as the pumping station at East Farleigh near Maidstone, Kent, built in 1860 (see p 209), and the valve house at Widdop Reservoir in Calderdale, built between 1872 and 1878 (see p 280).

The Egyptian style still failed to establish itself for residential buildings. One attempt to promote it in this area was made by Richard Brown,[33] who described himself as a 'Professor of Architecture' in his 1841 book *Domestic Architecture*. Brown ran an architectural academy in London but his address in retirement, given in the dedication of the book, was at Topsham near Exeter, and the volume was dedicated to the Earl of Devon. This connection is interesting, in the light of the number of examples of the Egyptian style found in the West of England. In his book, Brown gave examples of various styles of architecture from around the world, one of which was the Ancient Egyptian, with designs for residential buildings in each style. His dedication spoke of using the book 'to introduce … a more chaste and appropriate style into our native Architecture', implying that the Egyptian style met both criteria, and his preface quoted from Sir Uvedale Price's 1794 *Essay on the Picturesque*, showing that this movement was still influential in some quarters. Brown's book described what it believed to be the principles of Egyptian architecture, quoting from J G Wilkinson's influential *Manners and Customs of the Ancient Egyptians*, and illustrated Ancient Egyptian furniture, gardens, scenery, and an 'Egyptian Pavilion — Aboul's Palace'. Brown also quoted from Denon, who considered 'Medianal Aboul's palace' (Medinet Habu, the great temple complex of Ramesses III on the West Bank at Thebes) as a model for the palaces of the pharaohs generally. In an echo of Gandy's designs, but on a grander scale, Brown illustrated a design for a two-storey, nine-bedroom house in an Egyptian style (Fig 15), with an entrance hall, drawing room, dining room, morning room, library and servants' quarters, and also included illustrations of different Egyptian column styles and details of wall and ceiling decorations.[34] It remained a design, however, and when another architect or builder used Egyptian elements in 1840 or 1841, at Richmond Avenue in London (see p 191), they were purely decorative elements, sphinxes and obelisks, added to otherwise conventional terraced houses of the time.

If the Egyptian style was virtually unused for public, commercial and residential buildings during the late 19th and early 20th centuries in England, there was one area in which it became accepted. The collapse of the churchyard-based parish burial system in London led to the creation of huge new cemeteries run by joint stock companies, and the association between Ancient Egypt and funerary monuments was a natural one to make (Fig 16). Highgate Cemetery was established in 1838, with its first burials a year later, and although its entrance buildings were in a Gothic style, two of its most spectacular features were the Egyptian Avenue and Circle of Lebanon Vaults (see p 162). Abney Park Cemetery opened in 1840, with an entrance lodge in the Egyptian style designed by William Hosking and a hieroglyphic inscription composed by Joseph Bonomi Jnr (see p 89). The new cemeteries gave ample space for those with the means to commemorate themselves with impressive, and expensive, monuments with Ancient Egyptian features, and a significant number of large monuments and mausoleums displayed the key architectural features of the Egyptian style. There was clearly a 'pattern book' element operating as there are several in Kensal Green, for example, of a similar size and shape, with shared features such as battered sides, cavetto cornices and torus mouldings, but monuments such as those of Wilson Pasha at Hampstead (see p 156), the Gordon mausoleum at Putney Vale (see p 190), the Courtoy mausoleum at Brompton (see p 102) and the Kilmorey mausoleum, originally at Brompton, but moved

Fig 15
Despite attempts to translate them into practical dwellings, such as this design from Richard Brown's 1841 *Domestic Architecture* the features of the Egyptian style have seldom been adopted for residential buildings. [The Bodleian Libraries, University of Oxford, Shelfmark 2 Delta 343, Plate XXVIII]

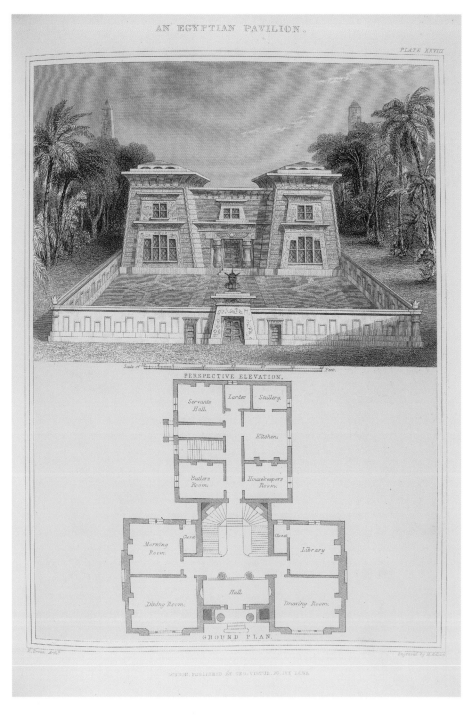

AN EGYPTIAN PAVILION.

PLATE XXVIII

PERSPECTIVE ELEVATION.

GROUND PLAN.

twice thereafter (see p 186), are either bespoke or very heavily customised from standard designs. Although they were always exotic rarities, Egyptian-style monuments continued to be built right up until shortly before the First World War.

Fig 16
The mechanisation of stone working produced a boom in monumental sculpture in the new urban cemeteries of Victorian England. While overtly Egyptian-style monuments were not common, uninscribed obelisks, such as this one seen here in Highgate Cemetery, are a common feature of many cemeteries. [AA074849]

Of all Egyptian architectural forms, the pyramid was the best known, and had always had funereal associations. The originals had inspired the monument of Caius Cestius and others in Classical Rome, and they in turn inspired individual monuments for wealthy modern counterparts, such as the mausoleum that Joseph Bonomi Snr[35] designed for the Earl and Countess of Buckinghamshire at Blickling in 1794 (see p 247). With isolated exceptions, however, such as the small pyramidal monument of John Shae Perring in Kensal Green (see p 183), the pyramid never became established as a monumental style in cemeteries. One reason for this was probably that when people thought of pyramids, they thought of the Pyramids of Giza and of architecture on a huge scale. When it came to national, rather than individual monuments, though, it was precisely this epic quality that led architects and designers to choose the pyramid. The end of the Napoleonic Wars saw two proposals, one in 1817 for a 205ft-high pyramid on Shooters Hill in London to commemorate British military heroes, and two years earlier one for an even bigger pyramid in Trafalgar Square, at 364ft almost as high as St Paul's Cathedral, also to commemorate British military victories. Both, however, would have been dwarfed by Thomas Willson's[36] proposed pyramidal mausoleum, to be erected around 1825 on Primrose Hill, to house the bodies of up to five million Londoners (Fig 17). It was to be nearly 80 years before the next such proposal, this time for a national gallery of sculpture and national mausoleum housed in a relatively modest 150ft-high pyramid in Hyde Park. The last attempt to erect an Egyptian-style monument in London was in 1920, when a 160ft-high pylon, flanked by temples, was proposed for Hyde Park Corner as a national war memorial for the dead of the First World War. Although it resembled a temple rather than being a pyramid, its monumental size links it to its predecessors and distinguishes it from buildings like those in Highgate and Abney Park Cemeteries. None of these designs were ever built, which emphasises the failure of the Ancient Egyptian style to ever become fully established or accepted in Britain. The only element to become truly vernacular was the obelisk. Only two genuine Egyptian obelisks were erected in England, the so-called Bankes Obelisk at Kingston Lacy in Dorset (see p 239) and Cleopatra's Needle on the Victoria Embankment (see p 105), but hundreds, probably thousands, of plain obelisks can be seen in older cemeteries, and outside cemeteries they were popular as war memorials. Although the obelisk is a quintessentially Egyptian form, when used for funerary and monumental purposes it is typically single, without hieroglyphic inscriptions, and owes more to the Classical tradition.

Freemasonry, particularly in its early history, was influenced by the Classical tradition that architecture originated in Ancient Egypt, and also by the Hermetic tradition that Egypt was the source of an occult wisdom restricted to an elite group of initiates. This led to an early association between Ancient Egypt and Freemasonry, and eventually to another use of the Egyptian style in architecture. In continental Europe,

Fig 17

An 1829 engraving showing two cross sections, at different scales, of Thomas Willson's proposed pyramidal mausoleum for the remains of 5,000,000 Londoners.
[City of London, London Metropolitan Archives]

THE PYRAMID.

the connection between Freemasonry and Ancient Egypt was given added impetus by the publication in 1731 of *Séthos*, a book attributed to Abbé Jean Terrasson which described the initiation of an Ancient Egyptian prince into religious mysteries and his eventual retirement to a temple of other initiates. The work was popular and influential, and was turned into a theatrical performance piece with music by Mozart, as well as being a major influence on Mozart's *Die Zauberflöte*. Ancient Egyptian iconography was used in stage designs, and incorporated into Masonic regalia. In the 18th century, many Masonic lodges met in taverns. It was not until around 1775 that the first purpose-built lodges began to appear in England, and most were built in the 19th century. When purpose-built Masonic lodges began to appear, several had Egyptian-style interiors, and one survives as a gymnasium in the basement of the Great Eastern Hotel near Liverpool Street in London. Egyptian-style exteriors were much rarer, but one dating from the 1860s survives at Boston in Lincolnshire, and also has some Egyptian features in its interior (see p 250).

Commercial pharaonic – the 20th century

The Victorian era was one of elaborate decoration in exteriors and interiors, and the Gothic and Italianate styles were both popular. Given this, it was hardly surprising that there was little enthusiasm outside monumental architecture for the Egyptian style with its relative simplicity and monumental geometric forms. It was not until the first half of the 20th century that English architects began to turn to the style again, possibly as a reaction against the elaborate styles of Victorian architecture, and because the Egyptian style was seen to lend itself to new materials and techniques of construction. When they did, it was largely for public and commercial buildings. Probably the first of these was a new print works for the newsagents W H Smith, built in London in 1916, whose façade had pylon entrances, torus mouldings, and cavetto cornices (see p 195). Given the fact that so few Egyptian-style buildings were constructed at any time, what followed amounted to a dramatic revival of the style. In 1920–2 Wallis Gilbert built a factory for GEC in Birmingham with strong Egyptian influences on the façade and interior decoration (see p 256). Adelaide House, near London Bridge, was built in 1925 with battered sides and a cavetto cornice, and was soon followed by Britannia House (see p 95) and the new Arcadia Works of Carreras, now Greater London House (see p 152), both with strongly Egyptian features. Between 1928 and 1930 four cinemas were built in London with Egyptian façades or interiors, and in one case with both, and the Pyramid Cinema, which had an Egyptian-influenced exterior and interior, was built in Sale near Manchester in 1930 (see p 286). Coloured faience tiling began to be used to mimic the painted decoration of Ancient Egyptian temples and tombs. Sometimes, as with the exterior of the Carlton Cinema in Islington (see p 103), or the Hoover Factory (see p 174), this was on a grand scale, but the back entrance to the Reliance Arcade in Brixton (see p 191) achieves the same effect on a much smaller canvas.

This interwar revival of the style in architecture is often attributed to the discovery of the tomb of Tutankhamun, but while this undoubtedly created huge popular enthusiasm for Ancient Egypt, the interior of the tomb was very modest architecturally, and it had no exterior, being excavated from the rock of the Valley of the Kings. While architects may have reflected public taste by using the Egyptian style, there is a lack of evidence to show that the forms they used in buildings were inspired by the contents of the tomb, During the 1920s and 1930s, however, a series of excavations were carried out by the Egypt Exploration

Society at Amarna in Egypt, the site of Akhenaten's capital city of Akhetaten. A number of those taking part in the digs were trained architects, and articles on the excavations appeared both in the popular *Illustrated London News* and in the Architectural Association's *Journal*. An equally significant factor may have been the development of new construction materials and techniques, and the tendency for these to be reflected in simpler forms and less ornament, to which the Egyptian style lent itself relatively easily. The advent of the Second World War, and the growth after it of full-blown Modernism in architecture, typified by the glass skyscraper, meant that it was not until the end of the 20th century that buildings were again designed in the Egyptian style.

In the late 1980s the designer and developer Ian Pollard planned a six-storey office building for a vacant site on Warwick Road in London, which would have had a glass pyramid covering a central atrium, and a full-height glass elevation on the north side with coloured Egyptian scenes sand- and shotblasted into the glass. A collapse in property prices meant that this project never got further than models and designs and this portion of the site was sold off, but on the adjacent site in 1988 Pollard designed and built a DIY supermarket for Sainsbury's, which had a number of Ancient Egyptian-style features, most prominent of which was a full-height carved frieze of Egyptian gods and goddesses on the main façade facing the car park (see p 167). Pollard also submitted designs for an Ancient Egyptian-themed sales area as part of a refurbishment of Harrods department store, but eventually withdrew from the project. In 1991 Harrods Director of Art and Design, William Mitchell, began creating two Egyptian-themed rooms and a seven-storey escalator with Ancient Egyptian designs on it and on the surrounding areas on the floors it passes through (see p 157). And some 120 years after the Egyptian-style pumping station had been built near Maidstone in Kent, the London Docklands Development Corporation commissioned three leading architects to design three storm-water pumping stations in East London. One of these was the so-called 'Temple of Storms' designed by John Outram. Opened in 1988, it was explicitly intended to echo the hypostyle, or columned hall of Egyptian temples, and also featured brightly coloured decoration (see p 193). Ten years later, in 1998, Outram returned to an Egyptian theme when he designed Sphinx Hill, a private residence at Moulsford in Oxfordshire. Described on his practice's website as 'a modern interpretation of an Egyptian House', it makes extensive use of coloured rendering and Ancient Egyptian symbolism, especially the winged solar disc (see p 225).

The impact of Imhotep – assessing Egyptian-style architecture

Both Herodotus and Aristotle credited the Ancient Egyptians with the invention of architecture, and the Egyptians did have, in the Step Pyramid of Djoser, the first large-scale use of stone masonry. Distinctive elements of the Egyptian style, particularly pyramids, obelisks and sphinxes, survived over thousands of years, and were used again in modern times. Why the style was revived, and what it meant to architects, their clients and the public, are not straightforward questions to answer.

When detailed information began to reach Europe about the surviving Ancient Egyptian monuments, attempts were made to assess their place in architectural history, and their contemporary relevance. Architects were familiar with the Egyptian elements that had been filtered through the Classical tradition, but now had to decide how far the Egyptians had

influenced the Ancient Greeks, and in turn the Romans.
This was not a trivial question. Opinions were sharply
divided between those who saw Ancient Egyptian
architecture and sculpture as possessing intrinsic merit,
and having inspired succeeding civilisations, and those who
saw it as at best a primitive and barbaric ancestor of the
aesthetically superior products of Greece and Rome. As
early as 1809, a writer in Rudolph Ackermann's influential
Repository of Arts magazine spoke of 'the barbarous
Egyptian style' being 'succeeded by the classic elegance
which characterised the more polished ages of Greece
and Rome' (although as late as 1822 the magazine was
illustrating a fireplace and chimney-front in the Egyptian
style). Early uses of the Egyptian style, like Thomas Hope's
interior at his Duchess Street mansion and Walsh Porter's
at Craven Cottage, were largely a personal statement by
members of the social elite, and despite their influence
as arbiters of taste, the Egyptian style achieved only a
relatively brief fashionable success. The dominant model
was still Graeco-Roman. When, in 1819, Sir Joseph Banks
wrote to Henry Salt about Salt's first collection of Ancient
Egyptian antiquities, intended for the British Museum,
Banks referred to the colossal statue of Ramesses II known
as the Younger Memnon, previously sent to England by
Salt, as 'a *chef d'oeuvre* of Egyptian sculpture', but tellingly
said that 'we have not placed that statue among the
works of Fine Art' in the museum's Townley Gallery, which
contained sculpture from Greece and Rome, and said that
it 'remains to be proved' whether any Egyptian sculptures
could compete with such 'grand works' (Fig 18).[37]

Fig 18
The colossal statue of
Ramesses II – known in
the 19th century as the
'Younger Memnon' – was
brought back to England
in 1818 by the pioneer
Egyptologist Giovanni
Belzoni on behalf of
Henry Salt, the British
Consul General in Egypt.
[© Trustees of the
British Museum]

The influence of Ancient Egyptian architecture was addressed by two 19th-century
professors of architecture at the Royal Academy, Sir John Soane and one of his successors,
Charles Robert Cockerell. Soane referred to it in his series of Royal Academy lectures
delivered between 1809 and 1820, and between 1841 and 1856 Cockerell used as a
teaching aid a large picture, 13ft by nearly 10ft, called *The Professor's Dream*, showing the
'evolution' of architecture, with Ancient Egypt in the foreground, implying that it had inspired
its successors. Neither of them was noted for their use of the Egyptian style. Soane had
produced a design in 1778 for a pyramidal Egyptian temple, flanked by sphinxes, but the
pyramid was of the steeply pitched Classical form and had a Neoclassical portico, and
Egyptian elements are absent from his later work. In his first lecture Soane, while admitting
that, 'It is impossible not to be impressed with the grandeur and magnitude so peculiar in the
works of the Egyptians in general, but particularly in their sacred buildings…',[38] still felt that
they were inferior to Greek architecture, and that 'instead of the graceful and harmonious
disposition of parts so visible in Grecian works, we have in these [Egyptian structures] only
uniformity and tiresome monotony in the general forms as well as in the details'.[39] He did,
however, concede that:

> The essential qualities of Egyptian works are prodigious solidity and wonderful magnitude … Indeed, in all their works everything seems calculated for eternity; and if solidity, quantity, mass, and breadth of light and shadow, were the only requirements in architecture, we should find all that could be desired in the works of the Egyptians.[40]

When it came to actual modern uses of the style, however, Soane was not impressed by what he saw:

> What can be more puerile and unsuccessful than the paltry attempt to imitate the character and form of their works in small and confined spaces; and yet, such is the prevalence of that monster, Fashion, and such the rage for novelty, that we frequently see attempts of this kind by way of decoration, particularly to many of the shop fronts of the metropolis. Nor does this evil … end here. The Egyptian mania has spread further: even our furniture is decorated with the symbolical forms of the religious and other customs of Egypt.[41]

What Soane thought of the Egyptian Hall, Foulsham's library, or the Egyptian House in Penzance is not recorded, and he died before the construction of Marshall's Mill in Leeds, but these were all public and commercial buildings, and this was to become established as the most popular use of the style. Foulsham's Civil and Military Library was explicitly part of a group of buildings inspired by the concept of the Picturesque, in which the utility or morality of structures was less important than their aesthetic qualities, and the architectural historian Professor Richard Carrott has referred to the architectural genre of the 'Commercial Picturesque'. Mills, museums (but private ones), pumping stations, cemetery buildings, factories, office buildings, cinemas and shops have all been built in England in the Egyptian style. Conspicuously absent are major public buildings and monuments. Where such buildings have been proposed, for example the various pyramidal war monuments, they have never been built, and in the case of the proposal in 1920 to construct a national war memorial at Hyde Park Corner in the Egyptian style, it was savaged by one critic as 'pure pagan swagger', redolent of pharaonic despotism.[42] This was introducing moral criteria to architecture with a vengeance.

It is difficult not to conclude that the architectural and cultural establishment, where it takes notice of the Egyptian style at all, does not like it. Augustus Welby Pugin, who was so influential in establishing the Gothic style in England, particularly for religious buildings, was a fierce critic of the Egyptian style in cemeteries, lumping it in with Neoclassicism as pagan and inappropriate for a Christian burial ground. Major office buildings like the new Arcadia Works of Carreras and the Hoover Factory fared little better. Both were accused of 'façadism' – the superficial use of design elements on the front of a building. The architectural critic Maxwell Fry referred to the front elevation of the Carreras factory as 'a piece of ponderous scenery secured to a factory for the purpose of advertisement', and its cavetto cornice as a 'sham'. The great architectural historian Nikolaus Pevsner simply described it as an 'abominable factory'. Such criticisms still persist, and the recent Egyptian-style Homebase on Warwick Road was described in one article as 'advertising, not architecture' (see p 172).

Perhaps that is the whole point. The Egyptian style has always been an exotic import, but its very exoticism makes it highly recognisable, and it lends itself to the symbolic. This is of little use for domestic buildings, where it has been confined to interiors, external decoration, as at Richmond Avenue in London, or bespoke designs for private clients such as Sphinx Hill in Oxfordshire. However, it blossomed in the great joint stock cemeteries of the 19th century where it could evoke not only the Egyptian belief in the survival of the individual soul after death, but the survival for thousands of years of the temples and tombs of the Egyptians, and of the bodies of their dead themselves. Individual monuments, and even cemetery buildings, could never be on the same scale as the Egyptian originals that inspired them, but for both the cemetery companies and the well off who erected lavish monuments, it was sufficient to have enough to evoke Ancient Egypt. In some cases, such as Perring's monument at Kensal Green or Wilson's in Hampstead Cemetery, the choice of style was because of the link between Egypt and the person who was being commemorated, but as a generalisation the larger and more elaborate the Egyptian-style monument, the more tenuous is the link between its occupant and Egypt.

Increasing pressure on space in cemeteries, the greater use of cremation and a trend toward simpler monuments led to the decline of the Egyptian style there, but outside the cemeteries, it was (if the phrase is appropriate) alive and well. For Marshall's Mill in Leeds, built to spin flax into linen, the Egyptian connection was an appropriate one, and to connect a pumping station like that at East Farleigh in Kent or the valve house at Widdop Reservoir in Yorkshire to a civilisation founded on a great river also made sense. The relevance of the style to office buildings and factories was perhaps less obvious, although Carreras could link their trademark Black Cat to the goddess Bastet, but the clean and monumental lines of Ancient Egyptian temples adapted well to steel-framed concrete buildings, and papyrus columns, solar discs and the like provided eye-catching detailing. The colourful decoration of Egyptian temples and tombs had not been reflected in funerary architecture and monuments in England, although it had been used for interiors, but its bright colours and forms could be used to good effect on the exteriors of cinemas and shops.

However, the lack of official public buildings in the Egyptian style made it easy to dismiss as little more than an exotic and attractive novelty, used as a matter of personal taste or to achieve a commercial effect. Seen in this way, there is little difference between a dramatic Classical mausoleum and one with battered sides, cavetto cornice, papyrus columns and winged solar discs, or between a Chinese-style cinema and an Egyptian one, and a striking factory or office building is still striking whether it is theatrical Art Deco or imitation Egyptian temple. This can profoundly irritate both those who object to a historically ill-informed use of Egyptian elements for what can be seen as frivolous applications, and those who dislike such elements on principle as façadism or shallow historical pastiche, or who simply consider them unsuitable, culturally and stylistically, for England. The creation of funerary monuments and cemetery buildings in the Egyptian style could evoke the biblical connections that meant so much to the Victorians, but by the time Adelaide House was built in 1925, these carried considerably less weight, and when a correspondent to *The Builder* magazine (echoing Pugin) criticised the tendency to erect in Britain 'modified Greek and Roman temples which originated in pagan worship in a Mediterranean climate', they would probably have extended this criticism to include buildings based on Egyptian temples.

In certain areas, however, use of the Egyptian style, even if divorced from the original function and symbolism of the elements in Ancient Egypt, was intended to be symbolic rather than simply decorative, although the conscious employment of symbolism was still rare, and in some cases surprising. A number of Masonic lodges had Egyptian-style interiors, particularly when they were built to serve Royal Arch as well as Craft masonry, but Egyptian exteriors were more typical of lodges in continental Europe and America, and the Freemasons' Hall at Boston (see p 250) is an isolated example in England. Egyptian-style elements, mainly battered doorways and window openings, but in the case of St Boniface Catholic Church in Tooting papyrus columns and cavetto cornices (Fig 19), were occasionally used on churches and chapels. They were presumably acceptable because of their biblical connection, especially the tradition of the Flight to Egypt by the Holy Family, but the creation of the Old Synagogue at Canterbury (see p 222) in the Ancient Egyptian style, given the biblical narrative of the Exodus, is eyebrow raising.

Architects who have consciously and explicitly exploited the symbolism of the style are rare, and Ian Pollard and John Outram are notable modern examples. Pollard's DIY superstore reflected his conviction that buildings should be made to last by evoking the creations of the Ancient Egyptians, while the frieze of deities on it was an ironic comment on consumption as a modern 'religion'. The Egyptian elements may have been decorative rather than structural but they were carefully researched, recalling the involvement of the Egyptologist Joseph Bonomi Jnr in the creation of the Crystal Palace's Egyptian Court. Outram's buildings are strikingly modern, but the design of the Temple of Storms pumping station was rooted in the symbolic design of Ancient Egyptian temples, particularly the columned or hypostyle hall. This approach is strikingly different to other Post-Modernist architects, who appear happy to use elements simply because of their form, rather than their significance. Robert Venturi, for example, used small Egyptian-style pillars with polychrome decoration on the National Gallery extension in London, but commented that he had done this primarily to provide eye-level detail and saw himself in not conforming to, or linking to, the architectural order of the existing building as no different to 19th-century architects who combined eclectic elements,

Fig 19
Designed by the architect William Williamson, later known as Benedict Williamson, St Boniface Tooting began as an Early Christian revival design, but was completed in 1927 with an elaborate west front featuring papyrus columns and cavetto cornices. Williamson was interested in Ancient Egyptian architecture and these features were his attempt to create a new style or order. [DP103945]

particularly those who introduced Classical elements into church buildings. In this he differed from John Foulston, who answered those who might criticise him for combining several styles within one view by observing that he had at least 'preserved himself from the abomination of having exhibited a combination of styles in the same building'.

All of which rather begs the question: what is an Ancient Egyptian-style building? The Four Seasons Hotel in London's Docklands has a striking cavetto cornice, easily visible from the river, but no other overtly Egyptian features. The Hoover Factory has slightly battered sides, reeded edges and polychrome decoration, but is suggestively, rather than outrightly Egyptian, and has strongly Art Deco elements in which the Egyptian is thoroughly digested. Adelaide House has battered sides and a cavetto cornice, but again lacks other clearly Egyptian elements. In the end, there is no objective way to decide, but as a rule of thumb, any building which uses explicitly Ancient Egyptian elements can be considered to qualify. This includes hieroglyphs, especially readable ones, and the distinctive Egyptian column shapes. Often, though, the Egyptian elements are primarily decorative, and sometimes decorative elements can become heavily stylised, or are absent altogether, and then the decision tends to come down to how many of the basic elements of Ancient Egyptian architecture can be found in combination. Use of battered sides and the pylon form are suggestive. Couple these with torus mouldings, even if they are plain, and the form is strongly suggestive. Add a cavetto cornice, even if undecorated, and most people would recognise something with its ultimate roots in Egypt.

It has been a long journey to England for the Ancient Egyptian style, over thousands of miles and thousands of years. It was never as commonly used as other historically rooted styles, like the Classical and Gothic, but if it remains an exotic import, it is one that shows no sign of disappearing. As long as there are public and commercial buildings, every so often someone is likely to design one in the Egyptian style, and every so often, someone will want to have a house that speaks of the Nile, even if it is beside the Thames.

Cemeteries: Catacombs and cornices

Before the 19th century funerary monuments in the Egyptian style were rarities and often, like the pyramidal mausoleum at Blickling in Norfolk (see p 247), inspired by Classical sources, and in particular by the pyramidal mausoleum of Caius Cestius in Rome (Fig 20). This might have remained the case were it not for a short Corsican and a very tall Italian. The traditional English place of burial for generations had been the parish churchyard, but the beginnings of the Industrial Revolution saw a massive expansion in the population of cities. In the first half of the 19th century the population of London grew from around one million to over two, pushing the parish burial system to the point of collapse, with up to 3,000 bodies per acre in some London burial grounds and an average of more than 200 new burials per acre per year. In some city churchyards the soil was raised several feet above street level. Twelve or more coffins could be buried one above the other, with the topmost sometimes only a few inches below the surface. In summer, congregations could be forced out of churches by the stench of decaying corpses in the vaults below (Fig 21), and as Charles Dickens wrote in one of his sketches:

Fig 21
A 1747 print by Hogarth
satirising the idleness of
apprentices also illustrates
the unsavoury state of
a parish burial system
already under severe
pressure in cities by
the mid-18th century.
[Photo © Victoria and
Albert Museum, London]

The opening of the service recalls my wandering thoughts. I then find, to my astonishment, that I have been, and still am, taking a strong kind of invisible snuff, up my nose, into my eyes, and down my throat. I wink, sneeze, and cough. The clerk sneezes; the clergyman winks; the unseen organist sneezes and coughs (and probably winks); all our little party wink, sneeze, and cough. The snuff seems to be made of the decay of matting, wood, cloth, stone, iron, earth, and something else. Is the something else, the decay of dead citizens in the vaults below? As sure as Death it is! Not only in the cold, damp February day, do we cough and sneeze dead citizens, all through the service, but dead citizens have got into the very bellows of the organ, and half choked the same. We stamp our feet to warm them, and dead citizens arise in heavy clouds. Dead citizens stick upon the walls, and lie pulverised on the sounding-board over the clergyman's head, and, when a gust of air comes, tumble down upon him.[43]

Some relief was provided by the establishment of private burial grounds but these were soon full, and with the inescapable pressure to accommodate new burials came the inevitable temptation to re-use graves. Employing an all-too modern euphemism, gravediggers spoke of the 'management' of graves. What this meant in practice was made all-too clear by the surgeon George Alfred Walker who wrote an exposé of burial practices in 1839.[44] Graves were emptied for re-use, not years after the last burial, but sometimes as little as four to six weeks after. Suspiciously large quantities 'hundredweights' of second-hand coffin nails and other fittings were sold, and coffin wood was sold or given away for firewood. Partially decomposed bodies seem to have been dumped in common pits to make room for new burials and there were accounts of basket loads of bones being piled under tarpaulins, probably to undergo the same treatment. Decomposing bodies polluted water supplies and led to outbreaks of disease.

Such a situation could clearly not be allowed to continue and the model for a solution presented itself in France. As far back as 1765 the Parliament of Paris had legislated against further burials within the city, and in 1786 huge quantities of bones were disinterred and moved to newly created underground catacombs in disused quarries. In 1804 an imperial decree by the Corsican-born Napoleon Bonaparte created several new cemeteries to serve Paris, including the cemetery of Père Lachaise on a hillside overlooking the city. Initially, there was no enthusiasm to be buried at Père Lachaise, but in a highly effective piece of marketing the remains of the famous poet La Fontaine and the dramatist Molière were moved there, followed 13 years later by the alleged remains of the tragic lovers Abélard and Héloïse. The ploy was successful and soon the cemetery was a sought-after spot for interment. It was also a new type of burial ground – a 'Garden Cemetery', laid out with pleasant paths and avenues, and planted with trees and shrubs (Fig 22). As London continued to grow and the problem of burying its dead worsened, the barrister George Frederick Carden was a leading campaigner for a London cemetery along the lines of Père Lachaise. In 1827 the architect Augustus Charles Pugin exhibited plans for a garden cemetery, and one suggested site for a new cemetery was at Primrose Hill. A new urgency was given to the problem of burials with the first major cholera epidemic in London in 1831, and in 1832 Carden's campaigning bore fruit when the General Cemetery Company was established as the first of a new breed of commercial cemetery companies and set up Kensal Green Cemetery. Between 1832 and 1847 Acts of Parliament authorised the creation of eight such companies, including the so-called 'Magnificent Seven' which surrounded London. These were Kensal Green (see p 177), West Norwood (see p 197), Highgate (see p 162), Abney Park (see p 88), Nunhead, Brompton (see p 97), and Tower Hamlets. Churchyard burial was not finally banned in London until 1852, but to alleviate the concerns of parish incumbents over their loss of income from burial fees when the dead were buried in the new cemeteries, a sum (between 1s 6d and 5s at Kensal Green) was paid to them for each burial.

The new cemeteries, like Père Lachaise before them, needed to attract custom. Although their pleasantly laid out paths and avenues helped (Abney Park at one time had the largest collection of tree varieties in Europe), it would be some time before the plantings matured and so the key focal point initially was the cemetery buildings. As the first of the 'Magnificent Seven', Kensal Green also saw the beginning of the controversy over the most appropriate architectural style

Fig 22
Père Lachaise Cemetery in Paris, the first of the modern 'Garden Cemeteries'.
[© Chris Elliott]

for the new cemeteries. George Carden, who had been elected Treasurer of the General Cemetery Company, favoured the Gothic style while Sir John Dean Paul, a banker who had found the prospective site and put up the capital for its purchase, favoured the Greek Revival. To complicate matters, a number of architects had also become shareholders and were clearly interested in the major commission represented by the cemetery buildings. One was Thomas Willson, who in 1824 had exhibited plans for a proposed pyramidal mausoleum to contain the bodies of five million Londoners, another was Augustus Charles Pugin, and a third was John William Griffith, whose designs for the main entrance and two chapels were eventually adopted. Several other architects were also approached or submitted designs and a competition was held to design the Anglican Chapel and main gateway. Griffith and Pugin were both judges and eventually a Gothic design by H E Kendall was selected. At this point the infighting which had probably been going on for a while already began to surface. The decision of the judges was challenged at a committee meeting of the company, which had not yet been incorporated, and at the first shareholder's meeting Carden was effectively demoted to Registrar and Paul was elected Treasurer in his place. During 1832 the rival architects lobbied and published plans but December of that year saw the death of Pugin, a strong supporter of the Gothic style, and early the next year Carden was first suspended from the Board of Directors for making statements prejudicial to the company, and then removed from his post as Registrar. Paul and the Greek Revival faction triumphed, and it was Griffith's designs that were built (Fig 23). The whole affair seems to have been a storm in a teacup, and as Kensal Green and the other cemeteries were laid out buildings were erected in a number of styles with Gothic prominent amongst them. West Norwood, the next to open, had Gothic buildings; Highgate had a Gothic entrance and lodges, but Egyptian-style catacombs as a centrepiece; Nunhead had Gothic buildings; and Abney Park had an Egyptian entrance and lodges, and a Gothic chapel. The struggle for the moral and aesthetic high ground in cemetery architecture, however, was by no means over.

Fig 23
While the Greek Revival style triumphed here at Kensal Green, the most appropriate style for the buildings of other cemeteries was still hotly disputed, and individual choice prevailed in the design of monuments.
[DP055987]

Everyone, even those to be buried in common graves, and those who survived and mourned them, could benefit from choosing the impressive buildings and pleasant grounds of the joint stock company cemeteries as the location for their interment, but it was the prosperous upper-middle and upper classes who could afford to be buried in their most select areas, and to erect correspondingly impressive monuments. In June 1830, before his fall from grace, Carden had recommended, and the committee of the General Cemetery Company accepted, that Kensal Green should follow the example of Père Lachaise and allow the public to erect 'what description of monuments they please'. True Egyptian-style monuments, rather than those modelled on Ancient Roman ones like the pyramid of Cestius, had already been built, but the popularity of the style was helped by a curious coincidence. Alexander MacDonald, an Aberdeen stonemason, had been manufacturing paving stones, hearthstones and tombstones from marble and other materials from about 1820. Around 1829 he began to experiment with polishing granite, and while in London visited the British Museum to see Ancient Egyptian statuary sent back to England by the pioneer Egyptologist, the 6ft 7in-tall Giovanni Belzoni (Fig 24). Inspired by these, MacDonald began to produce rounded and polished forms, introduced the use of steam-powered machinery, and in 1832 produced the first polished granite monument in an English cemetery for Kensal Green, and founded the modern monumental masonry industry. Plenty of monuments were still produced in Portland stone, marble and other materials, but mechanisation allowed the creation of granite monuments in quantity, and in particular of those in the Egyptian style, which was closely associated with this particular material, largely because of the tendency of museum collections at this time to focus on large sculptural pieces in granite. Some Egyptian-style monuments, like the family mausoleum with battered sides, cavetto cornices, torus mouldings and winged solar discs above their doors, benefiting from their position clustered along the main avenues at Kensal Green, are probably 'pattern book' monuments with limited customisation (see p 180). Others, however, were bigger, more elaborate bespoke monuments in prime locations, like the Kilmorey mausoleum, originally in one of the 'select' circular plots at Brompton (see p 98). Although it is not certain who produced it, the manufacturers were based in Scotland, and a number of Egyptian-style monuments have on them the name of MacDonald Field, the company founded by Alexander MacDonald. Kilmorey's plot alone was originally priced at around 2,000 guineas, or £2,100, roughly £120,000 in today's terms, and the mausoleum itself was rumoured to have cost £30,000, about £1,500,000 at modern prices. This was an era of high death rates from infectious diseases and of conspicuous consumption on the paraphernalia of mortality. For burial in vaults and catacombs, massive triple coffins with sealed lead

Fig 24

Giovanni Belzoni (1778–1823), who excavated and transported many of the first large Ancient Egyptian sculptures to reach England, and inspired Alexander MacDonald to create the first modern granite funerary monuments in the early 19th century. [Photo © Victoria and Albert Museum, London]

G. BELZONI.

linings were required, usually finished with dark velvet and upholstery nails, and hydraulic catafalques, or coffin lifts, were installed at Kensal Green and West Norwood to handle them. At Highgate, while burial in a common grave cost £2 10s, burial in the Terrace Catacombs ranged from £10 to £94, with interment fees in addition.

The profusion of monumental styles in the commercial cemeteries was not just a matter of individual whim. There was also a feeling that certain forms were particularly appropriate for emphasising mortality and the hope of survival after death, and that the cemeteries themselves could act to improve the general taste of the population in areas such as architecture and landscaping. In 1843 John Claudius Loudon, author of an influential work on cemetery design and management, noted:

> Some of the new London cemeteries might be referred to as answering in some degree these various purposes, and more particularly the Abney Park Cemetery; which contains a grand entrance in Egyptian architecture; a handsome Gothic chapel; a number, daily increasing, of sculptural monuments; and one of the most complete arboretums in the neighbourhood of London, all the trees and shrubs being named.[45]

He went on to observe:

> We have seen with what pains the most celebrated nations of which history speaks have adorned their places of sepulture, and it is from their funereal monuments that we gather much that is known of their civil progress and of their advancement in taste. Is not the story of Egypt written on its pyramids, and is not the chronology of Arabia pictured on its tombs? Is it not on the funeral relics of Greece and Rome that we behold those elegant images of repose and tender sorrow with which they so happily invested the idea of death?[46]

The association between Ancient Egypt, death, and the survival of the soul was well established. Before the first of the new cemetery companies was established, Belzoni had exhibited a reproduction of rooms from the tomb of Sety I in the Egyptian Hall in Piccadilly with huge success, and although there had been unrollings of mummies before to investigate them, the physician Thomas Pettigrew and others now began to conduct these as public demonstrations before audiences which included the social and intellectual elite of the day. In 1830 another physician, Augustus Granville, unrolling a mummy at the Royal Institution, took the opportunity to express his hope that a necropolis for 'great and illustrious men' would soon be created in England and mentioned a project for one 'details of which were already before the public', which may have been a reference to Carden's campaign. Alexander, 10th Duke of Hamilton, took things to their ultimate conclusion by being embalmed by Pettigrew and buried in a genuine Egyptian sarcophagus, albeit in a lavish mausoleum on his family estate in Scotland, modelled on the architecture of Imperial Rome and with bronze doors that were reproductions of those of the Baptistry in Florence.

Hamilton's eclectic mix of styles was echoed on a smaller scale by many Egyptian monuments in cemeteries. The structures themselves used elements of Egyptian architecture but did not aim for archaeological accuracy. The proportions could be altered to achieve the desired height within a given plot size, and the roofs made pitched instead of flat in deference to the British weather. Hieroglyphs were occasionally used but their forms were not always accurate, and although they might be appropriate, for example the feather of Maat obliquely referring to the Weighing of the Heart ceremony depicted on many funerary papyri, coherent and legible inscriptions are not a feature. What seemed to be important was the overall effect of a solid and enduring architecture, and a culture which not only worshipped its ancestors and believed in a life after death, but which had ensured the survival of their physical remains to the present day. Sometimes there was a link between Egypt and the person who commissioned the monument, even though this might not be immediately obvious. The showman Andrew Ducrow (see p 181) had created spectacles inspired by Napoleon's Egyptian campaign and Belzoni's discoveries, Sir Ernest Cassel (see p 185) had helped to found the National Bank of Egypt, and James Wilson (see p 156) had worked as an engineer for the Egyptian government for more than 40 years. In other cases, however, there is no apparent connection and the reason for the choice of style seems to have been a matter of fashion or personal taste. In this, the Egyptian style was simply one of a number of ways in which those with enough money could try to achieve immortality by erecting a suitably lavish monument in a good position in a fashionable cemetery.

In 1843 Augustus Welby Pugin, son of Augustus Charles Pugin, published *An Apology for the Revival of Christian Architecture in England* (using 'apology' in its strict sense of a formal justification). Pugin was a passionate advocate of the Pointed, or Gothic style, considering it the only one appropriate for England as a Christian country. In his book, he wrote of styles deriving from other eras and cultures:

> I believe them [pagan styles] to be the *perfect expressions of imperfect systems* … but I claim for Christian art a merit and perfection, which it was impossible to obtain even in the Mosaic dispensation, much less in the errors of polytheism. The former was but a type of the great blessings that we enjoy, – the latter, the very antipodes to truth, and the worship of demons.[47]

While he admired the achievements of those who had created 'the pyramid, the obelisk, the temple' he could not accept that their symbols had any place in the architecture of a Christian country, let alone in its graveyards:

> The new Cemetery Companies have perpetrated the grossest absurdities in the buildings they have erected. Of course there are a superabundance of inverted torches, cinerary urns, and pagan emblems, … but the entrance gateway is usually selected for the grand display of the company's enterprise and taste, as being well calculated from its position to induce persons to patronize the undertaking by the purchase of shares or graves. This is generally Egyptian, probably from some associations between the word catacombs, which occurs in the prospectus of the company, and the discoveries of Belzoni on the banks of the Nile; and nearly opposite the Green Man and Dog public-house, in the centre of a dead wall … a cement caricature of the entrance to an Egyptian temple, 2 inches to the foot, is erected, with convenient lodges for the policeman and his wife, and a neat pair of cast iron hieroglyphical gates, which would puzzle the most learned to decipher; while, to prevent any mistake, some such words as 'New Economical Compressed Grave Cemetery Company' are inscribed in *Grecian* capitals along the frieze, interspersed with hawk-headed divinities, and surmounted by a huge representation of the winged Osiris bearing a gas lamp.[48]

This was illustrated by a caricature of such a construction, combining features of the entrance to Abney Park and Kensal Green Cemeteries (Fig 25).

Pugin's attack is often quoted in discussions on Egyptianising architecture, and J S Curl felt that 'the damage done by Pugin to Neoclassicism in general and to the Egyptian Revival in particular was devastating'.[49]

However, by the time Pugin's book was published, all the 'Magnificent Seven' cemeteries had already been built, and despite his assertion that the entrance gateway for them was 'usually' Egyptian, only two, Highgate and Abney Park, had Egyptian-style buildings and of these only Abney Park had an entrance in this style. His attack may have caused Egyptian-style monuments to go out of fashion for a while but it certainly did not put paid to them, and some of the most spectacular were built after the publication of *An Apology for the Revival of Christian Architecture in England*. The Kilmorey mausoleum (see p 186) was built only 11 years later, the McLennan monument in Anfield Cemetery (see p 282) in 1893, and between 1906 and 1910 the Edwardian era saw the magnificent monuments of Wilson Pasha in Hampstead Cemetery (see p 156), the Illingworth mausoleum in Bradford Cemetery (see p 278) and the Gordon mausoleum at Putney Vale (see p 190). Those who commissioned private monuments were probably more likely to follow their own wishes than to defer to the

Fig 25
This savage caricature of a cemetery entrance in the Egyptian style by Pugin in *An Apology for the Revival of Christian Architecture in England* (1843) was as much aimed at the commercialism of the joint stock cemetery companies as their choice of architectural style.

ENTRANCE GATEWAY FOR A NEW CEMETERY.

taste of architectural critics, and Pugin probably had more influence in the public sphere. Despite numerous proposals no major public building or monument, such as a museum, town hall or war memorial was built in the Egyptian style in Britain, with the possible exception of the Wellington Monument, a triangular 'obelisk' to which Egyptian-style features were added in 1853–4 (see p 245).

Despite being tainted by paganism in the view of Pugin and those who shared it, the Greek and Roman styles had a high status amongst the wealthy and aristocratic. The Grand Tour of Europe, particularly Italy, and an education in the Classics had been traditional for generations, and the funeral monuments of the elite tended to reflect this. Although there was an increasing interest in Ancient Egypt during the 19th century, and particularly in its association with the Bible, the same was not true of the Egyptian style. Egyptian monuments, and Egyptian buildings in cemeteries, were always exotic rarities. Their relatively small numbers, and their survival into the early 20th century, make it difficult to talk realistically about a decline of the style. It may be more useful to consider them as one of a number of styles which could be chosen for larger and more expensive monuments, and to look at what happened to such monuments and to the private cemeteries in general over the years.

The scandals over cemetery 'management' and the re-use of graves in the 19th century meant that the new commercial cemetery companies offered the reassuring option of purchasing plots or catacomb cells in perpetuity. Ultimately, though, this was to be their Achilles heel. In effect, they only had one thing to sell, which was space, and as that began to run out, their cash flow dried up. Their early efforts to attract the wealthy meant that they needed to construct impressive buildings but this could be risky. Brompton Cemetery was consecrated in 1840, but by 1852, largely due to the cost of building the chapels and catacombs to ambitious designs, it had to be taken into public ownership by the General Board of Health. As time went by, the companies were unable to charge the premium prices they could in their early heyday. When the Earl of Kilmorey purchased the plot in Brompton on which he was to build his mausoleum, he was able to reduce the price from 2,000 to 1,000 guineas. However, by the time he came to move the monument only 10 years later, and wished to sell the 'select' plot, he eventually had to accept £150 for the space with the cemetery estimating they could make little more than £250 by filling it with graves. There were other problems as well; at Nunhead the first Superintendent carried out a share fraud which created a deficit of £18,179 3s 6d (approximately £950,000 at modern prices).

More significantly, there was the rise of cremation. Although it had been widely practised since antiquity it had become virtually obsolete from the 5th century AD, largely because of Christian emphasis on the resurrection of the body. (Hence Pugin's comments on the unsuitability of 'cinerary urns', which were based on those used to contain the ashes of cremated bodies in Greek and Roman times.) It was considered to be illegal in Britain, although the practice was not specifically proscribed and a few private cremations were carried out unobstructed, until the attempt by the eccentric Dr William Price to publicly cremate the body of his five-month-old son, Jesus Christ Price. The resulting landmark court case in 1884 legalised cremation and it became steadily more popular, leading to the Cremation Act of 1902. Without the need for a coffin, or series of coffins, to contain an embalmed body, monuments could be smaller and ashes began to be placed in niches in specially built columbaria, the word 'columbarium' itself coming from the Latin for dovecote.

Ultimately, however, it was probably the First World War, which saw a sea change in so much of British society, which marked the end of an era in cemeteries. Huge new cemeteries with impressive buildings were again constructed, but this time they were public monuments for war dead, containing acres of identical plots with standard headstones differing only in the details of their inscriptions. Most of them were abroad, particularly on the Western Front, but a battlefield tourism industry sprang up, allowing relatives and survivors to visit them, and war graves in England followed the same severely elegant design. There was monumental statuary, but on war memorials, which sprang up across the country. In an era of death on an industrial scale, closely followed by economic depression, the extravagant funerary architecture of the Victorian and Edwardian age must have seemed inappropriate. More and more cemeteries came under local authority control and restrictions were imposed on the scale and type of new monuments. As more and more people were cremated some began to go without any monument at all, simply having their ashes scattered.

Nowadays, the simple inscribed headstone is the norm, with possibly a small urn for flowers and maybe a discreet statue of an angel or saint. Sometimes there is a small photographic portrait of the deceased. In recent years, however, computer-plotted and sandblasted engraving on funerary monuments has largely replaced hand-carved inscriptions, and allowed texts to be in a far wider range of scripts and alphabets. With the increasing secularisation of British society it may not be too long before some monuments again display, like Joseph Bonomi's, the deities of Ancient Egypt or its hieroglyphs, even if they do not take the form of its temples.

Cinemas: The splendour of Luxor

The first cinema with an exterior in the Ancient Egyptian style was only the second in the whole country. It opened in London in 1896 and was housed in the Egyptian Hall in Piccadilly, itself a pioneer of the Egyptian style in public buildings, but the building had existed long before the invention of moving pictures and it was to be some time before the style was adapted to purpose-built cinemas. Most of these were in London and between 1928 and 1930 four cinemas with Egyptian themes were built in London – the Luxor in Twickenham, the Astoria in Streatham, and two Carltons at Upton Park and Islington. Of these, only the Islington Carlton now survives with its Egyptian features intact. Examples outside London were less common, although the Palace Cinema was built in Lytham St Annes, Lancashire, in 1930 with an interior combining Ancient and modern Egyptian themes, and Sale near Manchester had the Pyramid Cinema, designed by Drury, Gomersall & Partners which opened in 1933, with a cavetto cornice and four palm capital pillars over the entrance, and which still survives (see p 286.) They were designed to provide facilities in the suburbs or outlying towns to rival those in the centre of cities like London and Manchester.

The four London cinemas were large, the Islington Carlton seating 2,248 (although it advertised itself as having '2,500 luxury seats'), and the Astoria Streatham 'nearly 3,000' (*Clapham and Lambeth News* 27 June 1930). They were luxurious and employed state-of-the-art technology in heating and ventilation, sound and projection equipment, information systems and safety features. The Richmond local press spoke glowingly of 'Twickenham's Egyptian Palace … Marvels Of The New Luxor Super-Cinema … Colourful Design And Luxuries Equal To The West End', while the *Clapham and Lambeth News* commented of the Astoria, 'Everything that modern science can do to cater for the convenience and comfort of theatre audiences has been embodied in this beautiful building.'[50]

These cinemas were not the only ones to employ foreign or historical themes; others of the same era were built in Chinese, Moorish and Graeco-Roman styles. In critical terms, they were probably not seen as especially significant; in an article on the cinema architect Julian Leathart,[51] Robert Elwall refers to a scathing attack in 1930 by the architectural critic P Morton Shand, in which he praised Leathart and modern continental designs in Germany and Sweden, while condemning the 'clogging dross of period reproduction and that craving for mere gaudiness which still strangles original design'.[52] Nevertheless, they are still of great interest as examples of the continuing use of Egyptian styles and motifs in architecture, and of how these were used in the particular context of cinema design.

Although the four London buildings have their Egyptian theme in common, they used it in significantly different ways. The Luxor in Twickenham had an Egyptian façade and interior decoration, the two Carltons had Egyptian façades but more Classical or modern interiors, and the Astoria had an Italianate front but an elaborate Egyptian interior. Sometimes other cinemas employed isolated Egyptian-style elements as part of a composite style. Examples of these are the 1937 Woolwich Odeon, by George Coles, a prolific designer of hundreds of cinemas in a 50-year career, which had a tiled Art Deco exterior but featured a single large free-standing Egyptian-style faience column or *torchère* outside, and the Golders Green Lido whose exterior was described by *Architecture* magazine as 'a simple Roman design', but also featured pylon-shaped elements and winged solar discs.

Despite the fact that only a few 'Egyptian' cinemas were built, like others of the era they were large and important entertainment venues (the opening of the Carlton in Islington was attended by Prince Arthur of Connaught and the Mayor of Islington). The use of Egyptian elements was extensive, and went beyond the architectural and decorative; the cover of the Luxor opening souvenir programme featured a winged sun disc and *uraeus*, and the usherettes wore Egyptian-style costume. They employed an eclectic mix of styles and the overall lack of coherence that most of the designs display in their use of Egyptian elements may be irksome to Egyptologists, but it seems clear that the intention of their architects (and by inference of their clients as well) was to use these elements as part of an overall design which combined modern and ancient elements in a highly functional and luxurious building which was accessible, and affordable, to a wide cross section of the public. For their patrons the mix of styles that they displayed was probably unimportant, compared to their overall effect, and the way that this combined with the escapist entertainment on offer inside to offer a respite from the often unwelcome realities of everyday life. Not for nothing are the cinemas of this era referred to as dream palaces.

The Luxor, designed by J Stanley Beard, opened on Monday 18 November 1929, with the distinctly un-Egyptian *King of the Khyber Rifles*. The main elevation was described in the planning application as 'faced with Terra Cotta, the design being a combination of Egyptian and modern architectural details, with the introduction of deep and brilliant colours harmoniously blended'. In fact, the only strongly Egyptian elements were six columns with palm capitals across the front over the entrance, which projected from the rest of the building, and two winged pharaoh heads with *nemes* headcloths below the parapet of the main front. (Beard was to use quasi-Egyptian-style columns again in 1934 for the exterior of the Forum cinema in Kentish Town.) The rest of the decoration was a mixture of loosely Classical elements such as urns, borders with roundels, tapered glazed lanterns, and an Italianate tiled roof. Inside, the foyer was described in the planning application as being 'in a modern style', but as constructed actually had painted panels or frescoes to either side of the entrance showing a lion hunt from a chariot, and a lobby floor with an Ancient Egyptian vulture motif. In the auditorium, the Egyptian theme was repeated, with a cavetto cornice, low relief pillars with lotus bud capitals, and lotus flower decorative elements. The proscenium was framed by combination lotus bud and palm columns, a torus moulding, and a winged sun disc surmounted by a lotus bud. The safety curtain had archer and chariot designs either side and falcons in the top-right and left corner. The auditorium ceiling was painted to represent a sky and clouds.

The Streatham Astoria, designed by Edward A Stone, opened on 30 June 1930. It had a red-brick exterior with stone dressings in a hybrid Italianate style. Inside, however, was what the *Clapham and Lambeth News* described as

> …a vast auditorium adorned with Egyptian paintings and glass mosaics …The general design is based upon Egyptian traditions in pleasing tones of red, green and gold, … while the flank walls of the circle are enriched with highly coloured bas reliefs of Egyptian scenes.[53]

These wall decorations, by the firm of Marc-Henri and Laverdet, showed a pharaoh hunting lions from a chariot and extended along the wall behind plain engaged pillars. The auditorium also had an elaborate glazed roof with lotus flower elements. The Egyptian theme was continued in the café lounge where square pillars with lotus capitals formed a colonnade, and in the foyer. Here, a number of square engaged pillars with lotus capitals were topped with an exaggerated cavetto cornice and there were lotus flower bouquet designs below the cornice between them. The newspaper article mentioned above also emphasised the sophistication of the heating and ventilation plant, the sound system and the lighting. The stage was described as capable of staging '…any of the biggest of West End spectacular stage productions'.[54]

The two Carlton cinemas were both designed for Clavering and Rose Theatres by George Coles. The first of his 'Egyptian' Carlton cinemas to be built was in Upton Park, seating 2,117, which opened with *The Spy* on 29 October 1928. It incorporated part of an old school building but its front, set in a parade of single-storey shops, was strongly Egyptian in style with an inset entrance in which were set twin columns, a composite of palm and papyrus bundle, with a hoarding for cinema posters between them and the main entrance below. A cavetto cornice ran round the top and sides of the front. Above this was a parapet featuring an extended central section with winged sun disc and *uraeus*, surmounted by another (unpainted) cavetto cornice, and then a pedestal and flagstaff. Below the lower cavetto cornice, and on either side wall of the front, were large 'Carlton' signs and large tapered and glazed lanterns were set either side of the entrance about 12ft above pavement level.

Two years later, the Carlton in Islington (see p 103) opened on 1 September 1930. The exterior features pylon-shaped window openings, papyrus bud columns and polychrome tilework. The interior of the cinema was not in an Egyptian style. Although its layout is ultimately dictated by the function of the building, the Islington Carlton is the one that uses the most Egyptian elements and avoids the eclectic mix of elements found in the others. It is also the only one of the four whose Egyptian elements have survived. The Carlton at Upton Park was damaged several times by bombs during the Second World War, and a V2 rocket finally demolished the entrance in 1944. The interior of the Streatham Astoria was completely reconstructed in 1962, and despite objections from the local council the Luxor at Twickenham was demolished by its owners in the early 1980s.

Outside London, the Palace Cinema in Lytham St Annes, which closed in 1958 and was replaced by shops, opened on the Easter Monday Bank Holiday, 21 April 1930, less than six months after the Luxor in Twickenham. Although, like the Astoria in Streatham, its exterior was not in an Egyptian style, and the interior decoration included numerous Classical elements, there was a strong Egyptian theme with sphinxes on the dados of the side walls, a desert scene on the front panels of the lower balcony and a sculpted and coloured frieze depicting an Arab camel caravan halted at an oasis over the proscenium arch. Below this frieze was a winged solar disc, while the pilasters at the side of the stage had capitals in the shape of pharaonic heads (Fig 26). A souvenir programme was headed by a frieze design inspired by Ancient Egyptian tomb paintings, with another pharaonic head in its centre, and in a subtitle the 'New Lytham Palace' was actually described as 'The "Luxor" Talkie Theatre' (Fig 27). The Pyramid Theatre in Sale (see p 286) was possibly the last Egyptian-style cinema to be built in England, and while its Egyptian elements were impressive, they were more

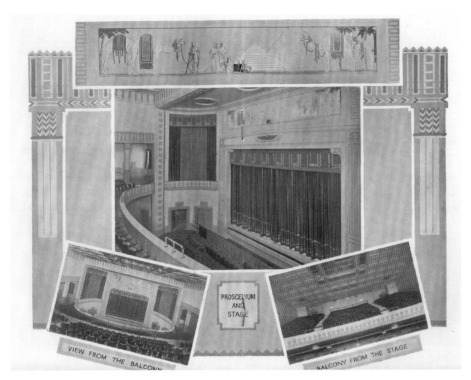

Fig 26
The decoration of the Palace Cinema in Lytham St Annes, Lancashire, mixed Ancient and modern Egyptian imagery. [Courtesy of Lancashire County Library]

understated than many of its predecessors and mainly consisted of moulded elements on the façade and interior. However, its impressive stage and sound system did include an organ with Egyptian decoration (Fig 28).

The Egyptian style seems to have appealed in the context of cinema design because it brought with it a bold use of colour, and a number of positive connotations which could be linked to the stress on modern comfort and convenience. Antiquity as such is not emphasised in contemporary documents, but the planning prospectus for the Luxor noted the 'many wonderful examples of ancient craftsmanship' that had emerged from Luxor in recent years, and went on to state: 'The "Luxor" cinema is giving all that is best in the workmanship and conception of modern cinema construction and organisation, and this, together with pleasing Egyptian design and colour, will bring some of the splendour of Luxor to Twickenham.'[55]

... THE NEW ...

LYTHAM PALACE

THE "LUXOR" TALKIE THEATRE

General Manager . . . . . . HARRY HALL
Phone . . . . LYTHAM 781

{ PROGRAMME SOUVENIR }

PERFORMANCES DAILY *at*
2-30 : 6-30 : *and* 8-40

PRICES *(including Tax)*

FRONT STALLS	9d.
STALLS	1/-
BALCONY	1/-
BALCONY STALLS	1/6

All Seats bookable in advance.

FOYER CAFE

Western **Electric**
SOUND SYSTEM

For the convenience of patrons there is a Special Booking Office in the Entrance Foyer, where seats can be obtained for the Blackpool Theatres: The Grand, Opera House, Winter Gardens, Palace, Tower Circus, Tower.

PROPRIETORS: THE BLACKPOOL TOWER CO. LTD.

Fig 27
The souvenir programme for the Palace echoed elements from the interior decoration, like the pharaonic head and wings from the proscenium arch. [Courtesy of Lancashire County Library]

Fig 28
The Pyramid Theatre in
Sale, near Manchester,
had a probably unique
Ancient Egyptian casing
for its Christie organ,
which could be used
on either of the
organ's consoles.
[The Lancastrian
Theatre Organ Trust,
www.ltot.org.uk]

The construction of Egyptian-style cinemas spanned the Wall Street Crash, from the Roaring
Twenties to the Great Depression, and maybe for both eras bringing some of the splendour
of Egypt to England was an appropriate objective.

Egyptiana: Silver-gilt services to sewing machines

It is not easy to make a clear division between architecture in the sense of the exterior and interior of built structures, the decoration that is applied to these structures, and the objects with which interiors are furnished. This is true whatever the style, and in this respect the Egyptian is no different to others. Many buildings that we think of as Egyptianising, like the former Carreras factory, are actually thoroughly modern steel-framed structures with Egyptian decoration. Similarly, interiors can be built in an Egyptian style, and not merely decorated, while others are Egyptian because of their decoration, and some lack any Egyptian elements other than the artefacts with which they are furnished. However, while exterior decoration can be changed, usually without affecting the essential structure, this affects the overall image of the building, while a building in one architectural style can have interiors in several, and a room can take on a character when it is home to artefacts in a certain style. Because of this, I have chosen to describe the more decorative aspects of the Egyptian style as Egyptiana, by analogy with Chinoiserie, the term applied to the European artistic style that reflected Chinese influences.

Imperial Rome was rich in Egyptiana, including Egyptian decorative elements such as columns, doorways, and mosaics applied to otherwise Roman buildings, statues, and cult objects associated with the worship of Egyptian deities, particularly the goddess Isis. The growing awareness of the legacy of the Classical world in the Renaissance saw a revival in the use of Egyptiana from the 15th century onwards, and excavated pieces were not only incorporated in contemporary interiors, but widely copied as well. From the early 18th century, works including Bernard de Montfaucon's *L'Antiquité Expliquée* published between 1719 and 1724, and the seven volume *Recueil d'antiquités égyptiennes, étrusques, grecques, gauloises* of Anne-Claude-Philippe de Caylus, published between 1752 and 1767, provided a source of Egyptian images for those wishing to use the style, and towards the end of the 18th century these influences began to make themselves felt in the British Isles.

In 1770 the first Josiah Wedgwood's library included Montfaucon's *L'Antiquité Expliquée* (which was available in an English translation by 1725) and the *Recueil d'antiquités* of the Comte de Caylus. From at least 1773, and possibly before, the Wedgwood pottery company produced items using Egyptian elements and both the Caylus and Montfaucon books, especially the latter, were the source of several designs (Fig 29). Later the company also used engravings of Egyptian vases from a 1721 comparative history of architecture by the Austrian architect Johann Bernard Fischer von

Fig 29
A pair of candleholders made by Wedgwood c 1830. Wedgwood's Egyptian-inspired designs drew on a variety of sources, but all of these sources presented Ancient Egyptian elements in isolation from their cultural background.

Fig 30
Wedgwood was not the only company making household items in an Egyptian style. These sphinx candleholders were made by Copeland c 1805–15.

Erlach, also in Wedgwood's library. However, although some of these engravings were depicted genuine Egyptian antiquities in the collections of Italian dignitaries, they were represented in a florid baroque style combining Classical elements with von Erlach's own fertile imagination. The resulting creations by Wedgwood may not have been archaeologically correct but they, and others like them produced by other manufacturers, were intended as fashionable items, not artistic reproductions (Fig 30). From around 1805 Wedgwood designs included hieroglyphs, but they were purely decorative, as it was not until 1822 that Jean François Champollion published the first of his ground-breaking works on the decipherment of hieroglyphs.

One of the most important sources of inspiration in the late 18th century for those wishing to use the Egyptian-style in interiors was Giovanni Battista Piranesi's 1769 *Diverse Maniere d'adornare i Cammini* (Various Ways of Decorating Fire Surrounds), in which 13 out of 36 plates were of Egyptianising designs (Fig 31), and in which the Italian text was accompanied by parallel texts in English and French. Some of his designs were executed as paintings on the walls of the *Caffè degli Inglesi* in Rome, where they would have been seen by those on

Fig 31
A plate from Piranesi's *Diverse Maniere d'adornare i Cammini* (1769). Piranesi's extravagant designs, although impractical for all but the grandest residences, did much to popularise images of Ancient Egypt such as mummies and inscribed obelisks. [The Society of Antiquaries of London]

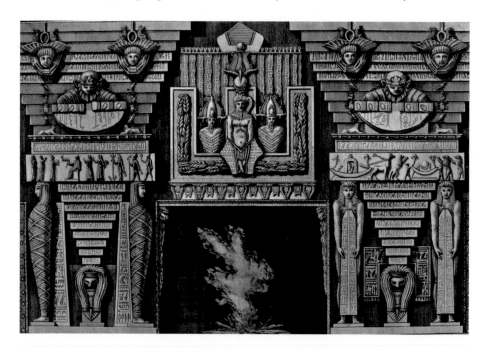

the Grand Tour. Piranesi was proposed as a member of the Society of Antiquaries of London
by the wealthy radical Thomas Hollis, who also donated a copy of Piranesi's work to the
Society's library. Into this copy, he inserted a manuscript quoting in Italian part of a letter he
had received with the book from Piranesi, which throws interesting light on the motivation
behind Piranesi's use of Egyptian elements. The sense of the passage is not altogether clear,
and so I have quoted it in the original Italian and in a fairly literal translation:

*Vi mando un saggio delle mie invenzioni, in una raccolta di 57 tavole di cammini ed altre
cose dipendenti dalla piccola ed elegante architettura, architettura per gl' usi della vita tanto
necessaria e per le manifatture. Vederete in quest' opera usato cio', che peranche in questo
genere non era conosciuto. L'Architettura Egiziana, per la [verso] prima volta apparisce; la
prima volta dico, perche [without an accent], fin ora, il mondo ha sempre creduto non esservi
altro che pirami[di] guglie, e giganti, escludendo non esservi parti sufficienti per adornare e
sostenere questo sistema d'architettura. Gl' Inglesi liberi vogliono qualche volta ogn'uno una
nuova specie di cose che si omogenea al suo temperamen[to]. Giudicarete.*

I am sending you a sample of my inventions, in a collection of 57 plates of chimneys
and other things appropriate in small and elegant architecture, architecture that is so
necessary for the purposes of life and for craft-work. You will see used in this work [the
Diverse Maniere] what was until now not known in this kind [of domestic architecture].
Egyptian architecture appears for the first time. I say, for the first time, because until now
everyone has always believed that there was not in such architecture other than pyramids,
spires [obelisks?] and giants [colossal statues?], ignoring that there are not in it [Egyptian
monumental architecture] sufficient parts to embellish and support this system of
architecture. The free [broad-minded?] English sometimes each want a new style of things
in keeping with the [individual] temperament [of each of them]. You be the judge.[56]

In Piranesi's time, the best known elements of Ancient Egyptian architecture would have
been the pyramids, obelisks (of which Rome had plenty) and monuments referred to in
Classical sources, such as the colossal statues of Amenhotep III at Thebes known as the
Colossi of Memnon. Little was known of temple architecture, and without knowing that
the domestic architecture of Ancient Egypt had been constructed almost entirely in mud
brick, little of which had survived, there must have seemed to be a puzzling lack of 'ordinary'
buildings. The first excavations at the Ancient Roman city of Pompeii had begun in 1748,
revealing well-preserved interiors with wall paintings and artefacts, but when it came to
Ancient Egypt there was a lack of similar material to draw on. Piranesi's aim seems therefore
to have been twofold; to supply the 'missing' decorative elements of Ancient Egyptian
architecture and to adapt it to domestic use in contemporary buildings. He also seems
to have believed, or hoped, that it would appeal especially to English tastes.

However, it was not until 1789 when probably the earliest interior in the British Isles with a
number of Egyptianising features was created in Scotland, where the architect James Playfair
designed Cairness House for Charles Gordon. Playfair travelled to Rome in 1792, and on
his return he prepared revised designs for the house, work on which had already begun, to
include a billiard room decorated in an Egyptianising style. A chimneypiece, window and door
surrounds and a frieze were painted with hieroglyphs, although, like those on Wedgwood's
pieces, these were purely decorative.

Another designer who, like Playfair, travelled to Rome was Charles Heathcote Tatham, who lived in the city between 1794 and 1796. He worked as an assistant to the Prince of Wales' architect Henry Holland and had been sent there by Holland to study Classical design. In 1799 Tatham produced *Etchings, Representing the Best Examples of Ancient Ornamental Architecture; Drawn from the Originals in Rome, and other parts of Italy, during the years 1794, 1795 and 1796.* He noted 'the calamitous events [the early battles of the French Revolutionary and Napoleonic wars] which have lately overwhelmed that beautiful country' and 'dispersed its treasures over the continent',[57] making it difficult for students of architecture to gain access to the original pieces shown in his book. He praises a number of architects and designers, including the Frenchman Julien-David Le Roy, James Stuart and Nicholas Revett, for producing works in the late 1750s and early 1760s which illustrated numerous models of Classical art 'having overturned that barbarous taste of architecture and decoration which prevailed some time back, and establishing in its stead the true principles of Grecian simplicity and perfection'.[58]

Fig 32
In semi-human form, Horus could wear the double crown, combining the white crown of Upper Egypt and the red crown of Lower Egypt, and emphasising his identification with the pharaoh.

Tatham also praised 'the celebrated Piranesi' as having produced 'the most valuable' of such works, but qualified this praise by noting that he had been:

> Fired with a genius which bad defiance to controul [sic], and rejected with disdain the restraints of minute observation, he has sometimes sacrificed accuracy, to what he conceived the richer productions of a more fertile and exuberant mind. This has betrayed him into much incorrectness of delineation.[59]

Tatham did not specifically mention Piranesi's *Diverse Maniere* with its extravagant Egyptianising fireplace designs, but is unlikely to have been thinking of these when he spoke of the 'chaste and beautiful examples' in his works. Despite his obvious preference for designs based firmly on actual Classical pieces, however, Tatham was not against the Egyptian style and his work contained plates illustrating two sphinxes, two lions, an 'idol' described as Osiris but more probably Horus wearing the double crown of Upper and Lower Egypt (Fig 32), and a human-headed canopic jar. One of the lions and one of the sphinxes had hieroglyphic inscriptions, and while these are not immediately readable in the plates, most individual hieroglyphs are copied with reasonable accuracy. Most of these pieces were in the Vatican in Rome, while the lions decorated the Fontana delli Termini and the Capitol in Rome. Whether these were Ancient Egyptian originals or Roman copies they were all described as Egyptian, and by including them with the purely Classical pieces Tatham indicated that they were also suitable models for designers and architects. He produced a number of designs for furniture and artefacts with Egyptianising elements himself, including pieces for Carlton House, the residence of the Prince Regent, which was extensively rebuilt between 1783 and 1796. Not all of these designs were actually created, but they would have influenced potential clients and other designers. Among the more than 200 subscribers to Tatham's book were the Duke of York and Sir Joseph Banks, as well as architects and designers like Joseph Bonomi Snr, George Dance, Joseph Gandy (see p 19), Henry Holland, Peter Robinson, John Soane and Samuel Pepys Cockerell.

Egyptian themes were already being used by designers like Tatham before the French invasion of Egypt, but after British victories at the Battle of the Nile and Alexandria, and the publication of *Voyages* by Vivant Denon, one of the scholars who had accompanied Napoleon's army to Egypt, conditions were right for the style to become the height of fashion for a while. Despite a lull in hostilities of just over a year following the signature of the Treaty of Amiens in 1802, the Napoleonic wars did not end until 1815, but France was still a powerful cultural influence and the Prince Regent, later to become George IV, was a Francophile in matters cultural, if not political.

The prince spent lavishly on his residences and one of his advisers on the remodelling of Carlton House was Walsh Porter, an arbiter of taste who in 1805 was to incorporate an Egyptian-style reception room into his own country retreat of Craven Cottage. Some of the Egyptian pieces created by Tatham and others for Carlton House or the Royal Pavilion at Brighton, including candelabra, desk sets, clocks and cabinets, were relatively modest in scale, if still expensive. But in 1806 the prince commissioned a magnificent silver-gilt table service, still in use for state banquets, with Egyptian decoration on a number of the items; it cost over £70,000, equivalent nowadays to around £3,000,000.

The elite craftsmen who supplied this market were happy to cater for the new fashion. The Vulliamy family produced a total of seven chimneypieces for Carlton House, and although none of these were in an Egyptian style, they made two with Egyptian decoration in 1805 and 1806, one for the Duke of Richmond and one for the Marquess of Blandford. They also supplied the Marquess with a clock case in the Egyptian style (Fig 33), and a piano made to resemble an Egyptian temple.[60] The first English furniture pattern books with pieces in the Egyptian style were produced by Thomas Sheraton between 1804–6, and around the same time Thomas Chippendale the Younger produced chairs and two tables with Egyptian decoration for a new library for Sir Richard Colt Hoare at Stourhead (see p 243), James Newton, one of the leading furniture makers of his day, produced two collector's cabinets with Egyptian decoration, and in his *Household Furniture* of 1808 George Smith also incorporated Egyptian elements.[61]

Another visitor to Rome at around the same time as the architect James Playfair was Thomas Hope, an immensely wealthy junior member of an Amsterdam banking dynasty of Scottish origin, whose Grand Tour lasted nearly seven years, between 1787 and 1795, and included Egypt, which he visited twice, returning just before the French invasion. His family fled

Fig 33
Black marble and ormolu
clock with Egyptian
decoration, one of three
in this style made in
1807–8 by Benjamin
Vulliamy. The one made
by them for the Marquess
of Blandford may have
been similar.
[Photo © Victoria and
Albert Museum, London]

Amsterdam in 1795, when it was occupied by the French, and like most of them Thomas Hope settled in London. In 1799 he purchased a Neoclassical mansion in Duchess Street and set about remodelling it. He coined the phrase 'interior decoration' and the decoration and furniture of the Duchess Street mansion were published in 1807 as *Household Furniture and Interior Decoration* in a conscious attempt to influence public taste, or at least the taste of the social elite. (The pieces by James Newton mentioned earlier are believed to have been inspired by a visit he made to Duchess Street in early 1804.) One of the rooms at Duchess Street was in an Egyptianising style. As well as a frieze of Egyptian figures, it included casts of genuine Egyptian antiquities, and Roman copies of them, made while Hope was in Italy, and a genuine Egyptian mummy. (At this time, not enough was known about Ancient Egypt to distinguish authentic antiquities from Roman copies or imitations of them.) In another, much smaller, room or closet Egyptian and other antiquities were displayed on an Egyptian-style chimneypiece. His country residence, Deepdene in Surrey also had Egyptian-style furniture.[62]

One spectacular application of the Egyptian style was a Sèvres porcelain dessert service with a 22ft-long miniature reproduction of some of the best-known temples of Egypt, taken from Denon's work, as its centrepiece (now at Apsley House, London, see p 91). Originally created between 1810 and 1812 for the Empress Josephine but rejected by her as 'too severe', it was given to the Duke of Wellington by Louis XVIII in 1818 after the defeat of Napoleon. Such ensembles were out of the reach of all but royalty and the most wealthy, but others could still commission more modest artefacts from the same firms and craftsmen who made them, and furniture, clocks, tableware, napkins, desk wares, vases, bookends, wallpaper and fabrics were all produced with Egyptianising details from the early years of the 19th century. In general, use of the Egyptian as a fashionable style in interiors was concentrated on public and reception rooms such as halls, libraries and dining rooms, reflecting changes in society during the 17th and 18th centuries. In the late 17th century, chimneypieces became lower, often incorporating mirrors and mantelpieces, allowing the display of clocks and similar items, and becoming a point of focus in a room. This helps to explain the production of items like clocks in an Egyptian style, and the particular theme of Piranesi's *Diverse Maniere*, as well as many of the designs in it, can probably be attributed to the fact that chimneys in Italy often had a truncated pyramidal shape.[63] From 1810, the traditional French style of food service, where all dishes were served at the same time, was replaced by so-called Russian Service where courses were served in sequence, creating space on the table for elaborate centrepieces and other decorations like the Sèvres service.

The sources which had inspired the use of Egyptian themes up to this point were an interesting mix. For example, in *Household Furniture and Interior Decoration*, Thomas Hope refers to specific Egyptian elements in his furniture as being derived from examples in the Vatican and Capitoline Museums and the Institute of Bologna, which he would have seen on his travels through Europe, and at the end of the work listed a number of works 'either representing actual remains of antiquity, or modern compositions in the antique style, which have been of most use to me…'.[64] These included the *L'Antiquité Expliquée* of Montfaucon and *Recueil d'antiquités* of Caylus, and 'Piranesi's works in general; and particularly his vases, candelabra and chimney-pieces'. (Although he did not cite it, Hope had been a subscriber to Charles Tatham's *Etchings … of Ancient Ornamental Architecture; Drawn from the Originals in Rome, and Other Parts of Italy*.) However, Hope did not need to rely purely on 18th-century sources like these, with their roots in the Classical tradition, as he had also travelled in Egypt, had first-hand experience of Egyptian architecture and antiquities, and could draw on the accounts of other travellers, such as the Revd Richard Pococke's *Description of the East*, which included material on Egypt, the *Travels* of Frederik Norden, the Danish naval officer sent to explore Egypt, and Vivant Denon's *Voyages*, all of which are mentioned at the end of Hope's book. It is not known when the Egyptian decoration and furniture and decoration at Duchess Street were created, but at least some of the furniture there had been designed by the beginning of 1803, suggesting that if Denon was an influence, it was at a fairly late stage.[65]

Elsewhere, however, although earlier authorities were still cited, Denon's work became an increasingly important influence. The chimneypiece that Benjamin Vulliamy and his son Benjamin Lewis Vulliamy created for the Marquess of Blandford in 1806 had heads modelled, according to their invoice, on ones from 'Ct. Caylos' (the Comte de Caylus), but another invoice for the piano created for him in 1811 specified that the ornaments had been copied from 'Denons Book'.[66] Denon was also cited as an inspiration for the central reception room in Craven Cottage, remodelled in 1806 for Walsh Porter. While this suggests an increasing reliance on sources with direct experience of the remains of Ancient Egypt, this did not necessarily mean an accurate or informed use of Ancient Egyptian elements. As long as hieroglyphs remained undeciphered, the meaning and function of Ancient Egyptian art and architecture could only be guessed at, or approached through the accounts of Classical authors. This made it easy to distort or misinterpret Egyptian source material, and the Picturesque tradition encouraged its use as part of eclectic interiors mixing Egyptian and Classical elements.

For a while, things Egyptian had been the height of fashion, but it is in the nature of fashion for it to change, and eventually the Egyptian style was replaced by others, particularly the Italian, Rococo, and Gothic, the latter coming to typify the Victorian period. By 1809 Rudolph Ackermann's *Repository of Arts* magazine, a barometer of contemporary taste, was comparing the 'barbarous' Egyptian style unfavourably with the Graeco-Roman, although this did not stop the magazine featuring a design for a chimney-front in the Egyptian style as late as 1822.[67] When the Sèvres Egyptian table service was given to the Duke of Wellington in 1818 there were fears that it might already be looking dated. The interior of the Egyptian Hall in Piccadilly was remodelled in an Egyptian style by J B Papworth in 1819 and Giovanni Belzoni's exhibition there in 1821 of reliefs from the tomb of Sety I was highly successful but by the time his wife Sarah tried to revive it in Leicester Square in 1825, after his death, it struggled to cover its costs.

Egyptiana went out of fashion for a while, but by the middle of the 19th century in addition to archaeological material in museums and private collections, numerous artists and archaeologists had visited and travelled in Egypt and a variety of authentic source material was becoming available which had not been refracted through the lenses of Classical and Renaissance culture. In 1837, J G Wilkinson published his impressively detailed *Manners and Customs of the Ancient Egyptians*, with hundreds of lithographic and woodcut illustrations by Joseph Bonomi Jnr, most of them drawn from reliefs and paintings in tombs and temples, and from surviving artefacts (Fig 34). In the preface to an abridged edition issued in 1854, Wilkinson noted that

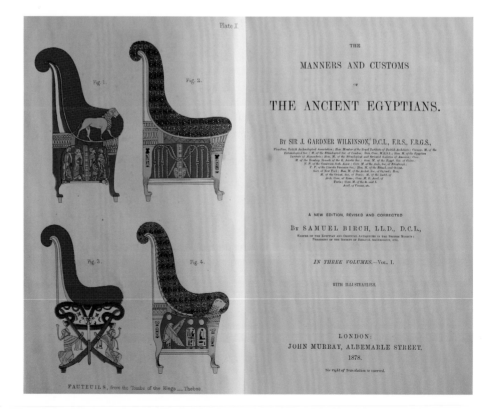

Fig 34
Ancient Egyptian examples, as depicted here in Wilkinson's *Manners and Customs of the Ancient Egyptians*, inspired contemporary designers in the 19th century after its first publication in 1837. [Courtesy of Museum Books]

…the impulse now given to taste in England has induced me to add some observations on decorative art, as well as on colour, form, and proportion … and as many of the ideas now gaining ground in this country, regarding colour, adaptability of materials, the non-imitation of natural objects for ornamental purposes, and certain rules to be observed in decorative works, have long been advocated by me, and properly belong to the subject of Egypt, I think the opportunity well suited for expressing my opinion upon them; while I rejoice that public attention has been invited to take a proper view of the mode of improving taste.[68]

In an industrial age, designers were needed, not just fine artists, and a system of design education began to emerge. Part of this was the production of pattern books and one of the first, George Phillips's 1839 *The Rudiments of Curvilinear Design*, covered the Egyptian as one of a number of national and historical styles. Perhaps the most influential, though, was Owen Jones's 1856 *The Grammar of Ornament*. Jones had not only travelled in Egypt, and worked there as an artist for Robert Hay, he was Superintendent of Works at the Great Exhibition, and created the Egyptian Court at the Crystal Palace with Joseph Bonomi Jnr and James Wild, who had both worked and travelled in Egypt, and who contributed illustrations to the Egyptian section of Jones's book.

While the design reformers never succeeded to the extent that they would have liked and public taste tended to remain obstinately unimproved, a number of designers adopted elements of the Egyptian style, although pattern books were often copied from directly, rather than being used, as they were intended, as sources of inspiration. Jones himself produced wallpaper for John Trumble and Co, and in 1857 Ford Madox Brown designed a chair based on an Egyptian original in the British Museum for the artist William Holman Hunt, who had visited Egypt. In the 1870s and 1880s, Edward Godwin's furniture designs, again inspired by British Museum originals, were produced commercially, and in 1885 Liberty and Co produced two pieces based on Ancient Egyptian furniture, both called 'Thebes'. One was a four-legged stool with a leather seat, yet again an almost exact copy of an original in the British Museum (Fig 35), although the design was registered, the other a three-legged stool with legs fixed directly into a solid wood seat. Both were highly popular and the three-legged stool appeared in the firm's catalogues until at least 1907. Clocks, tableware, jewellery and pianos with Egyptian themes and patterns were also produced. On a more prosaic level sewing machines were decorated with sphinxes; an 1897 watch retailing for 7s 6d was, for no apparent reason, unless perhaps its silent operation, called *The Sphinx*; a design of washbasin was called the *New Pyramid*; and a marmalade jar in the shape of Cleopatra's Needle, with decorative hieroglyphs, was produced. From time to time Wedgwood produced further 'Egyptian' pieces, and in 1978 it released a range inspired by the Tutankhamun exhibition at the British Museum six years before.

Fig 35
This genuine Ancient Egyptian stool in the British Museum was copied almost exactly in the late 19th century as the 'Thebes' stool by Liberty and Co, marrying the simplicity of Ancient Egyptian design to contemporary taste.
[© Trustees of the British Museum]

The use of the Egyptian style in architecture and interiors, as suggested initially, was often decorative, or non-structural. Much of its initial use for decorative wares and furniture was also superficial. The functional form of a candelabra, a desk set or a clock remained the same, but Ancient Egyptian decorative elements gave it an exotic gloss. The same sort of process can be seen at work in the use of other Oriental styles during the Regency period, such as the Chinese and Indian. This very exoticism made it first highly fashionable, but then susceptible to attack as barbarous and uncivilised. What attracted the design reformers to the Egyptian style from the 1840s onwards however was different. Reacting against what they saw as excessive decoration in contemporary styles, they valued Egyptian art for its conventionalised, symbolic and nonnaturalistic qualities.

The leading designer Christopher Dresser was well acquainted with Jones's *Grammar*, to which he had contributed a plate, and had visited both the Egyptian Court at the Crystal Palace and the British Museum to study Egyptian material. Unlike some other designers, he was prepared to design for mechanised production rather than limited craft production. He worked for the pottery and china firms Wedgwood, Minton, Royal Doulton and others in the second half of the 19th century and produced Egyptian-influenced designs for them. It was, however, what he called the severity and dignity of the style that interested him and fitted with his leaning towards abstract decoration, and he was not interested in directly copying Egyptian originals.

The simple geometric shapes of the Liberty stools, with their lack of human, animal or iconographic decoration, could be incorporated in modern interiors without clashing. The three-legged stool was sold in Samuel Bing's Parisian shop, *La Maison de l'Art Nouveau*, which gave its name to the movement and artistic style, and as early as 1896 one of these stools was purchased from the shop for a Norwegian industrial design museum. The use of increasingly stylised Ancient Egyptian elements can be seen to continue into Art Deco, which drew heavily on non-European traditions, and in which although Egyptian elements are suggested, they have been thoroughly assimilated and digested. The process of increasing stylisation did not, however, lead to the disappearance of recognisably Egyptian imagery on decorative and domestic items. Even at the time of writing, a modern Chinese copy of a vintage manual Singer sewing machine is still decorated with transfers showing a winged but recognisably Egyptian sphinx, based on those on the original machine.

Egyptiana can range, and has ranged, from simple reproduction to almost complete abstraction, and has been used in everything from complete interiors and royal furnishings to everyday household objects. It has been made of precious materials and metals, and of simple wood or pottery. It has been valued for its exoticism and its formality, become so iconic and familiar as to risk cliché, and appealed to both popular and high taste, but to this day the production of Egyptiana reflects the fact that our culture continues to find things of value in the material culture of Ancient Egypt.

Egyptology: From antiquary to Egyptologist

In the late 16th century those in the British Isles who began to study the relics of the past became known as antiquaries, and in 1572 a College of Antiquaries was formed in London by Archbishop Matthew Parker, Sir Robert Cotton, William Camden and others. It operated until 1604, when it was suppressed by King James I. This may seem surprising, but then, as now, the study of the past often has political resonances in the present day. Archbishop Parker was a leading Anglican theologian and his collection of early manuscripts was used to demonstrate the historical independence of the English Church from Rome. Cotton's library, donated to the nation by his grandson in 1701, and eventually acquired by the fledgling British Museum in 1753, was finer than any other of its time including the royal and institutional libraries but became seen as being used to support arguments in favour of an increased role for parliament, and it was confiscated in 1630 and only returned to his heirs after Cotton's death. Less controversially, Camden's great work *Britannia* was not only a geographical description but drew on his own researches, which included visits to sites and the study of artefacts as well as written sources, and it began to draw people's attention to the survival in the landscape of the remains of earlier civilisations, especially that of the Romans.

Fig 36
This book is an anonymous work of 1706, based on Greaves' *Pyramidographia*, of 1646, and its title refers to now discredited beliefs about the units of measurement employed to build Ancient Egyptian pyramids. [Courtesy of Museum Books]

At this period, there was little understanding in Europe of Ancient Egypt as a culture in its own right. Egyptian obelisks began to be unearthed and re-erected in Rome, and excavations on Roman sites uncovered Egyptian artefacts, or Roman versions of them, but these were interpreted almost exclusively with reference to Classical authors or biblical sources. Still further confusion was caused when so-called Hermetic texts were held to reveal occult secrets of the Egyptians and Ancient Egyptian religion was held to prefigure Christianity. In the absence of any understanding of hieroglyphic texts such as those on obelisks, vast edifices of erudite but misinformed speculation on their meaning were constructed by authors such as the Jesuit Athanasius Kircher. This situation persisted, despite a few reports from travellers who had actually visited Egypt such as the English mathematician and astronomer John Greaves. Both Greaves and Kircher studied oriental languages, Coptic and Arabic in the case of Kircher, Persian and Arabic in the case of Greaves, but Kircher was what would nowadays be called a desk scholar while Greaves actually visited Egypt in the late 1630s, staying there for four months. While in Egypt, Greaves studied and measured the Great Pyramid producing the first cross sectional plan of it, concluding that the pyramids were tombs and the structures in front the remains of funerary temples, rather than believing as many at the time still did that the pyramids were the granaries constructed by Joseph for the biblical pharaoh. Greaves drew on Classical sources, but tried to relate what they had to say to what he could actually see, and even though the book he produced in 1646 on his return to England, *Pyramidographia*, was poorly received his work was a sign of a new intellectual climate (Fig 36).

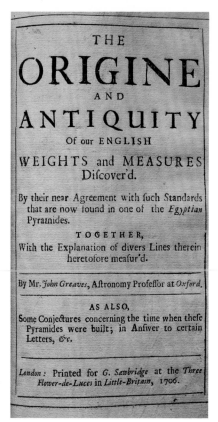

THE

ORIGINE

AND

ANTIQUITY

Of our ENGLISH

WEIGHTS and MEASURES
Discover'd.

By their near Agreement with such Standards that are now found in one of the *Egyptian* Pyramides.

TOGETHER,

With the Explanation of divers Lines therein heretofore measur'd.

By Mr. *John Greaves*, Astronomy Professor at *Oxford*.

AS ALSO,

Some Conjectures concerning the time when these Pyramides were built; in Answer to certain Letters, &c.

London: Printed for *G. Sawbridge* at the *Three Flower-de-Luces* in *Little-Britain*, 1706.

Gulielmus — Stukeley M.D.
Collegii Medicorum et Societatis Regiæ Londini Socius
G. Kneller Baronet pinx. 1721.   J. Smith Fec et ex. 1721.

Fig 37
The eccentric antiquarian,
Freemason and member
of the first Egyptian
Society in London,
William Stukeley. He
also helped to found the
Society of Antiquaries
and was its Secretary
for nine years, between
1718 and 1727.
[© Trustees of the
British Museum]

By the 18th century, although travel in Egypt was still difficult and hazardous, a few visitors to the country began to bring back reports and in 1741 the first Egyptian Society was founded in London. Its core membership was a select group of gentlemen who had actually visited the country, such as John Montagu, the 4th Earl of Sandwich, the Dane Frederik Norden, William Lethieullier, and the Revd Richard Pococke. Other members included the antiquary Revd William Stukeley (Fig 37), who believed that Druidism in the British Isles sprang from Egyptian colonies, that identifications could be made between biblical figures and pagan deities, and that Egyptian mummification sprang from the burial of the biblical patriarch Joseph. Although Stukeley was considered eccentric even in his own time, he and many if not most of the Society's members were also Freemasons and the belief that the origins of the Craft could be traced to Ancient Egypt was widely held then.

By the end of the 18th century there was a growing interest in the cultures of the Near and Middle East, and a new term, 'Orientalist', began to be used to describe those who studied them. A number of the 167 scholars who travelled with the French army when it invaded Egypt were Orientalists, and the work of their Commission, and especially that of Vivant Denon, was to revolutionise the study of Ancient Egypt. For the first time, information on the surviving material culture of that society was widely available, and when eventually supplemented by the successful decipherment of Ancient Egyptian scripts, meant that the culture could be studied through primary source material.

Limited excavations had taken place for centuries in Egypt, although they were little more than treasure hunting, an opportunity to acquire supplies of mummies as a medical ingredient or increasingly in later years an opportunity for travellers to take back souvenirs. However, after the French expedition there was a huge demand for Ancient Egyptian material, particularly large sculptures and papyri. Such items found their way into royal and aristocratic collections, many of which subsequently became the basis of the newly emerging national museums such as the British Museum (Fig 38). They were studied by scholars, but even then the emphasis was on removing material for study in the scholars' home countries rather than studying it in its country of origin. As a result, Egyptology is sometimes accused of exploitation, expropriation and exportation.

Much early excavation and collecting was driven as much by commercialism and nationalism as by scholarship. Items collected by the French savants accompanying Napoleon's expedition were confiscated by the British, and donated by George III to the British Museum. Without an occupational pension, the British Consul General Henry Salt aimed to fund his retirement by assembling and selling three large collections of Ancient Egyptian antiquities, one of which was bought by the British Museum, one on behalf of Charles X by Jean-François Champollion to form the basis of the Louvre's Egyptian collection, and the third sold at auction after Salt's death. The French Consul General, Bernardino Drovetti assembled a collection that was rejected by the French, but purchased by the king of Sardinia and became central to the present day Egyptian Museum of Turin. Another of Drovetti's collections went to the Louvre, while his third was bought by Richard Lepsius for the Prussian King Friedrich Wilhelm IV, and now forms part of the Berlin Museum collections. As well as this, many private individuals acquired their own collections of Ancient Egyptian antiquities. In the light of this, it is easy to assume that the accusations against Egyptology are justified. When set against the political and cultural landscape of the time, however, things are not quite so clear-cut.

If Egypt had been exploited, and its cultural heritage expropriated and exported, this was nothing new. There are more obelisks in Italy than Egypt, a direct result of the actions of successive Roman emperors, and even before the Roman conquest in 30 BC Egypt had been under uninterrupted foreign rule since the Persian re-conquest in 343 BC. Following the French invasion, Egypt remained a province of the Ottoman Empire but was ruled by Muhammad Ali Pasha with increasing independence, first as wali, or governor, and then under the self-assumed title of khedive, or viceroy (Fig 39). He, however, was of Albanian origin and had little interest in the remains of Ancient Egypt other than to use them to buy influence with the European powers. His ambitions led him to push through the rapid industrial

Fig 39
The de facto ruler of Egypt under the Ottoman Empire between 1805 and 1848, Muhammad Ali wanted to modernise the country, and had little value for the remains of Ancient Egypt except as building materials or gifts to cement relations with European powers. He is seen here in Cairo, in an 1844 portrait by the artist J F Lewis. [Photo © Victoria and Albert Museum, London]

development of Egypt and this was often at the expense of its past, Islamic as well as Ancient Egyptian. Joseph Bonomi Jnr noted the demolition of a temple at Armant to provide stone for a new sugar factory, and commented that the colossal statue of Ramesses II at Mit Rahina, ancient Memphis, could be 'entirely demolished at any moment that material might be wanted for the construction of a granary or a factory'. The most horrifying example of this nearly came in the 1830s, when Muhammad Ali proposed demolishing the Giza pyramids to provide ready-cut stone for Nile dams. This was only prevented by the shrewd actions of a French advisor who convinced him that quarrying fresh stone would be more economical. Muhammad Ali was succeeded in 1848 by Ibrahim Pasha, but little changed. In her letters from Egypt, written 1849–50, Florence Nightingale wrote of the destruction of a tomb at How (Hiw, in Upper Egypt) to make a sugar factory 'a private speculation of a son of Ibrahim Pacha'.

In such a climate, it was not surprising that some took the view that Ancient Egyptian monuments should be removed from the country for their own safety. The commercial exploitation of Ancient Egyptian antiquities may now seem objectionable and undoubtedly led to many sites being damaged or destroyed by uncontrolled excavation in search of antiquities, and to many items being acquired without significant information on their provenance or context, but without a commercial value many objects and sites would simply have been destroyed anyway, in the name of progress.

Gradually, things began to change. Egyptology began to emerge as a separate scholarly discipline, although the term itself was not used until 1859 and did not become common until the 1870s. Before then, those who studied Ancient Egypt were often simply referred to as Orientalists, or as Hierologists, Egyptologers or Egyptologues. The first attempts to set up a national museum in Egypt were made as early as 1835 but as fast as collections were assembled, successive khedives gave them away, usually to visiting European royalty. This was true of Khedive Said, but he was persuaded to appoint the French Egyptologist François Mariette as Director of an Egyptian Antiquities Service in 1858, and the first Egyptian Museum in Cairo was set up. By modern standards, Mariette's methods were crude. He excavated on an industrial scale, at one time having authorisation to recruit 7,000 labourers to work on various dig sites. European or Egyptian foremen were often left to their own devices for weeks at a time, and because money was not paid to workmen for finds that they made, objects often found their way into the hands of antiquities dealers, fuelling the commercial market. Sometimes, pieces were purchased and used to 'salt' unpromising sites so that excavations would be carried out there.[69] Despite this, Mariette was amongst the first, in 1877, to recognise the need to protect Ancient Egyptian buildings from damage from a rising water table and increasing salinity brought about by irrigation schemes.

A fundamental change began in the late 19th century. Flinders Petrie (Fig 40) first visited Egypt in 1880, where he carried out excavations at the Pyramids of Giza, and a year later, Major General Augustus Pitt-Rivers excavated near Thebes. Both men were pioneers of the systematic recording and publication of excavations, and Petrie combined Pitt-Rivers' use of stratification (the order of soil layers in the ground) with the use of artefacts to date the layers. Together with others, they laid the foundations of modern archaeology and Egyptology. Petrie in particular revolutionised archaeology in Egypt, through his emphasis on painstaking excavation, meticulous recording and prompt publication, and the creation of dated series of

objects, especially pottery, which could be used to date the layers in an excavation. He also recognised the importance of minor domestic objects and broken pieces. In the past, the emphasis had been on obtaining large monumental sculptures and other museum pieces, and much else had simply been discarded, and the information from it and its location and context lost.[70]

In 1883, a law was passed that made all antiquities the property of the Egyptian state. This did not, however, mean that nothing thereafter left Egypt. Excavations were increasingly carried out by institutions, such as the Egypt Exploration Society, and museums, which also loaned staff to other excavators, but it was still not uncommon for rich private individuals to sponsor them. Few of the latter, however, would have been happy with merely academic publications to show for their money. It was therefore the norm for finds from the excavation to be divided between the state (represented by the Egyptian Antiquities Service) and excavators, and then between the excavators and museums who had loaned staff, or the institutions and individuals who had sponsored their work. At the same time, museums routinely acquired material from the antiquities market.

Plenty of material was already in private collections, and surfaced at auction or through dealers from time to time, but illicitly excavated material was also widely available. Perhaps the most celebrated example was when in 1881, after the appearance on the market of a number of very fine papyri and other items, obviously from a common source, they were discovered to have come from a cache of royal mummies near Deir el Bahri in Thebes, exploited for years by a local Egyptian family. The acquisition of antiquities by museums through dealers, in England as well as in Egypt, continued for some time, but as the rules on exportation of antiquities were more strictly enforced, and museums became more concerned about establishing the provenance of the objects they acquired, less and less material left Egypt legitimately.

There has always been an uneasy tension between Egyptology as a scientific discipline and certain groups who wish to use its findings to bolster their own views, or those who attack it on political grounds. Much of the early impetus for excavation in Egypt came from a desire to confirm the truth of biblical accounts, and the first excavations of the Egypt Exploration Society concentrated on the Delta area because the possibility of finding sites named in the narrative of the Exodus made it easier to raise money from sponsors. As time went on, and society became increasingly secular, this became less important and more attention was paid to the culture and civilisation of Ancient Egypt in its own right, rather than as a supplement to biblical history or a foreshadowing of revealed religion.

In the late 19th and early 20th centuries, the physical remains of Ancient Egyptians were used in an attempt to bolster ethnological theories of the development of the human race, and often to assert the superiority of one ethnic group over another, and particularly of European over non-European culture (Fig 41). Thousands of skeletons, and especially skulls, were collected, measured and assigned to racial types. By contrast, between the two world wars, a short-lived theory known as Diffusionism held, in its most extreme form, that civilisation had spread out across the world from Egypt and some have even traced the origin of the Egyptians to a vanished prehistoric or Atlantean civilisation.

Fig 41
The allegorical sculpture representing Africa from the Albert Memorial in London, begun in 1864, but not completed until 1876. These romanticised images of pre-industrial cultures contrast with other sculptures representing Victorian agriculture, commerce, engineering and manufacturing, placed higher and nearer to the monument itself.
[© Nick White. Source English Heritage, K990321]

Egyptology has had to cope with political conflict since before the excavation of the tomb of Tutankhamun, and in recent years with demands for repatriation of antiquities on the grounds that they form part of the cultural heritage of Egypt. In a way, such tensions are endemic to any study of the past, whether recent or distant. The early study of Ancient Egypt was intimately associated with the occult philosophy of Hermeticism, and risked falling foul of religious orthodoxy, just as the original College of Antiquaries was suppressed on political grounds.

Modern Egyptology has seen the development from antiquary to archaeologist and from speculation to science. These days, it is as much about patient exploration by ground scanning, radar and soil and sediment analysis as spectacular discoveries, and much more emphasis is put on Ancient Egypt's links with neighbouring cultures and their influence on each other. Through a fortunate combination of circumstances, Ancient Egypt was not only a highly developed literate culture, but one whose remains have been exceptionally well preserved, and which can tell us much about it. We owe much in our civilisation indirectly to the Ancient Egyptians. The least we owe them in return is to listen to them with an open mind, and that is surely what Egyptology should be about.

Freemasonry: Wisdom from the east and the pharaoh's apron

Quite why Ancient Egypt should be associated with Freemasonry is not immediately obvious, as the central allegory in the series of ritual dramas through which Freemasonry teaches moral lessons and self-knowledge is the building of Solomon's Temple in Jerusalem. To understand why some Masonic temples were built in imitation of Ancient Egyptian ones and how Egyptian symbolism became associated with Freemasonry, it is necessary to delve back into the history of the Craft, a history which even the United Grand Lodge of England freely admits is 'still the subject of intense speculation'.

It is now generally accepted that Freemasonry as a secular fraternal society modelled itself on the 'operative' or working lodges of medieval stonemasons, using allegories based on their tools and customs, and that it may have evolved to counter the political and religious upheavals of the late 16th and early 17th centuries in Europe. Although the first documented creation of an English Freemason comes from 1646, the first Grand Lodge was not created until 1717 by the union of four London lodges. At this point, the ritual and ceremonies of the Craft were still relatively simple and passed on by word of mouth. There were also some documents setting out the supposed history of the mason's craft, and a series of rules or 'charges' to be followed by the mason. One of these documents, known collectively as the 'Manuscript Old Charges', dates to the late 14th century but all other versions are 18th-century copies attributed to lost earlier originals. These histories traced the use of stone in building from Adam and taught that the biblical Abraham travelled to Egypt, accompanied by Euclid who taught the Egyptians the practical application of geometry to work stone for building and rules of conduct to live and work by.[71]

The tradition of Ancient Egypt as a source of occult wisdom had already been present in biblical and Classical sources, and in the 15th century a text in Greek on hieroglyphs known as Horapollo was discovered and translated. Although the text is now known to be a medieval version of a 5th-century Graeco-Roman text, at the time and for long afterwards it was attributed to Hermes Trismegistus ('Thrice Great'), identified with the Egyptian god Thoth and believed to be a contemporary of Moses (Fig 42). Translated into Latin and Italian, the Horapollo text was used by Renaissance Humanist scholars to link Christianity with the philosophy and magic of Ancient Egypt and was the basis of the Hermetic view of hieroglyphs, which saw them as symbolic texts dealing with occult wisdom. In the 1770s, a Scottish-born

Fig 42
The legendary Hermes Trismegistus, teaching the principles of geometry and architecture to the Egyptians.
[Wellcome Library, London]

Hermes, of old, with mystic Science fraught,
Bade the proud Column rear its lofty Head;
And there engrav'd, the Wisdom that he taught,
To other Times and other Nations spread.

Fig 43
William Preston, whose
1772 *Illustrations of
Masonry* did much
to standardise the
ceremonies of early
English Freemasonry, and
which was also published
in America and Germany.
[Copyright and
reproduced by
permission of the
Library and Museum of
Freemasonry, London]

printer and Freemason called William Preston (Fig 43), who worked in London, developed the explanations (Lectures) of the symbolic pictorial representations (Tracing Boards) of the three main Masonic ceremonies by introducing more complex allegories and symbolisms, drawing on the Hermetic tradition. Included in his version of the Lectures was the idea of a 'near affinity' between the practices of Freemasons and those of the Ancient Egyptians, who concealed their wisdom in 'signs and hieroglyphical figures' which could only be understood by their priests. Preston was not only influential in British Freemasonry, but was in contact with Freemasons on the continent where the Craft is believed to have spread from Britain.

Freemasonry had become widely established in Europe by the 1730s but developed along significantly different lines to that in Britain. British Freemasonry was relatively inclusive and offered a way of overcoming or bypassing social barriers, but on the continent Freemasonry was more restricted within professional and aristocratic circles. In addition to the three degrees of Craft Masonry, those of Entered Apprentice, Fellow Craft and Master Mason, there are a number of 'side' orders or systems – that is those for which the status of Master Mason is a prerequisite, some based upon medieval orders of chivalry, and others of which draw their inspiration from Ancient Egypt. Continental Freemasonry was particularly keen on the creation of additional degrees and rites and it is therefore likely that Preston's development of the Masonic Lectures to include a greater emphasis on Ancient Egypt was influenced by continental ideas.

A key influence on the popularity of Ancient Egyptian elements in continental Freemasonry was the publication in 1731 of the Abbé Jean Terrasson's book *Séthos*. It described the life of an Egyptian prince whose trials prepare him for retirement into a temple of initiates of the Mysteries of Isis, which are described in detail, and it emphasised the Hermetic tradition of Egypt as a source of esoteric wisdom. It was a best-seller, and translations from the original French into English and German followed within a year and into Italian within three years. Library catalogues and inventories of continental Masonic lodges which mention it confirm that it was read in Masonic circles but Egyptian rites and iconography in Freemasonry did not become common until the 1780s.

The real impetus for the popularity of 'Egyptian' Freemasonry came with the invasion of Egypt by Napoleon in 1798. A number of the savants accompanying the army, as well as a number of its military officers, were Freemasons and they would have been receptive to any discoveries which could be seen as evidence of the origins of Freemasonry. Following this, French Masonic regalia such as aprons began to feature Ancient Egyptian architecture (Fig 44), and lodges began to adopt Egyptianising furniture and decoration and to display genuine Ancient Egyptian antiquities. A number of writers also attempted to trace the origins of Masonic Rites to the Mystery cults of the Ancient World, including those of Egypt; and the French archaeologist Alexandre Lenoir in particular did this with the 'French Rite', practised by the majority of continental lodges at this time.

In contrast to the continent, Egyptian elements in Freemasonry never really took hold in England and this may have been because they were seen as tainted by association with radical and republican politics. The liberal ideals of the Enlightenment found ready expression in Freemasonry, but could become politically uncomfortable in Georgian England when they became associated with the French and American Revolutions, and the enthusiasm of French Freemasons for discovering purported Egyptian roots of the Craft was perhaps too closely

Fig 44
A 19th-century French Masonic apron with images of Joseph-Napoleon Bonaparte, elder brother of the French emperor, and stylised Egyptian architecture in the background. [Copyright and reproduced by permission of the Library and Museum of Freemasonry, London]

linked with the Napoleonic cause, even though Bonaparte himself was not a Mason and his invasion of Egypt had been a military failure.

Even without Egyptian trappings, however, Freemasonry offered a powerful social networking system, reaching to the highest levels. The first Egyptian Society, which operated from 1741–3, was mainly composed of travellers who had actually visited the country, and most of its members were Masons. They included aristocrats such as the 4th Earl of Sandwich and the 2nd Duke of Richmond, but also military and naval professionals like William Lethieullier and Frederik Norden, and members of the clergy like William Stukeley and Richard Pococke.

An even clearer example of how the Craft could cut across social boundaries can be seen with the pioneer Egyptologist Giovanni Belzoni. It is not certain where and when he became a Freemason, but once he had achieved celebrity through his exploits in Egypt and his exhibition in London of casts from the tomb of Sety I, Freemasonry allowed someone who was not only a foreigner, but the son of a barber, and whose earlier career in Britain had been in the popular theatre, to mix with royalty. The Duke of Sussex was the first Grand Master of the United Grand Lodge of England (UGLE), formed in 1813 by the reconciliation and union of two rival bodies, and had created the Alpha (now Royal Alpha) Lodge, a private lodge under his personal control, set aside for Masons distinguished in some way, and selected and almost always proposed by himself. As the sixth son of the reigning monarch, he had little if any chance of acceding to the throne, but was noted for his liberal political views, and was called, 'A Prince among Radicals, and a Radical among Princes.'[72] Belzoni is believed to have joined the Alpha Lodge, and also became a Companion of the Royal Arch in Cambridge in 1820 and a Knight Templar during a visit to Norwich in 1821. Masonic records from this time are often sparse or non-existent, but whether Belzoni was already a Mason, having become one abroad and allowing him to fraternise with the social elite, or whether he was made a Mason in England to make this possible, the effect was the same. Thomas Pettigrew, whose interest in mummies was originally inspired by seeing Belzoni unroll them, was surgeon to the Duke of Sussex, and for 18 years a joining member (one joining an additional lodge or changing from that in which he was originally made a Mason) of the exclusive Alpha Lodge. The Revd George Adam Browne, Belzoni's sponsor in the Royal Arch and probably the Knights Templar as well, was chaplain to the Duke of Sussex, and another member of Alpha Lodge. After Belzoni's death in West Africa, his widow was assisted by a number of Masonic lodges, and individuals such as Browne who were also Freemasons.

Archaeological discoveries in Egypt encouraged the identification of links between Freemasonry and Ancient Egypt. As well as the simple presence of so much impressive ancient masonry there, the gradual deciphering of funerary texts such as the Book of the Dead fitted with the Masonic tradition that Wisdom comes from the East. Other discoveries, while less dramatic, could also be seen as significant. For example mimosa, which has a connection to Masonic funerals, was found in a wreath on the mummy of Amenhotep II. It was both easy, particularly with the support of Preston's Lectures, and flattering, to believe that Freemasonry could trace its roots back thousands rather than hundreds of years, and that the pharaohs themselves had been Masons.

This idea was given encouragement by Belzoni's widow, who believed that the kilt worn by pharaohs was related to the Masonic apron and that the paintings and reliefs on the walls of royal tombs showed the pharaoh being taken through the Degrees of Freemasonry (Fig 45). She wrote an essay on the supposed links between Freemasonry and Ancient Egypt, and was visited in Brussels by the American doctor and Freemason John Weisse, who later wrote a book on the subject, particularly the role of obelisks, drawing on her work. Sarah Belzoni's essay was also presented to the governing body of Dutch Freemasonry, who arranged for it to be printed and circulated to lodges in the Netherlands.

Still later, the transport to England of Cleopatra's Needle was largely financed by the surgeon, dermatologist and Freemason Erasmus Wilson, and carried out by the engineer John Dixon, another Freemason. When the Needle's twin was transported to New York, it was erected with Masonic ceremonies and the spectators included an estimated 9,000 Masons. Many collectors of Egyptian antiquities and patrons of Egyptology were also Masons, and their interest in Ancient Egypt may well have been influenced by their beliefs about Masonic history and heritage.

It was natural that those Masons who believed in the Craft's links to Ancient Egypt would want to celebrate them and one of the most obvious ways might seem to be through the decoration of lodges themselves. The first purpose-built Freemasons' Hall in England was not constructed until 1775, and most were built in the 19th century. Of these, however, very few were in an Ancient Egyptian style and the only one in England with an Egyptian-style exterior appears to be the Freemasons' Hall at Main Ridge near Boston in Lincolnshire, built in 1860 (see p 250). A number of Egyptian-style lodges were built in France and Belgium from 1840, and several in the United States in the late 19th and early 20th centuries. Egyptianising interiors were more common, especially in buildings that were not exclusively Masonic, and were created for the Masonic Hall in York, and lodge rooms at the Great Eastern Hotel, the Horseshoe pub, and Café Verrey in London. Where buildings were used for meetings of Royal Arch chapters, or served more than one Masonic order, especially the Royal Arch, rooms were sometimes decorated in an Egyptian style, and the Royal Arch Chapter Room in Edinburgh is an impressive example.

Fig 45
An illustration from Belzoni's 1820 account of his excavations in Egypt, showing the formal starched linen kilt which Egyptian pharaohs were often shown wearing. The resemblance that some saw between this and the apron of Freemasons encouraged beliefs that the Craft had its origins in Ancient Egypt. [Copyright and reproduced by permission of the Library and Museum of Freemasonry, London]

Fig 46

An 1857 certificate for the Ancient and Primitive Rite, derived from the Rite of Memphis, featuring imagery of obelisks and sphinxes, and conferring on Edward MacBean degrees including that of Patriarch of Memphis. [Copyright and reproduced by permission of the Library and Museum of Freemasonry, London]

Some Masons went beyond Egyptian themes in the architecture or decoration of lodges, and practised Orders that were inspired by Ancient Egypt. Prominent among these were the Rites of Memphis and Misraim. There is evidence for the operation of the Memphis Rite in England from the early 1850s, mainly in London and mainly by political exiles from France working the Rite in French (Fig 46). There is no global organisation regulating Freemasonry, and each Grand Lodge can choose whether to recognise others as Regular, or conforming to the same principles, or to consider them Irregular. English and continental Freemasonry split in 1877 when the Grand Orient of France adopted a constitution which did not require Masons to believe in God. UGLE recognised the Royal Arch and the so-called Chivalric

Degrees of Freemasonry, but the 'Egyptian' rites were tainted by their association with the controversial 18th-century figure calling himself Count Cagliostro, often described as an adventurer and charlatan, who claimed to have been initiated into one while in London and set up lodges allegedly following its teachings on his return to the continent. The Memphis and Misraim Rites were also associated with revolutionary politics in Italy and France, and were eventually unified by the Italian revolutionary Giuseppe Garibaldi. Orthodox, mainstream Freemasonry, heavily populated by members of the establishment from the royal family downwards, was not likely to recognise these Rites as Regular on such grounds alone, but there were additional causes for concern.

The Rites allegedly based on teachings stemming from Ancient Egypt also tended to emphasise the esoteric and even occult aspects of these teachings, and could unsurprisingly, as a result of this, attract the contemporary equivalents of Cagliostro, figures whose claims were enthusiastically embraced by some and dismissed as fraudulent by others. John Yarker (Fig 47), a Mason who had parted company with UGLE in 1862, sought to establish the antiquity of Masonic traditions, linking them with the ancient Mystery religions, set up his own Masonic organisations, and claimed to have been authorised to award degrees including those of Memphis-Misraim. He in turn nominated as his successor the occultist Aleister Crowley, who claimed to have been initiated as a Scottish Rite Freemason in Mexico, and to have been initiated as a Master Mason in a French lodge, which at that time was not recognised as Regular by UGLE. Crowley made several attempts to secure recognition by the Masonic authorities in Britain, but without success. Yarker may have been sincere in believing in the legitimacy of the Rites that he promoted; Crowley, adept at mythologising his own past, and with scant interest in any organisation that he did not control, was always an unlikely mainstream Freemason, and despite his occult epiphany allegedly being inspired in Cairo by an Ancient Egyptian stele, he developed his own occult teachings.

Fig 47
John Yarker, who before his break with the United Grand Lodge of England in 1862 was a Mark and Royal Arch Freemason, and at one point a member of the Quatuor Coronati Lodge, the research lodge of English Freemasonry. [Copyright and reproduced by permission of the Library and Museum of Freemasonry, London]

Others sought to make links between the architecture of Ancient Egypt, particularly pyramids and obelisks, and the teachings of Freemasonry. Reviewing the 1870 book *Papers on the Great Pyramid* in the *Masonic Magazine*, Brother William Rowbotham expressed the view that 'everything connected with the building lends itself in a remarkable manner to illustrate Masonic lore'. Later, Walter Marsham Adams, a barrister, attempted to establish a correspondence between the internal layout of the Great Pyramid and the journey of the soul described in the Ancient Egyptian *Book of the Dead*. In the preface to *The House of the Hidden Places*, published in 1895, he wrote

…in dealing with the ideas thus masonified, so to speak, in that mysterious structure, I have been led, or rather compelled, to employ phrases and symbols current among the Masonic brotherhood of the present day, such as Grand Arch, Purple Arch, Royal Arch, the Star, the Open Angle … and other insignia of the craft. Whenever therefore such expressions occur – and they run necessarily through the entire work – it should be remembered that they are here designed to refer to the actual masonry of the Grand Pyramid, and the analogous features in the Ritual of ancient Egypt. At the same time, whether any vestige of this secret doctrine of the Light may survive in the esoteric doctrine of which those subject to Masonic rules are not permitted to speak, is an interesting question which naturally suggests itself, though it evidently cannot be established by open discussion.[73]

Despite the hints in this passage, there is no direct evidence for Adams having actually been a Mason himself.

In 1886, several years before Adams's book had been published, the UGLE had founded a research lodge, the Quatuor Coronati, to study Masonic history systematically. Initially, theories of the origins of Freemasonry in the legendary past were not dismissed out of hand, and Yarker wrote a number of papers for its *Transactions*. Gradually, however, the origins of the Craft in the late 16th century were established to professional historical standards. The lack of central direction in the choice of architectural style for Masonic buildings had always meant that externally most of them mirrored the predominant styles of their era, which in Victorian times were Gothic or Classical, and the process of redefining Masonic history gradually removed the legitimacy of Egyptian features or furnishings. 'Egyptian' Freemasonry may only survive now in the form of the teachings of some Orders, but it has left the legacy of some spectacular buildings and interiors, in Britain and abroad, as reminders of a belief in the 'Pharaoh's Apron'.

Hieroglyphs: Writings of priests, words of the gods…

To the Ancient Greeks hieroglyphics were *ta hiero glyphica*, 'the sacred carved letters', and to the Ancient Egyptians they were *medoo netcher*, 'the divine words' (Fig 48). The last securely dated inscription in Ancient Egyptian hieroglyphs was written in AD 394 (Fig 49), and sometime after that the ability to read and compose them, even in the land of their birth, was lost. It was to be over a thousand years before the first attempts were made in Europe to decipher the scripts of Ancient Egypt, and more than 1,400 years before the attempts succeeded.

The ability to decipher a system of writing whose meaning has been lost depends on two things; an understanding of its principles and a knowledge of the language that it is used to write. For simplicity, writing systems can be thought of as falling into three main types. In phonetic systems, characters are used to record single sounds or groups of sounds. The Western alphabet with its 26 basic signs is an example of this, although variations on these and accents are often used to record the sounds peculiar to individual languages. In pictographic systems, characters are simplified drawings of the things they represent, and in ideographic systems characters are used to represent more abstract concepts. Chinese characters are a complex system but include pictographic characters and combinations of these to represent more complex and abstract ideas.

Fig 48 (far left)
A hieroglyphic inscription from Karnak, showing the different ways in which they can be written; in horizontal lines or vertical columns, and read left to right or right to left, depending on which way animal, bird or human glyphs are facing.
[© Chris Elliott]

Fig 49 (left)
The last datable hieroglyphic inscription, in the Temple of Isis at Philae, naming Merul, son of Horus, and showing the local Nubian sun god Mandulis. It can be dated, by a demotic graffito accompanying it, to 24 August 394 AD.
[© Chris Elliott]

Fig 50
Sketches by Albrecht Dürer illustrating the first symbols in a Latin translation of the Horapollo text, produced between 1507 and 1519. Taken out of context, it was easy to misinterpret the pictorial forms of hieroglyphs as esoteric symbols.
[© Trustees of the British Museum]

Fig 51
This stele, with a Coptic inscription carved on limestone, was excavated at the site of the Monastery of Apa Jeremias near Saqqara. From the 3rd century AD the Egyptian language was written in Coptic script, derived from the Greek alphabet. Because vowels are written and the spoken language was preserved in church ritual it was possible to deduce the sound values of hieroglyphs.
[© Trustees of the British Museum]

For centuries, the greatest obstacle to the understanding of hieroglyphs was the belief that they were primarily symbolic, rather than characters used to write an actual language. Around the same time that the last hieroglyphic inscriptions were being written, in the 4th century AD, a writer in Egypt called Horapollo produced a list of nearly 200 hieroglyphs with his interpretation of their meaning. By this time, however, he was writing about an archaic script which was probably only understood by a small number of priests of the traditional deities of Egypt, and although some of his information was accurate, much of it was mistaken, particularly his claim that the meaning of the signs was symbolic. In 1415 a version of the Horapollo text was discovered, and circulated first in manuscript copies and translations, then in a printed version (Fig 50). In his interpretation, not only were the signs thought to be symbolic, but their meaning was thought to be often allegorical and used to veil secret wisdom which had been revealed only to a select few. Despite the effort that was put into such interpretations, they were essentially castles in the air, but this approach was to dominate attempts to translate hieroglyphs until the 19th century. The 17th-century Jesuit scholar Athanasius Kircher studied documents from Egypt written in a language called Coptic, and recognised this as a late form of Egyptian, written in the Greek alphabet supplemented by extra characters (Fig 51), but still persisted in believing that hieroglyphs were a symbolic script used to convey esoteric wisdom.

With the dawn of the Enlightenment in the 18th century, a more sceptical and scientific approach began to be taken. In a book published in 1741 and soon translated into French, the English bishop William Warburton (Fig 52) set out his view that hieroglyphs had not been invented by Ancient Egyptian priests purely to conceal their secrets from the common people, but that they were used to record legal and business matters as well as religious material. He was also one of the first to recognise links between other scripts from Ancient Egypt and the hieroglyphic inscriptions carved on monuments such as obelisks.

Twenty years later, in an important development, the Keeper of Medals in the French royal collection, Abbé Jean-Jacques Barthélemy, suggested that the barred oval rings found in hieroglyphic inscriptions, now known as 'cartouches' after their resemblance to 18th-century musket cartridges, could contain royal names (Fig 53). This idea was further elaborated by Joseph de Guignes, Professor of Syriac (a Middle Eastern dialect) who had also studied Chinese, where similar rings were used to highlight proper names. The suggestion of links between Ancient Egyptian hieroglyphs and Chinese was also made by others, including the eccentric English antiquary William Stukeley, and the English Catholic priest John Turberville Needham, who attempted to translate the hieroglyphs on a bust in an Italian collection by comparing them to Chinese characters. Despite the fact that Coptic was of great antiquity and still in use in Egypt for church services, the fact that it was written with Greek letters, and some additional ones for sounds not found in Greek, led de Guignes in particular to conclude that it had been corrupted by Greek, and that Chinese was the language of an Egyptian colony, and remained closer to its source. This idea, although plausible, was to be another dead-end approach to the translation of hieroglyphs.

The Danish antiquarian and scholar Georg Zoëga learned Coptic, studied inscriptions on the numerous Egyptian obelisks in Rome and produced a corpus of nearly a thousand hieroglyphs, grouping them by type, for example birds and human figures. However, despite working out that hieroglyphic inscriptions were read in the direction the signs faced, and agreeing that cartouches contained royal names, he made no further progress with interpreting their meaning. Zoëga published his work in a book on the purpose and uses of obelisks in 1797. A year later Napoleon's armies invaded Egypt and a year after that, in July 1799, one of the most famous discoveries in archaeology was made by a French working party repairing defences at a fortification they called Fort St Julien, near the modern town of Rashid in the Nile Delta.

The Rev.d D.r Warburton

Fig 53

The shape, now known as a cartouche, used vertically or horizontally to enclose the names of Ancient Egyptian kings, was actually an extended form of the *shen* hieroglyph, a knotted rope signifying both eternity and protection. *See* Figs 48, 58 and 59 for examples of cartouches used vertically. [Mark Rudolph]

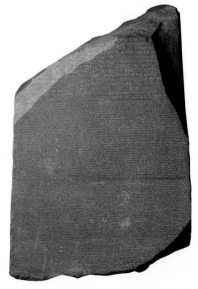

What the troops under the command of the engineering officer Pierre François-Xavier Bouchard unearthed was, of course, the Rosetta Stone (Fig 54), and what followed is the stuff of legend. The stone provided what had previously been missing; parallel versions of the same text in different languages, one of which, crucially, was Greek, which could already be read. The young French genius Jean-François Champollion was then able to decipher the hieroglyphs, and for the first time in more than a thousand years the writings of the Ancient Egyptians could be read again.

Except that it wasn't quite that simple. When the Stone was discovered, Champollion was only nine years old and it was to be another nine years before he began work on its inscriptions. When he did, it was to be another 14 years before he made his crucial breakthrough, and when he did the text that triggered it was not from the Rosetta Stone. Along the way, he several times pursued theories that were mistaken and flawed, and when he did succeed it was some time before his approach was generally accepted as correct.

Fig 54 (above)
Dated by our calendar to 27 March 196 BC, the Rosetta Stone records an agreement between the monarch and the priesthood rewarding their support for him during the suppression of revolts in the Delta area of Egypt and Upper Egypt. [© Trustees of the British Museum]

Fig 55
The demotic script was used mainly for legal, official and business documents, written on papyrus or fragments of pottery or stone, but was also used for magical and funerary texts such as this one. It probably dates to the 3rd century, when Egypt was under Greek and then Roman rule, and combines a vignette, or picture, showing divine figures, some 'pseudo-hieroglyphs' and a demotic text from the 'Book of Breathings', a collection of spells intended to protect the deceased and assist their passage to the afterlife. [© Trustees of the British Museum]

Despite the fact that the Greek inscription could be read, and that the significance of the Stone had been appreciated as soon as it was found, it was to frustrate some of Europe's finest scholars for years. The Stone is a large fragment of a round-topped slab, or stele, inscribed with three copies of a long and formal agreement between a synod of Egyptian priests and the 14-year-old ruler of the country, Ptolemy V, known by his title as *Epiphanes* or 'God Manifest', setting out his endowments to temples, remittances of various taxes, amnesties and reforms, and eulogising him as a living god and ideal ruler. The ruling dynasty of Egypt at this time, established by the first Ptolemy, one of Alexander the Great's generals, were Macedonian Greeks and so one of the inscriptions was in Greek. Another, of which the least is preserved, was in hieroglyphs, and the third in a script known as demotic, and initially also referred to as enchorial. Demotic, although the script is derived from hieroglyphs, is a very cursive form and used to write a late version of the language. It was employed for everyday documents, including business and legal ones, among the Egyptian-speaking population since by the time the Stone was carved and set up hieroglyphs were an archaic form of writing employed for religious inscriptions (Fig 55).

To us it now seems surprising, but initial efforts to decipher the Egyptian texts on the Stone focussed on the demotic section rather than the hieroglyphic. However, the demotic section was the most completely preserved, and the easiest point of entry to the text seemed to be to try and identify the demotic equivalents of the proper names which could be read in the Greek text. By 1802 the Swedish diplomat and Orientalist Johan Åkerblad had succeeded not only in doing this, but also in recognising from their Coptic forms the words for 'temples' and 'Greeks' and identifying the suffix pronoun for 'him'. At this point, however, he stalled and failed to make any further progress. The root of the problem, for him and for others who worked on the Stone, was that they still did not understand the principles on which either demotic or hieroglyphic texts worked. Åkerblad had managed to identify words which were written alphabetically, but this only worked for some sections of the text, and if demotic looked like the sort of scripts with which scholars of Middle Eastern languages were familiar, it was still possible that hieroglyphs were symbolic or decorative, and not the sort of script used, as the Egyptologist John Ray has remarked, 'to convey ephemera such as the price of donkeys'. Things were not made any easier by the fact that there was another script, hieratic, known from its use on papyrus documents (Fig 56). Although the Rosetta Stone itself was in London, taken there by the British as the spoils of war, casts and copies of the inscriptions were made, and scholars on both sides of the Channel vied to be the first to solve its mysteries.

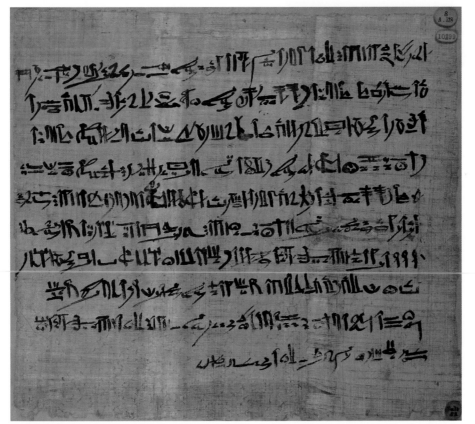

Fig 56
This papyrus with the text of a hymn to Osiris is written in hieratic script, a cursive and simplified form of hieroglyphs used from the earliest times in Ancient Egypt. It was still in use in the Third Intermediate Period, between 1069 and 664 BC, when this text was written.
[© Trustees of the British Museum]

Sir Thomas Lawrence. P.R.A. Pinx^t   Henry Adlard. Sc

Thomas Young

Fig 57
Thomas Young, shown here in an engraving of a portrait by Sir Thomas Lawrence, presented his first paper to the Royal Society at the age of 19, and by 28 was Professor of Natural Philosophy at the Royal Institution. [© National Portrait Gallery, London]

One of them, in France, was Champollion, and another, in England, was Thomas Young (Fig 57), a brilliant polymath whose achievements were astonishing. As well as being a gifted physician and familiar with at least 12 languages including Coptic, he anticipated the wave theory of light and established key formulae still used in life assurance and civil engineering. Unknown to either man, both were working on the texts of the Stone, and they only became aware of each other when Champollion mistakenly addressed a letter to the Royal Society, of which Young was the Foreign Secretary, rather than the Society of Antiquaries who were the first keepers of the Rosetta Stone when it came to London. Champollion was hampered by the lack of an accurate copy of the Stone and had written to ask if his copies, which differed in places, could be compared with the original and corrected from it. Both men also realised the importance of having copies of other hieroglyphic inscriptions to test their theories on. Young had been corresponding with Silvestre de Sacy, one of the first French scholars to study the Stone, Åkerblad, who had continued de Sacy's work, and Edmé Jomard, who was editing the massive *Description de l'Égypte*, the record of the work of the savants who had accompanied Napoleon's army. The *Description* contained many engravings of inscriptions, although like many copies at this time they contained errors created by artists or engravers unfamiliar with the scripts, but Jomard was reluctant to make any available to Young. The stakes for both Young and Champollion were high; the prestige of being the first to be able to read hieroglyphs again would be enormous, but both men also appreciated the risks of publishing too early. A partial solution might not only be wrong, but might give valuable clues to a competitor. Ultimately, this was to lead to an ill-natured dispute between Young, Champollion and the supporters of both men, involving wounded academic sensibilities and insinuations of plagiarism, compounded by elements of national pride, which has dragged on to this day.

Åkerblad had shown that some groups in the demotic text could be read alphabetically, but Young recognised that the Egyptian texts used both alphabetic and non-alphabetic signs, particularly those used to mark plural forms, and that some demotic signs could be seen to be related to hieroglyphs, as could some hieratic signs. This was still a long way from deciphering the scripts, but Young managed to identify word groups in the demotic and hieroglyphic texts, many of them correctly, and started to identify alphabetic hieroglyphs. By 1819 he had managed to identify the name of Ptolemy six times in the text of the Stone, and those of Ptolemy and Berenice, a Ptolemaic queen, in texts from the temple of Karnak, and had attempted translations of 218 demotic words and 200 hieroglyphic groups from the Rosetta Stone. Young published his results anonymously in a supplement to the *Encyclopaedia Britannica*, but at this point he still believed that alphabetic demotic and hieroglyphs were only used to spell out foreign words and names. Champollion originally believed that there were four separate scripts; demotic, used for business, hieratic, used for religious purposes, hieroglyphs for monumental inscriptions, and hieroglyphs with esoteric significance. He also originally believed that hieroglyphs were later than demotic and hieratic, and developed from them. By 1821, however, he had recognised that hieratic characters were a modification of hieroglyphs, although he still believed that they had no phonetic component, and published these results. They confirmed what Young had already deduced, and also published, but anonymously in a small and fairly obscure journal of which Champollion was probably not aware.

Around this time, the wealthy traveller and scholar William Bankes brought back to England an obelisk and its pedestal which had stood at the Temple of Isis at Philae in Upper Egypt. Young, who had set up an Egyptian Society to collect and publish all known Ancient Egyptian inscriptions, had encouraged Bankes not only to search for the missing section of the Rosetta Stone, but also to copy the names of kings and gods that he found. The obelisk had a hieroglyphic inscription, and its base, when cleaned, revealed a Greek inscription with the names of Ptolemy and two of the numerous Cleopatras (Fig 58). Bankes suspected that the obelisk texts would provide another valuable correspondence between royal names in their Greek and hieroglyphic forms. He published the inscriptions for private circulation, and in the margin of a number of the lithographs pencilled in the annotation 'Cleopatra', indicating that he suspected it appeared in the hieroglyphic text. This was not as simple a conclusion as it might appear, since the name appeared twice in the Greek text but only once in the hieroglyphs. Bankes drew on his observations of Egyptian temples, where he had recognised that Ptolemaic kings and queens were shown in relief carvings, and that their order reflected the order in which their names appeared in accompanying Greek inscriptions. Bankes copied an important list of royal names which he discovered at Abydos (Fig 59), and although he refused to make it available to Champollion, Young sent a copy to Champollion in 1823 without telling Bankes. A copy of the Philae obelisk inscriptions had also reached Paris, and Bankes's simple pencil annotation was to provoke a bitter dispute.

Fig 58
Phonetic hieroglyphs were used to spell out the names of foreign rulers of Egypt, like Cleopatra, as in this cartouche from a temple built under the rule of the Ptolemaic dynasty.
[© Chris Elliott]

Ironically, because of an artist's mistake while copying the inscriptions, Young believed that he had made an error in his identification of alphabetic characters and made little progress with the obelisk texts. Meanwhile, Champollion had been doing a numerical analysis of the Rosetta Stone texts. If hieroglyphs were ideograms, with each representing an idea, there should be some correspondence with the Greek text, but while there were less than 500 Greek words, there were many more hieroglyphs. If the hieroglyphs were grouped it made no difference, as he found only around 180 groups. He began to suspect that the script was neither alphabetic, pictographic nor ideographic, but some combination of all three. He had also firmly established a link between demotic, hieratic and hieroglyphs, and was converting texts between the different scripts. Using this process on a papyrus brought back to Paris (the 'Casati' papyrus), he was able to convert a name that he believed to be that of Cleopatra from demotic to its presumed hieroglyphic form.

In early 1822, Champollion obtained a copy of the engraving of the Bankes obelisk, and found in the inscription a cartouche with a name that closely corresponded to his version of the name of Cleopatra. This not only allowed him to confirm the value of numerous phonetic or alphabetic characters, but also to deduce that there could be more than one making the same sound, which would explain to some extent why there were so many different hieroglyphs. Later, Bankes would allege that Champollion had seen Bankes' pencil note on the obelisk text engraving and owed his identification of Cleopatra's name to it. It now seems clear that Champollion arrived at his conclusion independently and that Bankes' engraving only provided confirmation, but at the time, with the Napoleonic Wars not long past, nationalism, politics and a charged academic atmosphere meant that there were plenty ready to believe, and repeat, the allegation.

Young had correctly concluded that certain hieroglyphs appearing after the names of queens were there to identify them as royal female names. Now Champollion realised that some of the stars which appeared in a carving of a zodiac in the temple of Dendera did not represent actual stars, but showed that the hieroglyphs before them were used to write the names of stars. This was a crucial breakthrough, establishing another key principle of the script, that of determinatives or semantic markers. Champollion could now read the names of Greek and Roman rulers, and some of their titles, written in hieroglyphs, but it was still not clear whether the same principles would work with the names of Egyptian rulers.

In September 1822, he received copies of inscriptions from the temple of Abu Simbel in Nubia, which had only recently been rediscovered by Europeans and cleared of sand so that it could be entered. The inscriptions included new names in cartouches. In one of these, Champollion identified its first hieroglyph as a picture of the sun, Re or Ra in Coptic, and its final two hieroglyphs as that used to write an 's' sound. From Classical authors, he knew that well before the Greeks and Romans ruled Egypt there had been several pharaohs called Ramesses, and if the remaining sign was read as 'm' or 'ms', the name as a whole could be read as 'Ramesses' (Fig 60). Young had already suggested that a hieroglyph showing a sacred ibis bird on a standard might be used to write the name of the god Thoth, but when Champollion found another cartouche with this hieroglyph instead of the sun sign, he was able to read the whole as the name of Thothmes, another pharaoh (Fig 61). So excited was he by this crucial discovery that he ran to find his brother, but years of obsessively hard work, often in difficult personal and financial circumstances took their toll and after gasping out *'Je tiens l'affaire!'* (a bit like Archimedes' famous cry of *'Eureka!'*, or 'I have it!') he collapsed in a dead faint and was in a state of nervous and physical collapse for the next five days.

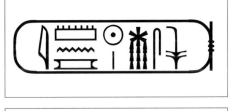

Fig 60
This cartouche of Ramesses II gives his birth name (as opposed to the name he took on acceding to the throne) and the epithet 'Beloved of Amun'.
[Mark Rudolph]

Fig 61
The 'Son of Ra', or birth name of one of the pharaohs called Thutmose (or Thothmes). The ibis hieroglyph can be read as 'Thoth', the Greek form of the god's name, and the second sign as *mes* (see Fig 165). The final sign is an extra 's', a process known as phonetic complementing.
[Mark Rudolph]

By 20 September 1822 he had resumed work and on the 27 September he read the main paper, on phonetic hieroglyphs, at a meeting of the Academy of Inscriptions and Literature in Paris. This was later expanded into a document sent to the Perpetual Secretary of the Academy, the landmark in Egyptology known by the short version of its title as the *Lettre à Monsieur Dacier*. Young was present at this meeting, and without knowing it initially the two men actually sat next to each other. As Champollion's paper had to be submitted in advance to be lithographed and copied for the audience there had not been time for it or the *Lettre* to mention the Abu Simbel inscriptions, but these had been a vital catalyst, as they proved that phonetic hieroglyphs had been used before the Greeks and Romans, and not simply to write foreign names and words.

Champollion now began to realise the full complexity of the system of writing with which he was dealing. It was one that used pictograms, ideograms and phonograms. Hieroglyphs could represent the object they depicted, an idea associated with it, or a sound, and sometimes the same hieroglyph could be used in more than one way. Some hieroglyphs, now known as 'determinatives', were used at the end of a word to show its sense, especially where words were otherwise written identically. Like a number of other languages with which he was familiar, such as Arabic and Hebrew, it largely ignored vowels, but a single hieroglyph could be used to write one, two or three consonants.

Initially, Young was gracious enough and even though he spoke of Champollion having 'borrowed an English key', he conceded that it fitted a 'dreadfully rusty' lock which few would have had the ability to open. Soon, however, relations between the two men soured. Young behaved as if Champollion were a junior colleague or protégé who had not sufficiently acknowledged his debt to the older man, and in an anonymous review of the *Lettre* maintained that Champollion had merely 'confirmed and extended' a system devised by Young. The question of how much Young had contributed to the decipherment of hieroglyphs became increasingly irrelevant as Champollion's progress became more confident, and further material confirmed the basic principles of his approach, while Young effectively abandoned the study of Ancient Egyptian scripts.

Both men had made important discoveries, in all likelihood independently, and both had made numerous false starts and mistakes. Young did not help himself by often publishing anonymously, and Champollion suffered from his reluctance to publish anything before he was certain of his findings. Young is remembered for his outstanding achievements in several fields of science, Champollion for one thing. Young was hampered by his rather mechanical approach and relied on the rare discovery of parallel texts, and in the end it was Champollion's obsessive dedication to the problem and his extensive knowledge of Coptic and the Ancient Egyptian scripts that was to prove decisive. If Young was a lighthouse Champollion was a laser.

Astonishing as it may now seem, for years after the publication of the *Lettre à Monsieur Dacier* there were still those who disputed Champollion's approach, and for even longer there were those who stubbornly continued to claim for Young the lion's share of the credit for deciphering hieroglyphs, and imply that Champollion's success was due to academic skulduggery. Some, including Bankes and Young himself, had questioned the value of what would be revealed when hieroglyphs were finally translated. What they wanted were historical records, what they worried about was that the texts would simply be religious. As a writer in the *Gentleman's Magazine* observed tartly in 1832, 'Little will be found but superstitious mythological trash.'[74]

Even when it became clear that as well as history and religion the writings contained laundry lists, love songs and the price of donkeys, the idea of hidden esoteric wisdom died hard. In 1936, in his book *A Search in Secret Egypt*, the philosopher and mystic Paul Brunton could still maintain that hieroglyphs had been communicated by an adept from Atlantis, before it sank, to the Ancient Egyptians, themselves descendants of an Atlantean colony. He also held that hieroglyphs had a threefold meaning, being used to record the sounds of the language, and the information communicated in it, but also having a hidden meaning known only to initiates.

Champollion died when he was only 41 but others continued to build on his work and system, which was championed by Samuel Birch (Fig 62) in England and by Richard Lepsius in Germany. A general problem was the lack of accurate copies of texts to work from, and although copies were often made under conditions of great difficulty, unreliable epigraphy was still a major stumbling block. There was also a lack of reference works, although the banker and antiquarian Samuel Sharpe began to publish a series of *Egyptian Inscriptions* from 1837 and a basic hieroglyphic vocabulary in the same year. In 1861, he published *Egyptian Hieroglyphs*, which had the first hieroglyphic fount in England, designed by the artist and sculptor Joseph Bonomi Jnr, who had travelled extensively in Egypt and studied its inscriptions *in situ*.

Fig 62
Samuel Birch, who worked at the British Museum for nearly 40 years, between 1846 and 1885, and was Keeper of Oriental Antiquities, which included the Ancient Egyptian collections. He did much to establish the systematic recording and cataloguing of the collections, and lectured and published widely. [© Trustees of the British Museum]

In 1857, Samuel Birch published his introduction to the study of hieroglyphs and followed it in 1867 with an Egyptian grammar and dictionary listing over 9,000 words. By 1892, Harrison and Sons, who published for the British Museum, could offer 15 different hieroglyphic founts, and in 1897 work began on the monumental *Wörterbuch der ägyptischen Sprache*, better known in English as the *Berlin Dictionary*. Begun by the German Egyptologists Adolf Erman and Herman Grapow, it aimed to cover all phases of the Ancient Egyptian language and was not completed until 1961, by which time it included around 16,000 words. There was also a need for accessible texts which could be used by students, and the British Egyptologist Alan Gardiner, who had studied with Erman, not only produced his *Egyptian Grammar* in 1927, but also funded the hieroglyphic fount used in it. In 1962, Raymond Faulkner produced *A Concise Dictionary of Middle Egyptian*, containing 5,400 words, and a standard student text since then. All this, and the patient work of scholars in the emerging discipline of Egyptology, allowed the Ancient Egyptians to speak again.

Although the written material that has survived from Ancient Egypt, like its other physical remains, is only a minute fragment of what once existed, it is still a massive amount, and every text that is translated adds a little more detail to our picture of the civilisation, and its legacy. Perhaps that legacy is even greater than most people would imagine. In 1905, the Egyptologist Flinders Petrie excavated at the Egyptian turquoise mines of Serabit el Khadim, in Sinai, and recorded a series of inscriptions in characters which resembled, but were not hieroglyphs. The limited number of characters suggested that they were alphabetic, and when he was preparing them for publication, Alan Gardiner realised their potential significance. Independently, both he and Kurt Sethe in Germany had theorised that Egyptian hieroglyphs representing consonants had been borrowed and used as the model for the alphabetic scripts used in Syria and Palestine around 900 BC. The Greeks adopted their alphabet from one of these, used by the Phoenicians, and substituted vowel sounds for a number of consonants not found in Greek. Although they were short and damaged, Gardiner realised that the inscriptions recorded by Petrie provided confirmation of this theory (Fig 63). Ultimately, if it is correct, our alphabet, which we owe to the Greeks, owes the shape of its letters to the Ancient Egyptians and their hieroglyphs.

Fig 63
Some of the inscriptions in the mysterious script found on objects from Serabit el Khadim in Sinai in 1905. Alan Gardiner theorised that the shapes were originally pictures, derived from hieroglyphs, of the objects which gave their names to the letters of early Semitic alphabets. The four signs on the right of the bottom inscription can then be read, left to right, as the name of the Canaanite goddess Ba'lat. [Courtesy of the Egypt Exploration Society, www.ees.ac.uk]

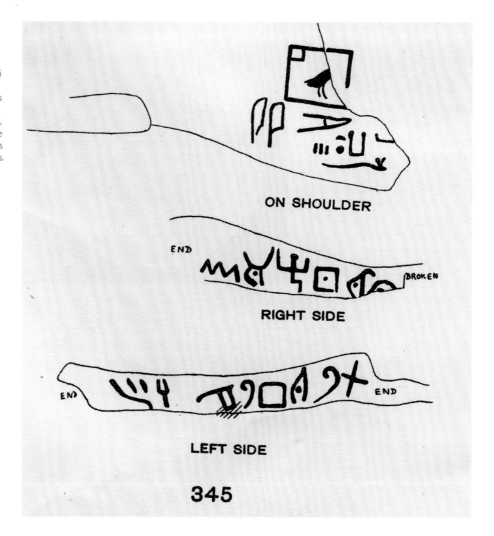

Nowadays, there are probably more people who can, at least to some extent, read hieroglyphs than there were in Ancient Egypt, where only a tiny minority were literate, but the language itself is extinct. In the modern world hieroglyphs are used primarily for decoration, and although occasionally readable only a few, such as the *ankh* and *wedjat* eye, or Eye of Horus, retain any vestige of the meaning that they were endowed with in Ancient Egypt. But through the decipherment of hieroglyphs, hieratic and demotic, the Ancient Egyptians can speak to us again, and we can share not only their religious texts and royal pronouncements, like the Rosetta Stone, but their literature, love songs, contracts, wills, legal wrangles, scribbled notes and gossip.

Finding Egypt in England

London

Bromley		**Lambeth**	

Bromley

Crystal Palace Park

Camden

Britannia House

Greater London House

Hampstead Cemetery

Highgate Cemetery

Ealing

The Hoover Factory

Hackney

Abney Park Cemetery

Islington

Carlton Cinema

Richmond Avenue

Kensington and Chelsea

Brompton Cemetery

Harrods

Kensal Green Cemetery

Lambeth

Reliance Arcade

W H Smith works

West Norwood Cemetery

Richmond

The Kilmorey mausoleum

Tower Hamlets

The Temple of Storms

Wandsworth

Putney Vale Cemetery

Westminster

Apsley House

Cleopatra's Needle

Homebase

Abney Park Cemetery

Stoke Newington
High Street,
London
N16 0LH

The 32 acres of Abney Park Cemetery were created from the grounds of two 17th-century houses, Fleetwood House and Abney House. It was one of the 'Magnificent Seven' cemeteries created by private cemetery companies as a response to the crisis in London's traditional burial grounds caused by the rapid growth of population as the city expanded in the 19th century.

The Stoke Newington area was home to many Dissenters and Nonconformists;

Methodists, Baptists, Wesleyans, Unitarians and members of other Protestant groups who rejected the teachings of the established Church of England. This prompted the Abney Park Cemetery Company to create the cemetery in 1840 expressly for Nonconformists, and explains the relative austerity of many of the monuments when compared to other Victorian cemeteries. Among these communities lavish and expensive funerary monuments were considered extravagant

Fig 64
The entrance to Abney
Park Cemetery. The
cornices on the main
columns between the
lodges feature floral
decoration combining
papyrus sheaths and
lotus flowers.
[DP103845]

and wasteful. Simple and sober designs
were preferred.

Drawing on the trees which were a
legacy of the original houses' grounds and
adding to them in collaboration with the
well-known Loddige's Nursery in nearby
Mare Street, the company turned the new
cemetery into an arboretum with 2,000
species when it opened. At its height, with
2,500 species, it rivalled Kew Gardens and
was an immediate attraction to visitors.

The layout of the cemetery, its chapel, main
gate and lodges, were designed by William
Hosking FSA, Professor in Architecture and
Civil Engineering. Hosking's membership
of the Society of Antiquaries may help to
explain his choice of an Ancient Egyptian
style for the entrance lodges and gate piers.
The lodges have battered sides with inset
upright window openings, cavetto cornices
with winged solar discs at their centre and
winged solar discs above the windows
(Fig 64). On the cornices, on either side of
the winged solar discs, are small hieroglyphic
texts (Fig 65). They were composed by

Joseph Bonomi Jnr, who had trained as an
artist and sculptor and worked in Egypt for
years with the leading Egyptologists of his
time, and who two years later was to design
the Egyptian façade for Marshall's Mill in
Leeds (see p 265).

In March 1840 Bonomi consulted Samuel
Birch, then a 26-year-old assistant in the
British Museum who was later to become
Keeper of Oriental Antiquities there. Birch
sent Bonomi two possible texts for the

Fig 65
The cornices above
the lodge doorways
have floral decorations
similar to those on the
gateway columns, and in
their centre hieroglyphic
inscriptions composed
by Joseph Bonomi Jnr.
[DP103851]

Fig 66
Birch's first suggestion to Bonomi for the Abney Park inscriptions was a text which he translated literally, read right to left, as 'the Gate of the abode of Eternity'.
[Mark Rudolph]

Fig 67
Birch also suggested this alternative text which could be read, right to left, as 'the wall-ramparts-enclosure etc. of the same [the abode of Eternity]'.
[Mark Rudolph]

Fig 68
Making the appropriate amendment to Bonomi's inscription, which is read top to bottom, its literal meaning is actually 'Door to the House of the Corpse'. The last two signs (the oval hieroglyph and mummy) are determinatives, or semantic markers, showing that the preceding word has to do with decay and death.
[Mark Rudolph]

Fig 69
Bonomi used a hieroglyph representing a papyrus stem, used in words related to papyrus, or the general sense of being green. It can also be used phonetically, but not in this instance.
[Mark Rudolph]

Fig 70
The hieroglyph Bonomi should have used is one representing a wooden column.
[Mark Rudolph]

Fig 71
One writing of the word for 'door'. The first sign is phonetic, and the second shows the part of the object referred to by the word itself, one leaf of a double door. Another writing adds an additional phonetic hieroglyph, and a determinative for wood, the material doors were normally made of.
[Mark Rudolph]

inscription, with three alternative writings of one and two of the other (Figs 66 and 67). Birch had composed them himself, as although he remembered seeing them in an Ancient Egyptian text somewhere, he had not been able to track it down.[1] Bonomi chose instead to compose his own text, which is usually said to read 'The Gates of the Abode of the Mortal Part of Man.' (Fig 68)[2] As it stands it does not make sense since Bonomi confused two similar hieroglyphs (Figs 69 and 70) in his writing of the word for 'door' (Fig 71), but as Birch observed in a posthumous tribute, while acknowledging the accuracy of his hieroglyphic

draughtsmanship, 'Mr Bonomi did not study Egyptian philology.' The gate piers also have cavetto cornice tops, and the railings have stylised finials, which were probably intended to resemble lotus blossoms.

Inside the cemetery is the plain, stone chest tomb monument of Samuel Sharpe and his wife Sarah. Sharpe, who lived from 1799 to 1881, was a successful banker and Unitarian who became interested in Egyptology through the work of Thomas Young. Sharpe went on to study the work of Champollion and Gardner Wilkinson, learned Coptic, and went on to write widely on Egyptian history and hieroglyphs, and to translate the Bible. He collaborated with Joseph Bonomi on a description of the sarcophagus of Sety I in Sir John Soane's Museum. Sharpe tended to work along his own lines and few of his contributions to the field have stood the test of time, but he was an important populariser, publishing a total of 37 titles. His monument can be found on the southern end of Dr Watt's Walk. The easiest way to find it is to follow the entrance drive from the main gates and take the right-hand fork, and then a left fork. Continue straight over a crossroads and at the chapel turn left into Dr Watt's Walk. Follow this down until just before it branches and Sharpe's monument is on the left of the path. He is commemorated with the simple inscription:

Samuel Sharpe
Author of the History of Egypt
And Translator of the Bible

As the cemetery filled up, many of the original trees were felled to make way for graves, and many elms were lost during the 1960s to Dutch elm disease. Like almost all the other commercial cemetery companies, the Abney Park Cemetery Company eventually collapsed when its income from new burials dried up and the cemetery passed into the control of the local authority. Lack of money led to what can most charitably be described as a policy of benign neglect, but in practice this meant abandoning the cemetery and what remained of the arboretum to the ravages of pollution and vandalism. A local trust now runs the cemetery as a community resource in partnership with the local authority.

To reach the cemetery from Stoke Newington Station, turn left outside it and walk about 150 metres down the hill. The cemetery is on the right-hand side.

Apsley House

Tabletop temples – the Sèvres Egyptian service

The house known for more than 200 years simply as 'No. 1 London', and formerly home to the 1st Duke of Wellington, is still home to an extraordinary porcelain dessert service which has as its centrepiece a 22ft-long miniature reproduction of some of the best-known temples of Egypt.[3]

The story of the Sèvres '*Service Egyptien*' begins with the colourful life of one of the earliest Egyptologists, Dominique Vivant, Baron Denon (1747–1825). He came to prominence at the court of Louis XV and in 1771 or 1772 was sent as *Gentilhomme d'Ambassade* to the court of Catherine the Great in St Petersburg, then to diplomatic posts in Sweden and Naples. While at Naples, he studied ancient art and

monuments, assembling a large collection of Etruscan vases and practising etching and engraving. After returning to Paris via Rome he settled in Venice in 1788 on the eve of the French Revolution, but had to leave in 1792 when Venice expelled all French residents. He moved to Florence, then to Bologna and then to Switzerland. On hearing that his property in Paris had been confiscated and his name placed on a list of the proscribed, he took the courageous, perhaps even foolhardy step of returning to Paris. Although he wisely changed his name from the aristocratic 'De Non' and now signed himself 'Denon', he risked sharing the fate of many others in the Terror. He sought protection from the painter Louis David, in favour with the current regime, who obtained for him a commission to design republican costumes. He also earned a

149 Piccadilly,
London
W1J 7NT

living by engraving, including an erotic series 'L'Oeuvre Priapique', inspired by material from Pompeii.

He became friendly with Josephine Beauharnais, who was to marry Napoleon in 1796, and through her intercession was able to secure a place among the savants taken to Egypt with Bonaparte's 1798 expedition, despite being over 50 at the time. He survived the hardships of a military campaign, including being shot at on at least one occasion, and on his return published the enormously successful and influential *Voyages dans la Basse et la Haute Égypte* (*Travels in Upper and Lower Egypt*), first published in French in 1802 and soon translated into English and German. In the same year that he published *Voyages*, Napoleon appointed him Director of the Musée Napoleon. Denon also became responsible for designing parades and state events, and supervising the erection of monuments.

In 1800, Lucien Bonaparte, Minister of the Interior, appointed a 30-year-old geologist and natural history professor, Alexandre Brongniart, as administrator of the former Royal Porcelain Factory at Sèvres. Once rivalling Meissen as the greatest manufacturer in Europe, its dependence on aristocratic patronage and the economic depression following the French Revolution had brought it close to ruin, and in 1798 it had been taken over by the government. Despite a lack of previous experience in this area, Brongniart was an inspired choice. Under his direction the factory developed the hard paste still in use today, which fired with fewer losses, a new glaze and several enamel colours. Denon, who became artistic adviser to the factory in 1805, wrote to Brongniart:

> The idea has come to me for a charming Egyptian group, easy to make, to carry fresh, glace or dried fruit and which at the same time would be part of the

service and of the centrepiece. Tell me if you could make architecture with some accuracy: tell me if you could maintain the strict lines of columns … If you can assure success with that, we will get a really monumental centrepiece.[4]

Denon was right about the centrepiece being monumental but more than a little optimistic in describing it as 'easily made'.

Denon suggested the architect Jean-Baptiste Lepère, who had accompanied Napoleon's expedition, as the designer of the *surtout* or centrepiece. In November 1805, Lepère submitted a design based upon the Kiosk of Trajan in the Temple of Isis at Philae, the Temples of Hathor at Dendera and of Horus at Edfu, the First Pylon and processional avenue of ram-headed sphinxes at Karnak, the Colossi of Memnon and the obelisks at Luxor (one of which was subsequently removed to Paris.). Plaster models, which still survive at Sèvres, were made from Lepère's design and moulds from these. The centrepiece was a technical challenge and the central model of the Kiosk of Trajan at Philae alone took four months to make. In April 1807 Denon, who was in Germany at the time, replied to a letter from Brongniart with a mixture of encouragement and admonition:

> But I come back again to the fact that if it is possible for something to be made, then the Imperial Factory can make it. If you make nothing of this kind, then others will make what you make, and you will no longer be Europe's premier factory. Courage then, because I have promised the Emperor that the service will be completed on his return.[5]

The centrepiece is made up of 17 separate units of biscuit porcelain mounted on a *tôle peinte* (varnished tinplated steel or sheet iron) plateau, painted in imitation of Egyptian

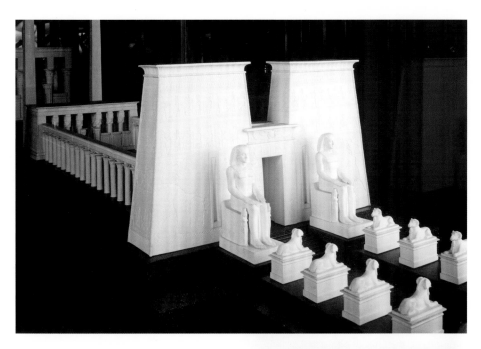

Fig 72
The centrepiece of the
Sèvres Egyptian service.
Denon's involvement
helped to ensure that
although it combined
elements from a number
of different sites, it
reproduced them with
reasonable accuracy.
[Photo © Victoria and
Albert Museum, London;
Source: English Heritage
Photo Library, K040691]

granite. A gilt-bronze plateau had originally
been suggested but may have been rejected
on grounds of cost. In the centre stands the
Kiosk of Trajan from the Temple of Isis at
Philae, flanked by four obelisks. Two smaller
temples, composites of elements from
Dendera and Edfu, complete the central
group. These are joined by colonnades to
two pylons modelled on those at Karnak.
At either end are pairs of seated figures,
modelled on the colossi of Memnon, at the
head of avenues of ram-headed sphinxes on
rectangular plinths (Fig 72). A number of the
pieces are decorated with hieroglyphs, which
although finely detailed are not readable.
The centrepiece was completed in July 1808
although the plateau was not finished until
some years later.

The centrepiece was accompanied by a
dessert service, originally consisting of 72
plates, 12 *compotiers*, 4 *sucriers*, 2 *confituriers*,
4 *seaux à glace* (ice buckets), 4 *corbeilles*
(porcelain baskets) in a lotus design, and
four Egyptian figures carrying dishes (Fig
73). The plates were decorated with gilt

Fig 73
One of the figures
from the dessert service.
The form of Egyptian
figures such as this were
influenced by depictions
of figures bearing
offering in Ancient
Egyptian tombs.
[Photo © Victoria and
Albert Museum, London;
Source: English Heritage
Photo Library, K040692]

hieroglyphs on a dark-blue background, with scenes in sepia after engravings in Denon's *Voyages* in the centre. They were painted by Jacques-François-Joseph Swebach-Desfontaines who was granted the unusual privilege of being allowed to sign his name on the work. Understandably, he restricted himself to scratching 'Swebach' or even just 'sw' through the enamel. The borders were designed by Brongniart's father Théodore, an architect. The *compotiers* have Egyptian zodiac signs on them, and the *sucriers* and *confituriers* were designed after illustrations by Denon. The plates were valued at 200 francs apiece and the *sucriers* at 280 francs each, with over half of this for gilding. (In contemporary prices, these might be as much as £400 per plate, and £560 per *sucrier*.) The final set had only two *seaux à glace* and additional *assiettes à monter* (side plates) decorated with scarabs.

This service is not the one now in Apsley House. It was intended as a gift for Tsar Alexander I of Russia, was delivered to St Petersburg in 1808 and is now in the Ceramic Museum at Kuskovo near Moscow. While it was being prepared, however, the Empress Josephine visited the factory to inspect its progress. Napoleon divorced her in 1809 – more because of his need for children of his own than on the grounds of her numerous indiscretions – and as part of their settlement offered her 30,000 francs worth of Sèvres porcelain. In February 1810 Josephine ordered a similar service to that made for the Tsar but with only two *sucriers*, two Egyptian figures and different scenes on some of the plates. The total cost was to be 56,134 francs (the equivalent in modern terms of around £111,912) and she was to pay the difference between this and Napoleon's credit of 30,000 francs. Firing and decoration of the new service continued until 1812. There were 76 plates in total, of which 67 survive, with one now in the Musée National de Ceramique at Sèvres.

It was delivered to Malmaison, Josephine's chateau near Paris, on 1 April 1812, carried in six litters by 12 men but Brongniart was summoned to be told that the Empress did not like it, finding it '*trop sévère*' (too severe). She had decided to have another made to designs by her protégé Louis-Martin Berthault. Brongniart's reaction can only be imagined. The Egyptian service was returned to Sèvres but his problems were far from over. Josephine had already spent over 3,000 francs of the money given to her by Napoleon and had only 26,606 francs credit. The service was now valued at 35,020 francs, which did not include the toleware plateau, ordered on her instructions but still at the manufacturers. By now, however, Napoleon's governmental credits had been cancelled and Brongniart refused to release any more porcelain without fresh orders, and presumably fresh credit.

Matters remained at an impasse while Napoleon abdicated, returned from exile on Elba, was defeated at Waterloo and was finally exiled again to St Helena. Such services, huge and hugely expensive, were not easy to dispose of even as state gifts. By 1817 it was still at Sèvres, although it had been considered as a gift for Cardinal Consalvi, Secretary of State to Pius VII. In 1818 the Duke of Wellington was based in Paris as commander of the occupying army, and gave a dinner during which he discussed the relative merits of hard and soft paste porcelain with Louis XVIII. Louis, who had every reason to be grateful to Wellington for restoring him to the French throne, wrote afterwards offering him '*quelques assiettes*' (several plates) and expressing the wish to 'do little gifts – keep friendship alive'. On the same day instructions were sent to Brongniart from the Comte de Pradel, one of Louis' courtiers, instructing Brongniart to deliver Louis' 'little gift', the Sèvres Egyptian service, without delay to the Tuileries where Wellington was based. It was delivered to the duke the next day, despite de Pradel's concern that it might now be considered unfashionable. The service in its final form had only two ice buckets but four Egyptian figures and was now valued at 36,300 francs.

Brongniart was finally paid two years later, 10 years after the original commission and 15 after the design was originally conceived. The service remained in the possession of the Dukes of Wellington until purchased for the nation by the V&A Museum in 1979. Time and several moves had taken their toll and extensive conservation was required, but it now forms a spectacular exhibit at Apsley House.

Britannia House

Designed by Leo Sylvester Sullivan, of the architectural partnership Hobden and Porri, and built for Museum Estates Ltd in 1928, Britannia House is a six-storey office block with striking Ancient Egyptian features. Constructed on a site previously occupied by the Westminster French Protestant Church and School, the rear of the building had to be laid out around a central light well and constructed with sloping roofs to avoid blocking light from neighbouring buildings, but the architect could make full use of the front elevation to Shaftesbury Avenue.[6] The building seems to have been named for its first occupants, Britannia Batteries (Fig 74). Originally set up in 1913 as Edison Accumulators to import and sell batteries from their American parent company, they were acquired in 1928 by Accumulatoren Fabrik AG and their name changed to the more patriotic Britannia Batteries.

Originally, the entrance to the offices was through the small doorway on the right, which has a cavetto cornice with winged solar disc and a pharaonic head with false beard and *nemes* headcloth above the cornice. (The carved details on the building are believed to be the work of Henry Poole, who three years earlier had worked with Sullivan on St Martin's House in St Martin's le Grand, which has some Egyptian inspired detailing.) The rest of the street level was a shopfront, with its own entrances on the outside of widely spaced simple fluted columns and a wide cavetto cornice above an architrave spanning the shopfront, with a frieze of *uraei* or cobras on the cornice and another winged solar disc in its centre. Above the cornice were four storeys topped by an architrave decorated with another, larger, winged solar disc, this time with flanking cobras, and finally another storey with a large cavetto cornice above it.

231–3 Shaftesbury Avenue, London WC2H 8EL

Fig 74
An early photograph of Britannia House not only shows how it got its name, but the original layout of the ground floor as a shop.
[C45/00149]

Technically, the building is steel framed with concrete filler joists or reinforced concrete floors and Portland Stone cladding to the front elevation and brick on most others. (The top cornice is actually reinforced concrete finished in artificial stone.) Around 1983 the building was extensively modernised and refurbished but without affecting the Egyptian-style elements. By this time the main entrance was through the former shopfront.

The architectural press at the time it was built was struck by the strong vertical emphasis of the building's front. Above the shopfront opening, whose relative lowness was emphasised by the wide architrave and widely spaced and fairly sturdy columns, long piers or pilasters rose four storeys before being topped off by Egyptian-style palm column capitals. Above the entrance door, three long channels with slit windows rose five storeys. The top cornice did not extend the whole width of the building and the channels were topped by a large star-shaped carving.

It is interesting to contrast Britannia House with Adelaide House (see p 25), built only a few years earlier. There, *The Builder* magazine had commented that:

> As it is essentially an office building, well equipped with elevators, one floor is as important as any other, and this has been a determining factor in the design, thereby leading to a sameness in the window treatment and the long vertical lines terminated by the large concave cornice.[7]

Although not as large as Adelaide House, much the same could be said of Britannia House. *The Architect and Building News* commented that while supporters of 'vertical emphasis' maintained that it was a logical expression of modern steel construction methods, the actual steel structure was a rectangular grid of relatively narrow vertical and horizontal girders. By adding wider stone-clad piers and using panels of a similar colour between windows to run them into each other, the architects of Britannia House were actually emphasising the vertical at the expense of the horizontal. The magazine, like *The Builder* saw its design as a logical outcome of its function as an office building – 'in the modern office building plurality of stories may be conceived as a single unit of accommodation, and there is no need to emphasise the floor levels which everybody knows to be present'.[8]

The magazine was generally approving of the design, saying that it 'expresses a high standard of craftsmanship, and exemplifies the new manner', but did not comment on the Egyptian elements other than noting that the cornice above the shopfront 'belongs to the same family as that which crowns the building'. *The Architects' Journal* talked of the 'strong vertical treatment', the way that the contrast between the low shopfront and the long piers gave '…a sense of strength and scale to the whole building', and how the strong horizontal lines generally gave to the whole front 'a sense of strength and repose'. It described the upper cornice as 'powerful', and noted the carved capitals of the piers but did not specifically identify them as Egyptian in style, simply saying that 'added interest is obtained by the judicious use of Egyptian motifs'.[9]

As with Adelaide House, contemporaries seem to have focussed on its modernity and seen the Ancient Egyptian elements as secondary – decoration rather than an integral part of the design. Now, when many office buildings are so similar, it is precisely these decorative elements which strike us.

Brompton Cemetery

This magnificent cemetery houses the graves of the Egyptologist Joseph Bonomi Jnr and the surgeon and antiquarian Thomas Pettigrew, as well as several fine Egyptian-style mausoleums.

In 1837, the West of London and Westminster Cemetery Company bought 40 acres of land from Lord Kensington, previously used as a clay pit and brick works, and the architect Benjamin Baud won the competition to design a new cemetery, which was consecrated in 1840. Baud created a formal layout with a wide main avenue leading from an arched gateway building to a large domed octagonal chapel, based on St Peter's Basilica in Rome, although the chapel was Anglican. Catacombs were built under colonnades that extended around the chapel, and there were plans for two other chapels, for Roman Catholics and Dissenters, to be built onto the colonnades (Fig 75). Baud's design proved costly to build and the company was soon in financial difficulties. In 1852 the cemetery was bought by the General Board of Health, becoming the first London cemetery to come under state control. It is now maintained by the Royal Parks.

The cemetery is laid out on a fairly regular grid pattern and a central avenue leads

Old Brompton Road,
London
SW10 9UG

Fig 75
Benjamin Baud's design for Brompton Cemetery had a more formal layout than some of the new garden cemeteries, as this aerial view shows.
[NMR 24410_009]

97

Fig 76
Thomas Pettigrew, whose unrollings of mummies led to him being nicknamed 'Mummy' Pettigrew. His interest in Ancient Egypt is shown here by the inscribed sarcophagus against which he is leaning. [Wellcome Library, London]

Thomas Joseph Pettigrew
FRS FSA FRCS

Died Nov 23 1865 Aged 74

His Family And Some Friends • Members Of The British Archeological Association.

To its immediate right is a similar tomb with a plainer cross marking the grave of his daughter Elizabeth and other family members.

Further along the path the next turning on the right leads back towards the central avenue, and through what was originally one of a number of circular plots set aside for particularly large monuments. This marks the original site of the Kilmorey mausoleum, now in Twickenham (see p 186). The impressive Ancient Egyptian-style mausoleum of Francis 'Black Jack' Needham, 2nd Earl of Kilmorey, was originally built for his beloved mistress, Priscilla Hoste. In September 1853, when it must have become clear that Priscilla was terminally ill, the earl met with the manager of the cemetery, J H Ruddick, to enquire the price of one of the 'select' plots, which a letter of Ruddick's describes as being in 'what were considered the most eligible portions of the cemetery'.[10] These had originally been priced at between 17s and 19s 11d (85p–£1) per square foot, which may not sound much at current prices, but as will become evident was a considerable sum at the time. Charges for most plots had been reduced to 12s and 10s (60–50p) per square foot if a suitable monument was erected, depending on whether it was a single or double plot, but the company was still trying to charge 17s for the most prestigious locations.

south from the gateway on the Old Brompton Road. Turning immediately left and then third right, two pine trees on the right help to locate the grave of Thomas Pettigrew, a surgeon whose interest in Ancient Egypt led to him becoming one of the most prolific unrollers of mummies in the 19th century (Fig 76). His interest in mummies began when he attended an unrolling by the pioneer Egyptologist Giovanni Belzoni in the early 1820s. Pettigrew went on to carry out numerous public unrollings at venues including the Royal College of Surgeons and the Royal Institution, which were highly popular and attracted audiences including scientists, politicians and bishops. His book on mummification was the first of its kind in modern times. In 1852, at the duke's request, Pettigrew mummified Alexander, 10th Duke of Hamilton, who was buried in a genuine Egyptian sarcophagus. Pettigrew's grave is marked by a granite ledger tomb, designed by his son-in-law Gordon Macdonald Hills, with a raised cross with foliated capitals. The inscription on his tomb reads:

Kilmorey may have been wealthy but he baulked at paying this much for a circular plot 51ft in diameter, which he proposed to enlarge to 54ft by taking part of the path surrounding it. The total area would have been 2,500sq ft and the cost around 2,000 guineas (£2,100). He offered 10s per square foot and pointed out the benefits of his mausoleum in influencing 'other wealthy persons to select this in preference to other cemeteries'. More practically, he noted that the circular plot would not be suitable for lucrative family graves as the water table limited the depth of graves to 7ft. The cemetery fretted about whether the mausoleum would interfere with the management of the cemetery but offered to reduce the charge to 10s 6d per square foot, lowering the price to £1,300, while the earl pressed for an answer, saying he was 'still undecided between Kensall Green [sic] and Brompton'.[11]

Matters, however, were complicated by the fact that the cemetery had now come under government control. Ruddick's immediate superiors were the Commissioners of Her Majesty's Parks etc, but ultimate control rested with Lord Palmerston, the Home Secretary. He had closed a large number of graveyards in London for reasons of public health, and felt that the sale of such a large plot to a single individual might limit Brompton's ability to make up for the loss of burial places elsewhere. Seven months after Kilmorey had first enquired about the plot Palmerston indicated that he was prepared to sell one but that, 'It appears to Lord Palmerston that it can scarcely require as much as 2,500 square feet.'[12]

This was in April 1854, and in an example of Victorian Civil Service bureaucracy at its finest was to be the start of protracted negotiations which were not completed until nearly five months later, in September.

Kilmorey, at one point even signing a letter 'Your very obedient humble servant Kilmorey' was at pains to emphasise that he only wanted to erect a single mausoleum, and did not want to occupy any more

space than was necessary for the building he planned. Following a meeting between Ruddick and Kilmorey and his architect, the younger H E Kendall, the revised size of the plot was estimated at 1,964sq ft and the cost, at 10s 6d per square foot, as £1,031 2s, which Ruddick rounded up to 'say one thousand guineas' (£1,050). Kilmorey accepted the rate per square foot, but then claimed his architect had estimated the plot size at 1,880sq ft and aimed to close the deal 'to save however further discussion I beg to offer one thousand pounds'.[13]

The Commissioners stuck to their estimate and Kilmorey eventually gave in and accepted this. By this time, though, Palmerston had become aware of Kilmorey's estimate and, without appearing to realise that the higher estimate came from the Commissioners' representatives, suggested that 'it appears to Lord Palmerston that Lord Kilmorey should be content with the 1880 feet'.[14]

Kilmorey, by this time, was beginning to become concerned. His solicitors wrote, pressing for the sale to be completed 'as the granite which has been ordered from Scotland for the building is arriving, and the architect has no place to receive the blocks as they arrive. The purchase money moreover is lying unproductive at Messrs Coutts.'[15]

The next correspondence from Whitehall, marked 'Immediate', reveals that Palmerston, having been informed that the plot was actually '1963½' sq ft, saw no objection to the sale. As Kilmorey fumed about waiting 'above three months for the decision of the Commissioners', they were recommended to issue their warrant so that the sale could proceed. At this point, however, someone pointed out that under the Cemetery Act, the Commissioners would have to get the approval of the Treasury as well as the Home Office before they could sell off a plot in perpetuity. A letter went to Kilmorey informing him of this, and with the effortless indifference of the true bureaucrat, requested a plan and elevation of the proposed mausoleum, which must surely have been provided at some point already. Kilmorey's reaction can only be imagined, but a terse letter from his solicitors on 25 August 1854 noted that 'Lord Kilmorey cannot be expected to be acquainted with your internal regulations.'[16]

It went on to note that no reply had yet been received to their letters of 3 and 20 July and that Kilmorey faced 'serious loss' owing to his contract with his builders. As late as 31 August the Commissioners were 'unable to state' when they would have the Treasury's decision, but on 2 September Gladstone gave his approval and the sale proceeded at a price of £1,030 16s 9d (£1,030 88p), with a further eight guineas for the preparation of deeds of conveyance. Priscilla died in October of 1854 and was buried in the mausoleum, which was reputed to have cost £30,000. Having been moved twice, the Kilmorey mausoleum can now be seen from the top deck of a passing bus on St Margaret's Road in Twickenham (see p 186).

Two things about this saga are of interest, apart from the light it throws on the operation of the cemetery companies and their relationship with their most prestigious clients. One is that the correspondence and other documents which survive make no reference to Kilmorey's choice of the Ancient Egyptian style for his monument, only referring to it as a 'handsome granite mausoleum'. The other is that despite the fact that his wife Jane, who he had married in 1814, was still alive (she did not die until 1867) and that he was openly living with his mistress, this does not seem to have affected the negotiations at all – although at least one source has tended to imply that this was the case by referring to the

need for Palmerston's 'intervention' before Gladstone gave his decision in favour of the sale. In 1863, when Kilmorey wished to move the mausoleum for the first time to his new residence at Woburn Park near Weybridge, at a cost of £700, his solicitors delicately referred to it as 'a cenotaph for the interment of himself and certain members of his family'[17] and went on to note, 'The remains of one person only are at present deposited within the cenotaph. [Technically an empty tomb, erected as a monument.] His Lordship would obtain a faculty if necessary for moving the remains with the building.'[18]

Despite the solicitors' discretion, as his wife did not die for another four years, the remains could hardly be hers, and when the faculty was granted by the Bishop of London it enabled Kilmorey to remove the remains of 'Priscilla Ann Hoste, spinster deceased' from the catacombs at Brompton, where they had been transferred when the mausoleum was dismantled. Even so, the identity of the mausoleum's occupant seems to have caused no difficulty, both the Board of Works and Sir George Grey, the current Home Secretary, giving their consent.

The final twist in the tale came when Kilmorey, having obtained agreement to move the mausoleum and Priscilla's remains, approached the Brompton Cemetery Company saying that he was 'much inclined' to dispose of the ground and asking if they would repurchase it. Ruddick was still manager of the cemetery and was approached by Kilmorey to see if he would advise him privately on the prospects of selling it at auction, but declined to do so and took the precaution of advising his superiors of the approach. The Board of Commissioners initially indicated that they were unable to repurchase the plot, but that they 'would afford him such facilities for disposing of it as they can consistent with the management of the cemetery'.[19]

The plot was advertised for sale at auction but bought in by the auctioneers on behalf of the vendor at £280. Ruddick, whose correspondence shows was aware of this, suggested to the Commissioners that the plot could be used for 90 private graves at £3 3s each. He wrote again to say that Kilmorey was now asking £315 for the plot and that £5 would be enough to clear any remaining concrete from the foundations. Within a few weeks Ruddick had revised his estimate to 80 graves at most, and noted the difficulty of disposing of 'alternate grave spaces' after the first 40 places had been sold because they could only have flat markers and people wanted upright headstones. Kilmorey by this point was asking £200 and Ruddick recommending £150 at maximum. The earl eventually conceded and accepted this offer. From an initial asking price of over £2,000 and a purchase price of over £1,000, the land was now worth at most just over £250 to the cemetery and possibly only half this. The era of the joint stock cemetery companies was over and with it the heyday of the private mausoleum.

Some of these can be seen by returning to the central path and turning left where there are four Egyptian-style mausoleums. On the east side are the sandstone Thompson mausoleum and that of Duncan Wilson, in pink granite (Fig 77). On the west side are the pink granite family mausoleum of Mrs George Morrison, and another in sandstone without inscriptions. All have battered sides and smooth cavetto cornices but are undecorated. The earliest burial in the Thompson mausoleum is that of Charles Thompson, in 1880, and other family members were subsequently buried or commemorated there until the early 20th century, including several from the First World War. (One of these was Major Donald William McPherson, of the 62nd Panjabi Regiment, killed in action in Sinai,

Egypt in November 1916.) The Wilson mausoleum has no date or inscriptions other than the name of Duncan Wilson. The Morrison mausoleum has an inscription over the door stating that it is 'The Family Mausoleum of Mrs George Morrison', but is otherwise without inscriptions apart from one on the lower left of the plinth mentioning 'Barker & Son North Entrance'. This presumably refers to the firm of monumental masons who erected it, although it may have been manufactured elsewhere.

The second turning to the left along the central path leads to another of the 'select' circular plots. On the way, to the left of the path on the corner of the second block in, is the monument of Joseph Bonomi Jnr

Fig 77
The Wilson mausoleum in Brompton Cemetery is situated inside an enclosure of stubby obelisk posts and decorative ironwork, elements that it shares with other large monuments, including a number of those in the Egyptian style. [DP103973]

Fig 78
Headstone of Joseph Bonomi Jnr who worked in Egypt with the major Egyptologists of his day, and illustrated the works of Sir J G Wilkinson, Samuel Birch and Samuel Sharpe. He was also involved with several projects such as the Nile Panorama and the Crystal Palace Egyptian Court that made Egyptology accessible to a wider public. [BB89/10341]

Fig 79 (right)
Anubis as a jackal. He is often shown in this pose on funerary chests or shrines, reflecting one of his titles 'Foremost of the Divine Booth [embalming booth or burial chamber itself]'.

(Fig 78). The round-topped sandstone headstone has a combination *chi* and cross monogram flanked by *alpha* (À) and omega (Ω) at the top. Its inscriptions begin poignantly by recording the deaths from whooping cough of four of his children within a single week in Easter 1852, two of them on the same day. The eldest was nearly six, the youngest was only eight months old. Below this are the names of Bonomi's mother-in-law, the wife of the painter John Martin, his wife Jessie, and then Bonomi himself.

Joseph Bonomi
Sculptor Traveller and Archeologist [sic]
Born 9th October 1796
Appointed Curator of Sir John Soane's Museum 1861
Died 3rd March 1878

Under this is a rectangular carving of Anubis on his shrine (Fig 79), wearing a ceremonial

tie and crossed by a flail, a symbol of Osiris. Beneath Bonomi's inscription is the final family member, Colonel J I Bonomi CBE of the King's Own Regiment, who died in 1930. Joseph Bonomi was involved with the Egyptian Court at the Crystal Palace (see p 146), Marshall's Mill in Leeds (see p 265) and designed the Egyptian Seat for Dr John Lee at Hartwell House (see p 219).

In the circular plot just ahead along the path is the Egyptian-style monument of Hannah Courtoy, who died in 1854 (Fig 80). It was built by her daughters Suzannah, Elizabeth and Mary, two of whom are buried with their mother. The monument itself is tall and fairly narrow, with battered sides, torus mouldings and a cavetto cornice with a repeating motif of blank cartouches surmounted by pairs of the curved ostrich plume feathers symbolic of Maat, goddess of truth and order. It is topped by a distinctly inappropriate pyramidal roof rather than the flat roof which would fit with the other elements. There were originally four of these circular plots, intended for a single mausoleum (the other two are symmetrically placed on the west side of the cemetery). Only this one and that originally occupied by the Kilmorey mausoleum were ever used for this purpose, and now only the Courtoy mausoleum survives, all three other circular plots having been used for smaller graves and monuments.

Fig 80
The Courtoy monument in Brompton Cemetery. Both the Courtoy and Kilmorey mausoleums were built by unknown architects, and for people who seem to have had no special connection to Egypt, but the choice of this style for such expensive monuments shows that it was considered prestigious. [BB89/10379]

Carlton Cinema

Polychrome picture palace

The Carlton, purpose built as a cinema and seating 2,248, was designed by the architect George Coles, and opened on 1 September 1930 with Harold Lloyd's first talking picture *Welcome Danger* and five variety acts. The occasion was graced by the Mayor of Islington and Prince Arthur of Connaught, and with the band of the Grenadier Guards, and the pipes and drums of the Scots Guards.

At street level the front of the building is plain with two entrances, the central one surmounted by a canopy. Above the level of the canopy runs a lotus frieze and from this rises pylon-like tapered window openings at either side, with a cavetto cornice moulding some way above them. Between the windows, a higher centre section forms a sort of entablature, slightly set back, with two large papyrus bud columns and abaci supporting a tall lintel surmounted by a cavetto cornice and plain low parapet. Behind the pillars, and between the lower pylons, is an upper register of five blank blue-bordered rectangular panels and below these a torus moulding and triangular frieze. Below this frieze is another row of five more blank panels, or 'false windows' surmounted by a lotus frieze, and with two central papyrus bud pilasters between the main columns. The cornices, friezes and other decorative details such as the pillar capitals and bases are in coloured relief tilework, or faience (Fig 81). The vestibule of the cinema was originally in a modernised Empire style, in tones of buff, peach and amber, which were continued in the auditorium; there used to be a tearoom and lounge on the first floor.

161–9 Essex Road, London
N1 2SN

Fig 81
The most distinctive features of the Carlton Cinema in Essex Road are its accurate use of an Egyptian column form and its colourful tilework. [DP148248]

The Egyptologist Dominic Montserrat considered that the papyrus bud columns and empty cartouche emplacements above them were characteristic of architecture from Amarna, site of the pharaoh Akhenaten's capital city of Akhetaten,

rather than generically Egyptianising (Fig 82). Amarna was excavated by the Egypt Exploration Society during the 1920s and 1930s and a number of those taking part in the digs were trained architects. Articles were written about the excavations in both the *Illustrated London News* and the architectural press. Periodic exhibitions of material from them were held and one of these in 1929 featured coloured tiles from the site of the city.

Later used as a Mecca bingo hall and vacant at the time of writing, the Grade II listed Carlton has survived remarkably well. The domed roof of the auditorium and much of the decorative plasterwork was destroyed by a bomb during the Second World War, and the vestibule is now painted in deep crimson and gold but the façade, for a time obscured by a large hoarding, is once more fully visible and now the only one of London's Ancient Egyptian-style cinema exteriors to survive.

The Egyptian features can all be seen from Essex Road.

Fig 82
The papyrus bud columns used on the Carlton have been linked with the architecture of Akhetaten, the new capital built during the religious revolution instigated by the pharaoh Akhenaten, in which the worship of the traditional Egyptian gods was replaced by worship of the sun disc. [DP103868]

Cleopatra's Needle

Nearly 3,500 years old, nearly 60ft high and weighing around 186 tons, the Ancient Egyptian obelisk which stands on the Victoria Embankment is not only London's oldest monument but must also be its most travelled, with perhaps the most eventful history.

Carved from a single block of Aswan granite, it was originally one of a pair erected in front of the Temple of the Sun at Heliopolis, now part of north-west Cairo, to commemorate the third jubilee of Thutmose III in about 1468 BC. Over 200 years later the obelisks were, like so many other monuments, usurped by Ramesses II, who added two additional columns of inscriptions to all four sides. Then in 10 BC, nearly 1,500 years after they had first been set up, they were transported to Alexandria and placed in front of the Caesareum, the temple to the deified Julius Caesar. Although they are known as Cleopatra's Needles, this was around 20 years after her death and was probably done on the orders of Augustus. For more than 1,000 years they remained standing there until one of them fell during an earthquake in 1301.[20]

Alexandria, one of the great cities of the ancient world, declined slowly over the centuries. Few European travellers visited it, and when Napoleon invaded Egypt in 1798 it had been reduced to a town of only 4,000 inhabitants. The fallen Needle had become half buried in sand (Fig 83), but after British forces defeated Bonaparte's army at the Battle of Alexandria in 1801 they found that the sand had been cleared from the fallen obelisk and a rope attached to the upright one – possibly to climb it, as was done with the nearby Pompey's Pillar, or maybe to topple it so that it could be transported back to France with the other antiquities collected by the French expedition. Perhaps inspired by this, after the withdrawal of

French forces the Earl of Cavan, who commanded the small contingent of British troops left in Egypt, approached the Turkish authorities and obtained their permission to take the fallen obelisk to England as a monument to British victories and those such as Sir Ralph Abercromby, victor of the Battle of Alexandria, who had died in them (Fig 84):

Cavan consulted his chief military engineer and a plan was drawn up for the construction of a stone pier or jetty against which a ship could be moored. The Needle, moved along rollers, was to be loaded into the ship by means of a specially cut stern port and then packed into place with bags of cotton. The troops were 'invited by their officers to subscribe a certain number of days pay' in the words of a later account,

Victoria
Embankment,
London
WC2N

Fig 83
The Alexandria obelisks, painted by Vivant Denon at the time of Napoleon's invasion of Egypt in 1798. By the time the fallen obelisk was finally moved to London, its survival had been threatened by the development of the modern city.
[Photo © Victoria and Albert Museum, London]

Fig 84
A posthumous portrait of Sir Ralph Abercromby, from 1815, probably based on an earlier portait by John Hoppner. Despite being over 66 at the time of the Battle of Alexandria, Abercromby was in the thick of the fighting, and was wounded twice, later dying as a result. His victory was the first by British forces against Napoleon's armies and made him a hero in England.
[Photo © Victoria and Albert Museum, London]

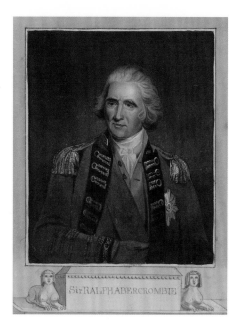

Sir RALPH ABERCROMBIE

which they apparently did with enthusiasm. One of the captured French frigates, *El Corso* (originally a Venetian vessel, the *Leoben*, sunk by the French in the eastern harbour during the siege of Alexandria) was purchased from the prize agents as a transport, raised and made seaworthy. All was going well, with working parties of troops being paid from the money they had themselves subscribed, and considerable progress had been made on the jetty when

> …the swell of the sea destroyed the quay he [Lord Cavan] had constructed to embark it from, and the funds are so exhausted as not to admit the formation of others … Lord Cavan was deterred from again prosecuting his designs of embarking the obelisk which was laying down, by the Commander-in-Chief in the Mediterranean declining to sanction and patronise the measure.[21]

Work on the project stopped, the contract for the ship was dissolved and the remaining funds were returned to the troops. Determined to leave some record of British

victories, Cavan had the top block of the fallen Needle's pedestal raised and a space about 18ins square chiselled out of it. In this space was deposited a brass or marble plate with an inscription setting out the principal events of the campaign, and complete sets of coins for the reigns of George III and Muhammad Ali. These remained there until 1830 when the base, which weighed around 40–45 tons (approximately 40–46,000 kilos) was demolished with explosives by an Italian engineer, Cassian Bey (another source names him as Chiandi), and the stone used in the construction of the naval arsenal. Following a protest by the Foreign Office, the return of the items was demanded and the inscribed slab or plate was returned to England where it was presented to William IV, who placed it in the Temple at Kew Gardens. Following the arrival of the Needle in England, the plate was given to the London County Council, by them to the War Department and it was finally fixed at the entrance to the Officers' Mess at the Mandora Barracks in Aldershot, Hampshire.

Over the next 77 years, as Egypt was transformed into a modern state with Alexandria as its commercial centre (Fig 85), there was a succession of proposals to transport the obelisk to London. It was twice offered as a gift to the Prince Regent by the de facto ruler of Egypt, Muhammad Ali; suggested as a suitable centrepiece and monument for Nelson in Trafalgar Square when that was being created; proposed for erection in Hyde Park to commemorate the Great Exhibition of 1851 and Prince Albert's role in promoting this; and put forward the following year as a highlight of the newly created Crystal Palace at Sydenham. Estimates of the cost varied from £5,000 to £18,000. A number of proposals, of varying degrees of practicality, were made by various individuals, some better qualified to do so than others, but several reports on the subject were also commissioned

1958. The Harbour. Alexandria. 1958

Fig 85
This photograph, taken in the mid-19th century by the photographic pioneer Francis Frith, shows how Alexandria had grown by then into a thriving modern city. Ultimately, the development of the city was to threaten the survival of the London obelisk. [Photo © Victoria and Albert Museum, London]

by the authorities from army and naval officers. One in particular, in 1851, included soundings and surveys in Alexandria harbour, indicating that the project was being given serious official consideration at least in some quarters. The uncertain state of the British economy at various times and doubts about the condition of the fallen Needle were both factors frustrating these plans, but there was a general perception that the Needle could and should be brought to England and that successive governments were dragging their feet. In 1846 *Fraser's Magazine* reviewed William Thackeray's account of his journey to Egypt *From Cornhill to Grand Cairo*. It echoed his view that the government had 'not shown a particular alacrity to accept this ponderous present', and described the Needle as 'the property of the British Public … which the unaccountable *nonchalance* of Government allows to remain in a most unseemly state … England appears from her apparent

bewilderment about the matter, to be in the position of the elderly lady who won an elephant in a lottery.'[22]

By 1859 Charles Dickens, writing about the Needle in his magazine *All The Year Round*, rhetorically asked why if we did not want it we did not tell 'the Pasha' so that it could be re-erected at Alexandria to save it from the attention of souvenir hunters, given to 'some other nation', or even 'offered to some first-class showman'. He noted that although it was the property of the British nation, the nation in general did not seem to care about it, and asked in frustration, 'Is it ever the intention of the British Government to bring to England Cleopatra's Needle?'[23]

The years went by with no progress. In July 1865 the British consul at Alexandria reported that the ground on which the obelisk stood had been 'given by the Viceroy to some Greek or Frenchman, who, intending to build thereon, sent a request to Mr Consul Saunders to remove the monolith or it would be broken up … Mr Saunders placed it under the safeguard of the local government, and there the matter rests.'[24]

Despite this, and continuing fears that the French still coveted the Needle, a summary of correspondence on the subject prepared for the Science and Art Department of the Committee of the Privy Council on Education in 1867 rather plaintively concluded, 'No further steps of importance have since been taken with reference to the removal or preservation of the obelisk.'[25]

Two years later, the intrepid Victorian canoeist John MacGregor paid his second visit to Alexandria while paddling round the Middle East. On his first, in 1849, the Needle had been half buried but in 1869 'it was so completely hidden that not even the owner of the workshop where it lies could point out to me the exact spot of its sandy grave!'[26]

It seemed as if, after nearly 70 years of apparently regarding the Needle as a white elephant, the British government had simply given up trying to get it to England and that it would disappear beneath the sand, or like its pedestal be broken up for building stone.

In the end, however, it was not the government that brought the Needle to London but a collection of individuals typical of their age – a Scots general who had served everywhere from Burma to the Balkans and Canada to the Crimea; a philanthropic dermatologist who had made a fortune from gas and railway shares and popularised the Turkish bath in England; a civil engineer who had lived in a tomb at Giza and excavated at the the Great Pyramid; and his brother, also a civil engineer, who constructed the first railway in China.

How, why and whether…

It was nothing new for Cleopatra's Needle to be used as an imperial trophy – both Ramesses II and possibly Cleopatra herself, or more probably Augustus, had either usurped it or transported it to a new site to serve their purposes. To extend the metaphor used by *Frazer's Magazine*, however, in these cases the elderly (and very autocratic) ladies had chosen to acquire an elephant, rather than finding themselves the owners of it, and in neither case would it have taken as long to complete delivery as the 77 years it took to bring the Needle to London and erect it. In ancient times decisions had been taken by divine rulers. In a more complicated modern era, although the Needle itself was the gift of an autocrat, many voices were raised in the debate over how, why and even whether the Needle could or should be moved. Right from the outset, there was a contrast between the enthusiasm of individuals for the project and a distinct lack of it from the British government, and although the problem was often assumed to be financial the real difficulty may have been political.

Causing offence to the Turks

The main reason the first attempt was abandoned was because the jetty was destroyed by a storm, but the project may originally have been undertaken largely on the initiative of the Earl of Cavan and inadvertently created a political embarrassment. An 1838 pamphlet by William Wilde (father of Oscar) proposing the erection of the Needle in Trafalgar Square quoted from letters written by the captains of two of the ships in the British force, Captain Larcom of HMS *Hind*, and Captain Hollis of HMS *Thames*. Larcom says that in March 1802 an order arrived from General Fox, commanding land forces in the Mediterranean, and Lord Keith, the naval commander-in-chief, 'forbidding the removal of the obelisk on the plea that it would give offence to the Turkish Government'.[27]

Hollis, who says that he himself carried the order to Egypt, says that the reason for it was not known, but that

> …the only public reason given for it was a supposition that it might give offence to the Turks, but this was not the case, as it had been previously guarded against, by a formal permission being asked, which was readily granted by the Aga who commanded in Egypt, he observing at the same time that the Turks cared not if we took every stone in the country; but he very sarcastically asked us if we had no stone quarries in England, that we were taking so much trouble to carry such a useless mass there as the obelisk appeared to him to be.[28]

Following defeat of the French by a joint British and Ottoman force, political anarchy reigned in Egypt. The Turkish Sultan's control was largely in name only, with both British and French backing rival power groups as the European great powers circled around the declining Ottoman Empire, whilst fearing the effects of its collapse. Eventually Muhammad Ali, originally second in command of ethnic Albanian troops from Kavala who formed part of the Ottoman forces, went on to take advantage of the power vacuum in Egypt to become de facto ruler (Fig 86). The Ottoman Sultan eventually granted him the rank of pasha, and recognised him as wali, or governor, of Egypt, but Ali claimed the higher title of khedive, equivalent to prince. While nominally a vassal of the Ottoman Empire, he acted as an independent ruler and eventually only military intervention by Britain and France stopped him seizing large chunks of the Middle East and threatening Constantinople (modern Istanbul) itself. In this highly charged political atmosphere,

Fig 86
A portrait of Muhammad Ali, painted by an unknown artist around 1840. Ali pursued his goal of turning Egypt into a modern state with ruthless commitment, creating state monopolies in important industries, and spending huge sums to create an army and navy.
[Photo © Victoria and Albert Museum, London]

officially accepting the 'gift' of Cleopatra's Needle from anyone in Egypt could send out the wrong signals to the Ottoman Sultan. By the time the obelisk finally came to Britain, Ismail had been recognised as khedive by the Ottoman government 10 years before, in 1867, and Egypt was effectively an independent state..

Our Egyptian obelisk

Various proposals over the years for bringing the Needle to London show that interest in it as a military trophy remained high. With the growing interest in Ancient Egypt, another powerful motive was the desire to possess one of the limited number of surviving obelisks, the largest Egyptian antiquities which could feasibly be transported abroad. In 1820, Samuel Briggs, the senior British merchant and banker in Alexandria, writing to George IV's private secretary, mentioned Rome and Constantinople as the only two cities in Europe which currently had obelisks and not only suggested the Needle as a monument to British military achievements, but also referred to its intrinsic merits as a work of art. The discovery in 1801 that the French had cleared sand away from the fallen obelisk and attached a rope to the top of its standing companion, fuelled suspicions that they had designs on one or both of them. The standing obelisk was actually offered to the French government by Muhammad Ali, but they chose instead to remove one of the two better preserved obelisks at Luxor (Fig 87), which was eventually set up in Paris in 1836. Not only did this emphasise that Britain, already offered the fallen obelisk, had done nothing to take up the offer for over 30 years, it gave grounds to suspect that the French would not stop at one obelisk. Writing to the Prime Minister, Lord Russell, in 1847, Prince Albert expressed his concern:

> I hear that the French Government are trying to get possession of it [the fallen obelisk] and to move it to Paris. This would be a real disgrace to our Government, moreover we possess absolutely nothing of this kind in England … Would you not undertake to have this national trophy and universally renowned work of Art brought to London? And have it erected as a principal monument to the Metropolis?[29]

Then, in 1867, the year of the great Exposition Universelle in Paris, Lieutenant Colonel Sir James Edward Alexander was in the city. Alexander was the great-nephew of Major Alexander Bryce, who as the senior military engineer at Alexandria had been consulted by the Earl of Cavan during the original attempt to move the obelisk. While in Paris, Alexander saw and admired the Luxor obelisk in the Place de la Concorde:

> I was then told that as good an obelisk, the property of the British Nation, lay imbedded in the sand of the sea-shore at Alexandria; that it was threatened with destruction by a M. Davray, the owner of the ground where it lay … I now determined to endeavour to save the national disgrace of the loss and destruction of the trophy – the prostrate obelisk, and I resolved to do my utmost to have it transported to London, to grace the Metropolis with a monument similar to those at Rome, Paris, and Constantinople.[30]

As good as his word, Alexander began his campaign. In 1868 he read a paper to the Royal Society of Edinburgh on how the Needle could be transported to London. Then, through his friend Sir William Stirling-Maxwell, he was introduced to the Chancellor of the Exchequer, Rt Hon Robert Lowe, who asked him to prepare plans and estimates. Working with City

Fig 87
One of two studies for plate 50 in Vivan Denon's *Voyages*, showing the two obelisks originally set up at the entrance to Luxor temple in Upper Egypt by Ramesses II. The slightly shorter one on the right was re-erected in the Place de la Concorde in Paris in 1836. [© Trustees of the British Museum]

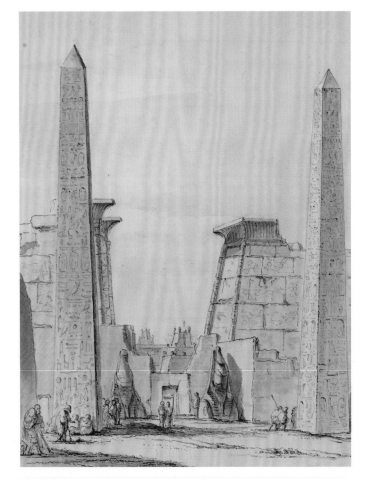

figures and the civil engineer William Eassie Jnr, Alexander prepared them but the estimated cost of £15,000 'induced Mr Lowe to postpone the undertaking to a more fitting season'. Alexander was told, by whom he does not say, that 'The obelisk was mutilated; was partly built over by the sea-wall of the fortifications; and besides, it was not likely that the Khedive would allow its removal after so many years, and that probably he might place it in the Museum at Cairo, in which he took much interest.'[31]

Undeterred by this, Alexander continued, reading papers to the British Association for the Advancement of Science in Glasgow and Belfast, and in 1872 *The Engineer* published a plan to move the obelisk suggested to him by a Scots civil engineer called Duncan. Three more years went by, and then Alexander decided to take matters into his own hands: 'I then resolved to go to the Land of the Pharaohs and ascertain the real state of matters.'[32]

To the land of the pharaohs

Alexander's friend Sir William Stirling-Maxwell was well connected politically, and during his career was an MP, senior university administrator and Trustee of the British Museum and National Gallery. He introduced Alexander to the Earl of Derby, Foreign Secretary in 1875. Derby in turn gave him an introduction to General Edward Stanton, the British Consul General in Egypt, who could then formally present him to Khedive Ismail.

On 19 March 1875, Alexander landed in Alexandria and secured the services of 'an intelligent dragoman' (guide and interpreter) Mustapha Adler Ali. Together they went to the site of the fallen obelisk but Alexander could see nothing, '…where was it? "There", pointing to a long trench, said Mustapha. "I see nothing", I answered. He called an Arab

boy, and directed him to clear off the sand with a stone, and soon a portion of the great mass was revealed.'[33]

Less than a week later Alexander accompanied General Stanton to the Abdin Palace in Cairo, where Stanton introduced him to the French-speaking Ismail as 'a zealous antiquary' who had come to examine the condition of the Needle and ask permission to remove it. In his account, Alexander quoted the khedive's response, ' "This obelisk was presented to the British nation by my ancestor Mahomed Ali Pasha, for services rendered to Egypt; it belongs to Britain, I give it up freely." '[34]

Ismail then asked how it was proposed to move the obelisk and Alexander outlined the plan that had been published in *The Engineer*, which involved casing the Needle in a wooden frame and moving it on rails into a waiting ship. Ismail asked about the size and weight of the obelisk but seemed satisfied, and said 'Take it by any means.' He and General Stanton then moved on to discuss other matters including the suppression of the slave trade in Egypt and the Sudan, but as they rose to leave Stanton, still anxious to confirm that the original offer by Muhammad Ali over 70 years before still held good, took the khedive aside and asked him, 'Is this your last word? We can take the obelisk?' 'You can take it, certainly', was Ismail's reply.

The khedive might have been willing to give away the obelisk, but despite his lavish spending in other areas it became clear that he would not, or could not, pay for it to be moved. However, his chief of harbours, Admiral McKillop Pasha, offered what assistance he could with materials from the dockyard on his return from official business on the Red Sea. Alexander therefore took this opportunity to make a brief visit to the Holy Land. News of his meeting with

Ismail must have circulated rapidly and on his return Alexander was soon receiving offers to move the obelisk. Hartly Gisborne, chief of telegraphs for the khedive, with whom Alexander was staying, suggested he consider a proposal to move the Needle for £12,000 by Mr Forrer, manager of the Engineering and Cotton Machinery Company of Alexandria. Hire of a towing vessel and the costs of erection in London would be additional. Another proposal came from 'Signor Cerioni, an ingenious Italian gentleman'. His estimate, which Alexander does not disclose, was 'modest' and he presented Alexander with a plaster model of the Needle. More importantly, an official of the Egyptian government, Chamberlain Bey, introduced Alexander to Waynman Dixon, C E [Civil Engineer] of the North of England Iron Company.

Enter the Dixon brothers

Dixon told Alexander that he and his brother John had been interested in the obelisk for some time and would be glad to be engaged to remove it to England. In 1872, Waynman had been Resident Engineer for the Giza Bridge near Cairo, designed by his brother, and had lived for some months in a tomb near the pyramids. During this time he investigated the pyramids and discovered the small shafts leading from the 'Queen's Chamber' in the Great Pyramid. John Dixon (Fig 88) came to Egypt for the opening of the bridge, and while they were in Alexandria the brothers went to see the fallen obelisk and discussed how it could be moved. Waynman suggested enclosing it in a cylindrical iron pontoon and rolling it into the sea, where it could be floated and towed to England. John was enthusiastic about the idea and on his return to England wrote to the papers saying that it could be done for £15,000. He asked Waynman to take soundings in Alexandria harbour and the plan was worked out in more detail

by Waynman, but nothing came of it until Alexander's arrival. Alexander insisted on inspecting the obelisk properly for himself and on 5 May Waynman employed men to clear away the sand and soil, 3ft deep in places, which covered it. The condition of the inscriptions was better than either of them had expected and afterwards Waynman gave Alexander a copy of what became known as the Dixon Plan. The estimated cost had now dropped to £10,000. The governor of Alexandria recommended that Alexander should meet with Signor Giovanni Demetrio, the owner of the ground on which the obelisk lay. Two meetings took place between Alexander and Demetrio, whose cooperation was eventually secured with the help of Mrs Gisborne, the wife of Alexander's host, and he gave his blessing for the obelisk to be removed. This was not to be the end of the matter, however, as Demetrio was later

Fig 88
Born in Newcastle-upon-Tyne, John Dixon was articled to the great railway engineer Robert Stephenson and later was to construct the first railway in China, although he specialised in bridges and harbour works. [Courtesy Institution of Civil Engineers]

offended by the Egyptian government's treatment of him and became embroiled in legal proceedings against them. For now, however, Alexander was free to return to London to pursue his campaign.

The fallen Needle's partial burial had actually helped to preserve it from damage but since the 18th century, when Frederik Norden had mistakenly concluded that it had been broken when it fell, doubt had been cast on the condition of the Needle and whether it was worth the expense of transporting to Britain. In 1843, the Egyptologist J G Wilkinson had commented in his book *Modern Egypt and Thebes* that the removal of the Needle had been 'wisely abandoned', and that because of 'its mutilated state, and the obliteration of the hieroglyphics by its exposure to the sea air, it is unworthy the expense of removal'.

In 1857, when the radical MP Joseph Hume was campaigning for the Needle to be taken to London, the Chancellor of the Exchequer rejected the suggestion in parliament on the grounds that, even at a then estimated cost of only £7,000, the inscriptions were so damaged as to make the expense of transporting it 'scarcely worth while'. Foreign Office papers from 1867 summarised the history of attempts to bring the Needle to London and noted in the context of the current estimate of how much it would cost to bring the Needle back that 'exposure and wanton damage' might have made the obelisk 'so injured as to be worthless as an object of Ancient Egyptian Art'. They commented that it was 'a great pity that so fine a memorial of antiquity should have been allowed to fall into this state, but it would appear to be throwing money away to spend so large a sum as £10,000 on a thing which after all is terribly defaced'.[35]

The writer, identified only as V D B, went on to suggest consulting 'the authorities

of the British Museum', which in practice meant Samuel Birch, the Keeper of Oriental Antiquities. Despite his considerable achievements as a scholar, Birch never visited Egypt and his report was therefore based on published sources and correspondence with others. One of these was H J Rouse (or Rowe) an engineer who suggested photographing the inscriptions on the fallen obelisk (which was eventually done by Waynman Dixon) but also mentioned meeting with a Mr Nash, who had been in Alexandria and described the fallen obelisk as 'much mutilated'. To this pessimistic assessment Birch added those of Wilkinson, Scott Tucker who had examined it in 1852, and Thomas Leverton Donaldson, Emeritus Professor of Architecture at UCL, who had visited Alexandria in 1861–2 and inspected the Needle:

> In the enclosed letter which he has written to me on the subject of its present condition states that when he visited Egypt in 1861 – 1862 the surface had been rubbed materially and the hieroglyphics almost indistinguishable although so deeply cut and that this obelisk as well as the other are so damaged that he does not consider them worthy the cost and labour of removal.[36]

The standing obelisk, which was eventually taken to New York, had indeed suffered from exposure to the weather and the inscriptions on one face were badly worn. Without clearing the fallen obelisk it was impossible to determine whether it really was in a similar state, and indeed if it was even intact. Such negative opinions of its condition from eminent authorities carried a lot of weight. Back in London, Alexander met with John Dixon. To finally settle the question of the obelisk's condition, Dixon asked his brother to completely uncover it and take photographs, and also to take extensive soundings in the harbour.

Waynman cleared three sides of the Needle and the middle part of the underside, washed and cleaned the inscriptions and photographed them. He found that although two faces were somewhat weathered, the hieroglyphs were 'perfectly visible'.

Armed with this information, Alexander approached the government but with no more success than when he had approached the Chancellor of the Exchequer in 1868. John Dixon was also enthusiastic enough to write to the papers, offering to contribute £500 to the cost of bringing the Needle to London as a memorial of the Prince of Wales's visit to India. Lieutenant General James Colbourne, the second Lord Seaton, introduced Alexander to William Cotton, Lord Mayor of London in 1875, and with his help Alexander prepared to try to raise the money to move the Needle privately in the City of London. In the course of this, in November 1876, Alexander wrote to a friend of his, Professor Erasmus Wilson, possibly to ask him for financial advice. Wilson was a leading dermatologist but shrewd investments in gas and railway company shares had made him a wealthy man. At Wilson's request Alexander then visited him and was asked to explain about the obelisk, its condition and the plans for bringing it to England. Alexander needed no further urging. The plans and calculations produced by William Eassie had been returned to him, but Alexander had the proposals of a London engineering firm Messrs King and the Dixon Plan, and it was the latter that he 'strongly' recommended to Wilson. Alexander's enthusiasm for the Dixon Plan may have been due to the fact that he himself, in his 1868 paper delivered to the Royal Society of Edinburgh, had suggested that the Needle could be transported by 'an iron casing or vessel built round it'. It is not clear whether Alexander had in mind the sort of fully cylindrical casing proposed by the Dixons but later

Waynman Dixon made a point of claiming full credit for the successful design. As a result of Alexander's visit Erasmus Wilson called on John Dixon a few days later, and although they were previously unknown to each other the common bond of Freemasonry allowed them to get straight to business. Dixon outlined his plan, which he estimated would cost £5,000 but which to cover contingencies he would contract to carry out for £7,000. Wilson recognised that there might be unforeseen problems and made an offer – the Needle to be set up in London for £10,000 within two years, 'no cure no pay'. Although this meant that if Dixon did not completely fulfil the contract he would be personally liable for all costs, as well as for any costs over £10,000, he willingly accepted the offer.

From this point on events, in contrast to the previous decades, moved quickly. A week later another meeting was held at the offices of Wilson's solicitor, Charles Swinburne. Also present, in addition to Wilson, Dixon and Swinburne, was Henry Palfrey Stephenson, a civil engineer, friend of Wilson and another Freemason, who was to give a second opinion on the plan. Stephenson's assessment was favourable, the terms of the contract were agreed and it was signed by the end of January. In 1872 Alexander had been offered a site by the Metropolitan Board of Works at the centre of what is now Victoria Embankment Gardens and he now confirmed with them that the offer was still valid. Together with Admiral Sir Erasmus Ommanney, he also visited the Admiralty twice in an attempt to persuade them to use a naval vessel returning from Alexandria to tow the obelisk vessel. The Admiralty refused to do this on the grounds that the safety of the towing vessel might be jeopardised in bad weather. Also, despite the fact that the khedive had confirmed that the original offer of the obelisk by Muhammad Ali still stood, and that its removal would be funded privately, the government still seemed to be dragging its feet. Ismail had given his approval to the Needle's removal but only verbally. After a month had gone by, John Dixon cabled his friend John Fowler, engineering advisor to the khedive, and on 14 March Hussey Crespigny Vivian, 3rd Baron Vivian, the British Consul General, was summoned to the Abdin Palace and presented with a letter officially presenting the Needle to Britain again and authorising John Dixon to remove it. Waynman Dixon, who had drawn up the initial designs for the vessel which was to transport the obelisk, was unavailable being in Somalia, and so Fowler also offered the services of Benjamin Baker, a junior partner in his firm of consulting engineers. Baker completed the detailed design work and in March 1877 a contract was signed with the Thames Iron Works, near East India Docks, for the construction of the prefabricated wrought-iron obelisk barge. By the beginning of June in that year it had been shipped to Alexandria ready for assembly.

Troubled waters

Over the years all sorts of suggestions had been made on how the obelisk could be transported to England. The original plan, in 1801, had been to move the Needle along a jetty and then load it into a naval vessel through a specially constructed stern port. (A variation on this technique was actually used to move the upright obelisk, now in New York, which was loaded into its vessel through a port specially cut in the bows, and the Luxor obelisk, now in Paris, whose transport ship was built with removable bows.) Several other proposals, inspired by a description of the transport of obelisks in ancient times by the Roman author Pliny, involved variations on the use of a dry dock and barges or caissons attached to the obelisk. The dock could subsequently be flooded and the obelisk floated to sea along a short canal. Some of these proposals would have been impractical, or have seriously underestimated the costs involved, but equally many of them were put forward by experienced professional engineers with the benefit of having seen the location of the Needle at first hand. In the end it was the Dixon Plan that was adopted, and although it had similarities to a number of the other proposals, its eventual success may have been due to its careful attention to the many problems posed by the location.

One of the principal reasons for Alexander the Great's choice of the small fishing village of Rhakotis as the site of the new capital named after him was that it offered one of the few natural harbours on an exposed coast. However, while the Eastern harbour was large it was also shallow. The Needle weighed in excess of 180 tons and any vessel large enough to take such a load as a single item was too large to come in close to the shore (John Dixon estimated that it could not come closer than half a mile), hence the need for a jetty. Not only that, but the bottom of the harbour was littered with broken columns and blocks, the remains of the ancient city. Despite some degree of protection offered by offshore reefs and natural limestone ridges, the city was still pounded by storms from time to time and the collapse of the first jetty in 1801 had shown what problems this could cause. An alternative solution was to dig a canal to take the obelisk into deeper water but John Dixon knew from the soundings carried out by his brother that beneath a few feet of sand the floor of the harbour was solid rock. He estimated the cost of constructing a canal at £40,000 because of the need to blast rock away and the problem of strong currents filling the canal with sand once it was created. The Dixon brothers' solution was to build a wrought-iron cylinder, 93ft long and 15ft across around the obelisk, with 10 watertight compartments and a tapering bow and stern. This would be rolled down timbers into the harbour, towed nine miles to the Western harbour, fitted with false keels, a superstructure, mast and rudder, and then towed to England.

Before this could happen, however, there was another problem to overcome. Alexandria was a booming city and the obelisk lay on a prime building site by the Eastern harbour near modern Saad Zaghloul Square. As far back as 1864, the owner of the land, possibly the 'Mr Bravay' from whom Demetrio bought it (Alexander's 'M. Davray' is probably a mistake), had threatened to break it up if it was not moved. The demolition of the obelisk's pedestal meant that this could not be treated as an empty threat and the British consul had placed it under the protection of the local authorities. Demetrio, who acquired the land in 1867, was an amateur archaeologist and unlikely to wantonly destroy such an important relic, but the Needle's presence on his land meant that he was unable to develop it. When Alexander met him, Demetrio had given his consent to the removal of the obelisk but was subsequently persuaded to claim compensation from the Egyptian government on the grounds that their failure to remove it had prevented him building on the land. He lost the court case and the Egyptian government disclaimed responsibility for the Needle. Like its British counterpart it seems to have been concerned that if it took any action to move the Needle it would assume responsibility for it, as well as incurring considerable expense.

Then, in April 1877, workmen arrived to begin clearing sand from around the obelisk and preparing a smooth pathway to the harbour. Had Demetrio been consulted beforehand he would probably have raised no objections but he must have been still smarting from his defeat in court and angered at what he saw as the high-handed

attitude of the government, which had first denied any responsibility for the Needle, then granted permission to remove it from his property without consulting him as the owner of the land. He promptly set up a fence around the site and, despite his previous claim for damages on account of the government's failure to remove it, refused to allow anything to be done until he had been paid an indemnity for its removal. When he was made aware of the situation, John Dixon sent a representative to Egypt. This was Captain Henry Carter, who had skippered P&O passenger ships for over 20 years and who was to be the master of *Cleopatra*, the obelisk barge. Carter took with him letters of support from Dixon and Birch among others, but it became clear that Demetrio's quarrel was with the Egyptian authorities. In a letter later written to *The Times* by Demetrio, but not published, he refers to one of the documents presented to him by Carter:

> No mention was made in it either of my name or of my land, as if some locality was in question which was either desert or abandoned or without an owner … I could not help being deeply mortified by such treatment, and I peremptorily refused to acknowledge the document as binding on me.[37]

Carter returned to Cairo where the Consul General persuaded the khedive to authorise a suitably diplomatic official letter to Demetrio. The change of heart was immediate and dramatic. Demetrio wrote to Dixon on 11 May assuring him that

> …I can have but one thought – that of at once acceding to your request and allowing you to remove the obelisk at present resting on my property … My sole object is to assist you in carrying out the artistic work you have undertaken, assistance which I owe you as a student of

archaeology, and as a Greek subject who cannot forget the debt of gratitude which his country owes to the English nation. I have therefore, the honour to inform you that from the present moment the obelisk is entirely at your disposal, and that I waive claim against the Egyptian Government in respect of it.[38]

Now work could begin. Using hydraulic and screw jacks, the obelisk was moved round until it was parallel to the sea wall, then raised and lowered back onto a bed of logs and railway sleepers to provide a firm and level base. Then the watertight bulkheads were assembled around it, the plates of the hull riveted into place, and two lots of ballast placed to evenly balance the craft. The path to the sea was cleared by removing the old quay wall, but the shore and the seabed were covered with what Alexander described as 'hundreds of building stones'. He noted that many of them 'were covered with hieroglyphics, but what these could have been it is difficult to imagine'. Thanks to recent archaeological investigations, particularly those by Franck Goddio and his team in the harbour, we now know that these would have been the remains of the royal quarters of the Ptolemaic city, including the palace of Cleopatra VII. Some of the larger stones and the foundations of a wall submerged in the shallows were blasted away with explosives. To protect the hull of the vessel as it was rolled towards the water, two 12ft lengths, one at each end, were covered with 'tyres' of 6in-thick timber planks clamped on by iron bands. Benjamin Baker described the result as 'a gigantic 270 ton road-roller'. Early in the morning of 28 August, the descent to the sea began. Despite the fact that there had been no official ceremony, thousands watched as winches on two lighters in the harbour began to haul a huge steel cable wrapped around the cylinder, while screw jacks pushed it forward down a timber slipway. After six hours the vessel had only made one complete revolution and the anchors on the lighters were failing to hold on the harbour bed, so the cable ends were attached to two steam tugs which steamed away from the shore. After nearly 12 hours the shoreline had been reached, and an hour and a half later it rested in 3ft of water, where it was left for the night.

The next morning work resumed but at midday, after picking up a burst of speed, the cylinder stopped dead in 7ft of water; two or three less than the depth at which she would float. All day the tugs tried to jerk the craft forward again but without success. The next morning Waynman Dixon went out to inspect the cylinder and opening a manhole in the deck found it half full of water. Pumps failed to make any impression and when a diver was sent down it was found that a hole 18ins long had been torn in the plates near one end. No one seems to have invoked 'The Curse of Cleopatra', but the culprit was a large squared block of stone weighing about 1,300lbs that had come from one of the ancient buildings and was now on the harbour floor. Embarrassingly, none of the watertight doors in the bulkheads had been closed so the cylinder had flooded from end to end and was now firmly wedged in place. Two or three days were wasted trying to pump out the craft before John Dixon intervened. A 9ft open-topped wooden box was constructed on the seaward side and filled with ballast. A jack placed between this and the cylinder then pushed it far enough back towards the shore for it to be patched and pumped out. On 7 September the attempt began again and shortly before midday the cylinder started to rise and fall in the swell, showing that it was afloat.

When the wooden 'tyres' and additional ballast were removed, the cylinder rolled upright just as it had been designed to do, and two tugs towed it nine miles around the headland to Alexandria Dockyard. An unusually strong northerly wind sent waves crashing over the harbour breakwater and the tugs rolled so heavily that those on their bridges had to cling to the rails. The obelisk cylinder rode the waves well but without a rudder veered violently from side to side, making the tugs dodge out of her way. The offshore reefs and shoals only added to the difficulties, but eventually the cylinder reached the Western harbour and dry dock. Here, Admiral McKillop was as good as his word and the hull was repaired, two 40ft-long bilge keels, a cabin, steering and hurricane decks were added, a mast set up and a rudder hung from the stern. After only 10 days the cylinder once again took to the water, this time as the *Cleopatra*, launched on 19 September in front of 150 dignitaries by McKillop's daughter breaking the traditional bottle of champagne, but on the stern rather than the bow.

Olga and *Cleopatra*

The *Olga*, a British merchant vessel, was due to leave Alexandria for Newcastle upon Tyne with a cargo of grain, and Carter arranged for her to tow the *Cleopatra* as far as Falmouth where a tug would then take over. The initial charge of £1,000 was reduced to £900 and a crew was signed up; five Maltese seamen at £20 for the trip, a carpenter at £25 and a boatswain at £50. This was generous pay at the time for a voyage estimated to take four weeks and probably reflects the nervousness of the crew at serving on such an unorthodox craft. Captain Booth was skipper of the *Olga* and Captain Carter of the *Cleopatra*. With brutal realism the contract stipulated that if the *Cleopatra* was lost at sea only the completed portion of the journey would be paid for. The *Olga* and *Cleopatra* sailed on 21 September, with Waynman Dixon as a passenger on the *Olga*. General Alexander

remarked about 'the old superstition of leaving on Friday not daunting the brave Captain Carter'. In the voyage to come Carter must have wondered more than once about this decision.

Despite some quirks, particularly a tendency to pitch suddenly and violently in rough seas as often as once every three or four seconds, the *Cleopatra* handled as her designers had predicted; and the small turret on her bows supporting the hurricane deck split the waves to either side, even though she rode very low in the water. Shortly after leaving port the boatswain was confined to his bunk by an inflammation of the liver (possibly cirrhosis brought on by heavy drinking). This meant that Carter had to stand watch all night every night and catch what sleep he could during the day. Then another crewmember injured his foot, leaving Carter with a crew of only five. Every six hours, he entered the interior of the vessel through a small hatch in his quarters and crawled through tiny hatches in the watertight bulkheads to check for leaks, and to ensure that the obelisk was firmly wedged in position. His only light came from a candle held in his mouth, which he once dropped when it started burning his nose leaving him to grope his way back from the bow in complete darkness for half an hour. Making between five and six knots, the two vessels communicated by messages chalked on a blackboard in daylight and by a combination of coloured lights at night. Once the shackle connecting the towing cable to the *Cleopatra* broke but was repaired. The weather began to worsen rapidly and the *Olga* had to battle along the North African coast against a violent storm. Running low on supplies of coal, Captain Booth made an unscheduled stop in Algiers where the crew proceeded to get fighting drunk. A day later, they were ready to depart again but one of the Maltese seamen was hospitalised after nearly severing his leg when it became trapped in a hawser, leaving the crew one man more short.

By 7 October they had reached Gibraltar, where letters were posted. John Dixon cabled England to report their safe arrival and two additional seamen were taken on. From Gibraltar they rounded Cape St Vincent into the Atlantic and in the evening of 14 October they entered the Bay of Biscay in fine weather. The next morning, however, there were signs of an approaching storm, and at 8 am a vicious squall broke on them from the south-west. As the day progressed, the weather continued to worsen, the wind rising to gale force and swinging to the west. At times the storm rose to hurricane force with thunder, lightning and hail. As long as the *Olga* and *Cleopatra* were running before the wind they could hope to ride out the storm, but it continued to move to the north and threatened to sweep away the deckhouse on the *Cleopatra*. Carter signalled to Booth to heave to, facing the wind. Booth was unwilling at first, fearing that it might put too much strain on the towrope, but eventually did so. The *Olga* made the turn successfully, but as the *Cleopatra* tried to follow she was struck broadside by an enormous wave and as she was hurled over Carter felt something shift below decks.

To keep the craft stable at sea, 20 tons of iron rails had been placed as ballast in the bottom of the hull. The ballast was secured by planks but they were only 1in thick, and the planks had just given way. The *Cleopatra* now lay at an angle of 45 degrees. Frantic efforts by Carter and his crew succeeded in moving much of the ballast back into place but just as the craft was beginning to right itself, another large wave hit and the ballast came loose again. Carter, fearing the vessel was foundering and would sink made the decision to abandon ship. His only lifeboat, 12ft long by 4ft wide, was on the windward side of the vessel and when the crew attempted to bring it round to the leeward side on the end of a rope, the rope snagged and the boat was smashed to pieces by the heavy seas. The *Cleopatra's* signalling lights had been washed away, but eventually the *Olga* made out that she was foundering and requesting a boat.

Six volunteers boarded a boat and attempted to reach the *Cleopatra*. A rope was thrown to them as they neared it, but the seaman who caught it was unable to hang on and the boat was swept past the obelisk barge and swamped by a huge wave. With no other option Carter and his crew tried again to replace the ballast. They had almost succeeded, bringing the craft nearly upright again, and also managing to turn her to head into the wind, when a gust of wind heeled the vessel back over and the ballast broke loose again. Throughout the night, with the *Cleopatra* heeled over even further than before, the Sisyphean struggle continued while the *Olga* slipped the towrope and attempted to close and put a line across (Fig 89). At 6.30 am the attempt was successful and an unmanned boat was sent to take off Carter and his crew. As soon as they were aboard, Booth cut the line between the two vessels and steamed back to look for survivors from the *Olga's* lifeboat. For three hours they searched but found only a boathook and some oars. Abandoning the search the *Olga* turned back to recover the *Cleopatra* but found only her mast floating in the water. After more hours of searching it seemed that she must have sunk, and the *Olga* set course for Falmouth, reaching it two days later.

Fitzmaurice and the hard-headed Scotchman

Waiting for them there was not only John Dixon but a telegram from the wife of the *Olga's* Second Mate William Askin announcing

Fig 89
In this 1878 painting by Edward Cooke RA, once owned by Erasmus Wilson, a fair degree of artistic licence has been used. It is meant to show the obelisk barge *Cleopatra* signalling to the *Olga* to cast off its tow line during the great storm, but there are a number of factual inaccuracies.
[Photo © Victoria and Albert Museum, London]

the birth of their first child. Askin had been one of those on the boat sent across to the *Cleopatra*. To his credit, one of the first things John Dixon did was to start a fund for the dependents of the men who had died, and donate £250. The atmosphere must have been grim. Six men had died and the obelisk was missing, presumed sunk. John Dixon and Benjamin Baker, however, had faith in their design and believed that as long as the hull of the *Cleopatra* was intact she would stay afloat. Waynman Dixon also later recalled that the report he had prepared for Alexander had foreseen such a situation: 'In case of bad weather and the towing ship being obliged to cast off the unwieldy mass, it could be let go with cable and anchor attached, and would probably strand or moor itself where it could be picked up again after the storm abated.'[39]

Carter confirmed that the *Cleopatra* had not been taking on water, her seams were tight and her hatches had been battened down before she had been abandoned. Alexander recalled that Dixon said to him, 'Cheer up, Carter, she'll float again,

and you shall bring her up the Thames.' Dixon contacted the Admiralty and urged them to despatch a ship to search for the *Cleopatra*. Lying low in the water she would pose a danger to shipping and if another vessel collided with her both might be sunk. Before this could happen, though, the lookout on the *Fitzmaurice*, a cargo ship from Middlesbrough bound for Valencia with a cargo of pig iron, spotted what looked like the bottom of a capsized ship. Through binoculars the master of the *Fitzmaurice*, Captain Evans, was able to make out the name 'Cleopatra' and recognised the obelisk barge. Evans was anxious to claim salvage rights, but the weather was appalling and none of his crew would volunteer to try to take a boat across.

All night the *Fitzmaurice* had to try not to lose sight of the *Cleopatra*, and the next morning the promise of a share of the salvage money was enough to tempt three volunteers to join the chief officer in an attempt to secure the barge – although the wind was still gusting and the sea heavy. *Cleopatra* was still heeled over at an acute angle, pitching and rolling, with her bridge plunging in and out of the water, and her rudder had jammed sending her round in a full circle every three or four minutes. After an hour and a half of trying, the chief officer managed to cling to the heaving bridge and get a line across. By noon wreckage had been cleared, two ropes attached and the *Fitzmaurice* began to tow the *Cleopatra* to the nearest port – the Spanish naval base of Ferrol 90 miles away. After two hours the ropes gave way, and when the barge had been secured again towing had to resume at a slower speed. The weather deteriorated again, the ropes parted a second time in gale-force winds, and for a third time a boat had to be sent across to secure the obelisk barge. Eventually, the *Fitzmaurice* brought the *Cleopatra* into Ferrol just after 9 pm on Wednesday 17 October.

Under maritime law a fee for salvage was due to the owners of the *Fitzmaurice*, Messrs Burrell and Son of Glasgow, particularly as Evans and his crew had exposed themselves to considerable risk in securing a vessel which was a potential danger to other shipping. John Dixon and Captain Carter went to Glasgow to negotiate payment but were shocked at the size of the fee demanded by Burrell and Son. Alexander

> …communicated with Mr Burrell and tried to induce him to be moderate in his charge for salvage on patriotic grounds … but Mr Dixon had no better success than I had. Mr Burrell claimed salvage to the amount of £5,000, and seemed determined not to abate the preposterous sum one farthing. Mr Dixon endeavoured to reason him out of his notions, and offered him a cheque for 600l [£600], but the hard-headed Scotchman could not be moved. In Glasgow there was a general feeling of shame at Mr Burrell's conduct.[40]

There was no other option but to settle the matter in court. A value had to be put on the obelisk itself and the court fixed this at £25,000, about £1,215,500 in today's terms. Some felt that this was excessive; *The Times* described it as 'very high', and said that:

> None have been more astonished than those who might be expected to set the greatest store by the monolith – viz., the Egyptologists themselves, who think that £2,500 would have been a fair estimate in appraising a monument, which, however interesting on account of its venerable inscriptions and history, is not a work of high art, like the Venus of Milo or the Apollo Belvedere.[41]

Two thousand pounds was awarded in salvage – £1,200 to the owners, far below what Burrell had claimed and only twice what he had been offered by Dixon, £250 to the master of the *Fitzmaurice*, and the balance divided between the crew with double shares for the volunteers who had first boarded the *Cleopatra*. While the matter of salvage was being decided, Dixon paid £5,000 to the Admiralty Court on 19 December to bail out the *Cleopatra* and allow her to continue her voyage. On the same day, Captain Carter arrived in Ferrol with a hand-picked new crew and materials to refit the barge. On inspection, it was found that the hull had remained watertight and that below decks everything was intact apart from the ballast which had shifted and caused so much trouble. Three weeks later the *Cleopatra* was refitted and this time no chances had been taken with securing the ballast.

The owners of the *Olga* were prepared to complete their contract but John Dixon would have had to wait for her to be available again, and he had been criticised in some quarters for entrusting such a valuable cargo to an ordinary merchant vessel in the first place. Whether or not a deep-sea tug would have fared any better in the Bay of Biscay, Dixon decided to enter into a fresh contract for £500 with William Watkins, owner of the *Anglia*, an ocean-going steam paddle tug known on the Thames as 'Three Finger Jack' because of her triple funnels. Built in 1866 she was the most powerful tug of her day and had previously brought vessels back from as far away as St Helena. By 12 January the *Anglia* had reached Ferrol and just after dawn on 15 January she left with the *Cleopatra* in tow.

This time, apart from a strong east wind on the first day, the weather was as calm as it had been stormy before. The *Cleopatra's* steering failed halfway through the voyage but in a flat sea this could be coped with. The weather deteriorated as the vessels came abreast of Dover and turned into the Thames estuary but by Sunday night, 20 January, they were safely moored near Southend. At Gravesend, John Dixon and his wife came aboard and a telegram arrived from Queen Victoria congratulating him on the Needle's safe arrival. On Monday afternoon the *Anglia* and *Cleopatra* made their way upriver. The nearer they came to the East India Docks at Blackwall, where a berth had been provided free of charge, the bigger the crowds along the banks of the Thames and the more small craft full of sightseers the skippers had to avoid on the river. At the entrance to the docks, the *Anglia* handed over to a smaller tug, the *Mosquito*, and by 5 pm the *Cleopatra* was safely moored.

The battle of the sites

Ever since the original attempt in 1801, attention had been focussed on if the Needle would come to England and how it could be transported. Less attention was paid to where it would be erected although it was clear that, in the words of an 1849 petition to Prince Albert 'some elevated

site in the Metropolis' was intended. Some specific sites had been suggested, such as the front of Carlton House, Trafalgar Square, Greenwich Hospital, and the Crystal Palace, but these were largely theoretical. Once it was clear that the Needle was indeed coming to England, though, what *The Times* called 'The Battle of the Sites' broke out. It noted in a leader, 'That our distinguished visitor is duly appreciated appears from the overwhelming number of invitations to every open space, every intersection of architectural lines, every bit of green, in and around the Metropolis; but everywhere there are objections.'[42]

All the previous sites were again proposed and other suggestions included Battersea Park, the British Museum, outside Buckingham Palace, Green Park, Horse Guards Parade, Hyde Park, Kensington Gardens, Northumberland Avenue, Parliament Square, Primrose Hill, Regent's Park, the Royal Observatory at Greenwich and Wellington Street. In reality most of these were never serious candidates. In 1872, the Metropolitan Board of Works had granted General Alexander a site at the centre of the ornamental gardens on the Victoria Embankment, which had only been completed two years before. (Before the creation of the London County Council, the Board of Works was effectively the local authority for London, and was responsible for major construction projects such as the Embankment and the new sewage system.) More importantly, the contract between Erasmus Wilson and John Dixon specified that the obelisk would be erected on a site 'on or near the Thames Embankment'. The 'no cure no pay' basis of the contract meant that Dixon would be liable for any expense over the agreed £10,000. He does not seem to have expected to make a profit, and the costs of salvaging the *Cleopatra* meant that any possibility of this had disappeared anyway, but he made it clear that he was not prepared to meet the costs of setting the Needle up at sites distant from the river. In a letter to *The Times*, he estimated the cost of transport to the British Museum, with the associated disruption to the public, as an extra £10,000. Sites even further away were 'as much out of the question as Salisbury Plain'.[43]

On 25 June 1877, the First Commissioner of Works, Gerard Noel, had been asked by Lord Ernest Bruce (who initially favoured Greenwich Hospital as a site) whether any site for the Needle had yet been selected. Noel replied that 'four important sites' had been suggested; two on the Embankment, opposite Northumberland Avenue and at Whitehall Stairs, one to the south of the Palace of Westminster, opposite Abingdon Street, and a fourth in Parliament Square itself (Fig 90). He stressed that no decision

had yet been taken, but mentioned the 'difficulty and risk' of transporting the Needle to a site distant from the river.[44] The Parliament Square site, favoured by both Dixon and Wilson, was a strong candidate until late in 1877, but the demand by the Metropolitan Railway for a perpetual indemnity against the Needle collapsing into the underground railway which ran beneath the square and the convenience of a site nearer the river, finally led to it being abandoned. The site originally granted to General Alexander would still have been available, but, 'It was now thought if the monolith was placed there it might not look sufficiently detached from the rear of the houses of the Strand, when viewed from the Embankment. So I went about alone and with Mr Dixon to observe the effect of other sites.'[45]

Fig 90
A full-sized wooden model of Cleopatra's Needle, complete with hieroglyphs, was set up in front of the Houses of Parliament to test public reaction to the proposed site, and was illustrated in a Special Supplement to the *Illustrated London News* in January 1878. [© Chris Elliott]

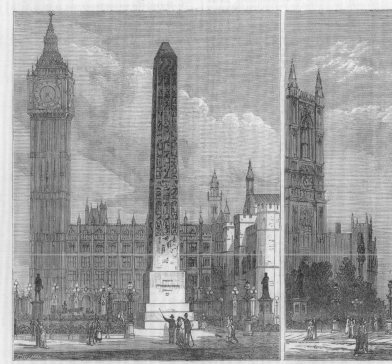
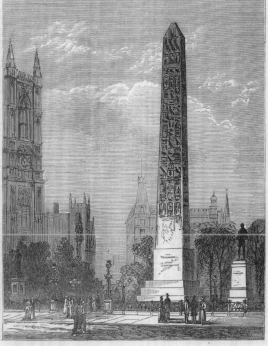

THE OBELISK AS SEEN FROM CANNING'S STATUE.   THE OBELISK FROM THE CORNER OF PALACE-YARD.

CLEOPATRA'S NEEDLE IN THE PROPOSED SITE.

Eventually, with the agreement of Erasmus Wilson, Dixon applied to the Board of Works to erect the Needle at its present site on top of the Adelphi Steps on the Embankment (Fig 91). This was chosen in preference to Northumberland Avenue and the Temple Gardens because of the presence of the railway at the former and of future buildings at the latter. Dixon wrote to *The Times* on 31 January 1878 announcing the reluctant decision to abandon Parliament Square and choose the new site. On the same day Gerard Noel was asked in parliament whether he proposed to 'take the opinion of the House' on the site of the obelisk. His diplomatic reply was that if the Adelphi site was found unsuitable, and another on a site under the jurisdiction of the Board had to be selected, he would 'give it careful consideration', and every opportunity would be given 'for public criticism before any decision is arrived at'.[46] In reality the Adelphi site was a done deal, although the debate rumbled on in the columns of *The Times* for several months and as late as 1911 an anonymous correspondent signing himself 'Anthony' urged that the 'original blunder'

of the chosen site be 'reconsidered' and the Needle moved to the centre of Oxford Circus.[47] However, despite the fact that most of the alternative sites were never realistic contenders, the Battle of the Sites was still significant. The choice of where to place Cleopatra's Needle was never going to be simply about where to best display a large Ancient Egyptian monument. It was going to be about Politics, Art, Religion and more besides, and was largely played out in the Letters columns of *The Times*. As General Alexander put it, 'Ancient Egypt, Egyptian enlightenment and refinement, scenes and acts of Bible history – are, as it were, realised by the presence of this stately object of art in the midst of our ancient, although compared with itself, very modern, city.'[48]

He went on to observe that the obelisk had gone on from Ancient Egypt to see the civilisations of the Greeks and Romans, and much later been witness to the 'brilliant exploits' of Nelson and the 'grievous loss sustained by Britain' in the death of Abercromby at Alexandria. The original motivation for bringing the Needle to London had indeed been military and

Fig 91
This picture shows the Needle on its final site at the Adelphi Steps, with Waterloo Bridge in the foreground. In the background can be seen the Adelphi Gardens (now part of Victoria Embankment Gardens), in the centre of which General Alexander was originally given permission to erect the Needle. [XA00144]

political. It represented, in the words of the 3rd Earl of Harrowby, writing in *The Times*, a 'monument of gratitude to England from liberated Egypt'.[49] Alexander himself commented in a letter to the paper, 'This was the chief reason why I did my best to save this precious monolith from threatened destruction in 1867.'[50] As a result, there was strong support from a number of quarters for sites such as Horse Guards Parade and St James's Park because of their military associations, and Alexander himself favoured the Park.

In addition to this, however, there were the views of those less concerned with the obelisk as military trophy and memorial, and more with what sort of surroundings were most appropriate for an Ancient Egyptian work of art. Here, there were two schools of thought: one felt that the Needle should be in an open space so that it was not overwhelmed by other buildings, the other that obelisks had originally been erected close to temples and thus should be placed in close proximity to other buildings. The critic and poet Francis Palgrave was of the former school, feeling that the Needle should be placed 'where it has some chance of being looked at in leisurely quietness and freedom from the bustle and hurry of the "Great City"'.[51]

He favoured St James's Park, other similar sites in, or adjacent to other London parks or in the long avenue of The Mall. John Dixon, however, whose opinion carried some weight, felt that the views of those that supported such sites were based on a misunderstanding, arising from sites like Heliopolis, that the Ancient Egyptians erected obelisks in open spaces as far as possible away from buildings 'Why they adopt such a conclusion I cannot imagine. The Egyptians always erected obelisks in close proximity to the giant masses of the buildings of their temples… '.[52]

Joseph Bonomi, however, felt that, 'Isolation for this solitary ancient monument seems to me to be an indispensable condition, indeed in one sense it is forced on us, for obelisks were invariably placed in pairs in front of the gate of a temple, and here the companion is wanting.'[53]

Even if the obelisk was erected in a built-up area, though, this did not mean that it could be placed anywhere there was space. Dixon rejected the site at the end of Northumberland Avenue because the Needle would be overwhelmed by inappropriate buildings and structures such as the railway bridge. Proximity to buildings was acceptable but they had to be the right sort of buildings with appropriate associations. Lord Harrowby felt that Parliament Square would be such a location and talked of the 'moral fitness' of a site that brought the obelisk into association with 'all that we are proudest of in our national history … The place would lend honour to the obelisk, the obelisk would lend honour to the place.'[54]

However, three days after Harrowby's letter in *The Times*, a response appeared from a colleague in the Upper House, identifying himself only as 'A Peer in Reply', who felt that, 'The Needle has no connexion whatever with British history, and therefore cannot, without a total disregard of moral fitness of site, make its appearance at Westminster.'[55] (Because of its role as the home of the national archaeological collection, the anonymous writer preferred the British Museum, which Harrowby had dismissed as being 'in a little-frequented quarter of the town'.) Such views were nothing new; in 1851, when there had been a flurry of proposals for the transport of the Needle, an anonymous writer in *The Builder* magazine (identified only as 'R', possibly the architectural critic John Ruskin) had been opposed to the whole idea, remarking of the Paris obelisk, 'It is no embellishment to the modern city, the representative of Celtic taste; its very form and meaning incomprehensible to the Celtic and European mind.'[56]

The writer proposed sending it back to Egypt, or at least re-erecting it on the shore of the Mediterranean. Considering the proposals then current to erect Cleopatra's Needle in London, he wondered where it would be set up, and went on to ask

> ...or will you turn it to account, as is your nature, and set it *somewhere* where it may be *useful?* – place a gaslamp on its summit, erase some of the hieroglyphics to make room for the letters V and A, and the name of the then Lord Mayor? From what you have already done none of these steps would surprise me or any other person who had lived some time in London.[57]

'R' then went on to suggest that it should be left in Egypt or set up at Southsea, near Portsmouth, as a memorial to Nelson.

Such extreme views aside, the style of surrounding buildings was also a factor to be considered. In a leader on 1 February 1878, *The Times* noted that:

> The Obelisk once out of Egypt, some violence to architectural congruity is inevitable; for the architecture of that country has never travelled, except for some such imitation as our Egyptian Hall in Piccadilly, built to receive BELZONI'S Exhibition. But if we take the rule of doing what others have done before us, and of avoiding an entirely new combination, we can only put the Obelisk among buildings of the Roman Empire or of the Italian style. The Obelisk has not yet fraternized [sic] with either Doric or Gothic.[58]

Yet another factor, and an important one, was the obelisk's biblical associations. Its original site, and that of its companion, had been outside the temple of Ra at Heliopolis (Fig 92), and this led Erasmus Wilson to describe it as being 'erected, as one of a pair, in front of the seat of learning wherein Moses received his education'.[59]

Others went even further. Two days after the Needle had finally been erected, William Macdonald Sinclair, resident chaplain to the Bishop of London, preached a sermon, later 'published by request' in which he described the obelisk as 'rich above all from association with the Saviour of the World ... Jesus of Nazareth, the babe who was carried past that time-honoured monolith'.[60]

Despite this, and despite the high regard felt for the achievements of Ancient Egyptian civilisation, in biblical terms Egyptian pharaohs were a byword for tyranny and oppression. *The Times* leader quoted above went on to note that:

> In this country the Obelisk has a formidable rival in its built-up imitator, the Church spire, which may be called the Christian obelisk ... The two things are characteristic of different social systems and political conditions. For its moving and raising, the Obelisk ... required immense numbers of slaves, captives, or persons in a thoroughly subject state. The spire, on the contrary, like the cathedral, represents an immense co-operation of voluntary agents ... under the influence of some kind of spiritual motives.[61]

The Battle of the Sites may ultimately have had little effect on the final site chosen for the Needle, but it reveals much about what this symbol of Egypt meant to the British.

Once Parliament Square had been ruled out as a site, attention shifted to the Thames, or

Victoria Embankment. John Dixon noted in a letter to *The Times* that:

> The Metropolitan Board of Works have repeatedly expressed their readiness to grant a site, but it is not an easy matter to select one, with due regard to future buildings and avoidance of the railway … With the cordial approval of Professor Erasmus Wilson, I have therefore applied to the Metropolitan Board of Works for permission to erect our obelisk on the top of the Adelphi Steps between Charing-cross and Waterloo-bridges.[62]

A full-sized painted wooden model of the obelisk, which had been set up in Parliament Square, was dismantled and re-erected on the Adelphi Steps site. This was one of a number of such steps for passengers to board and disembark from river steamers, which since the arrival of the railways had been less and less used. On 4 February, towed by two tugs of Page and East, the *Cleopatra* left the East India Docks and headed up river, cheered by crowds on the banks and bridges, to a berth on the south side of the river opposite the Houses of Parliament, where thousands came to see the obelisk. On 15 February, the Board of Works, having seen a smaller model submitted to them by John Dixon, and the full-size one on the Adelphi Steps site, unanimously agreed to grant the site without charge as the permanent home of the obelisk. Within a fortnight, the large model had been demolished and work began on the site. Because of the construction of the Victoria Embankment, the steps were built on a foundation of concrete 1,500sq yd in area and 12ft thick, set on a bed of London clay. The four large arches under the steps had been used to flush the steps, filling up at high tide and flowing out on the ebb tide, but were now filled with concrete.

On 30 May, the *Cleopatra* made the short voyage from her moorings near St Thomas's Hospital to her last berth at the Adelphi Steps, towed by two tugs, the *Era* and the *Trojan*. She was turned round so that her stern, with the top of the obelisk, was facing downriver. A timber cradle 65ft long had been fixed to the riverbed, and after waiting a day for a higher tide, the *Cleopatra* was floated over the cradle and when the tide ebbed was left resting in the cradle 7ft above the riverbed. At this point Captain Carter relinquished his command and passed the vessel over to the contractor,

Fig 92
Not everyone was awed by the monuments of Ancient Egypt, or their biblical associations, as this 1878 watercolour by William Simpson shows. Tourists gallop their donkeys past the obelisk of Sesostris I at Heliopolis, while a frantic donkey boy tries to prevent them.
[Photo © Victoria and Albert Museum, London]

George Double. From then on the *Cleopatra*, without further function, became so much scrap iron. The cabin and other superstructure were removed and the hull rotated a quarter turn so that eventually the best-preserved side of the obelisk would face the road. Then the top half of the hull plates were stripped off and by June the bulkheads had been cut away to expose the Needle.

A hoarding, guarded by policemen, was set up around the site and over the summer the pavement on both sides of the Adelphi Steps was lined with curious spectators watching the demolition of the obelisk barge, the construction of the granite pedestal and the slow progress of the obelisk itself from the river. On 11 June a visitors' book was opened and as *The Times* noted, 'Very few visitors were admitted, and these by card only within the hoarding.' Naturally, these included Erasmus Wilson and the Egyptologist Samuel Birch, as well as the Prince and Princess of Wales (the latter a former patient of Wilson's), and the Prime Minister, Benjamin Disraeli, Earl of Beaconsfield, who according to General Alexander, 'spent some time with Mr Dixon, seeking to understand the nature of the operations'. Waynman Dixon did not sign the book until 19 August, the same day that Marion Bonomi, Joseph Bonomi's widow, also visited, and on 13 September Hussey Crespigny Vivian, the British Consul General in Egypt, came to see the Needle which he had helped bring to Britain. It was not just Londoners who wanted to see the new arrival though. The visitors' book has names from across the United Kingdom (including the gloriously named Mark Napoleon Elliott from Manchester), and from around the world. There were visitors from Alexandria in Egypt, Melbourne and Sydney in Australia, Barbados, Berlin, Nova Scotia and Toronto in Canada, Cape Town, Denmark, Madras, Lisbon, Sweden, and in the United States

from Chicago, Grand Rapids, Indiana, La Porte, Michigan, New Orleans, New York City, Philadelphia and San Francisco.[63]

Getting the 180-ton monolith into the water in Alexandria had posed problems enough, but now it had to be manoeuvred up a set of steps. The timber cradle in which the barge had been placed ran parallel to the Embankment, facing the western steps, and the obelisk had to be moved up and along until it was opposite its plinth, which meant raising it up nearly 30ft and along nearly 100. To achieve this, the Needle, whose pointed end faced the steps, was first protected by a wooden casing and then jacked up with four pairs of hydraulic jacks. As it was raised, timber packing was placed underneath and four screw traversers dragged it up the steps. At intervals the obelisk was lowered onto an extra layer of timber packing and the jacks and traversers repositioned. This was slow work, especially at the beginning, as work could only be carried out at low tide when the cradle was exposed, and it took over two weeks to move the Needle 6ft up and 25ft along.

Once the Needle was up the steps and on the platform, 3in were trimmed off its base to square it off and a wrought-iron jacket, designed by Benjamin Baker and manufactured like the *Cleopatra* at the Thames Iron Works, was fitted to the monolith (Fig 93). The 20ft-long jacket, made in four pieces, had trunnions (projections or pivots) around which the obelisk could be rotated once it had been raised, and a wrought-iron strap or stirrup around the base to prevent it slipping out of the jacket. Then a huge timber framework, over 50ft high, was constructed around the granite base on which the pedestal would eventually stand (Fig 94). Two iron box beams were placed, one either side of the Needle, and the trunnions rested on these. Then hydraulic jacks lifted the beams, which

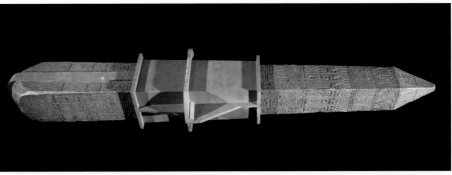

Fig 93
Made for John Dixon as part of a working scale model to demonstrate the process of erecting Cleopatra's Needle, this wooden obelisk clearly shows the wrought-iron box girder jacket and the strap passing around the base of the obelisk. The model is currently in the Large Objects Store of the Science Museum at Wroughton, near Swindon in Wiltshire. [DP114484]

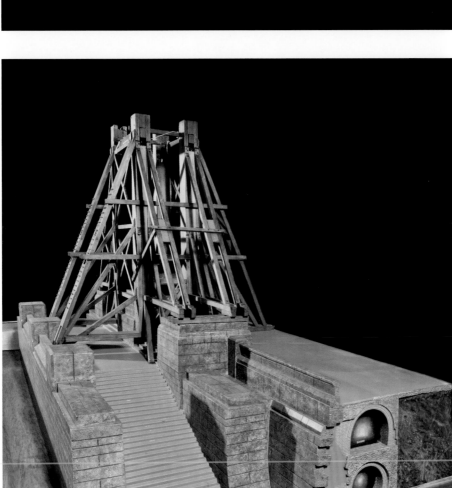

Fig 94
This view of Dixon's model shows the timber scaffolding used to raise and pivot the obelisk, as well as the construction of the Victoria Embankment, with an upper subway and an intercepting sewer beneath it. [DP114487]

ran in grooves in the timber scaffolding, 4in at a time. Timber packing was inserted and the Needle lowered back onto it, the jacks were raised and the process repeated.

By 7 September, the obelisk had been raised high enough and steel cables and

winches were set up to control the Needle while it swung into position (Fig 95). On 11 September, latches holding the obelisk horizontal were released and so finely was it balanced that John Dixon was able to move it a few inches by himself. On the following day, despite heavy early rain, thousands of

Fig 95
The Needle, ready to be swung into an upright position, showing its base, which had been trimmed and levelled.
[BB71/01648]

spectators watched from pavements and Waterloo Bridge while Sir James Alexander and other distinguished guests were on the steamer *Duke of Connaught*, which had been chartered by Wilson and Dixon. Inside the enclosure around the Needle were John Dixon, Benjamin Baker, George Double, Erasmus Wilson, Henry Palfrey Stephenson (who had advised Wilson on funding the transport of the Needle), Captain Henry Carter and Sir Joseph Bazalgette, responsible for the construction of the Victoria Embankment and Chief Engineer to the Metropolitan Board of Works.

Of the key players, only Waynman Dixon, out of the country on business, was not present. The Prince of Wales had been expected to attend but could not now do so for some time, and so shortly before three in the afternoon the latches securing the monolith were released, the winches started and the Needle began to turn. Within half an hour it was, to quote *The Times*, 'to any save a mathematical eye' upright. Engineers, however, deal with mathematics and there was a discussion between Dixon and others over whether the obelisk was truly perpendicular. To be sure, Dixon decided to leave lowering it the final 4in onto its pedestal until the following morning, and the cables were left in place and wooden wedges inserted under the Needle. Four inches was close enough for the good-natured crowd, and as the Union Jack and Turkish flags[64] were run up a flagpole fixed to the summit of the obelisk, three hearty cheers rang out.

If Captain Carter had been unconcerned about sailing from Alexandria on a Friday, John Dixon was even less superstitious, choosing Friday 13 September to complete the installation of the Needle. Without event the obelisk, which had been confirmed as vertical, was lowered onto the pedestal and settled into place with a final push from the

hydraulic jacks. Within a few days the jacket and straps had been removed and by early October the Needle stood in full view of London for the first time.

Pedestal, plumage and protection

In Ancient Egypt, the pyramidion or peak of an obelisk had often been gilded, and it was natural that a culture which loved decoration as much as the Victorians would be unable to resist embellishing Cleopatra's Needle. Its transport and erection were more than just an impressive feat of engineering – they could be seen as symbolic of British achievement in general. Even if the government had seemed less than enthusiastic about the whole affair and certainly unwilling to fund it, once the Needle was in place the Establishment could congratulate itself. On the first Sunday after it had been installed, William Macdonald Sinclair, in the sermon referred to earlier, spoke of it being set up

> …in the heart of the greatest city of the greatest empire of these days … at the zenith of the reign of Her who for more than forty years has been – noble contrast to Cleopatra! – the type of every virtue, constitutional, domestic, and personal, the beloved and revered Palladium and prototype of the purity of British homes; in a reign which has been one long and most glorious progress of solid improvement and rational reform… .[65]

His lavish encomium, rivalling those bestowed on the pharaohs, was given added significance by being preached in the Queen's Chapel of the Savoy. (The actual Chaplain of the Queen's Chapel was Revd William Loftie, an amateur Egyptologist and collector, who encouraged the writer Rider Haggard's interest in Egypt.) The chapel, situated not far from the Needle on Savoy

Hill, is unusual in that it is a 'free' chapel belonging to the monarch by right as Duke of Lancaster, and so particularly associated with Queen Victoria.

Before the obelisk had even been set up, a foundation deposit had been placed in two earthenware jars under the pedestal. (As *The Times* admitted 'drain pipes, in fact'.[66]) This Victorian time capsule contained a selection of objects which seem to have been intended to convey a picture of Victorian life to future generations in the same way that Ancient Egyptian tombs had done to the Victorians. The proprietors of *Engineering* donated copies of the magazine printed on vellum with details and plans relating to the transport and erection of the obelisk and its history, a parchment copy of Samuel Birch's translation of the hieroglyphs on the obelisk accompanied them, and there were specimens of wire ropes and cables from R S Newall, the company who had donated the towing cable for the *Cleopatra* as well as one of the hydraulic jacks of Messrs Tangye which had been crucial to the operation.

There were standard weights and measures presented by the Board of Trade, a standard gauge to 1,000th of an inch as a sample of accurate workmanship, a 2ft rule and a complete set of British coinage including an Empress of India rupee to commemorate the queen taking this title the year before. A portrait of the queen was no surprise, nor were a selection of bibles in various languages presented by the British and Foreign Bible Society, a translation of St John's gospel, chapter III verse 16 in 215 languages, the Pentateuch in Hebrew and the Book of Genesis in Arabic. There were also a map of London, copies of the main daily and illustrated papers, a London directory, the final edition for that year of *Whitaker's Almanack,* and that quintessentially Victorian publication,

Bradshaw's railway guide. Samples of Doulton ware represented the products of manufacturing, as did Mappin's shilling razor, a case of cigars, pipes, a box of hairpins and in the words of *The Times* 'sundry articles of female adornment'. An Alexandra feeding bottle and children's toys were presented by 'a lady'. Perhaps mindful of the fact that the Needle had now been moved twice and that it might not be in its final resting place, there was a one-half inch to the foot scale model of the obelisk in bronze, and a piece of its stone. Finally, keeping up the traditions of mariners throughout the ages, Captain Carter donated photographs of a dozen pretty Englishwomen.

The Egyptians had erected their needles without any form of support and the rounded corners had helped to pivot the obelisk on its base into an upright position. The Romans had preferred to add bronze 'crabs' for support on the corners. Dixon had mounted the obelisk directly onto its support after first having masons trim three inches off its base where the Romans had cut into it to install their crabs. Predictably enough, there was correspondence in *The Times*, started by an architect, John Holden, over whether the Needle would be able to withstand storms or be toppled by the wind. The matter was closed by John Dixon who estimated that it could withstand a force of 130 pounds per square foot while much less than this would level modern buildings. He did concede that the rounded corners of the obelisk gave it the appearance of being unstable, but described it as 'a half-finished design – a bird without its feathers…'.[67]

Dixon, on the basis of his fixed price, 'no cure no fee' contract with Wilson had to absorb not only the additional expense of the salvage and refitting of the *Cleopatra* when an initial decision in his favour and against his insurers was overturned in the Court of Appeal, but also his own legal costs and those of his opponents, and then the costs of erecting the obelisk on the Embankment. Although superintended by the Board of Works, the preparatory work on the site was funded by Dixon, as was the cost of the plinth. The final cost was probably at least £15,000 and may have come close to £20,000 of which Wilson, who got ample credit and eventually a knighthood, had only met the first £10,000.[68] Dixon felt that he had done more than his share and had been careful to stipulate in his agreement with the Board that they should be responsible for the remaining works. Now it was for 'the custodians who have accepted its charge (the Metropolitan Board of Works) to add to the framework the embellishments necessary to make it one of the finest monuments in London'.[69]

He outlined what they should be. The pre-existing plinths of the Adelphi Steps would be filled by sphinxes 'cast, I hope from real originals, not modern imitations'.[70] In this he had been supported by Joseph Bonomi. The visitors' book has an entry by G Farrell, describing himself as 'an intimate friend of the late Mr Bonomi' who had seen Bonomi a week before he died:

> Mr Bonomi was very anxious that the obelisk, if flanked with sphinxes, that these should be of the same date as the obelisk itself. Mr Bonomi said that there were only two he knew of that date, one in the Duke of Northumberland's collection at Alnwick – and the other he believed in the national collection at Paris … [and that] one of these should be used as a model.[71]

Dixon went on to recommend

> …bronze inscription plates on the pedestal itself, which should be crowned by a bronze fringe, each corner terminating in an appropriate bronze

ornament that would obscure the unsightly base of the monolith itself … If the Board will only give free scope to the artistic genius of their architect, Mr Vulliamy, and their engineer, Sir Joseph Bazalgette, I pledge my word the severest critic will have little to complain of… .[72]

It was indeed Vulliamy who designed the sphinxes, as Bonomi had suggested, from a small black diorite sphinx from the 18th Dynasty (about 1400 BC), about 11in long, in the collection of Lord Prudhoe, the 4th Duke of Northumberland. The duke's collection was catalogued by Samuel Birch and illustrated by Joseph Bonomi, and the sphinx was believed to be from the reign of Thutmose III who had originally commissioned the obelisk. It actually dated from the reign of his grandson, Thutmose IV, but the sphinxes on the Embankment have the cartouche of Thutmose III on their breasts (Fig 96). A full-sized plaster model coloured to resemble bronze was set up on one of the plinths to test the effect, and when this was successful the actual bronze sphinxes, modelled by Charles Mabey, were cast at the Eccleston Iron Works, Pimlico, at the foundry of H L Young & Co. In contrast to the original on which they were modelled, they were 19ft long, 6ft wide, 9ft high and weighed about 7 tons.

The sphinxes were originally intended to face outward from the obelisk, which would have been consistent with Ancient Egyptian imagery where the *akhet* hieroglyph, representing the sun rising or setting on the horizon, could be flanked by protective lions. The obelisk was a solar symbol and sphinxes, although solar symbols and representations of royal power in their own right, could be identified with the protective crouching lions. At a late stage, however, officials of the Metropolitan Board of Works made the decision that the sphinxes should face toward the obelisk as if they

Fig 96
The inscription on the sphinxes giving the throne name of Thutmose III is read as 'The good/beautiful god, Men-Kheper-Ra, given life.' The cartouche of Thutmose IV only differs in having three plural strokes below the scarab, meaning that his throne name is read as 'Men-Kheperu-Ra'. [AA79/01985]

Fig 97
The current orientation of the sphinxes, allegedly changed from the original on aesthetic grounds, was only one area of conflict between those who had brought the Needle to London and the Metropolitan Board of Works. [CC73/03083]

were studying its inscriptions. As *The Times* noted, this was 'contrary to the intention of the designer' and 'a position which they are never supposed to occupy' (Fig 97). The only explanation given was that with the heads of the sphinxes towards the monument, a line from the top of the obelisk to the tail of each sphinx would form an equilateral triangle.[73] The bronze decoration at the base of the needle combined torus mouldings, winged solar discs, the cartouche of Thutmose III flanked by protective *uraei*, or cobras and corner plates in the form of wings, which are protective aspects of a number of Ancient Egyptian deities, often goddesses (see Fig 100). Despite its sturdy appearance, this bronze is purely ornamental. Apart from the orientation of the sphinxes, these elements of the decoration proceeded without incident. The same, however, could not be said of the inscriptions.

Despite the fact that Dixon was paying for the plinth, the Metropolitan Board of Works decided at a meeting in September 1878 that no inscription of any kind was to be placed on the pedestal or its supports without their prior approval. When it was found that the date '1878' had been carved on the third course of the pedestal, it had to be planed out of the stone. Then, when it was found that some of the stones had been set back to create sunken panels for the eventual inscriptions, the course had to be torn down and rebuilt so that the stones were flush.[74] Even worse was to follow. Dixon, with the assistance of the Very Reverend Dean Stanley, Dean of Westminster, and Samuel Birch, had drafted the texts of the inscriptions. That intended for the north side acknowledged the roles in the transport and erection of the Needle of not only Dixon himself and Wilson, but also of the Khedive Ismail, General Alexander,

Consul General Vivian, Giovanni Demetrio, Charles Swinburne and Henry Stephenson, whose advice to Wilson had played a crucial part in securing his agreement to Dixon's plan, the engineers John Fowler and Benjamin Baker, Waynman Dixon, Samuel Birch, and even George Double as Manager of Works. However, despite the fact that it had been approved by Queen Victoria herself, the text was drastically reduced by the Board, so that only Wilson and Dixon were credited (Fig 98). Dixon was out of the country but a memo of protest was sent to the board by other concerned parties, objecting in particular to the removal of Alexander's name. It was to no avail. On his return to England, John Dixon wrote to the Board, asking them to use the original text, but was informed by its clerk that the Board 'having already decided on the inscription to be placed on the pedestal, cannot now reopen the question'.[75]

Fig 98
The final text of the plaque on the north side of the obelisk pedestal, which only credits Erasmus Wilson and John Dixon for their part in its transport. [DP026501]

So strongly did Dixon feel about what he described as a 'debt of honour' to those concerned, that he took the step of releasing his correspondence with the Board to *The Times*.[76] He must have realised that there was little chance of the Board changing its mind, but wanted to make clear, in a very public manner, that the decision on the text of the inscription was theirs entirely.

The Board was an appointed body, widely felt to be not only lacking in accountability, but also tainted by corruption, and became popularly referred to as the 'Metropolitan Board of Perks'. The real reason for its initial decision to drastically edit the original text, and its obdurate refusal to change its mind, may have been connected with the curious lack of official ceremony at the final stages of the Needle's erection. *The Times* had revealed that Queen Victoria 'was hoped' to attend but that 'to the great regret of Her Majesty' this was 'found to be impossible'.[77] Significantly, H C Vivian did not attend either although he was in London 'on leave'. He 'expressed his regret at having been unable to be present to witness the operation on Thursday',[78] but was able to visit the site in a private capacity the following day, as confirmed by his signature in the visitors' book. The real reason for the absence of both, and the lack of official ceremony, was almost certainly the tense political situation in Egypt.

At this time the country was still technically part of the Ottoman Empire and its ruler had the title of khedive or viceroy. This had been claimed by Muhammad Ali but not recognised by the Turkish sultan until 1867. The Khedive Ismail had been deposed by the Turkish sultan on 26 June 1878 following pressure from European powers including Britain, and within five years British forces would be landing in Alexandria. For the queen and her Consul General, in London for consultation under the flimsy pretext

of taking leave, to have attended official celebrations at such a time would have risked embarrassment and might have prejudiced ongoing negotiations. It would also have been unacceptable for the monument to have publicly commemorated Ismail, who was portrayed in the press as a profligate ruler who had bankrupted his country and was trying to avoid repaying his foreign creditors.[79]

In the end, four plaques were placed on the sides of the Needle's plinth, but not until 1882. That on the east side summarises the history of the obelisk up until its re-erection in Alexandria (Fig 99). On the opposite, west side, another plaque records the gift of the obelisk by Muhammad Ali and its role as a memorial of Nelson and Abercromby. The plaque on the north side records the roles of Erasmus Wilson and John Dixon in its transport and erection, and its near loss in the storm in the Bay of Biscay, while the plaque on the south side records the six sailors who died trying to reach the obelisk barge in the storm. The inscription on the north side was the Board's version but only minor changes were made to the others. In 1928 another tablet summarising the inscriptions on the obelisk was added by the London County Council.

If the debate over the Needle's stability had been unnecessary, there still remained one area of real concern. Before the Needle was brought to England, questions had been raised about its state of preservation and whether it was even worth bringing back. Once it was clear that it was concern began to be expressed over how it would be affected by the English weather, and particularly by the atmosphere of London. As many older buildings still testify, it was a city heated by coal and lit by coal gas, and the capital was noted for its dense fog, the 'London Particular'. This was more properly smog, often formed in the winter when

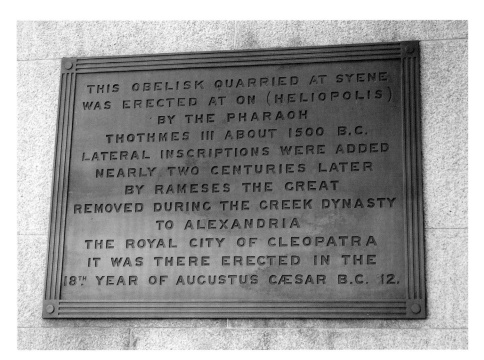

THIS OBELISK QUARRIED AT SYENE
WAS ERECTED AT ON (HELIOPOLIS)
BY THE PHARAOH
THOTHMES III ABOUT 1500 B.C.
LATERAL INSCRIPTIONS WERE ADDED
NEARLY TWO CENTURIES LATER
BY RAMESES THE GREAT
REMOVED DURING THE GREEK DYNASTY
TO ALEXANDRIA
THE ROYAL CITY OF CLEOPATRA
IT WAS THERE ERECTED IN THE
18TH YEAR OF AUGUSTUS CÆSAR B.C. 12.

Fig 99
The short but informative summary of the Needle's history on the east side of its pedestal was probably drafted by the Egyptologist Samuel Birch. [DP026498]

smoke from fires was trapped by cold air above it, and the pollution became so bad that in 1952 an estimated 4,000 people died prematurely as a result of one especially bad episode. Whilst the *Cleopatra* was still moored at the East India Docks, *The Times*, in one of its leaders, noted that:

> At every site suggested, the Obelisk would be covered with a thick coating of coal smut in ten years, and the hieroglyphics would have to be picked out – dug out, one may say – with sufficiently hard instruments in the hands of common workmen. That destructive process, accompanied with washing – perhaps a still more destructive process – has had to be repeated several times even on the sculptures of the Albert Memorial. The Obelisk would soon be as dark and unmeaning as a chimney-stalk [sic], unless the granite were polished and the inscriptions filled in with some material of different colour. This the critics would never hear of, but without it we

would soon incur the reproaches and forebodings of the Roman poet for allowing our idols to be grimed with smoke.[80]

Thankfully, none of the more drastic solutions mentioned by the leader writer seem to ever have been seriously considered, although several plaster casts, none of which seem to have survived, were taken to preserve the state of the inscriptions on their arrival in London. In the House of Lords, the Duke of Somerset asked the Lord President of the Council if 'the opinion of scientific men' would be taken 'As to the best mode of preserving the inscriptions from the destructive effects of the London atmosphere, either by glazing the monolith, as similar monuments have been glazed in the British Museum, or by other mechanical means.'[81]

In reply, the Lord President said that he would take immediate steps to enquire into the matter as there could be no doubt that the preservation of the inscriptions was a question of great interest, and that steps should be taken to prevent their 'obliteration'. Thankfully these did not include the recommendation of one correspondent who wrote to *The Times* in response to the duke's question suggesting that the inscriptions 'be filled up with lead',[82] which he felt would not only preserve them but make them more legible (Fig 100). The Metropolitan Board of Works took the advice of their Chief Engineer, Sir Joseph Bazalgette, and a consulting chemist, and after initial cleaning (probably by *The Times*'s 'common workmen') the obelisk was sealed

with two coats of Browning's Invisible Preservative[83] applied under the supervision of its inventor, Mr Henry Browning, in May 1879, and a retreatment was carried out in 1895. By 1911 it was again cleaned and treated with wax and in 1932 it was washed by the hoses of the London Fire Brigade. In 1949, 'a party of visiting Egyptian VIPs'[84] complained that it was being neglected and the London County Council spent £500 on a month-long cleaning. The obelisk was sprayed to remove dirt, cleaned with a detergent solution and then waxed. Although 1956 saw the first Clean Air Act, the waxing was felt to have been

Fig 100
The outer columns of inscriptions on the Needle, added by Ramesses II, are typical of that monarch, being carved unusually deeply so that they could not be erased and the monument again usurped by a later ruler. This may have inspired suggestions that they should be filled in to preserve the inscriptions from the polluted atmosphere of Victorian London.
[AA98/05960]

unsuccessful and the Needle was cleaned again in 1966, this time with low-pressure compressed air and abrasive grit, and finally it was cleaned with detergent and a proprietary stone cleaner. However, despite all this concern a recent study of assessments of the Needle's condition since it was brought to London and actions taken to clean and conserve it concluded that any erosion that had taken place was largely the result of fire damage in ancient times, probably around 525 BC during the Persian conquest of Egypt, and that the obelisk was not in imminent danger of major deterioration.[85]

The condition of the Needle is still closely monitored and in 2010 repairs were carried out to the fixings of one of the bronze wing castings (Fig 101), but the closest the Needle itself has so far come to real damage was during the First and Second World Wars. On 4 September 1917, in an air raid on London by German forces, a bomb exploded nearby on the pavement of the Embankment. Shrapnel broke a large chunk of stone off the steps of the obelisk and damaged one of the bronze sphinxes, leaving scars that can still be seen. In early 1941 there was some further damage from a flying bomb.

Sir Joseph Bazalgette was also responsible for the design of the benches on the Embankment with sphinx supports (although these are Greek female sphinxes, rather than the male Egyptian ones). The sphinx benches are in the London Borough of Westminster and those further east with camel supports, whose design is attributed to C H Mabey, are in the City of London (apart from one near Westminster Bridge). The original benches were made by Z D Berry and Sons at the Albion Works, Westminster, but the current ones are reproductions made in 1977 by the SLB Foundry in Sittingbourne, Kent.

Fig 101
In 2006 investigations began into the fixings of the bronze wing castings on the base of the obelisk after one at the south-west corner had become detached due to 'the presence of vegetation and the deterioration of the mortar joints over time'. However, the repairs were not made until 2010.
[DP026497]

Star of fiction, film, poetry, music, motor cars … and marmalade

Even before the arrival of the obelisk in London, Cleopatra's Needle had begun to make an impression on the popular imagination. In 1877, the annual parade to celebrate the installation of the new Lord Mayor of London featured a float preceded by two dromedaries from Sanger's Circus with riders in Egyptian costume, followed by two elephants (presumably from the same circus) and drawn by six horses. On the float, or 'ornamental car' was a model of Cleopatra's Needle, surrounded by representations of the sphinx and pyramids, and by costumed representations of Egypt. Sadly, the barrier on the route of the procession formed by the arch of Temple Bar meant that the model obelisk had to be horizontal and *The Times*, perhaps disappointed that it was not full-sized, described it as 'insignificant'.[86]

Once on its plinth on the Victoria Embankment, however, it was not long before the real monument began to inspire authors and poets. Indeed, its first literary appearance was in 1878 in Arthur Sketchley's humorous title *Mrs Brown on Cleopatra's Needle*. Sketchley was the *nom de plume* of the author and playwright George Rose (1817–82), who from 1866 published a series of popular comic works on topical issues of the day. They are delivered by the eponymous Mrs Brown and other stereotypical working-class Cockneys, in an equally stereotypical accent which makes Dick van Dyke's performance in *Mary Poppins* sound convincing:

> 'Well,' says Brown, 'If you want for to see it afloat, you'd better go afore as they lands it.'
> I says 'I shall go to-morrer arternoon, purvided always as there ain't no thick fog, as you can't see thro'.

> 'Well,' says Brown, 'They'll soon be a-settin' of it up.'
> I says 'I 'opes not like a gravin imidge, cos if they do, they'll 'ave the Bishop of London down on 'em, as won't 'ave no such goin's on.'
> Says Brown, 'It certingly 'as gravin imidges all over it.'[87]

In complete contrast, John W Bone FSA was inspired to verse in the same year, and wrote *Cleopatra's Needle by Moonlight*, a sombre meditation on mortality and religion, which was privately published. The Poet Laureate, Alfred Tennyson, had been asked to compose a poem expressive of the obelisk's history to be inscribed on its base, but this was not used, allegedly because Erasmus Wilson objected to a line which referred to 'your own citizens' bringing it from Egypt 'for their own renown'. Less controversial was a poem by Mathilde Blind, the political radical, feminist and early biographer of George Eliot, *To the Obelisk During the Great Frost, 1881*:

> Thou sign-post of the Desert! Obelisk,
> Once fronting in thy monumental pride
> Egypt's fierce sun…
>
> Now reared beside our Thames so wintry grey,
> Where blocks of ice drift with the drifting stream,
> Thou risest o'er the alien prospect! Say,
> Yon dull, blear, rayless orb whose lurid gleam
> Tinges the snow-draped ships and writhing steam,
> Is this the sun which fired thine orient day?[88]

Nor were musicians to be left out. Albert Hartmann composed *Cleopatra's Needle Waltz* in 1877, and expanded it with orchestral parts in 1879, while in 1878 Charles Williams (not the later composer of light music of the same name) wrote, composed, and sang 'with immense success' the comic song *Cleopatra's Needle*:

> I dearly loved a little girl who did not
> seem to care
> For anything unless 'twas novel exquisite
> and rare
> And Cleopatra's Needle seem'd in
> everybody's mind
> So I thought I'd see if this would bring
> my charmer to be kind.[89]

After this initial surge of interest, the obelisk had to wait until 1922 when the composer, conductor and violinist Percy Elliott featured *Cleopatra's Needle* as one of the four 'Thames Silhouettes' in his piano piece, *The Silent Highway*.

A year later, in 1923, the Needle featured more dramatically in an episode of the two-reeler serial *The Mystery of Dr Fu Manchu*. This was based on one of the stories by Sax Rohmer in which the eponymous doctor watches from Cleopatra's Needle as one of his minions unsuccessfully attempts to carry out an assassination from the roof of a nearby hotel (possibly the fictional New Louvre Hotel in the Strand featured in Rohmer's *The Si-Fan Mysteries*) by enticing the victim to lean out of his window and then dropping a noose around his neck.

Five years later, the obelisk had a major cameo role in *The Crimes of Cleopatra's Needle*, a 1928 detective story by the prolific author J M Walsh, who also wrote as H Haverstock Hill, Stephen Maddock, George M White and Jack Carew. Walsh, an Australian who settled in London, wrote at least 56 titles between 1928 and 1952, mainly spy fiction. This one begins with the heroine, Barbara West, witnessing a fatal stabbing by Cleopatra's Needle and the complicated plot involves an attempt to gain control of oil concessions in a small Middle Eastern state, several other murders and the Society of Cleopatra's Needle, a criminal organisation that sends its victims small visiting card-sized photos of the obelisk as a warning of impending doom, rather like the pirates' Black Spot in *Treasure Island*.

The Needle was becoming as much an icon of London as it was of Ancient Egypt. It had featured in *Cleopatra's Needle and Charing Cross Bridge*, one of a series of 37 views of London painted between 1899 and 1904 by Claude Monet, who stayed at the Savoy Hotel on the Strand and painted from the balcony of his room. However, Monet finished many of the paintings in his French studio and became more interested in atmosphere than topographical realism, eliminating the obelisk from one view of Charing Cross Bridge.

In Stanley Donen's 1958 film *Indiscreet*, Cary Grant and Ingrid Bergman are disturbed by autograph hunters at the foot of Cleopatra's Needle, and it makes another appearance in the 1963 musical from Michael Carreras *What a Crazy World*, starring Joe Brown and Marty Wilde, with an appearance from Freddy and the Dreamers. In a more sombre mood, it appears fleetingly in the 2001 Jack the Ripper film *From Hell*, starring Johnny Depp, despite the fact that the Ripper murders happened in Whitechapel, several miles away.

It continues to be associated with the uncanny and macabre. In *The Deeds of the Disturber* (2001), one of the popular series of Amelia Peabody Egyptological mysteries, the body of Jonas Oldacre, an Assistant Keeper in the Department of Egyptian and Assyrian Antiquities at the British Museum, is discovered at the foot of the obelisk with his throat cut and a scrap of paper clutched in his hand, and later Peabody herself is lured to a meeting at the Needle and narrowly escapes death. Even more recently, the Needle's guardian sphinxes feature in the children's fantasy *Stoneheart* (2006) by Charlie Fletcher, where London's statues come to life.

In real life the sphinxes were the inspiration for one version of the bonnet mascot on Armstrong Siddeley cars, one of which was owned by the 5th Earl of Carnarvon, who financed Howard Carter's search for the tomb of Tutankhamun. The sphinx was introduced as the Armstrong Siddeley trademark in 1910 after one journalist allegedly described the performance of a test car as being as silent and inscrutable as the sphinx. The first design was crouched, like the Greek sphinxes on Vulliamy's benches, but wingless, male and with an Egyptian *nemes* headcloth. In 1932 this was changed and the founder of the company, J D Siddeley, sent an artist to the Embankment to sketch the Needle's sphinxes as the basis for the new design. A less obvious connection than that between the sphinxes and Armstrong Siddleleys was made when the Needle was first set up, in 1878. In the Cuming Museum in Southwark

is a white china marmalade jar, made in Sunderland, in the shape of the obelisk, with hieroglyphic decorations.

No longer, in the words of *The Times*, a distinguished visitor, Cleopatra's Needle is now a resident, an Egyptian Londoner, although for a monument that spent well over a thousand years in each of its two previous sites, the 130 odd years it has spent here is barely enough time to get settled. In 1929, unidentified Egyptian Nationalist protesters pasted a placard on its base claiming that it was Egyptian property, but the notice was removed and nothing more was apparently heard of the matter. Whether or not this is the Needle's final resting place only time will tell. Musing on the obelisk that remained at Heliopolis, John Dixon referred to it as 'the only relic of a great bygone city'. He went on to suggest that 'when our obelisk has, like it, occupied its new position for 3,000 years, possibly it, too, may form the centre of a similar desolation'.[90]

We will not be here to know, but it, barring some catastrophe, should be.

Crystal Palace Park

Anerley Hill,
London
SE19 2BA

In 1854, a visitor arriving at Crystal Palace Station would have been able to walk through a 720ft-glazed colonnade into a magnificent structure dedicated, in the words of its official guidebook, to 'the advancement of civilisation and the welfare of her [Victoria's] subjects'.[91]

The original Crystal Palace was created for the Great Exhibition of the Works of Industry of all Nations, which was held in Hyde Park from 1 May to 15 October 1851. The first international exhibition of manufactured products, as its name suggested, it only included modern works

of art and industry. The building itself, designed by Joseph Paxton at an estimated cost of £80,000, two-thirds of that for a brick building, required 4,000 tons of iron, 400 tons of glass, 30 miles of guttering and 200 miles of wooden sash bars. After the close of the Great Exhibition a vigorous debate on the future of the building took place. A special commission was set up to report on possible options but eventually the government opted to leave it in the hands of Messrs Fox and Henderson, the builders and contractors who had erected it in the first place.

This was the age of the railway and the entrepreneurial partners of a firm of solicitors, Farquhar and Leech, spotting an opportunity, conditionally purchased the original Crystal Palace in May 1852 and then suggested a new 200-acre site at Penge Place on the Brighton Railway, to one of the railway's directors. It was not long before the Crystal Palace Company was set up, headed by Samuel Laing MP, Chairman of the Brighton Railway Company. Joseph Paxton became involved and £500,000 was raised by selling shares in the Crystal Palace Company. A new branch line was constructed from Sydenham Station to the Crystal Palace Gardens, and Fox and Henderson were contracted to re-erect the Crystal Palace. No time was wasted and work began on 5 August 1852.

This time the statistics were even more impressive. Over 9,641 tons of iron, 500 tons of glass, in excess of 175 tons of bolts and rivets, 103 tons of nails alone and more than 15,300cu yd of brickwork. As the official guide put it, 'nearly three-quarters of a mile of ground [had been] covered with a transparent roof of glass'. Laid end to end the glass would have stretched for 242 miles. The Hyde Park original was actually longer and wider but there was a greater area of galleries in the new building. Above a basement floor there were a grand central nave, two side aisles, two main galleries, three transepts and two wings (Fig 102), all with a sophisticated heating and ventilation system, and two 300ft water towers, one at each end of the building, to feed ponds and fountains. The floors were of boarding

Fig 102
A view from the nave of the Crystal Palace, with the North Transept on the left. The full-size models of the colossal statues of Ramesses II from Abu Simbel can be seen through the ironwork.
[FF91/00331]

1½in thick with ½in gaps between them so that dust could be swept into the void underneath. The masses of small change inevitably dropped through the gaps by thousands of visitors formed a useful bonus for the staff. On the parapet of the terrace outside were 26 allegorical statues of the most important commercial and manufacturing countries and cities in the world at that time – including Egypt.

From the start, the new Crystal Palace was intended to have an improving and uplifting function. A charter was granted by the government on 28 January 1853 binding the directors and their successors to, in the words of the official guide, 'preserve the high moral and social tone which, from the outset, they had assumed for their national institution'.[92]

Speaking of the workforce, up to 6,400 men at any one time, the official guide waxed lyrical about the effect on them of being involved in its construction:

> For the first time in England, hundreds of men received practical instruction – in a national fine arts school – from which society must derive a lasting benefit. It is not too much to hope that each man will act as a missionary of art and ornamental industry, in whatever quarter his improved faculties may hereafter be required.[93]

Owen Jones and Digby Wyatt[94] became directors of the Fine Art Department, and in charge of the decoration of the new structure. There were to be Fine Arts Courts with historical illustrations of the arts of sculpture and architecture from Egypt and Assyria to modern times, and other sections on geology, ethnology, sociology and botany in Courts of Art and Industry. Shortly after work started Jones and Wyatt left for Europe on a mission to collect examples

of the most important works of art there, including ones for the proposed Egyptian Court. They took casts of material in the Louvre, including a sphinx of Amenemhat II, and in Rome were to have also taken casts of one of the obelisks there – 'every arrangement had been made for procuring casts of the great Obelisk of the Lateran [in the Piazza San Giovanni in Laterano] … when an order from the Papal Government forbade the copies to be taken'.[95]

At the time of the Great Exhibition there had been moves to bring Cleopatra's Needle to London and to set it up in Hyde Park as a memorial to Prince Albert's work in promoting the Exhibition, but nothing came of these. In 1852, perhaps inspired by their failure to secure casts of the Lateran Obelisk, the directors of the Crystal Palace Company decided to transport the Needle, at an estimated cost of £7,000, and erect it in the great Central Transept. Samuel Laing wrote on 3 November to Lord Derby, who had become prime minister in February of that year, seeking the government's permission to do so. Lord Derby's reply, less than a week later, was clear; the government could not consent to part with the obelisk, which had been presented to the Crown by Muhammad Ali, but was willing to grant permission to the company to remove it at their own expense and erect it at the Crystal Palace. Two conditions were imposed; if at any time in the future the Crystal Palace ceased to be used for its original purpose, the government could repossess the obelisk without compensation, and if the removal of the obelisk became desirable 'for public objects', this could be done on payment of all expenses incurred by the company in transporting and erecting it.[96]

In the end there was to be no Needle at the Crystal Palace. In his book *Cleopatra's Needles*, Aubrey Noakes gave the impression that the directors of the Crystal Palace

Company were unwilling to bear the costs of transporting the Needle unless it became their property, and Labib Habachi, in *The Obelisks of Egypt*, describes the request as being 'refused' as it was considered that the obelisk should be brought to England as a national monument rather than the property of a private company. However, as well as publishing the letter from Lord Derby to Samuel Laing in which the government's qualified permission was given, *The Times* stated in 1852 that, 'The fate of this interesting monument has at length been decided', and noted that:

> Steps have already been taken to effect the removal of the column. It is understood that His Highness the Pasha will afford the directors every facility on his side of the Mediterranean, and that other interesting works of antiquity from Luxor and Karnak will accompany Cleopatra's Needle from the Egyptian shores.[97]

In March of the following year Mr Anderson, the managing director of the P&O shipping company, and also a director of the Crystal Palace Company, went to Egypt to make arrangements for the transport of the Needle to England. Even at the turn of the 19th century, however, when plans were first made to move the fallen Needle to England, it was already half buried (see Fig 83) and by 1852, with the rapid growth of Alexandria, it had vanished completely (Fig 103). As the *Illustrated London News* reported in 1853, the obelisk was partially built into the sea wall and ramparts which were part of the fortifications of Alexandria, and apart from the considerable cost of demolishing and then rebuilding these, the Khedive, Abbas I, had 'a very strong objection to a breach of such a nature being made or left open for any time, in the present state of European politics'.[98]

The timing was unfortunate. Muhammad Ali, who had originally given the obelisk to Britain

1770. Cleopatra's Needle.

Fig 103
By the time the photographic pioneer Francis Frith took this photo, around 1850, only the standing obelisk, also referred to as Cleopatra's Needle and now in New York, could be seen. The London obelisk was already buried, and would be further threatened by the expansion of Alexandria.
[Photo © Victoria and Albert Museum, London]

and who had always offered his cooperation in removing it, had become senile and was removed from power in 1848. His successor, Ibrahim, only ruled for four months before dying and was succeeded by his nephew Abbas, seen by many outside Egypt as a reactionary who reversed Ali's policy of Europeanisation. In July 1854, a month after the Crystal Palace opened, Abbas was strangled by two members of his bodyguard, but by that time the Crystal Palace Company had made alternative arrangements for the Egyptian Court.

Despite the vigorous urging of various parties over the years, governments had always resisted spending public money on transporting the obelisk and would probably have been quite relieved to have the problem solved for them (as it was eventually to be through the generosity of Erasmus Wilson), although for political reasons it would have been unacceptable to relinquish ownership of what had been a gift to the Crown from a foreign head of state. In practice, once the obelisk was on display in a prominent position in the capital, it was unlikely that they would want to incur the considerable expense of relocating it. (The cost of transport from the Thames was a major factor against many of the proposed sites when the Needle actually came to England.) For their part, the Crystal Palace Company would have a star attraction, and the government had undertaken to reimburse the costs of transporting and erecting the Needle if they reclaimed it. Only in the event of the Crystal Palace ceasing to operate as set out in its charter would they lose the obelisk. There had, however, been a number of unfavourable reports over the years on the condition of the Needle, from J G Wilkinson among others, and a report in 1853 seems to have been what tipped the balance, persuading the directors that it would not be sufficiently impressive to warrant the considerable cost and risks of transporting it.

However, the idea may not have been completely abandoned, or was revived later, as a board meeting of the South Kensington Museum (now the V&A Museum) in July 1865 received a report from the British consul at Alexandria noting a threat by the owner of the ground on which the Needle rested to break it up if it was not removed, and saying that it had now been placed under the protection of the local government.[99] In November of that year Anthony Panizzi, Keeper of Printed Books at the British Museum Library, wrote to Henry Cole, who would become the South Kensington Museum's first director, asking if the museum's trustees had any objections to a request by the directors of the Crystal Palace Company, presumably to transport the obelisk to the Crystal Palace. The trustees' reply made it clear, without actually saying so, that they would prefer that the government found the money for the obelisk to be transported to England, and erected at the museum, but this heavy hint was ignored by the government, and no further communication on the matter was made to the trustees.[100]

Despite the disappointing lack of an obelisk Ancient Egypt was to be a major theme in the new Crystal Palace. The Egyptian Court was set up just north of the great Central Transept on the Crystal Palace Parade side of the building, opposite the gardens. It was the work of Owen Jones, who had travelled in Egypt with the French architect Jules Goury in 1833, and Joseph Bonomi Jnr who had spent nine years in Egypt between 1824 and 1832. Both men could make use of original drawings and measurements they had made on the spot, and they also drew on the work of J G Wilkinson, J F Champollion and other Egyptologists.[101] Samuel Sharpe, who had written a successful *History of Egypt*, first published in 1846, contributed a historical summary to the published description of the Court, Wilkinson produced a companion to it, and the official guide to the Crystal Palace mentioned Samuel Birch's introduction to Egyptian hieroglyphs. The Court itself was a composite of art and architecture from different areas of Egypt and different periods of its ancient history, often on a reduced scale. Even in a building the size of the Crystal Palace this was a necessary compromise, but Jones was concerned in his guide to stress the authenticity of the display, noting the mixture of styles and dates in real Ancient Egyptian monuments. Sculpture and columns were created from casts of originals in the British Museum, Louvre and Turin Museum (now the Egyptian Museum in Turin), and the different areas of the Court combined elements from specific sites rather than being in the general style of a certain type of building or period. Most surviving Ancient Egyptian statues are unpainted but Jones believed that, like the Ancient Greek equivalents, both they and the Egyptians' buildings had originally been painted, so all the reproductions were coloured.

The authenticity of the displays was further enhanced by the way in which they were created. Jones referred in his guide to the techniques of Ancient Egyptian relief carving and painting, noting in particular how this could be seen in 'Belzoni's tomb', that of Sety I in the Valley of the Kings, and similar techniques were followed for the Crystal Palace display. Designs were drawn on squared grids, transferred to plaster slabs, corrected by Bonomi and then carved by 'a very small band of *mechanics* under his supervision and guidance'.[102] These '*mechanics*' were actually highly skilled specialist craftsmen, including 'M. [Alexandre] Desachy of Paris, assisted by a very intelligent body of French workmen'.[103]

From the nave of the Palace an avenue of eight lions, cast from a pair in the British Museum brought back by Lord Prudhoe from Nubia, led to a Ptolemaic-style temple exterior through which the Egyptian Court was entered (Fig 104). (One of the lions, greatly enlarged, was also to feature in Sir

Fig 104
The entrance to the Egyptian Court from the nave. On the lintel above the columns is the modern hieroglyphic inscription recording the building of the Crystal Palace (see Fig 105)
[DP004619]

E J Poynter's epic 1867 painting *Israel in Egypt*.) A hieroglyphic frieze over the temple columns, repeated with slight variations in the interior of the Outer Court behind, commemorated the erection of the Palace in the 17th year of Victoria's reign (Fig 105). Her name and that of Prince Albert were repeated elsewhere in the Court, and the directors of the Crystal Palace Company also had their names concealed among the genuine inscriptions. Above the hieroglyphic inscription was one in Greek for the safety and welfare of the royal family. The columns of the temple were copied from various sites but the arrangement was taken from the temple of Horus at Edfu.

A plan in the official guide suggested a route around the Court which took the visitor on a clockwise circuit (Fig 106). Entering the Outer Court, which featured copies of reliefs from Medinet Habu, the visitor faced a façade based on part of the Ramesseum at Thebes with a row of colossal statues of Ramesses II as Osiris, but also including reliefs of the king smiting enemies taken from Abu Simbel. Behind this was a hall with reproductions of columns from the hypostyle hall at Karnak. Turning left, the visitor passed into a court of Amenhotep III with columns cast from an original in the British Museum. To their right, an entrance led from this court into a reproduction of a rock-cut tomb from Beni Hasan. For the convenience of visitors the single entrance

of the original had been replaced by one in each wall. Outside one of these entrances were seated statues of Amenhotep III cast from a black granite original in the British Museum and restored by Bonomi to their original condition. Carrying straight on out of the tomb into the Inner Court, one entrance of which featured casts of a colossus of Sety I from what is now the Egyptian Museum in Turin, the visitor was faced by a reproduction of one of the porticos from the first court of the Temple of Isis at Philae, with some column capitals copied from examples in other parts of Egypt. Behind the portico was an Egyptian museum with exhibits including statues and a copy of the Rosetta Stone. Continuing on their circuit, the visitor could then admire a one-tenth scale model of the façade of the temple of Abu Simbel set in a recess and flanked by copies of a hieroglyphic list of kings. Turning back towards the nave, they passed through the Hall of Karnak Columns and back into the Outer Court.

The Ancient Egyptian features of the Crystal Palace did not end with the Court itself, however. In the North Transept, a grand avenue of 20 sphinxes led from the Mammoth Tree near the park-side entrance up to 65ft-high replicas of the colossi at Abu Simbel (Fig 107). Each of the sphinxes was a full-size copy of an original in the Louvre, from the reign of the 12th Dynasty pharaoh Amenemhat II, later usurped by the 19th

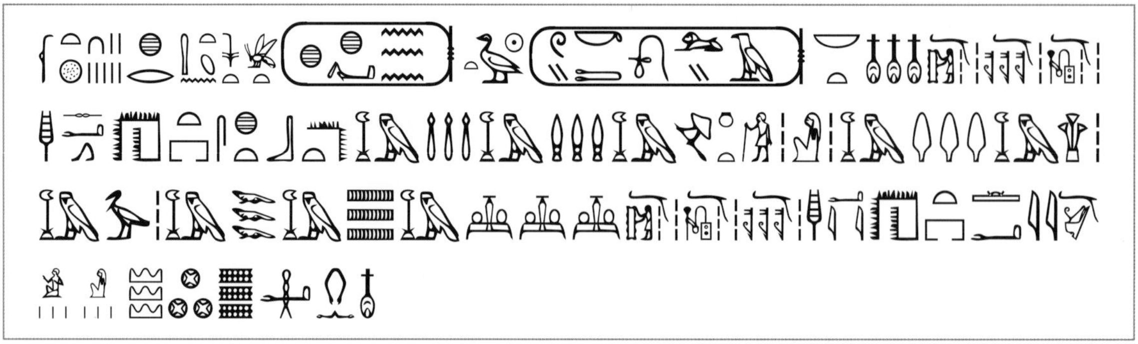

Fig 105
The inscription records that in the 17th year of the most gracious Queen Victoria, Ruler of the Waves, architects, sculptors and painters erected the Palace with a thousand columns, decorations, statues of 'chiefs and ladies', trees, flowers, birds and beasts, fountains and vases, building it as a book for the instruction of men and women of all lands, and wishing it to prosper. [Mark Rudolph]

Dynasty pharaoh Merenptah and the 21st Dynasty pharaoh Sheshonq I. Eight more copies stood outside the building guarding its park-side entrances. The inscriptions on them, dedicatory formulae calling divine blessings on the pharaohs, were partially restored, possibly by Birch, but at least one of the artisans who constructed the sphinxes, John Wigglesworth, had an interest in hieroglyphs and had lived in Cairo for two years.[104] The heads of the colossi were moulded from a cast taken at Abu Simbel by Bonomi while he was working for Robert Hay, and subsequently given to the British Museum. The bodies of the Crystal Palace copies were scaled up by pointing from a one-tenth size model by M Desachy and his team, and constructed of plaster on a brick core, and the figures of Ramesses' wives and daughters were modelled by M Monti. The magazine *Punch* was certainly impressed and suggested the figures were so big that a pub called 'the Rameses Head' could be started in one of them.[105] Others were

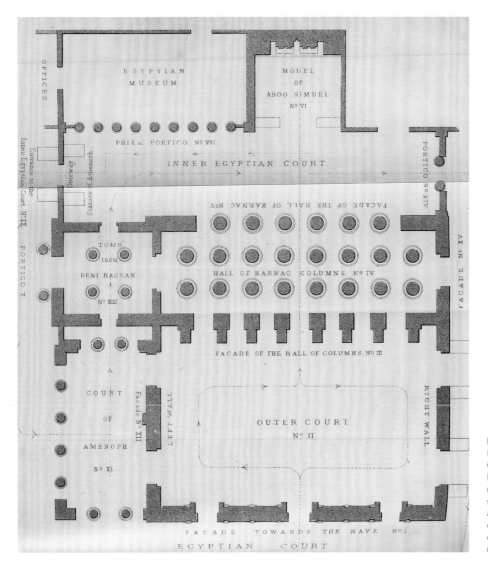

Fig 106
Plan of the Egyptian Court at the Crystal Palace. The Court recreated elements of sites hundreds of miles apart in Egypt, some of them, like the model of Abu Simbel, on a reduced scale.

Fig 107
This hand-coloured view of the Abu Simbel colossi in the Egyptian Court shows the colour scheme adopted for them, based on the view that like Greek sculpture, Ancient Egyptian statues were originally painted. [FF91/00333]

less impressed and the *Illustrated London News* described them as 'abnormal and idol-like figures', without either the exquisite proportions or emotional impact of Greek sculpture.[106] Above the Egyptian Court itself, a gallery contained casts of original wall sculptures used to make the copies in the Court and photos of Ancient Egyptian sites. The photos were described as French and may have been those of the traveller and amateur photographer Maxime du Camp, first published in 1852. To complete the experience, lotus and papyrus grew in the fountain basin at the north end of the nave.

The new Crystal Palace was opened by Queen Victoria on 10 June 1854. It became a national institution and a centre for the exhibition of fine art, particularly statuary. In the 1890s, this included a statue of General Charles George Gordon 'Gordon of Khartoum' on a camel, by Onslow Ford, which was placed in the

Outer Court of the Egyptian Court. The statue was commissioned by the Royal Engineers, exhibited at the Royal Academy in 1890 and then at the Crystal Palace, before being moved to the Royal School of Military Engineering at Chatham where it still stands. A second casting was at one point installed in Khartoum where it remained until 1958 when it was returned to this country and placed at the Gordon Boys' School in Woking, Surrey. The Palace was also used as an exhibition venue, and in July 1895 the Egyptian Court hosted the Centenary Exhibition of the London Mission Society. The *Crystal Palace Times* described how 'dresses, implements of war and industry, and many curios from every continent' were laid out in the Court. By this time, however, the Crystal Palace was facing competition from other venues, particularly the South Kensington Museum and the cost of maintaining the Palace and its landscaped gardens, and of staging events and activities, were a constant drain on the company's finances. A fire in the North Transept in 1866 destroyed some of the exhibits. Between 1880 and 1890, the building cost between £93,000 and £117,000 a year to run. In 1887 the company underwent financial restructuring, with shareholders (who had little choice) voluntarily surrendering half their rights. By 1911 the company was in serious financial trouble, and after public subscriptions were raised to save the Palace and park, it came into public ownership in 1914. On the night of 30 November 1936, however, it caught fire and was burnt down (Fig 108). At the time, there was not enough money for it to be rebuilt and before long the Second World War made this impossible, although an unsuccessful attempt was later made to use the site to celebrate the centenary of its construction.

Today, the glazed colonnade from the station is only a memory but the TV transmitter at the north end of the Palace's foundations provides a useful landmark to help find them. Steps still lead up from the park and

Fig 108
The remains of the Abu Simbel colossi after the fire in 1936 which destroyed the Crystal Palace. Compare this with the same view before the fire in Figure 107.
[sc00710/38b/01]

some of the sphinxes still survive, although suffering from the ravages of time and vandalism (Fig 109). The inscriptions on the right shoulder panel and chest are for Merenptah, while that on the left shoulder has been usurped by Sheshonq, whose

Fig 109
The Crystal Palace sphinxes have gone from being exhibits in a secular temple to Art and Science, to become guardians of an archaeological site, like their genuine counterparts in Egypt.
[DP104035]

restored inscription also runs around the plinth. The large central set of steps marks the site of the entrance to the Central Transept and on them is one of the allegorical statues. Sadly, it is not that of Egypt which was sculpted by Baron Marochetti, but one of Liverpool by Spence. Nearby is a lady representing the Zollverein by Monti, who worked on the Abu Simbel colossi, while the bottom half of another statue is all that is left of Birmingham. Opposite the stairs, and slightly to the right, is the site of the Egyptian Court, and further along the foundations towards the TV mast, another set of steps marks the entrance to the North Transept, at the head of which stood the colossi of Abu Simbel.

Greater London House

Hampstead Road,
London
NW1 7AW

A temple to tobacco

Eighty feet high and stretching 550ft along Hampstead Road, the former Carreras factory is one of London's finest Egyptian-style buildings and a spectacular example of the influence of Ancient Egypt on interwar architecture.

The factory opened on Saturday, 3 November 1928 as the new Arcadia Works of the cigarette manufacturers Carreras Ltd. It was not only visually striking with a brightly coloured 12-pillared façade, cavetto cornice, winged solar disc above the door and 10ft-high bronze cats either side of the entrance, but was also at that time the largest and most modern factory under a single roof in Britain, and one which pioneered modern construction methods in reinforced concrete.

The building was the brainchild of the company's chairman, Bernhard Baron. Born in Brest-Litovsk, Russia, in 1850, he emigrated from there to the United States where he became a cigarette manufacturer and the holder of patents for machinery that revolutionised cigarette production. After 30 years in the USA he moved to the United Kingdom. Here, in 1896, William Yapp had bought the tobacco business of Madame Carreras, a member of an old-established Spanish family tobacco business founded in 1788 by Don José Carreras-y-Ferrer, who had moved to England to escape political turmoil in Spain. When the business was floated as Carreras Ltd in 1903 Baron became a director, and later managing director and chairman. One of Don José's customers had been the 3rd Earl of Craven and Craven Mixture, later to give its name to one of the firm's best known brands, was originally produced for the earl. The Black Cat, which was to be another of the firm's best-known brands, was a Carreras trademark, first registered in 1886 (Fig 110). In 1904, Yapp and Baron opened the first factory in the UK to produce machine-made cigarettes and also introduced coupons and prize competitions to promote the Black Cat brand. In 1910 they opened a factory on the City Road, called the Arcadia Works, and in due course another one on Theobalds Road.

A new factory to replace these was planned in 1926 for Hampstead Road. The site chosen was controversial since much of it was open space. Indirectly this was to have far-reaching effects on the landscape of modern London as it led to the appointment of a Royal Commission on London Squares to prevent others being built on. The original design was by A G Porri, who as part of the partnership of

Fig 110
The spectacular façade of the former Carreras factory showing the company name and its Black Cat logo. The use of factory buildings to promote company brands led to accusations by architectural critics that this resulted in them being without architectural merit. [DP103856]

Hobden and Porri was responsible in 1928 for the Egyptian-style Britannia House on Shaftesbury Avenue, but his plans for the Carreras factory appear to have been for a building with a Classical elevation. Soon after these were made, however, Porri's plans were adapted into an Egyptian-style building by M E and O H Collins, who subsequently received sole credit for the design in the contemporary press.[107]

Although it is now celebrated for its Egyptian-style features, at the time the construction of the building was probably considered more impressive. Covering over 9 acres on five floors totalling 392,000sq ft it took over two years to build. It was the largest reinforced concrete building under one roof in Great Britain and employed innovative construction methods, such as running service ducts prior to the casting of concrete and constructing staircases in situ. A contemporary press release (then, as now, largely recycled by the local papers) reeled off the statistics: a workforce of 700–800 men, 26,000cu yd of reinforced concrete,

2,800 tons of steel rods, and emphasised that 'the conception and construction of the factory are entirely British'. This included not only the bronze window frames and all machinery, but even the nearly 400,000sq ft of Canadian maple flooring, from what was then a British dominion.

The façade was described in the press release as 'a conventionalised copy of the Temple of Bubastis, the cat-headed goddess of Ancient Egypt'. This confused the goddess Bast or Bastet with the city of Bubastis (in ancient Egyptian Per-Bastet, the House of Bastet), her great cult centre. The site, now known as Tell Basta, near modern Zagâzig, about 80km north-east of Cairo, was excavated in 1887 and 1889 by Edouard Naville, but the Temple of Bast was badly ruined and unlikely to have directly inspired the design of the Carreras factory. It is possible that surviving elements of the temple influenced an Egyptian-style design, but more likely that it was chosen to create a link between one of the company's best known brands and the Ancient Egyptian deity, since the architects had modelled the cat statues on either side of the entrance on originals in the British Museum (Fig 111). (But not on the iconic Gayer-Anderson cat statue, which was not presented to the museum until 1939.) Drawings by A G Porri and Partners had even described the building as Bast House, but what J S Curl describes as 'the somewhat unfortunate possibilities suggested in English by the name' led to it being changed. The company's Black Cat trademark was repeated across the façade in relief roundels. Handrails in the form of snakes supported by human hands ran alongside the entrance steps, and in front of the cat statues were tall lamps with bovine horns, symbols of the goddess Hathor. On the lintel of the entrance was a winged solar disc and Egyptian-style roll mouldings ran round the doorway. Another winged solar disc decorated the cavetto cornice. The external walls were rendered with Atlas White Portland cement, tinted with buff-coloured sand to simulate stone, and the papyrus bud columns were coloured with cement to which crushed Venetian glass had been added. Railings around the building incorporated *djed* and *was* hieroglyphs – symbols respectively of stability and power. Even the chimneys at the back of the building were shaped like obelisks.

Fig 111
The cat statues outside the building are Egyptian in style, and linked the well-known Black Cat brand on the façade with the culture of Ancient Egypt, giving the brand status by association.
[DP103862]

Internally, the only Ancient Egyptian elements of the building were the decoration and furniture in the ground-floor boardroom. Ventilation ducts with panels concealing light switches were styled to resemble columns, with capitals echoing the cavetto cornice on the building's front, and geometric designs. The boardroom doors and a dado frieze used a pattern echoing the niched façades of Old Kingdom architecture and false doors in tombs, and a frieze of stylised lotus blossoms ran along the sides of the beams running across the ceiling. The boardroom table was plain, but the chairs echoed the construction of Ancient Egyptian ones. Elsewhere, the building was a model of modern factory design, the key features being space, light and ventilation. The *St Pancras Chronicle*, reporting on its opening, noted:

> Spaciousness and light are the main features of the building, and this is due to the fact that the windows reach from floor to ceiling and that each machine – all are mechanical marvels – has its own motor and thus eliminate overhead shafting…The chief marvel of the factory, however, is the air conditioning plant built on the roof… .[108]

At the time the factory was built, the plant was the only one of its kind in the British tobacco industry. Air entering the building was washed, adjusted to the required temperature and humidified and each machine incorporated a dust extractor. An air vent on the roof was disguised to resemble a cigarette, with an end that glowed at night, forming an eye-catching advertisement for the company's products. The main purpose of the air conditioning was to ensure the quality of the tobacco used but there were side benefits for the workers involved. Baron was a paternalistic philanthropist, described by the *St Pancras Chronicle* as: 'The greatest philanthropist of our time, [who] has already given away a million and a half of money.'[109]

He provided his almost wholly female workforce with sick pay, lockers, rest room, welfare centre and sick room with doctor and nurse in attendance. The *St Pancras Gazette* for 9 November 1928 paraphrased Baron as saying that he now had the factory he had always wanted, one in which it was healthy and pleasant to work and which produced tobacco under hygienic conditions. Some idea of what had been more typical for the industry, and Carreras's previous factories, can be gained from the fact that the *St Pancras Chronicle* for the same date noted that even in the new factory 'through all these processes, a slight mist envelopes the workers, this being caused by the dust and sand contained in the leaves'.[110]

The opening ceremony for the building was a simple one at Baron's wish. In spite of this crowds stretched for hundreds of yards on either side of Hampstead Road. Baron opened the factory himself and presented each of his 3,000 employees with a silver commemorative medal. On the obverse was a head and shoulder left profile of Baron, identified as Chairman of Carreras. Around it was the text 'My Thanks For All Your Help'. On the reverse was a relief of the factory with its name, address and the date of opening. Around the bottom edge was the legend 'London's Most Hygenic Tobacco Factory'. Journalistic hyperbole reached a peak when the *Chronicle* asserted that: 'Mr Baron was, indeed, a happy man on Saturday, for he heard the cheers of three thousand employees and knew, as they knew, that he had provided them with a fairy palace in which to flit and work from day to day.'[111]

Seemingly absent from contemporary reports is any mention of another ceremony, which took place at night and was recalled in 2007 by the then Director of Art and

Design at Harrods, William Mitchell. As a very young child (he was born in 1925), he remembered being taken by his father to see a torchlight procession of people dressed in Ancient Egyptian costumes and with horse-drawn chariots, along the road in front of the factory. The two cat statues in front of the building had been supplemented for the occasion with smaller versions with gold earrings and glowing green eyes.[112] It may seem surprising that such a striking occasion was not mentioned in the press but there was also little coverage of the opening of Harrods' Egyptian Escalator, which was inspired by Mitchell's memory of this procession, and neither event may have been considered 'newsworthy'.

Bernhard Baron had seen his dream realised but he was to die a year later in 1929, and the Egyptian-style exterior was savagely attacked by modernist architectural critics. Maxwell Fry, noting the link to the company's trademark, observed that

> …apparently, the choice of a style was suggested by rather far-drawn reference to the sacred cats of Egypt. By employing an Egyptian mannerism for the main façade of the building it was possible to introduce the representation of a black cat in forms varying in size and importance, from the large figures that flank the main entrance to the myriad medallion reliefs that occur in monotonous repetition over the rest of the building. It was for purposes of advertisement, then, that this building gathered to itself the lotus, scarab, snake, and sacred cat![113]

Fry believed that the nature of reinforced concrete construction, which he believed 'flows towards lightness and rigidity, abhorring weight and mass and all the ponderousness of stone', were qualities which prevented the building having any close resemblance to the massive

Fig 112
Both the Carreras factory and Marshall's Mill in Leeds were pioneers of new construction techniques and materials. However, while the Leeds building was widely admired when it was built, for those who believed that a building's design should be dictated by its purpose and the materials used to construct it, decorative elements such as those shown here on the Carreras factory were considered not only unnecessary but undesirable. [DP103854]

architecture of Ancient Egypt and reduced the Egyptian elements to mere decoration. He described the main façade as 'a piece of ponderous scenery secured to a factory for the purpose of advertisement', and its cornice as 'a sham'. The boardroom he described as 'unsatisfactory in form and garish in its colour, decoration and lighting'.[114] Nikolaus Pevsner, author of the monumental 47-volume *The Buildings of England* described it as an 'abominable factory'[115] (Fig 112).

Primary cigarette manufacturing moved to Basildon in Essex in 1953, and the business was sold to the Rembrandt Tobacco Co in 1958 and merged with Rothmans. The Carreras factory was sold in 1959 for conversion to offices and renamed as Greater London House in 1961. Between 1960 and 1962, as part of the conversion, all Egyptian detail was obliterated. One of the cat statues went to the new factory at Basildon, the other found its way to Jamaica. In 1996, a new owner decided to restore the building and Finch Forman Chartered Architects made use of the original plans and drawings to restore 80–90 per cent of the original features and recreate one of the capital's most impressive buildings.

Hampstead Cemetery

Fortune Green
Road,
London
NW6 1DR

Wilson Pasha's monument

One of the most attractive of London's Ancient Egyptian-style funerary monuments is tucked away in this relatively obscure local cemetery. It is that of the Scots engineer James Wilson (1831–1906), who worked for the Egyptian government for 43 years.

Wilson held the senior rank of pasha, roughly equivalent to a knighthood.

His granite monument, about 4ft high, is shaped like an Egyptian temple, with battered sides, a torus moulding running along the edges and a cavetto cornice at the top (Fig 113). The centre of the monument is hollow apart from two rows of three papyrus bud pillars. On the end facing the path there is a winged solar disc on the cavetto cornice. The solar disc itself is flanked by what look like two vulture's heads rather than the more usual cobras. As well as Wilson himself, his wife Annie and James Hamish Wilson, probably his son, are also buried here.

On the front right of the plinth, a worn inscription reads 'A Macdonald Field design' followed by several letters which are indecipherable. This identifies it as a product of the Aberdeen company which pioneered the modern use of granite in architectural and monumental structures, and produced many of the Ancient Egyptian-style monuments in London's cemeteries. (In his book *The Victorian Celebration of Death*, J S Curl thought it was produced by Cramb, the monumental masons whose offices were opposite the cemetery at 128 Fortune Green Road. It is possible that it was manufactured by Cramb to a design by MacDonald Field.)

Fig 113
The granite monument of James Wilson in Hampstead Cemetery. As no other examples of this style of monument are known, it must have been specifically designed and manufactured for Wilson Pasha, and would have been correspondingly expensive. Despite its relatively modest size, it has some of the finest detail of all the Egyptian-style monuments. [DP103962]

The Wilson monument is visible from the cemetery gates, to the right of the path. Hugh Meller, in his *London Cemeteries* considers the house of the monumental mason Cramb, across the road from the cemetery, to be in 'Bastard Egyptian style' because of its stylised lotus flower decoration. The cemetery itself is entered from Fortune Green Road.

Harrods

Visitors to Harrods entering by door 3 from Basil Street used to be greeted by a startlingly lifelike waxwork of its then owner Muhammad al Fayed, standing on a plinth and flanked by four dark-green striding pharaonic figures holding staves. Acquired by the Egyptian Al Fayed family in 1985 for £615m, Harrods was a British institution, but one in need of a makeover. Fittingly enough for the first department store in London to boast an escalator, in 1898, what it got was a £300m refurbishment, with a £20m Egyptian Escalator and an Egyptian Hall on the ground and lower ground floor.

Initially, the designer and developer Ian Pollard, creator of the Ancient Egyptian-style Warwick Road Homebase (see p 167), was approached to submit designs for a single sales area within the store – a sort of Egyptian Room or Hall. The concept outlined by Muhammad al Fayed was of an area which would last as long as the famous Harrods Food Hall, at that time around 100 years old. Pollard was accompanied to the initial meeting by the stone carver and sculptor Richard Kindersley, who had previously been involved in the Homebase project, and a design evolved for a columned hall with a sandstone floor, with existing

87–135 Brompton Road,
London
SW1X 7XL

columns being encased in stone. An early computer-modelled design shows a large room with rows of columns supporting beams or lintels, with smaller beams running across the room. Both columns and beams are covered with coloured hieroglyphs and reliefs, and a deep frieze of offering scenes runs around the outside of the room. The intention was that stonework was to be stained with designs, rather than painted, to ensure that the designs lasted as long as possible. A Ptolemaic-style of column was chosen, which would have had the figures of three different gods around the circumference of each column, and square capitals with four heads below them similar to those of the goddess Hathor found in the Ptolemaic temple of Dendera.

At a subsequent meeting, feedback from Harrods' retail division was against round columns, preferring square ones. This may have been because they would be easier

to display merchandise around, but this would have rather defeated the point of decorating the columns. Pollard estimated that the work would take six months to complete, but the company was unhappy at losing the space for so long and the timescale was reduced to two weeks, and then six days spread over the course of three weekends. Some column models were made and Harrods suggested the idea of casting fibreglass column sections, each with three heads, torsos or legs, which could then be used in different combinations to create a variety of figures, but at this point Pollard and Kindersley withdrew from the project and were replaced by William Mitchell, Harrod's Director of Art and Design.

Mitchell's design for the Hall, which was built in 1991–2, eventually used fibrous plaster for the columns and friezes. The 'Hall' is actually two rooms, one on the ground and one on the lower ground floor (Fig 114).

Fig 114
The design of the hall on the lower ground floor of Harrods has had to accommodate the level of lighting needed in modern retail spaces. The pharaonic figure shown here is in the pose where a ruler offers to the gods in *nw* pots, often containing wine. [AA005432]

The decoration of the Hall features scenes of the *heb-sed*, or jubilee, and Opet festivals on its lower level, and daily life and funerary scenes on its upper level. Most of the scenes are based on 18th and 19th Dynasty originals, and although Mitchell, speaking to the author in 2007, then considered that the decoration of the Hall was 'fussy' and over detailed in comparison to what he saw as the simpler style of the reliefs around the escalator, the detail is impressive. Behind the escalator to the lower ground floor Egyptian Hall, the back of which is painted with a design of Egyptian-style stars on a dark-blue background, are full-sized copies of the Rosetta Stone and an inscribed sarcophagus lid. They are flanked by ram-headed sphinxes with small statues of a pharaoh between their paws, like those at Karnak, but gold painted.

The finished Egyptian Escalator, with the sky goddess Nut (Fig 115) depicted on the underside, rises through seven storeys (Fig 116). As Mitchell says on his website, 'I intended the staircase to be a walk-in-sculpture, the viewer would be transported on the escalator, as if travelling from the Lower Nile to the Upper Nile.' As it does, it passes a series of carved reliefs based on Ancient Egyptian originals whose themes were also chosen to mirror as far as possible the products sold on each floor – so that the floor selling musical instruments, for example, featured scenes of musicians. The handrail is coloured green, which can be seen as evoking the thin strip of fertile land bordering the Nile. Cartouches at the ends of the escalator contain hieroglyphs which can be read as 'Egyptian Hall of Harrods 1991' (Fig 117). Elsewhere are other cartouches with phonetic spellings of 'Al Fayed', and *uraei* above them, and the figures of the hieroglyphic 'alphabet'. Facing each other at the end of the escalator hall are two sphinxes – one with the features of Muhammad Al Fayed rests its paws on

a model of the building; the other with Mitchell's features has the tool used to carve the relief scenes in a small case in front of it. (According to Mitchell, the tool cost '7s 6d in old money' (the equivalent of 37½p

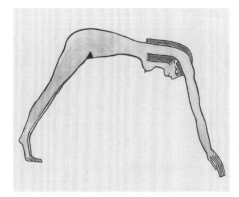

Fig 115
In Ancient Egypt the image of Nut as sky goddess may have originally been intended to personify the Milky Way. As the overarching heavens, her laughter was the thunder and her tears the rain.

Fig 116
Railings alongside the Egyptian Escalator feature cartouches terminated by hands and scarabs, naming the Egyptian Hall (see Fig 117).
[AA005451]

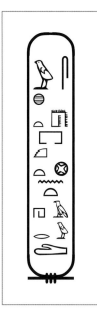

Fig 117
In ancient Egypt, cartouches were used to contain royal names, but the oval shape has been used here to make the hieroglyphic text (Egyptian Hall at Harrods) part of a set of railings (see Fig 116). [Mark Rudolph]

today.) Large pharaonic heads on either side of the escalator also have Al Fayed's features, and behind a pillar near a door on the third floor are the handprints of Al Fayed, his wife and children. On the mezzanine floor, a relief includes a quote from Shelley's poem *Ozymandias*. On the fifth floor, the escalator finishes and the columns alongside it terminate in Hathor-headed capitals supporting a lighted ceiling based on the Zodiac of Dendera, a copy of which was once exhibited in Leicester Square. Three large central light fittings were placed to represent the stars of Orion's Belt, and also the alignment of the three Pyramids of Giza. The constellation of Orion was personified in Ancient Egyptian times by the god Sah, known as 'The Glorious Soul of Osiris' (see p 296). A border of palm fronds surrounding this zodiac was intended to create the impression of looking up from Egypt into the night sky. Elsewhere, back-lit stained glass was used to create a dramatic effect (Fig 118).

Before work could begin on the Egyptian Escalator, the removal of the existing central lifts revealed the need for remedial building work and only once this had been completed could work begin on the escalator, which was started in 1996 and completed in 1997. Mitchell approached the British Museum for advice and James Putnam, who then worked at the museum, suggested sources for the Ancient Egyptian elements of the design and advised on the meaning of the hieroglyphs. Mitchell first created a small corner sample of the proposed reliefs, using a 'stucco' mix of one part cement to four of washed sand, which was brushed when semi-dry to prevent cracking and unify the finish. The reliefs were tinted using cement stain. Once this had been approved, the project began and took about 14 months to complete.

Mitchell worked on the panels off-site, in nearby Trevor Square, completing two

to four panels a day depending on the complexity of the design, starting with those at the top of the escalator shaft and working towards the ground floor. Each panel started as a galvanised steel frame reinforced with mesh. A first coat of cement was applied around 7.30 am for use the following day. Panels from the previous day were then set up one above the other, a second coat of cement applied, and reliefs carved back to the first coat which had by now hardened. Each panel took about two hours to carve. Other elements such as the 'granite' pharaonic heads, bronze balusters and ceiling panels were produced in outside workshops by specialist contractors. The ceiling figures were first carved from polyurethane, then cast in fibrous plaster and linked to frames in the ceiling before the ceiling panels were added. Light emitting diodes were used for the zodiac ceiling because of the difficulty of changing conventional bulbs if they failed.

The opening of the new escalator was marked by ceremonies attended by the president of Egypt, Hosni Mubarrak, which included a procession in loosely Ancient Egyptian-style costumes, complete with trumpeters and statues, including one evoking the famous 'Younger Memnon' colossus of Ramesses II in the British Museum. Part of the inspiration for these ceremonies was Mitchell's childhood memory of a similar spectacle at the Egyptian-style new Arcadia Works of Carreras, now Greater London House (see p 152).

The Egyptian Escalator and Hall were far from being the only involvement with Ancient Egypt of the store and its colourful owner. In July 1996 it sold a limited edition reproduction Ancient Egyptian beer brewed by Scottish and Newcastle Breweries and based on research by the archaeobotanist Dr Delwen Samuel. The beer, in a limited

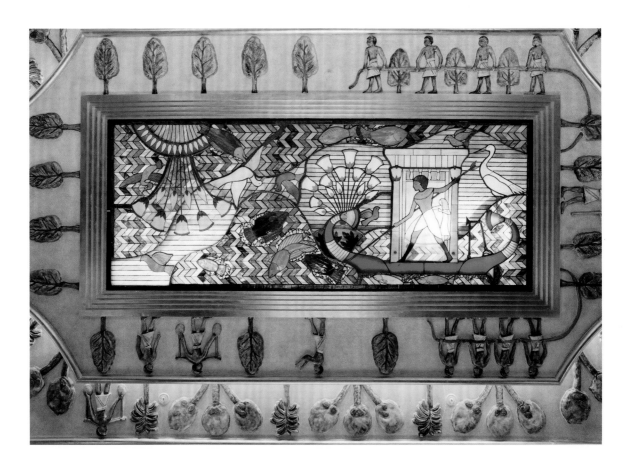

edition costing £5,000 for the first bottle and £50 for the remaining 999, raised nearly £28,000, donated to help fund Dr Samuel's continuing research. In 2007, there were plans for a rooftop pet shop with, almost inevitably, glass pyramids. These recall a previous and probably less serious proposal by Mitchell to erect a canvas pyramid on the roof with a mock pharaonic burial chamber inside it, invite the press to view the interior of the chamber but not enter it, and allow the rumour to gain credence that Muhammad al Fayed planned to be buried in a pyramid on the roof of Harrods. By the time the almost inevitable storm of protest and its accompanying publicity had

descended, the canvas pyramid would have been dismantled. Even more appealing was the idea of acquiring a huge sphinx around 10m high, used in Amsterdam as a prop in a production of Verdi's opera *Aida*, which was to have been towed back to London and up the Thames, with Tower Bridge opening for it. What would have happened then is unclear, although it would have made a spectacular addition to the store's decor. Even without it, the Harrods building and its interiors are now listed as Grade II*, and while they may not last as long as their Egyptian inspirations, they will still be one of the highlights of Egyptian London for some time to come.

Fig 118
In this stained glass 'relief' panel at Harrods, elements often found in Ancient Egyptian tomb paintings have been combined so that they can be viewed from a number of angles. [AA005450]

Highgate Cemetery

The Egyptian Avenue, the Circle of Lebanon and The Egyptologist

We must now enter the Egyptian Avenue: the ponderous cornice, the obelisks and pillars, the angular entrance, and the flying serpent, are all in excellent keeping with the place. We are now among the Cedars of Lebanon; talking of Ancient Egypt, of the pharaohs of old; of the custom of embalming; of Belzoni, and the mummy pits of Gournou.[116]

The Egyptian Avenue and the Circle of Lebanon Vaults of Highgate are London's largest and most spectacular pieces of Egyptian-style funerary architecture, and although Highgate has only one mausoleum in this style, it is also the last resting place of pioneer Egyptologists, Orientalist painters and others with a connection to Egypt, including the commander of the Nile Voyageurs, a group of Canadian boatmen who took part in the expedition to relieve General Gordon at Khartoum. Here, as in other cemeteries, it is interesting to note the general lack of Egyptian features on the monuments of such people.

The origins of the cemetery lay in an 1836 Act which established the London Cemetery Company. In 1838 the company, which also established Nunhead Cemetery, purchased 20 acres of ground that had previously formed the gardens and park of the 17th-century Ashurst Manor. (The house itself, which lay to the north of the cemetery, was demolished in 1830 to make way for Lewis Vulliamy's St Michael's Church.) Stephen Geary, who was also the architect of Nunhead Cemetery, designed the 'Undertaker's Gothic' brick entrance chapels (more properly 'Tudor Gothic'), and the grounds were landscaped by David Ramsay. The Circle Vaults, also designed by

Geary but in an Egyptianising style, were built in 1839 around a Cedar of Lebanon which already existed from the plantings of Ashurst Manor, and the first burial in the cemetery was on 26 May 1839. Between 1839 and 1842 the company's surveyor, James Bunstone Bunning, added the Egyptian Avenue leading to these vaults, as well as Gothic Terrace Catacombs on the north boundary and others in the Classical style in the outer bank of the eastern road. The cemetery's site on Highgate Hill gave it spectacular views across London, and although it lacked the cachet which royal burials gave Kensal Green, its position and the high cost of vault and catacomb burials ensured it a certain degree of exclusivity (Fig 119).

Following the 1852 ban which ended burials in London churchyards, a 19-acre eastern extension to the cemetery was opened, with the first burials taking place in 1854. Geary, the original architect of Highgate, died in the same year, but was buried in the West Cemetery. A hydraulic bier lowered the massively heavy triple caskets favoured by the Victorians from the south entrance chapel in the West Cemetery to a tunnel connecting with the East Cemetery. Classical catacombs, designed by Thomas Porter, were added to the outside of the Circle of Lebanon in the West Cemetery in the 1870s. The original Egyptian catacombs there, already beginning to suffer the effects of time, were repaired at the same time, but Portland cement was used instead of stone and proved only a short-term expedient. Highgate, like all the 'joint stock' commercial cemeteries, was eventually to fall into decline as it sold off its only real asset – the land on which it stood. After the Second World War, peripheral buildings and land were beginning to be sold off and 'pauper's graves', marked only by simple wooden

[Entrance to the Catacombs of the Cemetery at Highgate.]

Fig 119
An early engraving of
the Egyptian Avenue and
Terrace Catacombs at
Highgate West Cemetery,
with few mature trees
to obscure the view. The
woman in the middle
of the central group is
wearing mourning dress,
but the couple on the left
may well be sightseers.
[AA074863]

crosses, were replacing headstones and monuments. In 1960, the London Cemetery Company was absorbed into the United Cemeteries Company, but to no avail. The West Cemetery was closed in 1975, by which time it was no longer financially viable. The Friends of Highgate Cemetery was founded in the same year.[117]

Originally, the owner gave the Friends permission to carry out clearance work on Saturdays – removing invasive growth and opening access to graves. Restricted access and minimal funding meant that restoration of the cemetery to its original condition was not practical, and so the decision was taken

to manage it as a woodland park. In 1981, the freehold of both parts of the cemetery, and unrestricted access, was secured. A wholly owned subsidiary company was set up, and government funding through the Manpower Services Commission allowed conservation and restoration of the buildings and landscape to begin. Charitable status was established to secure the future of the cemetery and it is now a Grade II* Woodland Park, with two Grade I listed buildings, 2 Grade II* and more than 60 Grade II.

The Grade I listed Egyptian Avenue and Circle of Lebanon in the West Cemetery is entered through an archway with double torus mouldings flanked by four Egyptian-style columns, short projecting walls and a pair of plain obelisks (Fig 120). The columns are a florid composite of various Ancient Egyptian elements with a short section of cavetto cornice above them, and the double torus moulding is in stepped sections around a low pointed arch, rather than the classic trapezoidal or rectangular shape of an Ancient Egyptian pylon or doorway – but for once obelisks are found in a pair flanking an entrance as they should be. Beyond the archway, a covered passage slopes gently upwards, lined with entrances to catacomb vaults. The vault doorways are rectangular and the doors bear the classic funeral motif of reversed torches, but they are surrounded by torus mouldings in pylon shape. At the end of the passage is a wide path between the inner and outer circular vaults. The inner, Egyptian, vaults have projecting doorways similar to those in the Avenue, but with cavetto cornices above them, and a cavetto cornice with a low wall above it runs around the top of the Circle itself.

Above the outer circle vaults, not far from the Avenue, is the Egyptian-style Hartley mausoleum, designed by the Belfast-born sculptor Patrick MacDowell RA (Fig 121).

Fig 120
Entrance to the Egyptian Avenue, Highgate West Cemetery. The stepped arch, the cross shapes on the cornice and the shape of the pillars are not archaeologically accurate but were built to impress potential customers, and succeeded in this respect. [AA073788]

Fig 121
The Hartley mausoleum
in Highgate West
Cemetery, showing a
mixture of Egyptian and
other elements typical
of many monuments
in the Egyptian style,
and like them seemingly
chosen simply as a
fashionable style.
[AA073503]

It has battered sides and a cavetto cornice with what appear to be cartouches in it, and torus mouldings around the pylon-shaped doorway and the edges of the structure. A second torus moulding flanks the doorway and extends above it to include a winged solar disc with two rather plump cobras. The overall effect, however, is somewhat spoiled by the family arms in raised relief above the solar disc, which distort the proportions of the monument, and a plinth on the roof surmounted by a large funerary urn.

Also in the West Cemetery are the monuments of the Scots physician Robert Richardson and the artist and Royal Academician Frederick Goodall. Richardson, who visited Egypt and Palestine as travelling physician to Viscount Mountjoy and the Earl of Belmore in 1816–18, travelled as far as the Second Cataract and published *Travels along the Mediterranean, and Parts Adjacent: In Company with The Earl of Belmore During the Years 1816-17-18* in 1822. His grave looks to have once had a simple granite headstone, which has now collapsed and broken. Goodall, who was noted for his Egyptian landscapes, has a more substantial monument as befits the man who had the grand Mock Tudor residence which is now the Grim's Dyke Hotel in Harrow built for him. It is a raised granite ledger tomb on a curved stone base with floral decorations on the base corners, with a gabled top above a curved surround. He shares the monument with his wife Anne.

In the East Cemetery are the monuments of Henry Wallis and William Nassau Kennedy, and of the pioneer Egyptologist Samuel Birch. The artist and writer Henry Wallis, best known for his 1856 picture *The Death of Chatterton* depicting the youthful poet and Romantic icon who committed suicide by taking arsenic at the age of 17, was also a regular traveller to Egypt, collector of antiquities and an authority on Near Eastern ceramics. Wallis's headstone has a rounded centre section above flanking convex and concave profiles. It is visible from the path but the inscription is heavily weathered.

Kennedy's monument is a small tapering four-sided column on a plinth with a curved top, crowned by a stepped pyramidal capstone above a concave moulding. It commemorates the first Mayor of Winnipeg, who as a lieutenant colonel commanded the Nile Voyageurs, a unit of Canadian boatmen raised from the 90th Winnipeg Rifles in 1884 to assist Lord Wolseley in his ultimately futile effort to relieve General Gordon at Khartoum. The Canadians, who included Mohawk and Ojibway Native Canadians, were recruited because of their expertise in navigating rapids, as the whaleboats that formed part of Wolseley's expedition had to negotiate the Cataracts from Aswan southwards in order to reach Khartoum. Kennedy died in London, from smallpox, on his way home.

Samuel Birch ran the Department of Oriental Antiquities at the British Museum, which included Ancient Egyptian antiquities, from its creation in 1866 until his death in 1885. He wrote extensively, was an important populariser of Egyptology in its early days, founded the Society of Biblical Archaeology, which included Egyptology, and still found time for leisure interests which included mathematics, the theory of fortifications, politics, and writing and producing a play on Ancient Rome. His headstone is a handsome affair with a raised outer section resembling a Gothic window. In its centre is a large raised roundel with a relief head and shoulders portrait of Birch. Above the roundel is a relief of a laurel wreath with what may be the remains of a lion rampant in the middle. An inscription below the portrait gives his name, dates and titles, and commemorates him simply as 'The Egyptologist' (Fig 122).

The entrance to both cemeteries is in Swain's Lane. The West Cemetery is not normally open to the public but can be visited by booking a one-hour guided tour.

Fig 122
The headstone of Samuel Birch in Highgate East Cemetery. Birch's phenomenal output of work made important contributions to our knowledge of Ancient Egypt; however, although his headstone describes him as 'The Egyptologist', he was a classic desk scholar and never actually visited Egypt himself. [AA073659]

This should include the Egyptian Avenue and Circle of Lebanon Vaults, and may pass Goodall's monument, but Richardson's may not be on the tour route. If it is, the easiest way to locate Richardson's grave is to look for the distinctive monument of the sporting goods manufacturer Albert Prosser, which sports pairs of crossed tennis rackets on either side of cricket bails and stumps on a cricket bat, and which is at right angles to the path. Richardson's grave is at its foot. The East Cemetery is open to the public but there is a charge. Some burials still take place in the East Cemetery and it is closed when this happens. Kennedy's monument is easy to find by taking the Top Road from the gates to where it bends by Karl Marx's memorial. Almost opposite the huge bust of Marx is the Kennedy monument, behind the first row of graves and to the side of the monument of the philosopher Herbert Spencer. Some parts of the East Cemetery are still overgrown and the monuments of Wallis and Birch may not be visible from the main paths. Unless they are kept clear such memorials can be difficult to identify without a detailed grave map and reference to grave numbers on monuments, and inscriptions may be so heavily weathered as to be almost illegible.

Homebase

Few DIY superstores can boast a frieze of 10 Ancient Egyptian gods and goddesses, but at the northern end of Warwick Road a row of Egyptian columns with composite capitals and an entablature (Fig 123) mark the entrance to a unique branch of Homebase.[118]

In the 1980s, the developer Ian Pollard and his company Flaxyard plc set out to develop a vacant site on Warwick Road at a time when there were plans to alter the routes of Warwick and Cromwell Roads. The northern portion of the site was developed as a Homebase DIY superstore

195 Warwick Road, London W14 8PU

Fig 123
The columns at the entrance of Homebase have composite capitals, which combine a number of decorative elements and are typical of temples from the later period of Ancient Egypt. The store name covers the original winged solar disc over the entrance.
[DP103884]

for Sainsbury's and the rest of the site was originally to be occupied by an office development known within Flaxyard as the Ramesses II project. This was described in a 1991 special edition of the magazine *Architectural Design*, on Post-Modernist architecture, as 'an amalgam of I M Pei's glass pyramid [at the Louvre], Jean Nouvel's camera-lens windows [on the Arab Institute in Paris] and a glass version of the temples at Abu Simbel'. It went on to say that, 'The results will be deplored by the professional press and Pollard will take over the role, from Robert Stern, as the most Sincerely Hated Architect at Work (although in private many architects will grant his courage and inventiveness).'[119]

The building would have been six storeys high and 250,000sq ft, with a glass pyramid covering a central atrium with criss-crossed escalators at the front of the building. The glass pyramid was not merely to light the atrium and provide a strong Egyptian image; convection vents in the roof, combined with the use of the building's thermal mass and iris windows on the south side, were designed to make the building energy efficient. The east elevation, onto Warwick Road, featured the strong vertical emphasis, black glass and 'elephants' feet' columns used by Pollard in his earlier Marco Polo building on Queenstown Road opposite Battersea Park, to create an effect reminiscent of Ancient Egyptian temple pylons and colonnades. A stepped façade with regular gridded windows on the west elevation echoed the sloping south and east sides of the building, and was to be curved to accommodate a planned road scheme. The south elevation would have featured the Nouvel-inspired iris windows, which opened and closed during the day to adjust to levels of sunlight. On the north elevation, a six-storey glass façade would feature elaborate decoration in sand- and shotblasted glass with colouring. Viewed from the north, in a

scene reminiscent of the Temple of Medinet Habu, this would have shown a huge Ramesses II shooting a bow from his chariot, extending over the top three storeys from the right-hand (west) side and facing the Warwick Road. Ahead of him would have been a row of five smaller pairs of chariots on the upper storey, two pairs on the fifth and fourth storeys, and a pair below him on the third. On the first and second storeys, a parade of gods and goddesses would have echoed that on the wall of Homebase opposite. In another echo of the Homebase façade, the colouring of the figures on the Ramesses II building would fade away from west to east.

Sadly, a collapse in property prices meant that 'Ramesses II' was never to get further than the model stage and this portion of the site was eventually sold off, but by the time this happened the northern part of the site had already been developed. Originally it was to be the location for one of W H Smith's 'Do It All' DIY stores and was, like Ramesses II, intended from the beginning to have a strong flavour of Ancient Egypt. Pollard brought in the stone carver Richard Kindersley, with whom he had worked previously, and an early design featured an historical sequence of figures, the first of which would have been an Ancient Egyptian 'surveyor' with a knotted measuring cord and T-square with attached pendulum. This idea was soon abandoned, and when W H Smith ended their loss-making involvement in DIY Sainsbury's replaced them as the client. When overall details of the building had been decided, Pollard developed the idea of including a pantheon of Egyptian deities and temple elements (Fig 124).

There were a number of reasons for this. It expressed his belief (which would also have been embodied in the Ramesses II office block opposite) that buildings should be conceived as long lasting, in

Fig 124
The figure of the Goddess Neith, on the far right, has been adapted to fit over a service doorway. Behind her figure can be seen the hieroglyphic inscription giving the name of Pollard's company and the date of construction.
[DP103877]

contrast to some who felt that commercial buildings especially should have an intended lifespan of as little as 30 years. One way of expressing his belief was to adopt a stylised design which had been utilised over hundreds, if not thousands of years, with little change. The style also provided what amounted to a pattern book for Kindersley and his large workforce of stone carvers. (In an unfortunate comparison someone apparently observed that the frieze would be the largest carved surface created in Europe since Albert Speer's work for the Third Reich.) The temple-like image created by the Ancient Egyptian elements was also intended as an ironic reflection on the way in which shopping and retailing can be seen as being the new 'religion' of society.

Pollard developed the idea of a façade with Ancient Egyptian elements and rows of columns, and Kindersley began to research the concept. He visited the British Museum in London and the Ashmolean Museum in Oxford, and consulted Egyptologists including Carol Andrews. From this research, and discussions between Pollard and Kindersley, six detailed design drawings were developed and put to Sainsbury's select architectural committee. Not all included Ancient Egyptian elements but one which did had a frieze of gods and goddesses along the longest exterior wall, cobra water spouts (Fig 125), a cavetto cornice and winged solar disc over the entrance, coloured Egyptian columns with an entablature across the car park, and a row of Corinthian columns with an entablature along the end of the car park facing the road. Interestingly, in view of later events,

Fig 125
A water spout on the wall of Homebase in Warwick Road. As a symbolic opening in the wall of a temple, a water spout was often given some form of magical protection in Ancient Egypt. A rearing cobra, such as seen here, could symbolise the *uraeus* that protected the pharaoh, or the water could flow from between the paws of a lion.
[DP103892]

it was this design which was approved by the committee, with one anonymous member quoted as saying '…a bit over the top, but does it matter? Let's go for it!'

Building began in 1986 and at the beginning of 1988 Richard Kindersley and others began carving the frieze of 10 gods which ran across the main façade facing the car park. From left to right, they are Khnum, Ra-Horakhty, Thoth, Sobek, Bastet, Osiris, Nefertem, Seth, Heryshef, and Neith (Figs 126 and 127). The figure of Neith is simply carved, but moving across the frieze to the left, the deities are partially and then fully coloured, and finally gilded in places. The changes are marked by zigzag-carved lines based on 'break lines' in architectural drawings. Seth was originally carved holding an *ankh* – the faint outline of the *ankh* can still be seen behind the drill. However, Pollard thought that, since it was a DIY store and stories were circulating within the media at the time which claimed that the ancient Egyptians might have had electrical tools since they drilled holes through hard

stone, which it was thought could only be achieved by drilling at very high speed, then why not equip Seth with an 'Ankh & Decker' power drill? The *ankh* was duly recarved as a power drill.

Each deity had their name inscribed in hieroglyphs in a cartouche above their heads, and in its English form at the base of the figure. In a subtle typographical joke Kindersley suggested a typeface for these names from a group of fonts known as 'Egyptian', even though there is nothing overtly Egyptian about their form. The size of the wall, 29m long by 6.5m high, and the proportions of the figures meant that there was space at the right-hand side which needed to be filled, and it was decided to do this with a panel giving the name of the company, Flaxyard, and the date of construction in hieroglyphs. There were two options for the company name – to spell it out phonetically or as pictograms (hieroglyphs of the objects named). Both methods were employed by the Ancient Egyptians, with foreign names usually written

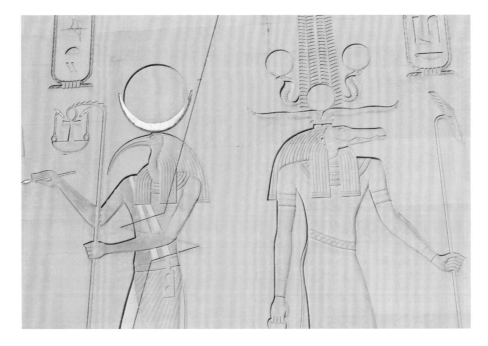

Fig 126
Part of the frieze on the main façade of Homebase showing Thoth on the left and Sobek on the right. The staff held by Thoth, and the symbols on it, are read as 'All Life and Power for 100,000 years', Sobek was often depicted as a crocodile crouched on a shrine or altar, and became linked with the sun god Ra. [DP103881]

phonetically, but the decision was taken
to use the hieroglyphs for 'flax' and 'yard'
(technically a courtyard rather than the
measure of length) for the name, preserving
the English word order. Numerals for the
date underneath represent 1 thousand,
9 hundreds, 8 tens and 8 ones. There was
much discussion between Pollard and
Kindersley about which gods would be
shown and how, but the final decisions
were taken on aesthetic grounds rather
than Egyptological ones. Some were for
practical reasons as well. The wall is broken
on its right-hand side by a double door
to a generator room and whichever deity
was shown at this point would have to be
seated. As it happened, it was the goddess
Neith, balanced in the composition by a
seated Osiris in the centre, and Ra-Horakhty
at the left. The façade was constructed
from Lepine limestone especially imported
from France because of its high quality and
fine carving potential, and the cobra water
spouts were each carved from a ¾ ton
block of St Bees sandstone. The design of
the rearing and open-mouthed cobras was
based, according to Kindersley, on Ancient
Egyptian examples found near the Step
Pyramid of Djoser.

As the building neared completion in 1988,
plans were well advanced for its opening.
A ceramic sphinx, about 150cm long, had
been commissioned to stand inside the
store. Booklets were to be produced for
adults and children showing each deity on a
separate page and with notes about them.
Those for children were to have been made
from actual papyrus, which was actually
sourced, cut and thonged. Special offers on
tourist flights with Egypt Air had been set up
to offer to customers. Then, 10 days before
the opening was due to take place, the
chairman of Sainsbury's, Sir John Sainsbury
(now Lord Sainsbury of Preston Candover),
arrived unannounced and ordered that
many of the pillars and columns be pulled

down, including a v-shaped group of large
Corinthian columns forming the entrance
to the car park, some decorative features
painted over, including the originally
polychrome Egyptian columns, and that
the winged solar disc over the entrance
be removed and replaced with a large
Homebase sign.

These actions, apart from causing a widely
shared feeling of betrayal among those
working on the project, are difficult to
understand. A statement subsequently issued
by the chairman claimed that the decision
to demolish the 'Corinthian' columns was
taken by the Homebase board, and that
only elements which were 'inappropriately
dominant and overwhelming' or, like the
Egyptian colonnade in the car park, 'not
considered to be in keeping with the
Homebase style' had been altered. It also
claimed that, 'We had little opportunity to
influence the design of the building. Once
it had been built we felt that its decorative
features over dominated the Homebase
trading style.'

Fig 127
The gods Seth (on
the left) and Heryshef
(on the right) depicted
on the frieze. As well as
symbolising destructive
forces, Seth accompanied
the sun god in his boat
journey through the
underworld at night
and speared the Apep
serpent to protect Ra.
In Ancient Egyptian,
Heryshef's name means
'He who is upon his lake',
but its derivation and
meaning are uncertain.
[DP103879]

These comments are surprising, not only in view of the fact that the design was chosen from several considered by the company's architectural committee, but also that a scale model of the building was displayed for around eight weeks in the entrance to the company's offices. This would presumably not have been the case unless they considered that it was in keeping with the company's trading style, although the architectural critic Colin Amery, chairman of the design committee and personal architectural advisor to Sir John Sainsbury, apparently claimed to have only seen the designs briefly. It is also interesting to note that the Corinthian columns, approximately 9m high, were intended by Pollard to carry a Homebase sign, so that it could have been seen far enough along the Warwick Road to enable motorists to change lanes in time to turn into the store.

The Warwick Road Homebase is fascinating, both as an example of the use of the Ancient Egyptian style in modern buildings and of the controversy that this can produce. The Hoover Factory (see p 174) and other highly decorated factories built during the interwar years by Wallis Gilbert and Partners, which also incorporated Egyptian elements, were criticised for vulgarity, novelty seeking and 'façadism', the superficial use of design elements on the front of a building. The 1991 issue of *Architectural Design* quoted earlier had predicted that Pollard would become 'the most Sincerely Hated Architect At Work', and this may have reflected an earlier editorial and news item in the *Architects' Journal* in June 1988. Both these were harshly critical of Pollard himself and the building. His previous work, including the distinctive Marco Polo House, was described as having attracted 'the business media as well as hitherto discriminating clients and critics'. The Homebase building, like its predecessor, was felt to

...rely on precedent, but in a way that betrays neither learning nor art. The plagiarism [probably a reference to the glazed wall on Warwick Road based on James Stirling's Staatsgalerie in Stuttgart] is mechanical, the 'wit' heavy-handed ... The façades are mere graphics, the interiors mundane ... His [Pollard's] buildings are advertising, not architecture.[120]

The news item, headed *Manqué Business*, described Pollard as 'an architect *manqué*' who 'insists on designing his own developments', and the Homebase building as 'a structure that is more of a built drawing than a piece of architecture', 'a profoundly depressing little structure' and one of a number of 'debased and bankrupt pastiches' produced by the then current revival of architectural decoration. Both pieces, interestingly, also mentioned the 'mundane' and 'interminable' openplan interior.[121]

One response to these criticisms would be that 'advertising', or 'publicity generating self-promotion' as it was put in *Manqué Business*, is entirely appropriate for a building which is not only a retail outlet, but a DIY one aimed at the public rather than trade customers. It could also be said that expecting the interior of a DIY superstore (or any other sort of supermarket) to be anything other than functional seems unrealistic. *Architectural Design*, having predicted that Pollard would become 'the most Sincerely Hated Architect At Work',[122] went on logically enough to describe the building itself as 'The most sincerely hated building in London'. However, it also conceded that it was 'better than one might think', acknowledging that the figures of the gods were based on research at the British Museum, even if the writer of the article did mistakenly think that several of them, and not just Seth, held 'various equipment on sale within – including a power drill'. Ian Pollard himself has called the Homebase building 'populist architecture' and 'something that people would like'. He also commented at the time in an article in *Building Design*, 'People are already using the building as a landmark to direct people. The building attracts people – and if that isn't what retailing is about I don't know what is.'[123]

The use of Ancient Egyptian elements in the building was not superficial. The images of the gods were researched in museums, not simply taken from readily available published sources. The ceramic sphinx, which stood inside the building for a single day, drew on an example in the British Museum and the sphinxes by Cleopatra's Needle, which themselves were modelled on an example in the collection of the 4th Duke of Northumberland, Lord Prudhoe and the hieroglyphs are accurate and legible. Ian Pollard, in choosing the Ancient Egyptian style, intended to express his belief that modern buildings, even commercial ones, should be conceived as long lasting. The Corinthian columns, allegedly criticised by Sir John Sainsbury as incompatible with the Ancient Egyptian elements, were chosen on pragmatic grounds of cost and time as it would not have been possible to have Egyptian-style columns of such a size specially produced. Neither Pollard nor Kindersley had problems with this, however, as during the Graeco-Roman period in Egypt, particularly in Alexandria, Classical and Egyptian architecture co-existed.

It is difficult not to detect the taint of snobbery in criticisms of the Warwick Road Homebase; cultural – in the implication that the aims of architecture and commerce are incompatible (see p 28), and that popular buildings lack architectural substance, and professional – since Ian Pollard is a designer and developer rather than an architect.

(The *Architects' Journal* began its editorial by pointedly drawing attention to the fact that 'Ian Pollard didn't finish architecture school', but a few paragraphs later could still say, 'Whether or not Pollard is an architect is irrelevant.') In a revealing phrase the *Architects' Journal* spoke of 'references to the work of the man who is currently master of the Egyptian coved cornice – James Stirling'. It went on to talk of the 'mechanical-looking reproduction of Stirling's Staatsgalerie banded masonry walling' and then described the curving glass wall to the north of the building as 'the most shameless and direct Stirlingesque detail'. Certainly, as Pollard himself has made clear, the glass wall was deliberately intended to echo the façade of James Stirling's Neue Staatsgalerie in Stuttgart, but much of its attraction to Pollard was that it was done at a fraction of the cost of its inspiration. Pollard may have been felt to be guilty of *lèse majesté* towards a pillar of the architectural establishment, but his greater crime may have been creating popular buildings. The *Journal* described Marco Polo House as 'popular not only with the public, but even with certain architectural pundits' and, as previously mentioned, his work as attracting 'hitherto discriminating clients and critics'. In a rather nervous tone, the editorial ended by describing Pollard as presenting 'a real challenge to architectural values – and standards' before going on to say that architects 'must recognise the needs he seeks to satisfy but must find more attractive, appropriate and profound means of doing so'.

It is one of the hallmarks of an exotic style, like the Ancient Egyptian, that its use may be popular or unpopular, but can probably never leave people indifferent. Londoners and visitors passing along the Warwick Road can make up their own minds.

The Hoover Factory

Western Avenue,
London
UB6 8DW

Built only three years after the clearly Ancient Egyptian-styled Carreras factory (now Greater London House, see pp 152–6), the Hoover Factory is a fascinating contrast in the use of Egyptianising elements. Between 1927 and 1935, the firm of Wallis, Gilbert and Partners were responsible for designing 10 so-called 'Fancy' factories of which nine were built before economic recession meant that they became too expensive. Despite its name, chosen initially to create an impression of established solidity, the firm began as the practice of one man, the architect Thomas Wallis. In a study of his work,[124] Joan Skinner dates Wallis's first use of Egyptian-influenced ornament in his designs to around 1918 in the works of GEC at Witton in Birmingham (see p 256), and also refers to its use, around the same time, in the offices of his own practice. Paradoxically, however, there is a lack of overtly Egyptian-style elements in Wallis's Fancy factories when compared with a building such as Greater London House. It has also been suggested (for example by the Egyptologist Dominic Montserrat) that all these buildings and others, with their emphasis on the use of natural light, were influenced by the results of excavations at Tell el Amarna, site of the capital of the pharaoh Akhenaten. Compared, however, to the work of a modern architect like John Outram, designer of the Temple of Storms pumping station, who is explicit about his use of Ancient Egyptian elements, there is a frustrating lack of material for interwar buildings to confirm how, when and why Egyptian influences were used.

In 1916, Thomas Wallis closed a practice in his own name and left a post in the Architects and Surveyors division of HM Office of Works and Public Buildings to set up Wallis, Gilbert and Partner. There never seems to have been a Gilbert, and until Frank Cox was recruited in 1917, no partner either. (Later, the practice became Wallis, Gilbert and Partners.) Wallis, over 40 at the time and married with several children, had taken a risky decision to work on the design of factories with Trussed Concrete Steel (Truscon), the British outpost of an American company formed to promote a system of concrete reinforcement developed and patented in America by the Kahn brothers, and their Kahn Daylight System of factory design. Initially, because such systems were relatively new, Truscon itself tendered for commissions, appointed architects and dealt with contractors. Wallis, whose offices were in the same building as Truscon, rapidly became a specialist in its use.

Professionally Wallis was taking a risk since the design of factories lacked status within his profession, and the use of an architect was believed to be viewed as an unnecessary extravagance by manufacturers. Set against this, the Kahn system 'Model' factories were quick to design and build, fire resistant, had large and uncluttered interior spaces and good ventilation, their glass-filled external wall spaces gave them good natural lighting, and compared to existing factories they had good working conditions for staff. Another key factor in their success was that during the First World War new factories and extensions needed a government license and had to use as little timber and steel as possible. Concrete, however, was not in short supply, giving the Kahn reinforced concrete system an advantage.

Around 1927, Wallis began designing the series of factories that were to become known as the 'Fancy' designs. Key elements were their use of coloured decoration, often in faience, novel decorative elements and motifs in addition to familiar ones from the Classical tradition, and elaborate and impressive main entrances incorporating landscaping. From the start, they seem to have been popular with the companies who commissioned them, attractive to the workforces, and popular with the general public because of their bold and colourful design. Wallis himself believed strongly that well-designed façades on main routes, such as the Western Avenue on which the Hoover and Firestone Factories were situated, were powerful advertisements for the firms that built them (Fig 128). The same factors seem to have made them equally unpopular with many in Wallis's profession and with architectural critics. Most of this criticism was directed at the façades, and the planning and layout of the factory interiors themselves was widely praised. The general implication of the criticism seems to have been that factories, as utilitarian buildings, could be modern, hygienic, efficient and pleasant to work in, but should have the decency to know their place and not aspire to the status of Architecture. The main accusation thrown against the Fancy factories was that of 'façadism'.

Such criticisms ignore the fact that to Wallis, the façades were an integral part of the overall design. In her book on Wallis's factories, *Form and Fancy*, Joan Skinner suggests that the façade, with its monumental scale, was not only intended to give an impression of permanence but also to function in the same way as an Egyptian temple with its processional way leading up to it and a pylon-flanked entrance leading to the temple proper, where the rituals of religion were carried out on an industrial scale supported by processing areas and storehouses. However, while it is tempting to draw parallels between the production-line process in factories, the way that a succession of rooms and courtyards in an Ancient Egyptian temple lead from the entrance to the sanctuary of the god, and the fact that these temples were surrounded by storerooms and workshops, this may be reading in more than the modern architect intended. For the analogy to hold in the well-lit factories of Wallis, any comparison would have to be with the sun temples of Amarna rather than the classic Ancient Egyptian temple, which became darker as the sanctuary was approached.

Fig 128
The Hoover Factory is distinguished not only by its design, but by the striking use of colour; white enhanced by green window frames and blue, orange and black detailing.
[DP103896]

Fig 129
The façade of the Firestone Factory was dominated by engaged columns with elaborate polychrome decoration on their capitals and bases. These features, particularly the extensive use of colour, suggest Egyptian influences on Wallis's design. [J930087]

The Hoover Factory does not have such clearly Egyptian elements as Wallis's now demolished Firestone Factory (Fig 129), but the columned façade is framed by slightly battered sides with a reeded edge, both suggesting, rather than imitating, the shape of temple pylons with torus mouldings along their edges (Fig 130). The strong clean lines and the use of vivid coloured faience on a white background are again suggestive of Ancient Egypt, especially at the base of the façade sides where curled elements are flanked by red and green banded faience. Whether or not, as Skinner suggests, these are intended to represent the curled ram's horns associated with the god Amun is less certain. Other elements of the building, however, especially the doorways and railings, owe much more to the Art Deco movement in which Ancient Egyptian elements were only one of several influences.

A total of 10 buildings were constructed on the Hoover site between 1931 and 1937, originally for finishing, repairing, servicing and packaging vacuum cleaners made or part-assembled elsewhere in London and Canada (to avoid punitive import duties). Full manufacturing began in 1934. The site was vacated by Hoover in 1987 when manufacturing was relocated to Cambuslang in Scotland and the head office to Merthyr Tydfil in Wales. The site was redeveloped in the 1980s and the rear of the factory became a Tesco supermarket in an Art Deco style. The original No. 1 building, restored by Lyons, Sleeman and Hoare, remains offices. The Hoover Factory is on Western Avenue in Perivale, not far from Perivale tube station.

Fig 130
One of the towers of the Hoover Factory. Wallis used flanking towers in a number of his industrial buildings. While these may suggest the pylon form typical of Ancient Egyptian temples, the proportions of the factory fronts are quite different. [DP103906]

Kensal Green Cemetery

Kensal Green, founded in 1832 and more correctly known as the General Cemetery of All Souls, was the first, and is among the most splendid, of London's seven great Victorian cemeteries (Fig 131). Today it is unique as the only one still being run by a joint stock company, the General Cemetery Company. It was one of the most socially desirable cemeteries due to its royal connections, and boasts an impressive collection of Egyptian-style monuments. Many of its other monuments, not in this style, commemorate people with connections to Egypt, and the diversity of these connections remind us that the use of the Egyptian style in architecture and interiors is only the most visible indication of the influence of Ancient Egypt on British culture.

George III had, as was usual for the time, a large family, with six sons and five daughters, but his relations with them were strained – possibly because of the effects of the hereditary porphyria from which he suffered. This, and the bickering over protocol at William IV's Windsor funeral, eventually led his youngest son, Prince Augustus Frederick, Duke of Sussex (and patron of the pioneer Egyptologist Giovanni Belzoni) to take the unusual step of choosing to be buried at Kensal Green on his death in 1843. He was followed in 1848 by his sister Princess Sophia, George's fifth daughter, and finally by Prince George, Duke of Cambridge (a grandson of George III) in 1904. For the social elite of Georgian and Victorian England proximity to the royal family, even in death, was highly desirable. Indeed, it was probably considered especially desirable since plots were sold with perpetual freehold guaranteeing in theory that those able to afford it would enjoy their status for all eternity, as if in some modern version of the royal necropoli of Ancient Egypt.

Harrow Road,
London
W10 4RA

GENERAL CEMETERY, KENSAL GREEN.

Fig 131
Kensal Green Cemetery in 1847, showing the Ducrow monument. Before their trees matured, the buildings of the garden cemeteries were a much more prominent feature. [AA074857]

Kensal Green Station is nearest the West Gate entrance but the layout of the cemetery is best appreciated by entering through the main entrance (where a photocopied map of the cemetery is available on request), further along Harrow Road to the left. Centre Avenue is to the right of the entrance and not far along it on the right is a pink granite obelisk. Uninscribed obelisks are common in English cemeteries but this one is unusual in being 20ft high, and the monument underneath it records the death in 1855 of the founder of the world's first rock band, which once performed at the Egyptian Hall.

Joseph Richardson, a Cumbrian stonemason, discovered in 1827 that the rock of Skiddaw, one of the Lake District peaks, could be tuned by chipping and shaping to produce musical notes when struck. For 13 years he worked to produce an instrument with a five-octave range, which was known as the Rock Harmonicon. It was played like a xylophone using sticks with round padded heads and can still be seen today in the Keswick Museum in Cumbria. He and his three sons toured with the instrument in the North of England and then began to perform at venues in London, including in 1846 the Egyptian Hall in Piccadilly (see p 18). Their repertoire ranged from Strauss waltzes to overtures and arias by Mozart, Handel, Rossini and Bellini. The 'Original Monstre [sic] Rock Band', as it was described on the cover of the programme for a performance in Barnet, north London, was an immediate success. The original harmonicon or lithophone was supplemented by steel bars, Swiss bells, drums and other percussion instruments and became Richardson & Sons Rock, Bell and Steel Band. A Royal Command Performance in 1848 before Queen Victoria, Prince Albert, and British and foreign nobility was followed by two more, and further touring in Britain and the continent.

Following Joseph's death in 1855, his sons Joseph, John (d 1886) and Robert (d 1870) continued touring, but on the eve of an American tour Robert died of pneumonia and after that the concerts were abandoned. Only Samuel Richardson, who died in 1888 aged 63, is actually buried under the obelisk, Joseph himself being buried under a 4ft 9in white headstone in plot 47 near Owen Jones, but Samuel's monument has an inscription in Joseph's memory. It is unclear exactly what the relationship between Samuel and Joseph Richardson was.

A little further along Centre Avenue is a Classical-style marble pedestal monument on a grey granite plinth surrounded by a privet hedge. It commemorates John Robinson McClean, a civil engineer who worked on the Suez Canal, was also first president of the Institute of Civil Engineers and an MP, and his astronomer son Frank.

To the left, on South Avenue, almost opposite the McClean monument, can be seen the tomb of William Makepeace Thackeray (1811–63). Best known as the author of *Vanity Fair,* he travelled to Egypt in 1844, visiting the painter J F Lewis in Cairo and recording his travels in a book, *From Cornhill to Grand Cairo* (Fig 132). To find Thackeray's tomb, look for a low raised red-brick tomb. Thackeray's is the plain flat stone ledger tomb next to it with metal rails.

Carry on along Centre Avenue for a few metres until it branches into three. At this point, as the cemetery begins to broaden out, probably the least confusing way of seeing the rest of it is to return to Centre Avenue after locating individual monuments, even if this involves some backtracking.

Just down the left-hand branch (South Branch Avenue) is the monument of Owen Jones and his two sisters. Look for an elaborate columned Gothic-style monument

OCTOBER 20, 1855. ILLUSTRATED TIMES. 325

WILLIAM MAKEPEACE THACKERAY.

Mr. Thackeray sailed for New York last Saturday, the 13th inst. He is to lecture on the "Four Georges,"—(not on the Kings' only, but on their respective eras)—and expects to return to his own country next summer. Meanwhile, we present our readers with a portrait of him taken from the best extant, that by S. Laurence; and we accompany it by a memoir, written by a literary man who knows him personally very well, and who writes with no reserve except that which s properly due to a living writer.—Ed.

Mr. Thackeray is of Saxon descent, and of a landed family settled from the earliest period in the county of York. From that county's families came Swift, and Cleveland, and Dr. Garth, and Pope's mother, and Bentley, so that it has produced its share of the humourists and satirists of England. The Reverend Richard Thackeray, rector of Hadley, in Middlesex, was the novelist's grandfather. His father was in the service of the East India Company, and he was born in Calcutta. He was educated, first at the Charter House, afterwards at Cambridge; and on attaining his majority, succeeded, I believe, to a good fortune.

Mr. Thackeray's bent towards art has always been as strong, or stronger, than his bent towards literature. He knows art and artists well, and loves them and their pursuit. One can see that, and all his personal tastes, in his books—which is the reason his books are so *real*. For, as I shall observe presently, it is conspicuously *reality* which constitutes the merit of his fiction—as of all fiction that is not hollow and untrue. Rembrandt, they say, learned to paint light and shade because they were so vividly exhibited in the room of his father's mill. And just as the romances of Europe all originated in its actual history, so life will always supply better subjects from its real truths than the most lively and vagrant fancy can inver t.

Having studied art and travelled in his youth, Thackeray found himself drawn to letters by that combination of instinct within and accident without — which somehow brings all able men to their proper sphere sooner or later. When he first entered on literary life, poor old Maginn was the great gun of magazines and journals, and I dare say Thackeray looked up to him with the admiration due to scholarhship and fame. Of Maginn I cannot even say *vidi tantum*, for he had gone "early to bed" (as Lockhart writes in his epitaph), in the little church-yard of Walton-on-Thames, while I was yet a bungler over the tougher bits of Cicero's orations. But I can understand that he was a charming though dangerous companion,—for he talked and drank like the old school in their—

———",Tavern hours of mighty wits,
Our elders and our betters."

I know stories about Thackeray's kindness to him which he would be the las man to allow to be published, but which please me like a bit of "Vanity Fair" or "Pendennis."

Thackeray then became connected with "Fraser's Magazine," where he wrote for many years,—wrote likewise (reviews and fancy chiefly) for the "Times," and elsewhere. He served his apprenticeship to Fame like most of those whom that goddess intends to patronise for any extended period. He was some 12 or 15 years writing before he became famous. No doubt, there are people now who pretend to have thought wonderfully of him all along. But the fact is, he was not famous, or generally read, till about 1847, when "Vanity Fair" made its hit. His "Chronicle of the Dream"—a comic poem quite equal to Hood, and far beyond the range of Anti-Jacobins, Peter Pindars, Colmans, Smiths, and such like—scarcely excited the commonest notice. How many wonderful "last new novels" glittered and crackled (and disappeared) with three times three, during the years when the great philosophical novelist was obscurely preparing for his substantial renown! Yet, turn to those volumes of "Fraser"—read the "Barry Lyndons," "Yellow-Plush Papers," "Hoggarty Diamonds," and so forth; they are quite worthy of him in sense, observation, humour, and light, commanding vigour of touch. There are many capital critical papers, too,—quite worthy of the author of the "Humourists." His travels—published under his favourite pseudonym of Michael Angelo Titmarsh—were, indeed, considerably successful. The "Cornhill to Cairo" is the best man-of-the-worldly and modern view of the East which we possess,—but it never attained a tithe of the success of the "Crescent and the Cross." Thackeray had to bide his time. Canting people said he was bitter, and dull people said he was "slow." Of the cleverer section, some feared his penetration, and some dreaded his rise; some disliked him because he steered clear of cliques, and some hated him because he was a gentleman.

The "Snob Papers" in "Punch" first showed to a wide section of the English people that a satirist was among them such as they had not had (in prose, a least) since Henry Fielding went to his grave in the Protestant churchyard in Lisbon. The leading idea of these papers —(the only things ever published in "Punch," except Jerrold's and the "Song of the Shirt," which will live in our literature)—is the exposure of the servility to rank, wealth, and fashion, which characterises the English middle-classes. He gave a new meaning to the word "snob," and added a new word of description to our social vocabulary. Like the word "bore," "snob" expresses (thanks to this satirist) what no other word in our language does. It implies a mean, cowardly, servile form of character, quite indescribable otherwise, except in detail. Of old, it simply meant a low fellow—what the French call a *manant*, and university-men a "cad." Thackeray extended and deepened the meaning,—made it quite another affair, and a very subtle word too. A man

"WILLIAM MAKEPEACE THACKERAY, AUTHOR OF "VANITY FAIR."

Fig 132
A newspaper portrait of William Makepeace Thackeray. Writing under the pseudonym of 'Michael Angelo Titmarsh', William Thackeray suggested in *From Cornhill to Grand Cairo* that if the British government did not want Cleopatra's Needle 'I wish they would offer the Trafalgar Square Pillar to the Egyptians; and that both of the huge ugly monsters were lying in the dirt … side by side'.
[Photo © Victoria and Albert Museum, London]

on the left of the path and then count 14 graves along from it. Jones was author of the highly influential book on design and colour theory *The Grammar of Ornament*, which featured Ancient Egyptian designs drawn from material in the British Museum, and he designed the Egyptian Court at Crystal Palace with Joseph Bonomi Jnr. Jones himself designed the ornate Ancient Greek style marble headstone above his grave on which he is described as 'Owen Jones Arch[t]'.

Return to the spot where Central Avenue forks and this time take the right-hand branch (North Branch Avenue). Follow it and look for the tall columned Graeco-Roman-style Collett monument on the left surrounded by stone railings. To the left of this is the monument of John Gordon of Newton, Aberdeenshire (1802–40), usually tactfully described as a West Indian 'landowner' (Caribbean slaves were not fully emancipated until 1833). The elaborate monument is very similar to an illustration of the tomb of the Bouchée family in Père Lachaise Cemetery in *Views of Paris* by Augustus Pugin, who became a director of the General Cemetery Company. On a stepped plinth a short central column supports a funerary urn. Four heavy tapered pillars support a pedimented canopy in the centre of which is a relief of a butterfly, a symbol of resurrection. On the corners of the canopy are four acroteria in the form of heads wearing Ancient Egyptian *nemes* headcloths (Fig 133).

Continue along North Branch Avenue to the point where a small gate on the right connects to Harrow Road. Opposite the gate is a splendid monument with a tall square plinth on which stands a

Fig 133
Apart from the pharaonic heads on the corners of the canopy pediment, the style and imagery of the Gordon monument are solidly, even heavily Classical.
[AA97/01160]

slightly larger than life robed female statue representing an allegory of Faith. Now rather battered, she originally carried a cross in the crook of her left arm and raised heavenwards a right arm which held a gas jet to illuminate the monument. Below the figure of Faith two large cherubs or *putti*, one holding a quill pen, hover above a relief portrait of a woman in an oval

frame. Below the portrait frame is a relief artist's palette and brushes. At the bottom of the plinth, in huge letters (originally of bronze) is the inscription 'TO HER'. The woman so commemorated is the popular artist Mme Emma Elizabeth Soyer who died after a miscarriage aged only 29. She was the wife of Alexis Benôit Soyer, chef for 13 years at the Reform Club, who created the sumptuous dessert *Crème d'Egypte à l'Ibrahim Pasha* at its banquet for Ibrahim Pasha in 1846, and also designed her monument. Alexis' inscription is on the back of the monument. Also buried there are Francois Simonou, Emma's stepfather and mentor, and Lady Isabella Watts, Simonou's grandniece, who launched the first English submarine.

Return to where Central Avenue forks and this time take the centre branch. On the left is the Ashbury mausoleum, in the Egyptian style with battered sides, a cavetto cornice and a winged solar disc over the doorway. There are a number of other similar monuments in the cemetery such as the Dredge mausoleum (Fig 134).

Fig 134
The Dredge mausoleum is a good example of what could be called 'Pattern Book Egyptian', having battered sides and a cavetto cornice but no detailed Egyptian-style decoration.
[DP103919]

However, some, while using Ancient Egyptian architectural elements, lack any of the decorative and symbolic elements associated with Egypt, such as the winged solar disc, and sometimes incorporate non-Egyptian elements, as in the mausoleum of the Duke of Cambridge (see p 185).

Centre Avenue continues until it reaches the beginning of the Quadrant. To the left of the Avenue, on the corner of the south-east section of the Quadrant, is the family tomb of Andrew Ducrow (Fig 135). Often described merely as a 'circus owner', he was known to his contemporaries as 'the Colossus of Equestrians', and was described by William Wallett, Queen Victoria's jester, as 'the Shakespeare of the Sawdust'.[125] He was legendary for his performances, especially *The Courier of St Petersburg* during which he performed the *Grand Écart,* controlling five horses at the gallop and straddling three of them with one foot on each outside horse while they were in motion. Later in the routine up to four more horses were introduced, with Ducrow catching the reins as they passed between his legs, finally controlling up to nine horses at once. He was also a rope dancer, and performed *poses plastiques* – striking poses often drawn from Classical mythology, art, or statues. One of his most successful tableaux, *Raphael's Dream*, or *The Mummy and Study of Living Pictures* included impersonations of a mummy and several Ancient Egyptian statues.

The monument was originally built in 1837 for Ducrow's first wife Margaret, and is said to have cost £3,000 when it was set up, the equivalent of £150,000 in today's terms. An extraordinary mix of styles, it combines Ancient Egyptian elements with traditional Christian and Classical funeral motifs and personal symbols. It was designed by his stage designer George Danson and built by the mason John Cusworth, and

is said to have been cited as an example of monumental vulgarity even in its own day.[126] Building and alterations continued for several years and Ducrow left £800 in his will for additional alterations and £200 for its perpetual upkeep, including flowers and shrubbery.

The monument is flanked on its corners by sphinxes on pedestals. At the four corners of the monument, palm leaf capital columns support a cavetto cornice topped by a Classical pediment with shell-shaped

Fig 135
The railings around the Ducrow monument in Kensal Green Cemetery feature funerary motifs of wreaths, swags, and inverted torches.
[DP103912]

acroteria at each corner and carved beehives at the centre of the pediment. Above the pediment is a two-tiered tapering pedestal, with a torus moulding around the top edge of the bottom pedestal and a large stone vase decorated with horses' heads on top of the upper tier. Below the cornice and between the columns are sloping Egyptian-style torus mouldings, and the door facing the paths has a torus moulding round it, a winged solar disc and *uraeus* above it, and inverted torches on either side at the base. Over the entrance, a phoenix supports a tablet with the inscription 'The Family Tomb of Andrew Ducrow Erected Anno Domini 1837'. Above the cornice, built into a Greek-style pediment, a relief panel shows Genius weeping over the ashes of her favourite son, and the masks of Comedy and Tragedy, while a riderless Pegasus ascends to Heaven. The motif of Genius weeping was repeated on a plate on Ducrow's outer coffin, of oak covered in purple velvet and studded with silver-gilt nails. Elsewhere on the monument angels flank inscribed tablets.

Tablets on the south side commemorate his first wife Margaret, his second Louisa and her remarriage to John Hay, her daughter, also called Louisa, and her husband Surgeon Major Henry Wilson. A single tablet on the north side records Ducrow and Andrew, his posthumous son by his second wife. In guides that mention the monument (such as Culbertson & Randall's *Permanent Londoners*), a phrase from the inscriptions is sometimes quoted which suggests an enormous sense of self-importance on the part of Ducrow: 'This tomb erected by genius for the reception of its own remains.'

In fact, although the epitaph was originally drafted for Ducrow by C A Somerset, who wrote the dialogue for many of his productions, the final version on the monument was revised by his widow Louisa and reads:

Within this tomb
erected by genius for the reception
of its own remains are deposited those of

Andrew Ducrow

It goes on to eulogise him, and concludes '…and to commemorate such virtues his afflicted widow has erected this tribute'.

Ducrow died of a stroke in 1842 aged only 48. His youngest son Andrew died in 1863 at Rangariri in New Zealand during the largest battle between Maori and European forces, hence the crossed banners, shako and sabre under the inscription commemorating him. On the same side of the monument, and separate from it but within the metal railings which surround it, is a broken column, a traditional funerary symbol. On the broken fragments are a stone hat and gloves. In his will, Ducrow left instructions for 'two Marble truncated or broken Obelisks or Columns … the column on the right dedicated to me and that to the left to my dear deceased Wife Margaret Ducrow'. The hat and gloves on Ducrow's column are believed by his biographer Saxon to be replicas of those worn by Ducrow in *The Royal Cotillion of Days Gone By, or The Court Beauties of Charles II*, one of the last pageants in which he appeared.

Diagonally opposite the Ducrow monument, on the other side of the Avenue, is the Egyptian-style family mausoleum of Sir George Farrant who died in 1844. It is interesting for its mix of Ancient Egyptian and contemporary elements, such as the family coat of arms and reversed torches on the side facing the Avenue, and also for the quasi-Egyptian 'solar disc' and other decorative elements on the cavetto cornice. The peculiar form of the winged head in the centre of the upper cornice suggests that Denon's *Voyages* was a design source (Fig 136). Farrant was a wealthy barrister and magistrate, and Deputy Lieutenant for the county of Middlesex, who owned land and property in Kent and Lincolnshire, but had no apparent connection with Egypt.

Continue past the Ducrow monument towards All Souls Chapel, (more generally known as the Anglican Chapel to distinguish it from the Dissenter's Chapel at the eastern end of the cemetery), but at the crossroads in the centre of the Quadrant take the left path and follow it across the curving path which forms the outside of the Quadrant. Not far along, on the right, is the massive mausoleum of the Dunlop family and just past that a fairly small Portland stone monument with a rectangular base topped by a pyramid. This belongs to John Shae Perring, a civil engineer who wrote *On the Engineering of the Ancient Egyptians* (1835), and subsequently went to Egypt to assist Galloway Bey, the manager of public works for Muhammad Ali. While in Egypt, Perring helped Colonel Howard Vyse to survey and explore the Pyramids of Giza and Perring later wrote the three-part *Pyramids of Egypt* in 1839.

Back at the crossroads, continue to the left along Central Avenue to the far side of the Quadrant. Here, on the right of the slope that leads up to the Anglican Chapel is the large low ledger tomb of Prince Augustus Frederick, Duke of Sussex, surrounded by squat tapered bollards which originally had chains between them. The sixth son of King George III and Queen Charlotte, he had no realistic chance of ever succeeding to the throne and solved the problem that this has always posed younger princes by becoming a patron of the arts and sciences. He was partly educated on the continent, and after being taught by a Masonic professor at Göttingen was initiated as a Freemason into the Lodge of the Glorious Truth in Berlin in 1798. This may have influenced his political views, which were considered

remarkably liberal for a prince but which led to him being unwelcome at Court. He was instrumental in the foundation of the United Grand Lodge of England in 1813, and through Freemasonry had connections with both Giovanni Belzoni and the architect Sir John Soane.

To the left of the Avenue is a group of tombs including the impressive Ancient Egyptian-style granite mausoleum of Lieutenant Colonel Charles Seton Guthrie (1805–74), his wife Sophia and Florence

Fig 136
By the time Sir George Farrant died, archaeologically accurate Egyptian-style buildings were being built, such as Marshall's Mill (see p 265), but his mausoleum has more in common with those from the Regency period.
[DP103914]

Ingliss, probably a married sister (Fig 137). It has lotus bud pillars, a torus moulding round the door, a cavetto cornice and a winged solar disc flanked by *uraei* wearing the white crown of Upper Egypt above the doorway, which faces the Anglican Chapel. Guthrie served in the Bengal Engineers between 1828 and 1857, the year of the Indian Mutiny, and assembled an important collection of Mughal jade, including a number of objects from the imperial household which may have been acquired during or after the sack of Delhi. His rank was not particularly senior, and although he may have been of independent means, this would often imply a titled background. Guthrie may have paid for his monument, which would have been expensive, from the sale of his collection, much of which was bought by the South Kensington Museum (now the V&A) in 1868. The Guthrie mausoleum makes a very brief appearance in a funeral scene filmed at Kensal Green in the 1980 mummy film *The Awakening*, based on Bram Stoker's book *The Jewel of Seven Stars*.

On the slope leading up to the chapel, just below Terrace Avenue, is the monument of Sir Ernest Cassel, in the form of an Ancient Egyptian pylon with a cavetto cornice and winged solar disc with *uraei* at the front of the cornice (Fig 138). Cassel was one of the great private financiers who bankrolled governments in the late 19th and early 20th centuries. He was a founder of the National Bank of Egypt, played a major role in the development of the country's industry and agriculture, even if this was largely for the benefit of European shareholders, and was fond of spending his winters in Egypt.

The catacombs under the Grade I listed Anglican Chapel are not normally open to

Fig 137
The Guthrie mausoleum in Kensal Green Cemetery and the smaller but equally elaborate Egyptian-style monument of Wilson Pasha in Hampstead Cemetery (see p 156) were manufactured in granite by the Scottish firm of MacDonald Field. [© Chris Elliott]

the public but can be visited on alternate Sundays on the tours run by the Friends of Kensal Green Cemetery. Here, in whitewashed passages originally lit from above by glass pavement lights and lined with rush matting to deaden footsteps – now gloomy and echoing since repaving after bomb damage during the Second World War covered the glass lights – rows of coffins line arched vaults from floor to ceiling behind rusting grilles and engraved slabs, or are simply laid across iron beams. In Vault 65, just above head height, can be seen the coffin of the Rt Hon William Pole Tylney Long-Wellesley, 4th Earl of Mornington, nephew of the Duke of Wellington, former occupant of Wanstead House, and last known owner of important Ancient Egyptian antiquities brought back to England by William Lethieullier. The faded nameplate on the grille is difficult to read but the coronet on the end of the coffin marks the resting place of a member of the peerage, and of one of the blacker sheep of that exalted flock.

Passing through the chapel, carry straight on along West Centre Road and take the second minor path on the left. Approximately 60m down it, on the right and in the first row of graves, next to a tomb with a large black Celtic cross, is a pink granite ledger tomb with a horizontal cross – the monument of Anthony Trollope. It is strange to think of such a very English author writing one of his classic novels of ecclesiastical life in Cairo, but Trollope, although he wrote a total of 48 novels and 18 books of travel and biography, worked for the Post Office from the age of 19 until his retirement and was responsible for the introduction of the classic British red pillar box for post. He was sent to Egypt in 1858 to negotiate a treaty for the conveyance of British mail through the country, finished

Dr Thorne, one of the novels collected as *The Chronicles of Barsetshire*, at Shepheard's Hotel in Cairo and started *The Bertrams*, part of which is set in the Holy Land.

Back on West Centre Road, the mausoleum of George, Duke of Cambridge (1819–1904), a grandson of George III, can be seen on the right. Although it has battered sides and a cavetto cornice, it is undecorated apart from a series of small low relief circles on the cornice with simple 'Maltese' crosses inside them. Further along West Centre Road, a sign points to the West Gate entrance and Kensal Green Station.

Fig 138
The Cassel monument is an unusual shallow pylon-shaped design. It is also one of the latest Egyptian-style funerary monuments, being erected in 1921 after the First World War. [© Chris Elliott]

The Kilmorey mausoleum

St Margarets Road,
London
TW1 1NN

Originally erected in a select plot in Brompton Cemetery, one of London's finest and most elaborate Egyptian-style mausoleum can now be found discretely tucked away behind brick walls in Twickenham and normally only visible from the top decks of passing buses. Its story has elements of Victorian melodrama; an earl with a dissolute past, elopement, a mistress and an illegitimate child. Not only that, but the mausoleum itself has been moved twice and is now on its third site.[127]

This magnificent monument was the creation of the Hon Francis Jack Needham, Viscount Newry and Mourne and 2nd Earl of Kilmorey, also known as 'Black Jack' and 'The Wicked Earl'. Born in 1787, he was educated at Eton and in 1814 married Jane, née Gun-Cuninghame, of County Wicklow, by whom he had three sons and a daughter. Behind this façade of respectability, however, there were already a few skeletons in the future earl's closet. Details of his early life are scarce but it is claimed that he ran away from school, fought with Wellington in the Peninsular War against Napoleon and was a member of the Hell Fire Club. He was friendly with Captain William Hoste RN and his wife, Lady Harriet Walpole, who lived nearby in London, and after Captain Hoste died seems to have become a trustee or guardian for the Hoste's six children. However, his relationship with the youngest daughter, Priscilla, went beyond the professional, some said with the connivance of Lady Harriet, and eventually he and Priscilla eloped together. Priscilla's brothers pursued them but the couple had gone abroad and either could not be traced or were beyond the reach of the law. Eventually they returned to Britain and she bore him a son in 1844. Although Needham had separated from his wife in 1835, she did not die until 1867 but he and Priscilla lived

together openly for at least a decade, his name appearing on the birth certificate of his illegitimate son Charles.

A discreetly kept mistress was one thing, a publicly flaunted extramarital liaison quite another, and an account of the earl written by his solicitor refers tellingly to his client having committed 'errors which society does not easily forgive'. Despite this, there can be little doubt that he was genuinely devoted to Priscilla and when it became clear that she was terminally ill with heart disease, he wrote to the Brompton Cemetery Company in 1853 requesting a prime site for her burial there. He also commissioned a mausoleum, designed in the Ancient Egyptian style by H E Kendall Jnr, of the firm of Kendall and Pope, which is reputed to have cost £30,000. There is no obvious reason for his choice of the style, other than it being fashionable. The full story of the monument's construction at Brompton can be found on p 98.

After Priscilla's death the earl moved from Twickenham, first to Sunbury and then to Chertsey, both in Surrey. Throughout his life he was an almost obsessive purchaser and improver of properties, and at various times owned five in the Twickenham area alone. One of these was Gordon House, an extension of which had, in 1758, been the architect Robert Adam's first English contract. In 1856, Needham leased it to Judge Thomas Chandler Haliburton who had retired to England from Nova Scotia in Canada. As well as being a Supreme Court judge, Haliburton was also the author of a successful series of humorous books about a clockmaker called Sam Slick. (Coincidentally, it was an encounter with Haliburton, a distant relative, which led the Egyptologist James Burton to change his surname to Haliburton.) In 1862, Needham moved the mausoleum from Brompton, at a cost of £700, to his new residence at Woburn Park, near Chertsey, where it was consecrated by the Bishop of Winchester for interment. Haliburton died in 1865 but his widow remained at Gordon House until 1868, when Needham moved back there bringing the mausoleum with him – this time at a cost of only £400.

Now in its own final resting place, the mausoleum, already containing Priscilla's remains, was ready for those of the earl himself, which joined them in 1880. Set in an octagonal enclosure 47ft in diameter, with a dwarf wall, pointed granite posts and railings, it measures 15ft square and approximately 16ft high. It is made from pink and grey granite, and the posts in the surrounding wall are of pink granite (Fig 139). Plans preserved in the National Archives show that the sections of the mausoleum are held together by concealed dovetail pieces. It has battered sides with torus mouldings and a cavetto cornice. There are winged solar

discs with *uraei* on the cornice, flanked by blank cartouches resting on the hieroglyph for 'gold' (Fig 140). Engraved relief panels with floral motifs and five-pointed stars surround the door and false doors on the other three sides. Overall the architecture is strongly in the Ancient Egyptian style but the decorative elements are less so. The floral motifs, although featuring lilies, are only loosely Egyptian and the stars are not in the Egyptian style. The posts of the enclosure wall are engraved with serpents wearing the dual crown of Upper and Lower Egypt, coiled round lotus flowers. Here, there is a combination of authentic Ancient Egyptian elements with more Graeco-Roman ones such as the staff of Aesculapius. The bronze door and false doors feature square panels with relief stars and a 'ball and stick' rampart motif above these. At the top of the door and false door areas are rectangular slots and ventilation holes made up of groups of four stars. The decorative ironwork on the railings is in a stylised floral pattern but not an Egyptian style.

Fig 139
The Kilmorey mausoleum in Twickenham. It is unclear whether the dwarf wall and posts around the mausoleum were present when it was first erected in Brompton Cemetery (see p 98) or whether they were added later.
[DP103922]

Fig 140
The cornice of the Kilmorey mausoleum. The decorative motif of the blank cartouche on a 'gold' hieroglyph occurs on several Egyptian-style buildings (see Marshall's Mill in Leeds, p 276, the Egyptian Dining Room at Goodwood, p 218 and 42 Fore Street in Hertford, p 249). [DP103925]

There are no Ancient Egyptian elements inside the mausoleum, which is not normally accessible to the public. On the wall opposite the door is a large marble relief panel carved in Rome by the sculptor Lawrence Macdonald, who also carved a semi-nude statue of the earl as Ulysses that was shown at the Great Exhibition of 1851. The mausoleum relief shows the dying Priscilla recumbent on a chaise longue, the earl kneeling beside it and holding her hands, while their son Charles leans on the back of the chaise with his head in his hand. Above them all an angel hovers. A low stone bench runs around three sides of the mausoleum. The matching coffins to left and right of the doorway are covered in now faded crimson velvet with panels and crosses marked out by dome-headed brass upholstery nails. Lead plaques on them identify their occupants. To the left, on the smaller coffin, the inscription reads, 'Francis Jack, Second Earl of Kilmorey born 13th December 1787 died 20th June 1880'; to the right, on the other coffin, 'Priscilla, the beloved of Francis

Jack Earl of Kilmorey born 26th June 1823 died 21st October 1854'. The interior is lit by four roof lights in the shape of five-pointed stars. Originally they all had orange-yellow glass in them but one was broken by falling trees in the great storm of 1987, which also broke the enclosure railings. The broken roof light and later damage from tree roots allowed water to leak into the mausoleum which damaged Priscilla's coffin.

In 1867, 23 years after Priscilla's death, the earl's first wife died and in the same year, at the age of 80, he remarried Martha, daughter of John Foster of Lenham in Kent. This seems to have been deeply unpopular with the rest of his family, already unhappy with the debts run up, in spite of a sizeable income, by his lavish spending. One of the many anecdotes told about him in later years is that to ensure his body only crossed his own land on its way to burial, he built a tunnel from Gordon House to the mausoleum and would be pushed along it on a trolley by his servants, dressed in a shroud and lying in his coffin. For years this was thought to be a myth but in 1966 research in the local authority's log of sewer construction from the 1880s, and subsequent excavation, revealed some truth in it. Either side of Kilmorey Road, near the mausoleum, a sloping entrance led down to a tunnel, plastered and painted with a green trellis-work design, and subsequently bricked off, which led under the road. Whether the earl ever rehearsed his final journey through it is another question.

In 1936, a family agreement with Hounslow Borough Council resulted in the mausoleum and its grounds passing in perpetuity to the council, who undertook to maintain and allow access to it. Following boundary changes in 1994, the responsible local authority is now the London Borough of Richmond upon Thames. The mausoleum, listed Grade II, can be found approximately midway between the junction of St Margarets Road and St Margarets Drive, and St Margarets Road and Kilmorey Gardens, near the Ailsa Tavern.

Putney Vale Cemetery

Established in 1891, this 47-acre cemetery surrounded by Wimbledon Common houses the grave of Howard Carter and the spectacular Egyptian-style mausoleum of Alexander Gordon.

From either the main entrance or the pedestrian entrance near the petrol station on the main road head towards the roundabout on Central Avenue. The office, just before the roundabout on the branch of the Avenue leading from the main entrance, has a useful map of the cemetery. From the roundabout, walk along Central Drive towards the chapels and crematorium at the back of the cemetery, and take the first path on the right. Carter's grave is on the right just before the next junction.

His monument is simple, without any overtly Egyptian features, consisting of a rectangular headstone, white marble curbing and a low rectangular footstone. The original headstone had merely recorded him as: 'Howard Carter, Archaeologist and Egyptologist, born 9 May 1874, died 2 March 1939', and his funeral had only been attended by nine people, none of them representatives of the Egyptological establishment. Despite his achievements as

an archaeologist, Carter had been involved in political controversy more than once in his career and could be a difficult person to deal with, but his discovery and painstaking excavation of the tomb of Tutankhamun ensured him popular recognition as well as a place in the history of Egyptology (Fig 141). The current headstone is a modern replacement erected in 1994 following concern that the original was deteriorating and that its text was almost illegible. The cost of renovating the grave and replacing the headstone was met by donations from academic institutions and private individuals, including a number of Egyptologists. The inscription on the headstone reads:

Stag Lane,
London
SW15 3DZ

Fig 141
In 1999, 60 years after Carter's death, an English Heritage Blue Plaque was unveiled at 19 Collingham Gardens in London, where Carter lived during visits to England in the 1920s. He is one of only two Egyptologists (the other being Flinders Petrie) who is currently commemorated in this way.
[K040068]

Howard Carter

Egyptologist

Discoverer of the tomb of Tutankhamun 1922

Born 9 May 1874
Died 2 March 1939

"May your spirit live, may you spend millions of years, you who love Thebes, sitting with your face to the North wind, your eyes beholding happiness."

Fig 142
The Gordon mausoleum in Putney Vale Cemetery has a similar design to the Freemasons' Hall at Boston in Lincolnshire although on a smaller scale. Both may have been inspired by the Temple of Dendur. [DP104364]

The text is taken from a cup found among the objects in Tutankhamun's tomb. At the foot of the grave is another text, quoted by Carter in his account of the opening of the sarcophagus: 'O Night spread thy wings over me as the imperishable stars.'[128]

From Carter's grave return to Central Avenue, turn right, and head towards the chapels and crematorium. Walk around them on either side and continue on for a few metres. On the slope to the left is the Egyptian-style mausoleum of Alexander Gordon, a large building made even more impressive by its position (Fig 142). Two palm-leaf capital columns with a water design on their base flank a door above which is a winged solar disc and *uraeus*. On the bronze door is a roundel with a central cartouche-shaped oval flanked by downward pointing wings and rearing cobras. Below this are triple lilies or lotuses and below them two six-petalled flowers. The keyhole cover is a downward pointing lotus flower. There is no name on the outside but on the slab above the crypt inside is the single word 'Gordon'. It contains the remains of Alexander Gordon, who died in September 1910 – 'On the 11th Sept, at "Woodfield", Lytton-Grove Putney, SW, the residence of his son. Col. Alexander Gordon, late of President McKinley's staff, of Shrewsbury Park, Seabright, New Jersey, and Hamilton, Ohio USA, aged 69. No flowers, by request.'[129]

Alexander Gordon originally worked for James and Jonathan Niles, brothers whose business, among other things, repaired steamboats on the Ohio River. During the Civil War, when this side of the business boomed, they needed another lathe, but none were available. Two of their employees, of whom Gordon was one, built the lathe and were so successful that the company started a machine tool department. After the Civil War, Gordon and his fellow employee went into partnership with a wealthy local businessman and bought the machine tool business from the Niles brothers. The Niles Tool Works, as it was called, moved from Cincinnati to Hamilton and went on to become part of a conglomerate which at the time was the biggest machine tool company in the world.[130] The company's extensive contracts with the US military would explain Gordon's involvement with President McKinley, although Gordon's title of 'Colonel' seems to have been a courtesy one. Gordon was a technical expert and travelled all over the world for the company, including to Egypt. In retirement he may have moved to London to live with his son. The design of Gordon Snr's monument may have been inspired by his experiences of Egypt or by the name of his company, but there is a Cairo in America, on the Ohio River, and a Thebes in Illinois, a Memphis in Tennessee, and the Mississippi has been called 'The American Nile'.

Reliance Arcade

Apart from its resemblance in size and contents to an Egyptian souk, the Reliance Arcade seems an unlikely place to find Egyptian-style architecture. Its front entrance, which has a modern rainbow façade over it, can be found fairly easily by turning left out of Brixton tube or rail station into Brixton Road, and then left again into the arcade. The far end of the arcade leads into Electric Lane and is decorated outside with an Egyptian-style polychrome tile façade, with a cavetto cornice along the roof level and columns with Egyptian-style decoration in a small central window (Fig 143). It was built in 1929 on the site of a house at 455 Brixton Road. The upper part of one of the original houses, built around 1810 on what was then Brixton Place, still survives above the arcade. The Carlton Cinema on Essex Road in north London (see p 103) was built a year later, and features similar tilework, so it is possible that both were the work of the same architect, George Coles.

Electric Lane,
London
SW9 8JZ

Fig 143
Looking like a cinema in miniature, it is possible that Reliance Arcade has a link with the Carlton Cinema in north London, but the arcade's architect is currently unknown.
[DP148246]

Richmond Avenue

In this street, among the otherwise typical Victorian terraced houses of Islington are rare examples of Ancient Egyptian themes in private dwellings. A row of 13 houses are decorated with an assortment of obelisks, sphinxes, and originally with pharaonic head doorknockers.

The houses in Richmond Avenue, originally known as Richmond Road, were built in 1841 by William Dennis, probably a local speculative builder. In 1866, the name was changed to Richmond Avenue and the houses renumbered alternately. All the houses except one from 46 to 72 inclusive

London
N1 0NA

have some Ancient Egyptian elements, but there is a considerable variation (Fig 144).

The most complete examples appear to be 58–62. On either side of the steps leading from street level to the front door of each house are broad walls. At the top of each of these, adjacent to the house, is a stubby obelisk inscribed 'Nile' on a pedestal. Together they are about 4ft high. In front of each obelisk is a sphinx with a *nemes* headcloth and scaled chest. The sphinxes draw on Classical influences as well as Ancient Egyptian and do not seem to be based on archaeological examples. On the front door is a knocker attached to a pharaonic head with *nemes* headcloth. The head and knocker originally had a gilded finish.

Other houses in the terrace have sphinxes and obelisks, but without inscriptions, sphinxes but no obelisks, and obelisks with and without inscription but without sphinxes. The houses are otherwise without Ancient Egyptian elements and enquiries

suggest that there are none in the interiors. Although the sphinxes were described in a letter by Islington's Chief Librarian in 1972 as being 'of graven stone', this expression was probably for effect, and their number and the degree of their similarity make it unlikely that they were carved. It is probable that they are made from Coade stone, a form of ceramic sometimes referred to as artificial stone which could be moulded into elaborate shapes, although by the time the houses were built production of Coade stone items was coming to an end.

The most likely explanation for these isolated examples of domestic Egyptiana is that they were added by the builder to otherwise standard properties in an attempt to cash in on patriotic sentiment at the time. Between 1832 and 1840, Egyptian forces led by Ibrahim Pasha, the son of Muhammad Ali, had occupied large areas of the Middle East as far north as Syria. Technically Muhammad Ali was a subject of the Ottoman Sultan, but in effect he was asserting his independence and trying to annex a large chunk of the

Fig 144
Sphinxes and obelisks guard the door of 66 Richmond Avenue. There are actually two versions of the sphinxes, left- and right-handed, distinguished by their tails, to go either side of an entrance. [DP103937]

crumbling Ottoman Empire. In the spring of 1840, a revolt broke out in Syria and additional Egyptian troops were sent to suppress it. The European powers were already concerned by the expansion of Egyptian power in the area, which threatened their interests, and in the case of the British their communications with India. Britain, Russia, Austria and Prussia met in London, condemned the occupation and drafted the Convention for the Pacification of the Levant. Muhammad Ali refused to accept its terms and in September 1840 the fleets of the European powers bombarded coastal cities in territories occupied by Egypt. The bombardment of Acre forced an Egyptian withdrawal, and Muhammad Ali was obliged to accept a settlement which effectively put paid to his dreams of a new Egyptian empire. However, none of this prevented Ibrahim Pasha being warmly welcomed at the Reform Club in July 1846 on a state visit to Britain.

The houses are private but the Egyptian features can be seen from the street.

The Temple of Storms

In an unremarkable side street on the east side of the Isle of Dogs is one of London's most remarkable Egyptian-inspired buildings – the architect John Outram's Temple of Storms. By the 1980s, the closure of London's remaining up-river docks had led to the decline and dereliction of huge areas of East London. The former docks and their surroundings were described by the then Secretary of State for the Environment, Michael Heseltine, as '6,000 acres of forgotten wasteland'. The government of the day believed that conventional local authorities were incapable of the radical action needed to transform these areas, and so created the London Docklands Development Corporation (LDDC) in 1981. This was an Urban Development Corporation whose role was to regenerate the area by bringing land and buildings back into use, encouraging new and existing industry and commerce, and creating an attractive environment, including housing, so that people would want to live and work in the area. It could acquire land, grant planning permission, renew infrastructure and channel funds from central government, but it had severely limited powers to carry out work itself and was expected to work through other agencies, particularly the private sector.

There was one small and apparently insignificant area where the LDDC could actually award commissions themselves and they took full advantage of it. They were allowed to build infrastructure such as roads and sewers, and three storm-water pumping stations were needed in Docklands to prevent flooding. Rather than commission a conventional civil engineering design, the LDDC, in the form of its Director of Planning Ted Hollamby, took the extraordinary decision to have the buildings designed by three prominent Modernist architects – Richard Rogers, famous for the Pompidou Centre and new Lloyds of London building, Nicholas Grimshaw, architect of the Berlin Stock Exchange and the Eden Centre, and John Outram.

Outram has been called a 'Philosopher-Architect' and the *Sunday Times* described his practice as 'Britain's most eye-catching architects'. He is both an explicit user of ideas and themes, and a creator of striking interior and exterior decoration. All three architects commissioned by the LDDC

Isle of Dogs Storm Water Pumping Station, Stewart Street, London E14 3ET were faced with the same challenge. Their job was to provide a superstructure to house controls and provide room for maintenance in an unoccupied and windowless building, which had to last for at least 100 years, and be vandal and terrorist proof. The substructure, of tanks into which the water flowed for sewer debris to settle out, before the water was pumped to be stored and then returned by gravity into the Thames, had already been designed and in Outram's case constructed. Added to this was the requirement to incorporate large fans to ventilate the building and prevent the build-up of potentially explosive methane gas. Rogers' building was a pyramid of concentric cylindrical tanks decorated with his trademark external piping, and Grimshaw's resembled an upturned boat hull, cut in two asymmetrically and slid apart. Outram chose to create a Temple of Storms.

For a relatively small building, it is monumental both in appearance and concept, intended to put into practice the architect's belief that the role of Architecture with a capital 'A' is to build a civic space which situates human beings in the Cosmos, or 'Kosmos' as he sometimes spells it, alluding to its Classical roots. What is interesting is that in doing this, he has explicitly drawn on Ancient Egyptian architecture. From the street, the two most striking features of the building are a pair of giant red columns with elaborate coloured capitals, and the huge fan over the small doorway (Fig 145). The 3m-diameter columns resemble Egyptian ones in their shape, but not detail, while the fan has an element of the solar disc to it, the polychrome decoration recalls that of Egyptian temples, and the base of the walls is sloping or battered. Despite lacking some typical features of Ancient Egyptian architecture, it is a powerful modern interpretation of the style.

Central to Outram's design is the concept of the hypostyle, or columned, court which is a defining element of Ancient Egyptian temples. In these temples the columns of the hypostyle represented the papyrus swamp around the primeval mound, which rose out of the formless waters of chaos.

Fig 145
While lacking what are normally thought of as Ancient Egyptian architectural features, the Temple of Storms is explicitly inspired by elements of Egyptian temples, and built by an architect who has returned to Egyptian themes elsewhere. [DP104355]

The entire temple was seen as representing the process of creation in miniature. The columns of the Temple of Storms begin with the headless ones that bracket the gate, and continue with those either side of the doorway and with smaller fluted columns down each side of the building. Outram has written at length on the symbolism of the building and its representation of the 'Time of Foundation', recalling the Ancient Egyptian *sep tepy* or 'First Time of Creation'. The Temple of Storms was opened in June 1988, and 11 years later Outram was to return to Egyptian themes when designing the private residence known as Sphinx Hill in Oxfordshire (*see* p 225).

The Temple is not accessible to the public, and in any case its interior is purely functional, but the exterior can clearly be seen from the gate in Stewart Street and through gaps in the surrounding brick walls created to allow surveillance of the area behind. Outram intended the gate itself to form a giant eye and the fan above the doorway can be aligned to form the missing eyeball, recalling the Ancient Egyptian symbol of the *wedjat* eye.

W H Smith works

Erected in 1916 to a design by C Stanley Peach, 127 Stamford Street was built to house the printing department of the newsagents and booksellers W H Smith, known as the Arden Press. Writing in *The Burlington Magazine* A E Richardson called it 'another noteworthy addition to London architecture' and, noting that Peach had 'reverted to Egyptian models for his elevational treatment', expressed the view that he had 'evolved the [sic] building thoroughly expressive of its purpose'.[131] Its front elevation features two Ancient Egyptian-style pylon entrances, one at either end, with battered or sloping sides, torus mouldings along their edges and a decorated cavetto cornice at the roof level (Fig 146). Although clearly showing Ancient Egyptian elements, the centre of each pylon is almost filled with windows, apart from a large decorative panel with a roundel in it, and the entablature over the entrance is Classical in style, as are the pilasters along the front. The pylon entrances extend to the level of the attic storey and their cavetto cornices are decorated with stylised elements probably intended to resemble ostrich feathers, or possibly palm fronds, with a central WHS logo in place of a solar disc (Fig 147). There is another plain cavetto cornice running along the main roof level.

A period of expansion for the company had meant that a new print works was required, and plans were made for construction of a reinforced concrete and brickwork building with a large window area in the cement-finished front elevation and a large iron and glazed roof on the ground floor on a site around 40,000sq ft. At the time it was one of the largest print works under one roof in London. The site was opposite buildings being erected to house the government Stationery Office, and a W H Smith company history by Gwen Clear described the print works as 'to be broadly in keeping' with the architectural features of the Stationery Office, without mentioning any Egyptian-style elements on the print works. Building began in 1915, and because of wartime requisition of other premises the Arden Press had already moved in before it was fully completed, followed by the printing department from Fetter Lane in 1916. According to *The Burlington Magazine*, it was also used temporarily as a hospital for wounded soldiers in 1917.

127 Stamford Street, London SE1 9NQ

Fig 146
Although the front entrances to the Stamford Street print works of W H Smith have some of the elements of Ancient Egyptian temple pylons, the battering on them is very slight, and there are no other battered elements on the street elevation.
[DP103948]

Fig 147
The Egyptian-style decorations on the pylons of the W H Smith building contrast with the Classical motifs employed elsewhere on the front.
[DP103951]

By 1939, the building had become too small, especially as there were plans to amalgamate the Arden Press with another works at Duke Street, and work was needed to bring it up to modern standards. Attempts were made to sell the building, but the printing industry was starting to move out of London and so eventually it was put up for auction, but withdrawn beforehand and sold privately to the proprietors of the *Daily Telegraph*.

This building may be the earliest example of the use of the Ancient Egyptian style in London in a commercial or industrial building since the Regency. Other examples of the style, in cinemas, offices and a factory, were not begun until after the First World War. It is mentioned by the great architectural critic Nikolaus Pevsner in *The Buildings of England*, but he describes it simply as a straightforward modern commercial structure.

West Norwood Cemetery

The Norwood or South Metropolitan Cemetery opened in 1837, and covers 39 acres. The land was bought for £75,000 and then built on by the South Metropolitan Cemetery Company. It had two chapels, designed in the Gothic style by Sir William Tite, for Anglicans and Nonconformists, both now demolished after wartime bomb damage, as well as catacombs for 2,000 burials under the Anglican chapel. A crematorium was added in 1915. The cemetery lodge was replaced in 1936, but also suffered from bombing, and both it and the current crematorium are modern replacements. A Greek Cemetery was begun in 1842, with a magnificent Greek Revival chapel built by the merchant Stephen Ralli in 1872 in memory of his son who had died of rheumatic fever at Eton. The architect of the chapel is not known for certain, although Oldrid Scott, son of the better known Gilbert Scott, has been suggested. The cemetery was acquired by the London Borough of Lambeth in 1966.[132]

Among the splendid tombs of the great and famous at this cemetery (it has 65 Grade II and II* listed monuments), can be found the more modest memorial of the painter David Roberts, famous for his paintings and engravings of Ancient Egyptian monuments. Also buried here are the Arabist Edward Lane, his sister Sophia Poole, his nephew Edward Stanley Poole, and the painter and sculptor William Woodington, who designed the bronze relief of the Battle of the Nile on Nelson's Column in Trafalgar Square, although their monuments have been destroyed.

From West Norwood Station, turn right down Knight's Hill, past St Luke's Church on the right, bear right, and the cemetery entrance is just past a library on the right. A map of the cemetery showing the main features and square numbers is available from the office. Once inside the cemetery, follow the path up the left-hand side of the cemetery towards its north-east corner. Continue round the top of the cemetery to the railings and entrance of the Greek Cemetery. Go through the entrance and straight ahead to the large chapel built in the style of an Ancient Greek temple. Turn right along the path and just before the railings is the impressive Grade II listed Ancient Egyptian-style mausoleum of P A Argenti (Fig 148). Built in white limestone, it has square engaged Egyptian-style pillars at the corners and a cavetto cornice above. Despite having vertical, rather than battered sides, small circular windows in the sides and a stepped doorway rather than the pylon-shaped one typical of Ancient Egyptian-style architecture, it is

Norwood Road,
London
SE27 9JU

Fig 148
The architect of the Argenti mausoleum in West Norwood Cemetery is unknown, but the lack of any overtly Egyptian elements, such as hieroglyphs or a winged solar disc, may have been intended to help it harmonise with the Classical style of other monuments nearby. [DP104032]

still clearly in this style, and an elegant and well-proportioned structure. It is ironic that while Roberts, whose name is forever linked with Egypt, has a plain traditional headstone, this splendid monument belongs to someone of obvious wealth but about whom nothing is currently known and who has no known connection to Egypt. The Greek Cemetery was established in 1842 when the Brotherhood of the Greek Community in London acquired the land from the South Metropolitan Cemetery Company, and was enlarged by a further purchase of land in 1872. The Brotherhood was made up of merchants and shipowners, whose wealth is demonstrated by the size of the monuments in the cemetery, and it is possible that Argenti had connections with Alexandria, which led him to choose an Ancient Egyptian style for his monument.

From the Greek Cemetery, walk towards the crematorium, then round the back of it past the terracotta vault of Sir Henry Tate of Tate and Lyle fame, who made a fortune from sugar refining and gave his name and collection of Victorian paintings to the Tate Gallery (now Tate Britain). On the right, just past the rear steps to the crematorium, is the simple round-topped marble headstone of David Roberts:

In Memory
of
David Roberts RA

Painter

Born in Edinburgh
October 24th 1796
Died November 25th 1864

The 247 lithographs produced by Roberts in six volumes after his journey through Egypt, Nubia and the Holy Land in 1838 and 1839 include some of the best-known images of Ancient Egyptian monuments, and of 19th-century Cairo. Although he made

comparatively little from the series due to the high cost of production, they helped to secure his critical and commercial success and have been reproduced ever since. His monument was replaced to the original design in the late 1990s as the original was in poor condition.

Next to Robert's grave, on the left, is that of his only child Christine, born in 1821, and married to Henry Bicknell 'of Clapham Common' who is buried with her. In contrast to her father's monument, that of her and her husband is an elaborate vault superstructure with a cenotaph coffin on top.

The graves of Edward Lane, Sophia Poole, Edward Stanley Poole and William Woodington are in the cemetery but they are currently unmarked. Like many other London cemeteries, West Norwood was the victim of vandalism and looting but during the 1960s over 10,000 monuments and memorials were removed and destroyed by the local authority in a programme designed to create low maintenance 'lawn cemetery' areas. Lane was the leading European Arabic scholar of his day and produced a great Arabic dictionary with the support of Algernon Percy, 1st Baron Prudhoe and 4th Duke of Northumberland. Lane, who lived for a number of years in Egypt, knew the pioneer Egyptologists of his day, including J G Wilkinson, and wrote *Manners and Customs of the Modern Egyptians*, first published in 1836, a companion work to Wilkinson's on the Ancient Egyptians, and a book which is a fascinating record of Cairo before many vestiges of its medieval past were lost forever as Egypt modernised. Lane's collection of antiquities was acquired by the British Museum in 1842.

Sophia Poole was Lane's sister and lived in Egypt with her brother for seven years. Her letters home were published in 1844 as *The Englishwoman in Egypt*. Her sons were Edward, who edited editions of Lane's translation of *The Thousand and One Nights*, originally published in 1840, and his *Manners and Customs of the Modern Egyptians*, and Edward's younger brother Reginald Stuart Poole, Keeper of Coins and Medals at the British Museum, and an Egyptologist who was actively involved in the foundation of the Egypt Exploration Fund, later Society. Sophia Poole spent her last years in her son's official residence at the British Museum, and died there. No record exists of the inscription on Lane's grave but Edward Poole, his wife Bertha, his daughter Eleanor and his mother Sophia were commemorated by a simple inscription giving their names, relationship and dates of birth and death, one of many copied by a local historian before the destruction of the original memorials. The site of Lane's, his sister's and his nephew's graves can be found by locating the new Garden of Remembrance not far south of the chapel and crematorium. Passing the Garden on the left, continue to the next junction, which has the remains of a granite sundial on its corner. On the south side of the road is a bay for rubbish skips and behind it a tree. The approximate sites of the graves are in front of and slightly to the right of the tree.

Following the path up along the south side of the cemetery from the sundial there is a sign for 'Dalton's Path'. Following this as it bends round to the left, the monument of Israel Thomas can be found in Square 34, a little distance to the left of the path. Biographical information on Thomas is scant but he may have been the founder of a local firm of printers. The monument, which must originally have been painted black (traces of paint still remain), sits above a vault topped with a slab, and consists of a square pedestal, a coved base, battered sides and cavetto cornice, with a stepped flat top above that. On the front of the cavetto cornice is a

stylised winged solar disc flanked by very thin serpent shapes. Square panels on the battered sides have inscriptions on the front commemorating Thomas, who died in 1842, and his widow who died in 1865, and on the right-hand side commemorating Henry Thomas, probably Israel's son, who died in 1843 aged 37. An inscription on the edge of the slab covering the vault records it as the family vault of Israel Thomas of Clapham.

Returning to the cemetery entrance along the south side, the path bends to the right going downhill, and a few metres along a turning to the right which leads back towards the chapel and crematorium is the railed monument of Gideon Mantell. The surgeon and geologist Gideon Mantell, known as 'The Wizard of the Weald' for his pioneering discoveries of fossil dinosaurs, especially *Iguanadon*, around his home town of Lewes in Sussex, is buried in West Norwood beneath a simple Egyptian-style monument with a cavetto cornice top and battered sides (Fig 149). The monument was probably designed by Amon Henry Wilds who designed much of Regency Brighton and also Mantell's house in Lewes. In October 1841 Mantell visited

Fig 149
Despite its lack of decoration, the Mantell monument in West Norwood Cemetery has two key features of the Egyptian style, battered sides and a cavetto cornice.
[DP104361]

the novelist Sir Edward Bulwer Lytton, author of *The Last Days of Pompeii* (1834), at Craven Cottage, his house in Fulham. The house, originally built by Walsh Porter, had an Egyptian Hall based on illustrations from Denon's *Voyages*, and the house or monuments illustrated in Denon's book may have been one factor that influenced the design of Mantell's monument. The original monument was surrounded by railings and had a large swamp cypress tree planted in the enclosure. During the hurricane of 1987 the tree collapsed, smashing the monument. It was restored in 1992 with the help of funds from the Geologists' Association, with the original base and capping stone, and replacement side panels. A ginkgo tree is now planted in place of the original cypress.

The cemetery is open to the public.

South East

Brookwood Cemetery

The origins of what is still one of the largest cemeteries in Europe and one of the few still run by a private company lie in the collapse of the parish burial system in English cities, particularly in London, and in the growth of the garden cemetery movement, originally inspired by Père Lachaise Cemetery in Paris. Church graveyards in cities had been unable to cope with the sheer scale of burials created by rapidly rising populations and a succession of epidemics, and the close proximity of the dead and the living created risks to health that only made matters worse. The creation of the first private cemeteries brought some improvement, but there was still a move to take cemeteries out of cities altogether. An Act of Parliament allowed the state to become involved in burials and in London there were proposals first for a Great Western Cemetery, based around Kensal Green, and a Great Eastern Cemetery at Erith, then for a huge national necropolis at Woking, with links by rail and water to London and other cities. Lack of money and political will put paid to all these schemes

but in 1852 a private company, the London Necropolis and National Mausoleum Company, was incorporated by Act of Parliament and purchased 2,000 acres at Brookwood, near Woking in Surrey, where 500 acres were landscaped and a new cemetery was established. It opened for burials in 1854.

In an almost unique arrangement the cemetery had two private train stations – one serving each major part of the cemetery for Anglican and Nonconformist burials. The so-called Necropolis Railway (actually part of the London and South Western Railway) ran from a private terminal, with its own chapel, in Westminster Bridge Road near Waterloo bringing corpses and mourners to Brookwood until the London terminal was bombed in 1941. In the 1850s many city graveyards and church crypts were emptied of human remains and although some were re-interred in public metropolitan cemeteries like the City of London Cemetery in Manor Park, many were transferred en masse to Brookwood.

Brookwood,
Woking
GU24 0BL

One of the most distinctive features of Brookwood, however, is the way in which its sheer size has allowed different religious, ethnic, institutional, military, professional and fraternal groups to create their own enclaves within it.[133]

There is only one monument in a fully Egyptian style at Brookwood, that of the Hughes family on the corner of Plot 19. It is an upright *naos* style monument of pink granite with lotus capital pillars at the corners. The roof is curved or segmental with a low parapet or cornice at the front. This is carved with nailhead motifs, and under them a 'v' shaped frieze which could be intended to represent lotus flowers. The doorway is very slightly battered, with a plain surround and lintel topped by a dentil moulding and a segmental pediment echoing the profile of the roof. J S Curl points out that the segmental form of the

pediment was not Egyptian but was used by the Romans to suggest Egypt, particularly on Temples of Isis.[134] There is a small circular boss in the middle of the pediment. The original door or gate is now missing but may have had Egyptian decoration. The sides of the monument are plain but the back has an interesting false door, the two leaves of which appear to be slightly ajar (Fig 150). Like the front, it has a simple surround and lintel, but no pediment. The monument contains the ashes of Rosalind Ormond Hughes (d 1907), Sybil Ormonde Bell (d 1911), John Hughes (d 1934) and Major Otto Joseph Bell (d 1939). No biographical information about them has yet come to light, and the designer and maker of the monument are unknown.

The Hughes monument is not the only one with Egyptian features at Brookwood, however. Almost opposite the American Military Cemetery is the Parsee or Zoroastrian section. The Parsees are a distinct religious and ethnic community in India, concentrated in and around Mumbai, who are descended from Iranians who migrated to India around the 10th century AD. They have preserved the Zoroastrian religion in which water and fire are both ritual elements, and prayer usually takes place in the presence of fire. The community has traditionally been associated with business and finance, and noted for its prosperity which is reflected in the size of these monuments at Brookwood. A number of them combine Græco-Roman elements such as triangular pediments and dentil mouldings, with the coved cornices and battered door and window openings that are associated with Ancient Egypt. A number also feature the winged figure which is a symbol of the religion, known as a *faravahar*, over doorways, but sometimes this is replaced by a winged solar disc. The use of Egyptian elements is most striking in a group of three mausoleums belonging to

Fig 150
The partly open false door on the Hughes mausoleum in Brookwood Cemetery may be intended to evoke the false doors in Ancient Egyptian tombs, through which the *ka* or spirit double of the deceased was believed to be able to pass to receive offerings, although these were a series of stepped and recessed niches, and not double-leaved doors. [Chris Elliott, by permission of Brookwood Park Ltd]

the Tata family at the front of this section and standing on a stone platform, with a low stone wall around them. The middle mausoleum has a flat roof, battered sides, a cavetto cornice, and a torus moulding on its corners and below the cornice. There is a simple winged disc above the doorway and the gate has bars which end in lotus flowers, small *uraei* near the bottom and a stylised winged scarab in the centre of its base (Fig 151). The neighbouring mausoleum to the left, although it is extensively decorated with Zoroastrian symbols, also has the same distinctively Egyptian elements in its gate. There are obvious links between fire and the sun and so the use of solar discs, scarabs, *uraei* and lotuses, all of which can have solar associations, is logical, but the monuments are highly unusual in their fusion of different architectural and symbolic elements.

The cemetery can be visited by the public.

Fig 151
Despite their stylisation and combination with other features, such as the rosettes, the Egyptian elements on this gate in Brookwood Cemetery are still clearly recognisable, and may well have been chosen for their symbolic significance of transformation, protection and rebirth. [Chris Elliott, by permission of Brookwood Park Ltd]

Buscot Park

Thomas Hope's Egyptian furniture

Its title is simple enough, even prosaic, but Thomas Hope's 1807 work *Household Furniture and Interior Decoration* was the work of a man with a mission – and that mission was to single-handedly raise the aesthetic taste of Georgian England, or at least the parts of it that counted (see p 207). Hope's London house in Duchess Street was designed by the architect Robert Adam for General Robert Clerk, who died in 1797, and was purchased by Hope in 1799. It was extensively remodelled between then and the end of 1803, and by February 1804 Hope was issuing printed invitations to view the house. The first 60 were sent to members of the Royal Academy, allowing them to visit and bring up to three friends. Had Hope followed the normal social protocol and simply issued personal invitations that would have been perfectly acceptable, but this smacked of admission by ticket and was considered presumptuous especially from one so young who, whatever his wealth, had only moved to London a few years before. Hope was not known for his social skills and was later to cause further outrage by his insensitive lobbying of the Duke of Wellington, when the duke was prime minister, to try to obtain a peerage. However, his wife Louisa was a skilled hostess and they were part of a social set which included two future monarchs (George and William IV) and their spouses. As well as his London mansion, Hope had a country seat at Deepdene, near Dorking in Surrey, which he purchased in 1806, and this was extended to house other parts of his art collections. Duchess Street was demolished in 1851 but most of its contents

Faringdon
SN7 8BU

were transferred to Deepdene and a new family home in London. Deepdene was sold in 1917, when its contents were sold at auction, and the house itself was demolished in 1969.[135] A number of pieces of furniture from Duchess Street are now at Buscot Park.

There were two Egyptian-style areas in Duchess Street. One was a small 'closet or boudoir' where a number of Egyptian, Indian and Chinese objects were displayed, the other, one of the two main drawing rooms in the house, a room with Egyptian decoration and furniture (Fig 152). As Hope himself observed, the main reason for this room was to segregate the 'several Egyptian antiquities' in his collection, many of which were in coloured stone, from his collection of Greek sculpture, which was mainly of white marble. He also felt that the 'workmanship' or style of the Egyptian pieces would be better appreciated separately in a room that was themed to its contents. In

this room, a repeated frieze, inspired by the vignettes on papyri, showed a priest making offerings to various deities, and the patterns on the ceiling were based on those found on some mummy cases. The predominant colours were pale yellow and 'bluish green' – by which Hope probably meant the turquoise colour of faience. Extensive use was made of black and gold, and the room was known as the 'Egyptian' or 'Black' room.

The Egyptian room, and its fittings and furniture, were all designed by Hope. He based some elements of the decoration on monuments he had seen at Thebes, Dendera and other sites during his visit to Egypt, but many others were copied from Egyptian antiquities in collections in Italy or illustrations in Denon's *Voyages*. Even genuine Ancient Egyptian antiquities, such as a grey basalt statue of a lion and a stone vase, had been excavated from the ruins of the palace of Tiberius at Capri and the

Fig 152
An engraving of the Egyptian room from Hope's *Household Furniture and Interior Decoration* (1807). The couch now at Buscot Park can be seen in the centre, and the armchairs to either side of the room.

villa of Hadrian at Tivoli. The room had a criss-cross patterned ceiling and two sets of double doors on three sides of the room. The furniture included an Egyptian-style couch (Fig 153) and armchairs (Fig 154) in mahogany painted black to imitate ebony and with gilt bronze mountings. On the chairs, the arms were supported by seated figures with *nemes* headcloths, their knees drawn up and their arms folded on them, copied from a genuine Egyptian example in the Vatican Museum. Finials on the back of the chair were in the style of canopic jars copied from examples in the Capitoline Museum, the front rails were decorated with winged Isis figures copied from a mummy

Fig 153
The couch from Duchess Street, now in Buscot Park, with panels depicting the deities Horus and Anubis, and scarab motifs on the feet. The crouching lions also resemble Ancient Egyptian examples. [The Faringdon Collection Trust, Buscot Park, Oxfordshire, England. Photograph by Bruce White for The Bard Graduate Center, New York]

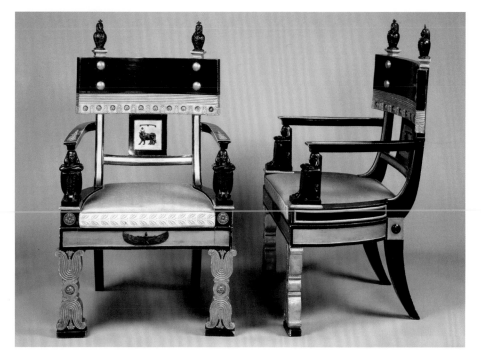

Fig 154
The Duchess Street armchairs, now in Buscot Park. The seated figures have decorative hieroglyphs carved on their fronts, imitating the inscriptions on the originals, and the cow shows the goddess Hathor in cow form suckling the pharaoh. [The Faringdon Collection Trust, Buscot Park, Oxfordshire, England. Photograph by Bruce White for The Bard Graduate Center, New York]

case in the Institute of Bologna, and a there was an image of a cow, associated with the goddess Hathor, on the back (Fig 155). In the centre of the room, a small mummy was displayed in a glass case mounted on a block with sloping sides and a gateway like opening at its centre. Above the openings on the sides were winged figures of Isis and to either side were animal-headed human figures representing priests wearing masks. Above the openings at either end were more figures of Isis and below, and to either side, winged griffins. In the opening itself was an antique alabaster cinerary urn used to hold the ashes of a cremated body. A simple table at one end of the room supported a basalt vase or 'cup', and to either side of this were small ædiculæ or shrines containing Egyptian figures, called 'idols'. On top of the shrines were two Classical copies of Egyptian canopic jars. The basalt lion statue was placed under the table. The mantelpiece was of black marble and its shape was copied from a Greek tomb. It had crouching lion statues on pedestals to either side of the mantel and an Egyptian-style figure in the centre. The rest of the fireplace lacked Egyptian features apart from two kneeling Egyptian figures on either end of the fender and a funerary boat in its centre.

The Lararium, the small closet-like room or boudoir referred to by Hope, was on the same floor of the house. In it, cotton drapes were hung from a bamboo arch and behind this was a large mantelpiece backed by a mirror. The back part of this, or chimneybreast, was rectangular, and stepped on its upper part, and a number of reliefs were fixed to its front. To either side were Classical-style stands with antique oil lamps on them. In front of the chimneybreast was an oak fireplace, painted to look like porphyry, with a rectangular grate but battered sides and a coved top. Above the grate was a winged solar disc, to either side were Classically influenced figures of Egyptian deities probably representing Isis and Osiris. Two fire irons were of Egyptian scribal figures, with knees drawn up and arms folded over them, in the same pose as those on the chairs in the Egyptian Room, and below these were two scarabs and the central figure of a winged goddess.

Not all the Egyptian pieces were in these two rooms. In another, Classically themed room, Hope had created stone seats where the sides were formed by sphinxes and the back was decorated on its corners with stylised lotus flowers. The sphinxes were a mix of Greek and Egyptian reflecting the lack of distinction between the types at this period. They were seated, winged and female in the Greek style rather than crouched or *couchant* as Egyptian sphinxes, but they wore Egyptian-style *nemes* headcloths. Elsewhere, in the Flaxman room, whose furnishings were dedicated to Aurora, the Roman goddess of the dawn, was a table with four female figures for its front legs. These, according to Hope, represented the four 'Horae, or parts of the day'. A frieze on the rail of the table had medallions showing the deities of Night and Sleep, while on top of the table were two antique vases and a clock in patinated and gilt bronze and antique marble. The face of this was

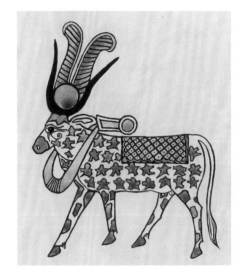

Fig 155
Hathor as a cow, wearing the *menat*, a broad beaded necklace or collar with a counterweight, which together with the *sistrum* or rattle was shaken as a percussion instrument during temple ceremonies.

carried by a figure representing the goddess Isis wearing the horns which she could share with Hathor, and a disc, interpreted by Hope as the full and crescent moon. To either side of Isis were two rectangular panels in gilt bronze with short obelisks and decorative hieroglyphs. Above these were tablets decorated with more pseudo hieroglyphs and behind these jars capped by bovine heads with *nemes* headdresses. Patrick Conner has linked elements of the decoration, particularly the jars, to plate 10 of Piranesi's style book *Diverse Maniere*.[136]

Despite the Ancient Egyptian elements, Hope's furniture was essentially in a rather heavy Neoclassical style and the Egyptian Room itself mixed Egyptian and Classical elements, was also used to display some of Hope's collection of pictures. Strangely, for one who had used hieroglyphs, or imitations of them, to decorate the relatively confined spaces of his rooms, and who had not been averse to using bamboo and cotton in the Lararium, he warned young artists

…never to adopt, except from motives more weighty than a mere aim at novelty, the Egyptian style of ornament. The hieroglyphic figures, so universally employed by the Egyptians, can afford us little pleasure on account of their meaning, since this is seldom intelligible: they can afford us still less gratification on account of their outline, since this is never agreeable; at least in as far as regards those smaller details, which alone are susceptible of being introduced in our confined spaces. Real Egyptian monuments, built of the hardest materials, cut out in the most prodigious blocks, even where they please not the eye, through the elegance of their shapes, still amaze the intellect, through the immensity of their size, and the indestructibility of their nature. Modern

imitations of those wonders of antiquity, composed of lath and of plaster, of callico and of paper, offer no one attribute of solidity or grandeur to compensate for their want of elegance and grace, and can only excite ridicule and contempt.[137]

At the time of the sale of the contents of Deepdene in 1917 by Hope's descendents, among the pieces of furniture there which could be attributed to Hope were the couch and two armchairs from the Egyptian Room at Duchess Street, which were bought by a dealer for £24 3s. For a while they were at Southwick House in Hampshire and having come back on the market they were acquired by the 2nd Lord Faringdon in 1954. They are now part of the Faringdon Collection Trust and are displayed in the entrance hall at Buscot Park along with a clock similar to that shown in Hope's book (Fig 156). In the gardens of Buscot Park is a pair of Coade stone Antinous statues (see p 14) which acted as supports for a small temple folly on an estate of Hope's near Deepdene. They date from around 1801.

Fig 156
The clock at Buscot Park. It does not have the horns and solar or lunar disc of Hope's design, but a number of examples of this clock are known to exist in museums and private collections, and even the clock at Duchess Street may have differed in detail from the design shown in the book. [The Faringdon Collection Trust, Buscot Park, Oxfordshire, England. Photograph by Bruce White for The Bard Graduate Center, New York]

Church of St Thomas a Becket

Brightling
TN32 5HE

Mad Jack's pyramid

Both this mausoleum and that at Blickling in Norfolk (see p 247), are of Classical inspiration and modelled on the tomb of Caius Cestius in Rome, and both, coincidentally, were built for men called John. The Blickling mausoleum, however, was built for John Hobart, 2nd Earl of Buckinghamshire – a comptroller of the royal household, ambassador to Russia and Lord Lieutenant of Ireland, whose aunt had been a mistress of George II. This one, in the churchyard of St Thomas a Becket in Brightling, was built for plain John Fuller who was a staunch opponent of the sinecures and corruption that were part of the Georgian political landscape, and a man so eccentric that he was known to his contemporaries as 'Mad Jack' Fuller.

John Fuller came from a family who had originally been London cloth merchants but who became Sussex landowners, made their wealth in the Wealden iron industry, particularly as gun-founders, and then diversified into sugar plantations in the West Indies. John Fuller inherited a fortune from his uncle including an estate near Brightling, Rose Hill (now Brightling Park), and sat in parliament first as MP for Southampton, then between 1801 and 1812 as county member for Sussex. During this time, as well as speaking on behalf of plantation owners and against the abolition of slavery, he became notorious for his wildly eccentric and outspoken interventions in debates, outbursts which probably owed much to the culture of heavy drinking which was typical of the time. (He is said to have drunk three bottles of port a day and to have eventually weighed 22 stone.) On one legendary occasion it took the Serjeant-at-arms and four messengers to eject him from the Commons and he spent two days in custody as a result. Having retired to his estates in 1812, he began to build a variety of architectural follies for which he is now perhaps best remembered, including his own mausoleum. These projects, including an obelisk north-west of Brightling Park visible from the Burwash road, and a 35ft-high building in the conical shape of a 'loaf' of sugar, were actually useful sources of local employment at a time of economic depression, as was the 4-mile wall he had built round the Rose Hill estate. He was a patron of science and art, endowing the Fullerian chairs of Anatomy and Physiology and Chemistry at the Royal Institution, and commissioning several works from the painter J M W Turner.[138]

His monument in Brightling churchyard (Fig 157), visible in his day from his house, was built in 1810 or 1811. It was designed by Sir Robert Smirke, who also designed an astronomical observatory for him around the same time, but who is better known for designing, with his brother Richard, the British Museum. It is a plain 25ft-high ashlar structure, probably built from the local sandstone, with a square base and a simple battered entrance with an arched top built out from one side of the pyramid. Inside, two lines of verse are carved on a tablet on the wall: 'The boast of heraldry, the pomp of power, And all that beauty, all that wealth e'er gave.'

They are from Thomas Gray's *Elegy Written in a Country Churchyard* (1751) and the full quartet runs:

The boast of heraldry, the pomp of power,
And all that beauty, all that wealth
    e'er gave,
Awaits alike the inevitable hour.
The paths of glory lead but to the grave.

Fig 157
Fuller's monument in Brightling churchyard is plainer than the Blickling mausoleum (see p 247), and only has a single entrance and no other openings in the side. It also lacks any external decoration. [AA98/04111]

For a long time, there were stories that Fuller had been buried sitting at a table with a bottle of wine and a roast chicken, but sadly these were proved to be false when the monument was opened to carry out restoration work. The churchyard is accessible to the public and the monument can be seen from the road as well.

East Farleigh Pumping Station

Still apparently known locally as 'the Egyptian House', the former Maidstone Waterworks building which stands beside the River Medway at East Farleigh is one of relatively few industrial buildings associated with water in the Egyptian style. Given that Ancient Egyptian civilisation was fundamentally shaped by its relationship with the River Nile, it is perhaps surprising that there are not more. Two others are the valve house at Widdop Reservoir (see p 280) and the Temple of Storms pumping station in London (see p 193).

The East Farleigh building is a two-storey rectangular building in Gault brick, which

Maidstone
ME16 9NB

has now been converted to office use (Fig 158). It was designed by the civil engineer James Pilbrow and an inscribed plaque on the east side suggests that it was constructed in 1860, the same year that the Maidstone Waterworks were created by an Act of Parliament. The Egyptian character of the building is created by a few simple features, notably battered pilasters and coved cornices. Viewed from the river the pilasters can be clearly seen, and seen end on, the single battered pilasters at the corners and paired ones in the centre of the building give it a definitely Egyptian profile. A parapet runs round the building at roof level, with a shallow coved cornice in cement render with a deep roll or torus moulding under the cornice, and most of the windows and doors also have coved cornices. In a fully Egyptian style the cornices would be deeper and have flat tops, and the whole sides would be battered, but this was intended as a functional building rather than an architectural statement.

The south, or river facing side, has two large rectangular windows with coved cornices on the ground floor, and on the upper storey there are smaller circular windows above these, and a small rectangular window with a coved cornice in the centre of the building between the battered pilasters. On the opposite, or north side of the building, the paired pilasters in the middle slope out from the building initially but are then perpendicular. Between them is the entrance, with a rectangular window above matching that on the other side, both with coved cornices. Rectangular and circular windows on either side match those on the south of the building. The west end of the building has two tall rectangular windows with cornices on the ground floor, and two smaller rectangular windows without cornices on the upper storey. The east side of the building, which faces the road, has two doorways, now blocked off, again with shallow covings. Between them a rectangular section extends outwards and is continued above the parapet to form a stack, which used to have a tapering top. The cornice extends round the stack. In the centre of the projecting section, an enclosure resembling a blind window frames an inscribed plaque

Fig 158
The former Maidstone Waterworks from the south, showing the shallow cornice and battered brick pilasters that give it an Egyptian appearance.
[DP139351]

recording the construction of the building and identifying Pilbrow as its architect. The cornice on this side has the only piece of decoration on the building, made up of tapering horizontal bands, a bit like a truncated pyramid, and superimposed on this a symbol like the Greek letter *Phi* (Φ). Its meaning is unclear. It has been suggested that it is meant to represent a *sistrum*, the rattle used in Ancient Egyptian temples, but it might equally well be a P monogram referring to the architect's surname. The interior of the building is plain and without any Egyptian features, although modern alterations have obscured some parts.

As with so many buildings in the Egyptian style, unless new information emerges the reasons for the architect's choice must ultimately remain a matter for conjecture. However, as with Bateman's valve house at Widdop Reservoir (see p 280), the intimate connection between Ancient Egyptian

civilisation and the River Nile must have had special appeal to architects specialising in hydraulic infrastructure, especially if they had antiquarian leanings. James Pilbrow (1813–94) had taken advantage of the 1848 Public Health Act to move into sanitary engineering and carried out a variety of drainage and water supply works, mainly in the south of England.[139] He was City Engineer for Canterbury around 1868 and recorded and published archaeological information, mainly on Roman sites unearthed during work on drainage systems. The inscription on the East Farleigh Waterworks shows him to have been a Fellow of the Society of Antiquaries of London, and it was probably through his antiquarian interests that he became familiar with Ancient Egyptian architecture.

The building can be viewed from a number of angles from the road.

The Egyptian Hall

Despite being almost an architectural footnote to one of the most magnificent buildings in England, the Egyptian Hall at Stowe is an early and interesting use of the Egyptian style. Like many mansions created in the Classical style in the 18th and 19th centuries, the main floor or *piano nobile* of Stowe was the first floor, reached by an imposing staircase from outside the building, and the ground floor was made up of service rooms. In 1803, a *porte-cochère* or carriage porch was created under the north portico, with ramps to the forecourt of the house, allowing carriages to pull up under cover, especially during the winter. From here, passengers could walk into a small hall and from there up a short spiral staircase into the North Hall. The house was essentially complete by this date but the

new entrance and hall provided a chance to use the fashionable Egyptian style.

The architect responsible for the Egyptian Hall is not known although Sir John Soane, who designed the Gothic Library at Stowe in 1805, implied in one of his Royal Academy lectures that it was the brainchild of the then owner, George Nugent Temple Grenville, 1st Marquess of Buckingham.[140] In John Seeley's 1817 guide to the house, he attributed the details of the design to illustrations in the work of Vivant Denon, almost certainly his *Voyages* (see p 15), a work often cited as the inspiration for early 19th century Egyptian-style architecture. Seeley mentions 'Denon's designs of remains in the interior of one of the small temples of *Tintyra*'[141] and later writes of the design

Stowe House,
Buckinghamshire
MK18 5EH

of two pillars coming from the same temple. He also refers to 'hieroglyphics and various designs, correctly copied from the Temples and Sepulchres of Tintyra and Thebes'.[142] Denon wrote in glowing terms about the Temple of Hathor at Dendera, which he called Tintyra, describing it as the finest of Egyptian temples, and it is probable that anyone designing an Egyptian-style interior in the early 19th century would want it to benefit from the prestige conferred by association with Dendera, whether or not the temple's features were reproduced with scrupulous accuracy.[143] At this time, few of the craftsmen who created the interiors of houses like Stowe would have had experience of this style, and it would have been rare to find anyone able to copy the Ancient Egyptian originals without almost unconsciously allowing themselves to be influenced by their training in the Western artistic tradition. The Hall was illustrated in one of a series of watercolours by Jean Claude Nattes in 1805, where it was described as 'The Egyptian Entry'. Although

this is valuable as the only currently known illustration of the Hall in its original state, comparing Nattes' painting with surviving details shows that he 'classicised' the Egyptian hieroglyphs.[144]

The Hall is about 24ft long and 6ft wide. Its sides are battered inwards but the roof is vaulted and the doorways are rectangular. Two doorways with part-glazed twin-leaf doors leading to the *porte-cochère* are cut into the walls and roof on the north side, and opposite them is a similar entrance leading to the ground floor of the house. At the east end of the hall two stone plinths flank the entrance to a spiral stairway leading to the North Hall. Originally, two sphinxes stood on these plinths. They seem from Natte's watercolour to have been Greek-style female ones rather than male Egyptian sphinxes.

At the west end of the hall, the walls become perpendicular, and there is an elliptical bay (Fig 159). The entrance to this is framed

Fig 159
The Egyptian Hall at Stowe from the stairs leading up to the entrance hall. The house is to the left, and the doors to the *porte-cochère* to the right. [DP103953]

by two columns and a lintel, forming an open segmental arch above. In Seeley's guide he describes them as 'fluted pillars, taken from Tintyra'. Again, like the sphinxes, they are more Classical in inspiration than Egyptian. They have a leaf design around their bases and a fluted swelling at the top, and are probably intended to be papyrus bundle columns, but the proportions are not those of Egyptian columns and the fluting and decorative bands around them are not obviously taken from Egyptian models (Fig 160). The bay originally had a stone sarcophagus with a stove in it, which supported an antique decorated white marble cinerary urn, used to contain cremated remains. As cremation was not an Ancient Egyptian custom, this would have been Graeco-Roman. The bay now contains a modern granite statue. The lintel between the two columns has a section of tiles on the underside, which may have been to prevent the wooden lintel scorching or catching fire from the stove below, and the moulded frieze from the top of the walls continues across the lintel and the top of the segmental arch, and round the back of the bay.

The dado rail that runs round the hall is a later addition. When it was built, seven framed sepia paintings on canvas were placed around the walls just above where the dado rail now runs, and a frame on the east wall shows where one of them would have been. Nattes' watercolour shows them to have contained a frieze of figures, one of which is recognisable as a harpist. This, and the other paintings, may have come from one of the plates in Denon's work (plate 55) which shows reliefs from tombs in the Valley of the Kings, including several of harpists. One of them is probably taken from the Tomb of Ramesses III in the Valley of the Kings at Thebes, visited and cleared by the traveller James Bruce in 1768. His account of his travels was widely read, and the tomb was known as 'Bruce's Tomb'.

Fig 160
Despite supposedly being modelled on examples taken from a specific Ancient Egyptian temple, details like the rosettes on this column at Stowe show that archaeological accuracy was not of prime importance to their designer, or presumably to his client. [DP103955]

A moulded frieze runs round the top of the walls and doorways, except for the east wall. It is made up of a repeating pattern of *ankh* hieroglyphs, symbolising life, between pairs of *was* hieroglyphs, symbolising power or dominion, a combination often found in Egyptian temples with the *neb* hieroglyph. The group is then read as 'all life and power' (Fig 161). At Stowe, the *ankh* and *was* glyphs are alternated with winged solar discs flanked by *uraei*. Mistaking the solar disc for an egg, Seeley wrote that 'the cornice is relieved by the Egyptian emblems of the Egg and the Serpent'. Seeley also wrote that 'the ceiling is … ornamented with the celebrated Egyptian Zodiac found in the ceiling of that temple [Dendera]'.[145] This is initially puzzling, as Natte's painting of the hall does not show any decoration on its ceiling, and the Zodiac of Dendera, a relief carving dating from the period of Greek rule in Egypt and showing many signs of the zodiac still in use today, is circular and nearly 8ft across. The frieze was illustrated in plate 48 of Denon's work,

Fig 161
The *ankh* and *was* hieroglyphs are often found in Egyptian temples as a group above the *neb* hieroglyph, which can mean 'all', to form a rebus or visual pun, reading 'all life and power', that is to the pharaoh. [Mark Rudolph]

and the Zodiac was widely admired in the early 19th century. Napoleon commissioned a copy, and the original was eventually removed and purchased for a considerable sum by Louis XVIII. However, another plate in Denon's work, (plate 132) illustrates a rectangular relief, also from Dendera, and which also shows constellations. In the second of two sales of the contents of Stowe House which took place in 1922, the catalogue refers to one long canvas and seven short ones. The short canvases would have been those on the wall and the long canvas would have been on the roof of the hall. Running along the length of the roof of the hall at Stowe, and shown in Nattes' watercolour, is a rectangular moulding with parallel raised edges a few inches apart, and between them a repeating pattern of floral rosettes inside diamonds, which would originally have framed the canvas. On the south side of the hall, a doorway leads under the main house. The frieze on the wall continues round the doorway, and above it is a semicircular lunette, with a moulding of a large winged disc flanked by *uraei*. In this case the solar disc is formed

Fig 162
This view of the illuminated solar disc also shows one side of the diamond and rosette friezes which originally framed the canvas panel on the ceiling.
[DP103954]

by a large hemispherical glass lens like that found in an old-fashioned bullseye lantern. This was originally lit by a gas lamp behind but now has an electric light instead (Fig 162). The house has been home to Stowe School since 1923 and because there are toilets just down the corridor through the doorway, boys excusing themselves to use them would say they were, 'Going to Egypt.'

In the 18th century, the gardens of Stowe House were developed by Richard Temple, 1st Viscount Cobham, who employed the finest architects and landscape gardeners of his day. As part of this massive project, John Vanbrugh, the architect and dramatist, designed a 60ft-high pyramid which was erected in 1726 in the north-west corner of the garden. It was of the steeply pitched form used in the tomb of Caius Cestius in Rome, and also used for pyramids at Blickling (see p 247) and Brightling (see p 208), with a rusticated arched entrance. Despite resembling this Classical inspiration, it was described in a 1756 engraving by George Bickham as an 'Egyptian Pyramid'.[146] It was demolished in 1797 but the foundations still survive. In 1805, when the Duke of Clarence visited, a bedroom was apparently fitted up for him in the Egyptian style. This could have involved furniture, fabrics and wallpaper, but no other information seems to have survived, and the decoration of the room was probably changed again later for a more currently fashionable style.

The lavish spending of the 2nd Duke of Buckingham and Chandos plunged the estate into debt estimated at £1.5 million, a colossal sum in those days, and in 1848 the moveable contents of the house were sold, but only raised £75,000. The house, an expensive white elephant, had to be closed up and despite attempts by successive generations of the family to restore their fortunes and those of the house it subsequently had to be put on the market twice, but unsuccessfully. Further pressure on the family finances from income tax and death duties forced another sale of contents in 1922 when more artefacts and statues inside and outside the house were sold off. These included the sarcophagus stove, the two sphinxes and the paintings from the Egyptian Hall. By 1922, the house was under very real threat of demolition, like so many other country houses between the two World Wars, but it was bought as the home for a new public school and in 1923 the first pupils at Stowe School enrolled there. In 1989 the National Trust took over the gardens and began a programme of longterm restoration. A Preservation Trust was created for the house itself in 1997 and the buildings leased back to Stowe School. A massive restoration programme started in 2000 and in 2011 restoration of the Egyptian Hall began. Preliminary investigations showed that both the columns and parts of the walls had a textured surface probably intended to mimic sandstone, and uncovered beaded borders in niches and on the upper parts of the walls. Additional windows opening onto the *porte-cochère* were also reopened.[147]

The main rooms of the house can be visited by the public although access may be restricted by the operation of the school and other events.

Goodwood House

The 2nd Duke of Richmond (1701–50) was a soldier with antiquarian interests whose collections included Ancient Egyptian antiquities, among them statuettes of Isis and Osiris, which he bought in 1740, and which had previously belonged to Edward Harley, Earl of Oxford. The duke was also a member of the first Egyptian Society, which met in London between 1741 and 1743. Modelled on the Society of Dilettanti, created a few years before as a dining club for those who had travelled to Italy, the Egyptian Society included, but was not limited to, those who had visited Egypt. Around 1743, he commissioned two sphinxes, similar to those designed by William Kent for Chiswick House (see p 14), to flank a two-storey garden building on the Goodwood estate, and these may also reflect his interest in Egypt at this time. His successor the 3rd Duke (1735–1806) commissioned the architect James Wyatt to design an ambitious extension of two wings to Goodwood House. This was begun in 1800 and was still incomplete when the duke, massively in debt, died in 1806. Before the duke's death, however, the first major room to be completed in the first new wing to be added was a dining room decorated in the Egyptian style, then the height of fashion.[148] Surprisingly, no paintings or photographs of it seem to have survived and in 1906 it was redecorated in a Classical style, allegedly at the instigation of Edward VII who visited Goodwood regularly for the horse racing.

Luckily, the room had been described in 1822 by the House's librarian, D Jacques.[149] According to him, the design 'is said to have been suggested by the works of Mons. Denon, particularly, his description of the Temple and Palace discovered at Tintyra'. The *Voyages* of Dominique Vivant Denon, who had accompanied Napoleon's expedition to Egypt as one of the savants charged with recording its archaeological remains as well as its modern state, was a highly influential design source. It was cited in the design of the Egyptian Halls at Stowe,

Chichester
PO18 0PX

Piccadilly, and Craven Cottage, the latter being the home of Walsh Porter, an arbiter of taste and confidant of the Prince Regent, and a number of other buildings have design elements which are very probably drawn from Denon's work. Jacque's description of the room is fairly brief but mentions a cornice and skirting of grey and white marble, gilt bronze wall ornaments, girandole (candelabra) figures of Isis and Osiris, and an Egyptian-style chimneypiece which was one of its outstanding features. This was one of two such designed and manufactured by the Vulliamy family, the other being for the Marquess of Blandford.

The fireplace created by the Vulliamys for Goodwood was described by Jacques as being of 'the finest statuary marble, adorned with bronze Egyptian hieroglyphs'. The decorations were designed by the sculptor J C F Rossi and consisted of two standing figures, a beetle, two birds with extended wings, two with their 'wings fixed with Beasts heads' and a 'Bull with wings extending 3 feet from the tip of one Wing to the tip of the other'. The standing figures would clearly have been gods or goddesses but the other figures are less easy to interpret. Although they are far from common, animal-headed birds are not unknown in Ancient Egyptian art and Re, for example, could be shown as a ram-headed falcon. If Denon was used as a source, however, these were probably based on the two *ba* birds (Fig 163), representing part of the spirit of an individual, that were shown by him. Winged bulls are not an Egyptian form but again Denon shows an illustration of a column capital with a bull's head and this could have been combined with wings. The Vulliamy's invoice book records payments for the carving of 'an Egyptian Eagle' and 'an Egyptian Beetle ', from which moulds were made to cast the bronze fittings. The beetle would be a scarab and the 'Egyptian Eagle' almost certainly a vulture, which might

easily be confused with an eagle by people who had seen eagles, but never a vulture. We know, from a description of the other Egyptian fireplace created for the Marquess of Blandford, that the Vulliamy's, like Josiah Wedgwood, used the Comte de Caylus's *Recueil d'antiquités égyptiennes, étrusques, grecques, gauloises* as a source of designs as well as Denon's work, and it is possible that the less archaeologically accurate images, or elements of them, were taken from the older work as well as Denon.[150] An English translation of Denon's work was available by 1803 and a first edition of the French language text is in the library at Goodwood.

In 1996, a two-year restoration returned the room to its original Egyptian decoration (Fig 164). The basic layout of the room had remained, with three windows along one side, two doorways in the opposite wall either side of the fireplace, one of them false, a door at one end, and a matching mirror at the other end of the room. The walls had originally been covered with elaborate yellow and black, or 'siena' scagliola, and although this had been painted over, most had survived underneath. Other fragments of charcoal-coloured scagliola elsewhere allowed the skirtings, the frieze, and the architraves of the doors and mirror to be recreated.

The original mirror and overdoors had left outlines on the wall, which allowed their shape to be deduced. (Similar outlines also indicate that there was once something over the fireplace, and this may have been one of four gilt bronze trophies of Egyptian objects which originally hung on the walls.)[151] When the set of false doors leading to a shallow cupboard were unlocked, it was found that graining and door furniture had survived on their backs, allowing the doorplates, escutcheons and handles to be copied and recast. The original chandelier was recognised elsewhere in the house by a

Fig 163
One of the five components that made up an individual, the *ba* was similar to our concept of the personality, but also closely linked to the physical body. Physical manifestations of a god could be described as the *ba* of that deity. [Mark Rudolph]

Fig 164
The restored Egyptian Dining Room at Goodwood. Original features were found behind the false door shown here to the right of the fireplace. [Photograph by Clive Boursnell, by permission of The Goodwood Estate Co Ltd]

lion head, also present on the door furniture and replaced along with a new second one copied from it. The original pelmets for the windows had simply been moved to an adjacent room, and could be replaced.

The dining table and 20 dining chairs had stayed in the room, but bronze mouldings of crocodiles had been removed from the backs of most of the chairs. Fortunately, new castings could be made from some that had survived. The original mahogany cellarets were supplemented with side tables in the style of Thomas Hope. A new carpet was specially made in Egypt, and tall torchères added, copied from examples of around 1810 in the Royal Pavilion in Brighton. Jacque's description had also mentioned an Egyptian porphyry vase and girandole (ornamental branched candleholder) figures of Isis and Osiris in bronze and gold. The girandoles may have incorporated the genuine Egyptian statuettes acquired by the 2nd Duke.[152] Two pairs of ormolu candelabra or girandoles in an Egyptian style, by Rundell, Bridge and Rundell, the royal goldsmiths, made for the 3rd Duke

of Richmond, came up for auction in New York in 2004 and one pair of them was purchased for the room. Their stems are formed from triads of Egyptian figures holding stelae in front of them inscribed with decorative but unreadable hieroglyphs. These figures are supported by winged female sphinxes and rest on separate table bases bearing the Richmond coat of arms. They may have been designed by an emigré French designer called Jacques Boileau and reflect the influence on him of Piranesi's *Diverse Maniere*. Four similar girandoles were made for the Prince Regent for Carlton House, and another similar pair was made for the 1st Marquis Wellesley.[153] Small Egyptian-style statues of offering bearers, which have sockets in their heads suggesting that they may originally have supported candleholders, and porphyry vases were replaced on the mantelpiece. A new cavetto cornice with gilded details was created for the restoration based on elements in Denon's work, and the fireplace itself was also recreated, with details based on plates from Denon identified from Jacque's description.

The battered overdoors and mirror have scagliola or black granite surrounds, banded torus mouldings and flared cavetto cornices with gilded winged solar discs at their centres and gilded palm leaves on their corners. The same torus mouldings are found on the doors, and on the window cases where they are painted to imitate verdigris, but the doors and windows are not battered. The handles and escutcheons of the doors are decorated with a lion's head on each, and the doorplates have Egyptian term figures similar to those on the Chippendale desk at Stourhead (see p 244) with a 'Greek Key' border, with five stars in an arc above and a winged solar disc below. Above the windows are gilded pelmets in the form of winged solar discs flanked by uraei. The distinctive curving, almost circular, form of the wings is found on a number of Egyptian-style architectural features from the early 19th century. The crocodiles on the backs of the dining chairs, with their straight bodies carried on dog-like legs, are also typical of this period and can be found on a number of military monuments such as the carriage created for the Turkish cannon brought back as a trophy from Sir Ralph Abercromby's 1801 campaign, and now on Horse Guards Parade in London.

The cornice around the ceiling of the room has a repeating design of vertical banding, with panels of winged solar discs with a form of the mes hieroglyph (Fig 165) below them, and flanked by birds (looking, it has to be said, more like pigeons than vultures), taken from plates in Denon's work illustrating the cornice of the portico of the Temple of Hathor at Dendera, or Tentyris as he refers to it. Below the birds are small uraei. In the centre of each wall is a panel with a head of the goddess Hathor and a version of the nbw hieroglyph for gold beneath it (see Fig 207). These images were taken from Denon's work but reveal the difficulty artists at this time, unfamiliar

with the canons and conventions of Ancient Egyptian art, had in suppressing their artistic training in the Classical style.

The recreated fireplace is not battered but has a banded torus moulding running around its inside and outside. The mantelpiece is in the form of a cavetto cornice with vertical banding. The bronze mounts have been based on Jacque's description and plates in Denon's work, and consist of vultures carrying the shen hieroglyph (see Fig 215), symbolising both eternity and protection, across the top, with a winged bull's head between them. Below this is a winged scarab with only two legs visible, and to either side of this ba birds, representing one of the five parts, including their physical body, that made up each individual (see Fig 163). These are modelled on plates 44 and 61 in Denon. Either side of the fireplace are figures representing Isis and Osiris, and their bases have hieroglyphic writings of 'Lennox', family name of the Dukes of Richmond, and 'At Goodwood'. The fireback and grate have also been restored with appropriate decoration and a pair of antique French sphinxes flank the fireplace.

Elsewhere in the house, in the now demolished Old Dining Room, was a well-preserved Egyptian mummy in a glass case. It had been sent from Egypt as a gift to the 3rd Duke, and was that of a female, about 5ft high. As well as the inner case, it had also been accompanied by the bottom of a sarcophagus, of which the lid was missing. Even then, the provenance of the mummy was unknown, and it is no longer at Goodwood but is believed to be the one donated to Brighton Museum by the then Duke of Richmond in 1935. It inspired Jacques, in his description of the house, to quote (perhaps unaware of the difference in gender) the last three stanzas of Horace Smith's *Address to the Mummy at Belzoni's Exhibition*:

Fig 165
The mes hieroglyph represents three fox skins tied together, and was used phonetically in the writing of a variety of words with the 'mes' sound.
[Mark Rudolph]

If the tomb's secrets may not be confess'd,
The nature of thy private life unfold;
A heart has throbbed beneath that
   leathern breast,
And tears adown that dusty cheek
   have roll'd;
Have children climbed those knees, and
   kiss'd that face?
What was thy name and station, age
   and race?

Statue of flesh – Immortal of the dead!
Imperishable type of evanescence!
Posthumous man, – who quitt'st thy
   narrow bed,
And standest undecay'd within our
   presence!
Thou wilt hear nothing till the Judgment
   morning,

When the great trump shall thrill thee
   with its warning.

Why should this worthless tegument
   endure,
If its undying guest be lost forever?
O, let us keep the soul embalmed
   and pure
In living virtue, that when both
   must sever,
Although corruption may our frame
   consume,
Th' immortal spirit in the skies may
   bloom.

Goodwood House can be visited by
the public.

Hartwell House

The Egyptian Seat

Three of the most important figures in British Egyptology are linked by a modest folly now tucked away in a lane near Hartwell House. Writing in 1851, in his description and history of Hartwell House and its estates, Captain (later Admiral) W H Smyth RN, a close friend of its owner, Dr John Lee, wrote that:

   While these sheets are in the press, Dr Lee has raised an edifice over the Hartwell Spring mentioned at Page 41; a view of which will form the tail-piece to this chapter. It is erected in the Egyptian Style, from a plan by Mr Bonomi, with inscriptions after the sacred hieroglyphics of the Mizraimites [the Ancient Egyptians] by Mr Birch of the British Museum.[154]

The small 'edifice', an ædicula or shrine in a simple Ancient Egyptian style, was duly illustrated by Smyth's son Charles Piazzi

Smyth.[155] He had often visited the house as a child and was to become well known in later years as the author of works on pyramidology, maintaining that the sacred cubit of the Bible was integral to the dimensions of the Great Pyamid and that the British inch was derived from it.

Lee was a traveller, collector and patron of science and archaeology. Born John Fiott in 1783, he changed his name by royal licence in 1815 after inheriting from an uncle on his mother's side (such name changes were not uncommon in the 18th and 19th centuries), and in 1827 inherited Hartwell House in Buckinghamshire and other estates from Revd Sir George Lee, another relative of his mother's. Between 1807 and 1810, he travelled in the Middle East, including Egypt, and acquired the beginnings of his collection of Ancient Egyptian antiquities. Later, his wealth allowed him to acquire many items from the sales

Oxford Road,
Aylesbury
HP17 8NR

of major collections. He trained as a lawyer and practised ecclesiastical law. He was a founder member of the Astronomical Society, later its president when it became the Royal Astronomical Society, and built an observatory at the house. As well as being a member of numerous learned societies, meetings held at Hartwell House were instrumental in setting up not only the British Meteorological Society, but the Syro-Egyptian Society, the Anglo-Biblical Society, the Palestine Archaeological Association and the Chronological Institute. The latter four were absorbed in 1872 by the Society of Biblical Archaeology.[156]

Samuel Birch, who was Keeper of Oriental Antiquities at the British Museum, and ran the Department of Oriental Antiquities from its creation in 1866 until his death in 1885, was also a founder member of the Society of Biblical Archaeology. He wrote extensively, and as well as being one of the most important Egyptologists of the 19th century was an important populariser of the subject in its early days.[157] It was he who remarked, in a posthumous memoir of Joseph Bonomi Jnr in the *Transactions of the Society of Biblical Archaeology*, that 'It will be a long time before we shall have an Englishman who will know Egypt so well.'[158]

Bonomi was the son of the architect Joseph Bonomi, who in 1794 had designed a pyramidal mausoleum on the Classical model at Blickling Hall in Norfolk for the Count and Countess of Buckinghamshire (see p 247). Initially, his son trained at the Royal Academy in London as an artist and sculptor, but in 1824, having travelled to Rome to continue his studies, he accepted a post as an artist and draughtsman on Robert Hay's expedition to Egypt, and remained there for nine years, working initially with Hay, then with other Egyptologists, and then again with Hay in 1838. He was to return to Egypt from

1842 to 1844 with the great Prussian expedition of Richard Lepsius. Bonomi was primarily a draughtsman and artist rather than an expert in Ancient Egyptian philology or an excavator, but he illustrated the works of Birch and several other Egyptologists, creating for Birch's *Sketch of a Hieroglyphic Dictionary* the hieroglyphic fount which at the time was the first in England, designed the Egyptian Court for the Crystal Palace with Owen Jones (see p 146), and catalogued Lee's Egyptian antiquities.[159]

The ædicula at Hartwell House was not Bonomi's first exercise in Egyptian-style architecture. In 1840 he had composed the hieroglyphic inscriptions for the gate lodges of Abney Park Cemetery, designed by William Hosking (see p 89) and two years later designed the carved stone façade of Marshall's flax mill in Leeds (see p 271). The Hartwell ædicula, which he designed in 1850,[160] was a much more modest affair of stone and brick covered with stucco. It is an open-fronted structure, with low flanking walls extending to the front and enclosing a pavement area, a low bench seat running inside round the side and back walls, two square pillars in front, and above them a hieroglyphic frieze (which extends to the sides of the structure as well), a reeded moulding, and above this a cavetto cornice with an inscription in Greek running along its top (Fig 166). The simple design and square pillars suggest the square colonnades of Hatshepsut's mortuary temple at Deir el-Bahri, the portico of the Ramesseum, or the second court of the temple at Medinet Habu, although the latter two would originally have had statues of the pharaoh as Osiris on the front of the square pillars. A spring runs out of the bank to one side, through a narrow channel in the floor of the ædicula into a square sunken basin, originally equipped with a chained drinking mug, and then overflows through another channel, this time angled to take the water

Fig 166
The Egyptian Seat is one of a number of buildings which link the Egyptian style to water, but its function has no clear parallel in Ancient Egypt. It also has associations with Ancient Greece and the many springs and wells in England which have had religious significance.
[DP103872]

out past the flanking wall on the far side. Although the style of the ædicula is firmly Egyptian, the Hartwell Spring was popularly supposed to cure weak eyes, rheumatism and other ailments,[161] and the routing of the spring through the structure suggests that it was intended to have the character of a small shrine like those associated with sacred wells and springs. This is emphasised by the Greek inscription on the top of the cornice, which reads 'Ariston men hydor'. It is a quote from the Ancient Greek lyric poet Pindar, also used on the Pump Room in Bath, and translates roughly as 'Water is best/greatest.' Temples built during the Ptolemaic period, when Egypt was under Greek rule, often had an inscription in

Greek in the same position and the same convention was followed for the Egyptian Court at the Crystal Palace (see p 148).

The hieroglyphic inscription on the front and sides (Fig 167) was composed by Samuel Birch.[162] The side elements are an equivalent in hieroglyphs of the quote from Pindar. The main inscription on the front is a dedicatory text that combines standard Ancient Egyptian formulas and titles with other elements which are the equivalents of English names and titles. It can be translated as follows: 'Year 13 under the majesty of [in the 13th year of the reign of] the Lady of the Rites, Ruler [Mistress] of the Waves, Lady of Appearances, Victoria, Most

Fig 167
The first cartouche appears to be a title, which can be translated as 'Ruler of the Waves', because of its similarity with the writing of that title in the hieroglyphic inscriptions at Crystal Palace, with which Birch was also involved (see Fig 105). The hieroglyphs repeated at either end, and inscribed on the sides of the structure, are translations into Ancient Egyptian of the quote from Pindar.
[Mark Rudolph]

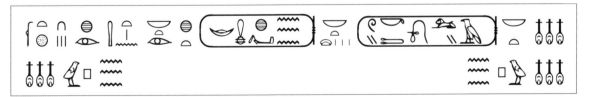

Gracious Lady'. This would date the structure to 1850, although it may have been designed then and built the following year. The shrine is listed Grade II.

Hartwell House was subsequently bought by Ernest Cook, grandson of the founder of the travel company which did so much to popularise tourism in general and travel to Egypt in particular. The house, listed Grade I, became a hotel in 1986 and the *ædicula* was rebuilt in 1989 as part of a general restoration of the house and grounds. By this stage it had badly deteriorated and errors had been made to the inscriptions in an earlier restoration.

The inscriptions were reconstructed with the assistance of Dr Carol Andrews of the British Museum using remaining fragments and the illustration in Smyth's history of Hartwell.[163] The Egyptian Seat, as it is known, is accessible to the public and can be found by turning off the Oxford Road towards the hotel, bearing left when the road forks along what used to be known as Weir Lane leading to the 'Heydun Mille'.[164] The trees along the roadside have grown since the Seat was built, but from the bench inside the sky above can still be seen reflected in its central basin and it is easy, sitting in it, to imagine Dr Lee doing the same and contemplating the reflection.

The Old Synagogue

King Street,
Canterbury
CT1 2AJ

Given the biblical narrative of Exodus, the choice of the Egyptian style for a synagogue seems strange to say the least but was made for logical reasons. This building is unique in Britain and one of only a few anywhere in the world.[165] Although there had been a Jewish community in Canterbury since medieval times, the first modern synagogue was established in 1763. In 1845, the land on which this stood was taken by the South-Eastern Railway Company for the construction of a new railway line. There were problems over compensation due to the absence of lease documents but it was eventually paid and contributions for a new synagogue were solicited from Jewish congregations in the United Kingdom and its dependencies. There were also donations from private individuals and the non-Jewish community in Canterbury. Sufficient funds were raised to enable the decision to be made in 1846 to purchase the freehold of a piece of land in King's Street and to build a new synagogue on it.

In January 1847 a local architect, Hezekiah Marshall, about whom little is known, was appointed to design the new synagogue. His initial design had to be modified to bring it within budget but it seems that the choice of the Egyptian style was a deliberate one on the part of his clients. It was only four years since Augustus Welby Pugin had published *An Apology for the Revival of Christian Architecture in England*, which championed the Gothic style in church and secular buildings, and his views were highly influential. To Jews, however, in the words of Jacob Jacobs, a contemporary historian of the Canterbury congregation, 'Our every tradition associates Gothic styles with recollections of persecution and cruelty.'[166]

By August 1847 bids had been received from local builders one of whom, Thomas French Cousins, was selected. The cornerstone was laid on 23 September 1847 by the prominent financier and Jewish community leader Sir Moses Montefiore and the occasion was attended by a large crowd of Jewish and non-Jewish spectators.

The building finally erected was about 30ft high, 27ft wide and 40ft long. Seen from King Street, its most prominent feature is a cement-rendered Egyptian-style façade, battered, with two engaged papyrus bud columns and a cavetto cornice (Fig 168). The Egyptian features form a sort of shallow portico, inset from which is a plain elevation with three plain rectangular window openings between and to either side of the columns. There is no entrance, as this is actually the Ark wall of the synagogue (the east or south-east wall.) The rest of the synagogue is built of red and grey brick laid in alternate courses to produce a striped effect, with a slate roof. There are two doors in the north wall, the rear being the main entrance. This is flanked by short cement-rendered obelisks and takes the form of a stepped arch. While this is not an Egyptian form, it is closely associated with Piranesi whose extravagant designs popularised the Egyptian style in the late 18th century. The doors are decorated with stylised lotus flower handles. The other doorway on this side is much plainer but has a slightly stepped top continuing this motif. Above the line of the doors are three tall, plain, rectangular window openings, with diamond-paned windows like those on the east elevation. The south side of the building has more window openings and a door at the far end leads into a service area with kitchens and toilets. Short cement-rendered obelisks stand either side of a gate on the north side leading to a garden area and the back of the building and similar ones flank the gateway into the garden area that leads to the synagogue.

Inside, the same motifs are continued. The Ark surround takes the form of a battered arch, pointed on the top and stepped inside, with floral decoration on the capitals. The doorway at the opposite end of the synagogue is without decoration and has slightly battered sides, and reverses

Fig 168
This view of the Old Synagogue in Canterbury shows the effect of the 'false front' created by its architect to take account of the layout of the site. [DP139129]

the elements of the Ark surround, having a shallow pointed arch with a stepped top. Either side of this doorway, battered pilasters lead up to two obelisks which break through the line of a railing along the front of the former women's gallery (originally the gallery was also latticed). The stepped motif is repeated in the elements at the base of pilasters leading to the roof beams. The Ark itself was in imitation marble and there was a stained-glass window above with a Hebrew inscription. The approach to the Ark and the reading desk in the centre of the building were carpeted, the rest of the floor covered by matting.

Outside the synagogue, and just to the north, is a mikveh or ritual bathhouse, which was built in a matching style in memory of their mother by the La Mert brothers in 1851 (Fig 169). (The date on the stone inset above the door is incorrect.) Here, the battered corner pilasters in cement render are shorter than those on the main synagogue and pointed at the top to form an obelisk shape. The doorway has a shallow pointed top and a stepped arch, and the door has decorative ironwork across it ending in lotus flower shapes. The main building is in banded brickwork to match the synagogue with two simple window openings on each side with shallow pointed tops and horizontal glazing bars. The roof is pitched and slated.

The decorative elements of the synagogue are sometimes clearly Egyptian, as on the east elevation, but elsewhere they are Egyptian by association, like the stepped arches, or simple stripped down forms. The overall effect has been described as 'almost modern' and compared to Art Deco.[167] Even in 1889, when repairs were carried out, the *Jewish Chronicle* spoke of the building '[presenting] in its interior an appearance of chaste beauty quite in keeping with its Egyptian style of architecture'.[168]

Repairs, which included painting the columns and work on the gardens and paths, had become necessary because of the decline of the Jewish community in Canterbury, and the last recorded minutes of the congregation were in 1896. By 1911 there were only three Jewish families in the city, and M Adler, lecturing to the Jewish Historical Society of England referred to 'the synagogue, with its quaint Egyptian exterior [being] now threatened with demolition'.[169]

A brief revival followed in 1913 when it was reopened for services for troops (presumably Jewish) stationed nearby, but in 1931 it was transferred to the Charity Commissioners and sold. The money was given to the Board of Deputies to maintain the Jewish burial ground in Canterbury, and the scrolls given to the Oxford Jewish community. In 1982, the synagogue and mikveh were sold to the King's School and after restoration are now used as rehearsal and recital spaces by its music department, although occasional Reform-style services are held by the reconstituted Canterbury Jewish Community. The interior of the building is not normally open to the public but the Egyptian-style elevation can be seen from the street.

Fig 169
The architecture of the mikveh shares the banded brickwork of the main synagogue, as well as the stubby obelisk forms used inside and flanking the entrance, the stepped arch form, and the use of lotus elements for decoration, here on the door hinges.
[DP047121]

Sphinx Hill

Designed and built as a private residence in 1998 by John Outram, the architect who also designed the Temple of Storms in London's Docklands (see p 193), Sphinx Hill is a strikingly modern interpretation of the Egyptian style. Its Egyptian inspiration is unmistakable and yet it has few of what might be thought of as the canonical features of the Egyptian style. Its sides are not battered and there is not a cavetto cornice in sight unless one counts the mirror in the hall. Instead, its Egyptian character comes from the bold use of colour and the extensive use of symbols associated with Ancient Egypt.

It was created on a riverside plot by the Thames that had previously been occupied by an architecturally undistinguished 1970s house. Structurally, it is fairly straightforward being constructed of blockwork with precast concrete floors and a rendered exterior finish. The couple for whom it was created, a QC and his wife, both shared an interest in Ancient Egypt and she has a degree in Egyptology, worked extensively on the various revivals of Middle Eastern antiquity and contributed a chapter on sphinxes to a British Museum book about mythical beasts. They deliberately looked for a location that they hoped would allow them, and the architect that they chose, to create a building which could have its own definite personality without clashing with the predominant style of neighbouring towns and villages. This building, the ultimate design of which was arrived at by a process of dialogue between the clients and the architect, was to be 'Egyptian' but modern – not simply using Egyptian motifs or forms but interpreting and adapting them in a contemporary residence. This is not so very different from the motivation of John Foulston who when designing his Civil and Military Library and other buildings in a

variety of historical styles (see p 229), spoke of making 'such various modifications as he conceived might render them suitable to the immediate purposes of those Buildings which he has been commissioned to erect' and also recognised the problems of using a pure historical style in buildings which 'neither emulate the character, or serve the purposes of [those they are based on]'.

John Outram has referred to himself as an 'iconographic engineer' and talked of combining influences from a variety of architectural traditions in 'synthetic iconography'. As well as his Temple of Storms, a storm-water pumping station in London's Docklands (see p 193), he also designed Duncan Hall, part of the School of Engineering at Rice University. Both buildings display the same bold use of colour and Egyptian elements (particularly columns) as Sphinx Hill.

The great modern architect Le Corbusier once famously defined a house as a machine for living in, and the interior of Sphinx Hill had to have all the requisite components to function as a home so it has a hall, dining room, kitchen, two bathrooms, three bedrooms and dressing room, drawing room, two studies, a swimming pool and garage. Apart from small extensions to one side and the rear, the basic shape of the house is defined by its roof into three rectangular blocks with curved or segmental tops, two set forward and the middle one set slightly back (Fig 170). The curved roof is unusual but what really sets this house apart, inside as well as out, is the bold use of colour and shapes and the underlying symbolism. None of this was casual or accidental, and many elements of the house can and are intended to be interpreted in more than one way. Rather than seeing the multiple layers of meaning as confusing or

Fig 170
The front elevation of Sphinx Hill, showing how colours and shapes work together to create multiple layers of symbolism.

a dry exercise in esoteric architectural theory, however, it is well to remember that one of Outram's clients remarked about the house that it was intended to 'prove that mild eccentricity is still alive and well amongst the world of the Egyptomaniacs'. If there is complexity there is also a sense of fun and it can be thought of by analogy with a complex piece of music where basic themes are developed, elaborated and repeated. A good way of appreciating Sphinx Hill is by looking at the way it uses columns, the way it uses colour and the way it uses visual metaphors and symbols.

From the front or back of the house, the viewer's eye is immediately caught by the triple curve of the roof and the four bold shapes that seem to support the outside curves, two on each side. Almost entirely created by shape and colour, and nearly flush with the building, they give the impression of giant columns or pilasters. They also resemble an Ancient Egyptian hieroglyph which can be a phonogram making the sound *in*, or acting

as an ideogram for *iwn*, a column with a tenon. Pillars and columns are a signature element of Outram's architecture and here they work to define the building and give it a rooted and solid appearance. The doorway is framed by short curved brick and concrete columns. The window frames, of wood sheathed in aluminium, are intended to evoke the trabeated order, or post and lintel system of building, which was characteristic of Ancient Egyptian architecture. Inside, repeated use is made of palm capital columns and pilasters. Palm capital columns are a distinctively Egyptian form but here they are deliberately square rather than round. Some columns upstairs are free-standing (Fig 171), and in other buildings (for example, Duncan Hall at Rice University in Texas and the Temple of Storms) Outram has used the idea of 'invisible' columns, where the presence of a column is suggested by their pattern but no column is actually there. In many places downstairs the columns are at either side of curved window openings echoing the outside appearance of the house. Modern three-bedroom detached houses do not tend to have columns, still less on such a generous scale as here, and they are one of the key elements that give the building an Egyptian feel, but also work to define the living area, creating an unexpected feeling of space.

When designing the house, Outram researched Ancient Eyptian art and artefacts in the British Museum and was particularly struck by some of the funerary material such as mummy cases and coffins. Much of this is brightly painted and the colours have survived well due to the climate and the absence of light from tombs. Unlike the European artistic tradition which has been characterised since the Renaissance by the use of shaded colour to indicate perspective, in Ancient Egypt colour was usually flat, although different tones could be used. The whole of Sphinx Hill, inside and out, is characterised by the use of strong areas of colour and the use of colours together. Many of these have links to Egypt; there are sandy walls and ceilings suggesting the desert, blue evoking the sky and water, red standing for both the sun and the desert, and the greens associated with vegetation. Downstairs, the palm capitals are subtly gilded. The symbolism of colour in Ancient Egypt was complex and still not completely understood today, but the house draws on links made by the Egyptians between colours and solar and lunar aspects of the cosmos, the idea of the sky above and water below, growth, life and rebirth.[170]

Even as an empty house Sphinx Hill would have an Egyptian flavour, but the eclectic furnishings amplify the theme and provide a rich supply of Ancient Egyptian images. There are a number of pieces of custom joinery with Egyptian motifs, like the dining table and chairs, a sideboard with Egyptian-headed terms similar to those on Thomas Chippendale's 'Philosophers' table

at Stourhead (see p 244), a book lectern, and table and mirror in the hallway. With the architect's blessing, two sets of small stained-glass windows with sphinxes were added to lunette windows upstairs and downstairs. In the upstairs drawing room there is a pyramidal hearth, combining the practical and the symbolic. Outside, pairs of sphinxes are set alongside the formal water garden that leads down to the river. There is a larger symbolism at work in the building, however, related to the role of hieroglyphs in Ancient Egypt.

Egyptian hieroglyphs were not simply a system of writing. They were highly symbolic and considered to have magical powers. They could also be used as decorative

Fig 171
Contrast the use of elements of the Egyptian palm column here with the more traditional form used for the Freemasons' Hall in Boston (see p 251).

and architectural elements, bringing their meaning with them. What seems to be a border around the top of many Ancient Egyptian stelae, or inscribed slabs, is actually an extended *pet* hieroglyph representing the sky or heavens. The *akhet* hieroglyph, representing the horizon where the sun rose and set, could be formed by buildings so that the twin pylons at the entrance to temples, which were theoretically aligned east and west, formed this shape, with the sun either literally appearing between them or being symbolically represented by the display of the statue of the sun god

Fig 172
The rear elevation shows the house's side wings, as well as the way the water garden creates a 'symbolic Nile'.

from the terrace between them on special occasions.[171] At Sphinx Hill, both colours and shapes have symbolism. The blue under the roof can represent the sky and the two red circles at either end the progress of the sun across the sky during the day. The two circles can also be seen as beams resting on the column shapes at either side. The circular central windows can also represent the sun, and there are stylised winged solar discs below the first-floor windows and over the door. The grid pattern of the courtyard, repeated at the base of the column forms, can suggest the network of canals which covered Egypt in ancient times and still irrigate it today. Outside the house, a formal water garden, its pools flanked by sphinxes, leads down to the river and Outram has commented that he sees this as a symbolic Nile leading down to its delta (Fig 172). It is also worth noting that the Thames when it flows through Oxford is known as the Isis. J S Curl has pointed out (see p 12) that the segmental pediment, although not Egyptian, was associated by the Romans with Egypt, particularly in temples of Isis, and the segmental shape is found throughout the house. What is important is not that any part of the house or indeed combination of parts has a single meaning, it is that they *can* be read and often are read in different ways and on different levels. It is perhaps this symbolic richness which is the most attractive feature of Sphinx Hill. It is a modern building which refers back to Ancient Egypt in an informed way, and without simply reproducing that culture's forms. At the heart of Outram's architectural philosophy is the principle that buildings should work, should be functional, and this house is a good demonstration that, in John Foulston's words, a building inspired by Ancient Egypt can be 'suitable to the immediate purposes' for which it was intended.

South West

Civil and Military Library

John Foulston's Civil and Military Library, built in Devonport in 1823, was one of a number of highly distinctive Egyptian-style buildings designed in the early 19th century, including the Egyptian Hall in Piccadilly, a shopfront at 42 Fore Street, Hertford (see p 249) and the Egyptian House in Penzance (see p 233). Originally intended for a Classical and Mathematical School, the building was purchased to house a Civil and Military Library of about 4,000 volumes, and a collection of minerals donated by Sir John St Aubyn. (Interestingly, the St Aubyn family home was on St Michael's Mount, across the bay from Penzance where the Egyptian House was created to house the private geological museum and dealership of John Lavin.) The library was one of a collection of buildings designed by Foulston for the civic centre of the town that had grown up around the Royal Naval Dockyards. The buildings were grouped around a square and consisted of a town hall or guildhall, a commemorative column, a chapel and the library itself. Foulston was already an established architect, having designed the Royal Theatre and Hotel in Plymouth, and he took advantage of the scope that this commission offered him by combining an extraordinary variety of styles. As he himself put it:

> It occurred to him that if a series of edifices, exhibiting the various features of the architectural world, were erected in conjunction, and skilfully grouped, a happy result might be obtained. Under this impression, he was induced to try an experiment (not before attempted) for producing a picturesque effect, by combining, in one view, the Grecian, Egyptian, and a variety of the Oriental... .[172]

As good as his word, he built a Neoclassical guildhall and column, the now demolished Indian-style Mount Zion Chapel (reminiscent of the architecture of the Royal Pavilion in Brighton) and the Civil and Military Library. Collectively, they were designed to achieve, as he noted, a 'picturesque' effect – literally like that of a picture (see p 19). Individually, they represented an attempt to combine what he considered to be the best examples of the various styles with 'such various modifications as he conceived might

122 Ker Street,
Devonport,
Plymouth
PL1 4EH

render them suitable to the immediate purposes of those Buildings which he has been commissioned to erect'.[173]

The dominant influence on architects at this time was the Classical architecture of Ancient Greece and Rome, and Foulston admitted his 'partiality to the Grecian style' and its 'grandeur and exquisite proportions'. Sensitive to the criticism that might be levelled at him for his bold experiment, he noted that:

As objections may be made to the introduction of pure Grecian, Egyptian, or Oriental Architecture, in modern English Buildings, which neither emulate the character, or serve the purposes of a Parthenon, a Memnonium, or Indian Temple; he begs to intimate, that he has only followed the example of other architects, in the hope that the precedents they have afforded might warrant him in making similar experiments … Should the critic be indisposed to admit the full propriety

of thus congregating, within one view, several buildings of different styles, the author trusts he has preserved himself free from the abomination of having exhibited a combination of styles in the same building.[174]

Like the other buildings, the Library was intended to show that exotic styles could be adapted to what he called 'modern and domestic purposes'. The building which resulted was rectangular and had two storeys with a stuccoed front and sides, two windows on the ground floor either side of a central porch and entrance, and three windows on the upper floor (Fig 173). To achieve the desired Egyptian effect, two plain cavetto cornices were added to a parapet which concealed the roof. From these, torus mouldings, with the characteristic Egyptian pattern of horizontal and diagonal banding, led down to ground level to create the outline of the entrance pylon to an Egyptian temple. Another section of moulding joined these across the centre of the building. The three windows equally spaced across the

Fig 173
This oblique view of the former Civil and Military Library shows how the Egyptian appearance derives entirely from the façade and the rest is of conventional design.
[DP130084]

upper storey had their own plain cavetto cornices and although the openings were rectangular, the torus moulding around them repeated the battered profile. On the ground floor the battered central doorway was flanked by papyrus bud columns with a winged solar disc flanked by *uraei* on the lintel above. The inset side windows have rectangular central sections and slightly lower side sections, whose outside edges are angled so as to maintain the battered profile from the storey above. There are decorated cavetto cornices above the entrance and ground-floor windows, almost joining to form a continuous line across the front. The decorations on these are particularly interesting as they may confirm that an important source for the design were plates of the Temple of Hathor at Dendera in Vivant Denon's *Voyages*. Each cornice has a central Egyptian head, surrounded by wings and flanked on either side by other wings enclosing what look like *mes* hieroglyphs (see Fig 165). The form of these wings, with their almost circular downwards curve, is not particularly Egyptian but very closely resembles Denon's drawings of the cornice on the temple at Dendera (see Fig 12). They are also similar to decorations on the Farrant monument at Kensal Green (see p 182), suggesting that Denon's plates were also the inspiration for that.[175] Below the wings are shapes like hieroglyphs but which do not correspond to any specifically. The twin-leaf entrance doors are three-quarters glazed with carved decorations vaguely resembling solar discs crowned with ostrich feathers below. The glazing bars of the windows are used to create elaborate geometric patterns, a feature that they share with the Egyptian Hall and Egyptian House, although these are not identical (Fig 174).

The original interior layout of the building featured a central entrance hall on the ground floor, with a doorway on the right to a reading room and on the left

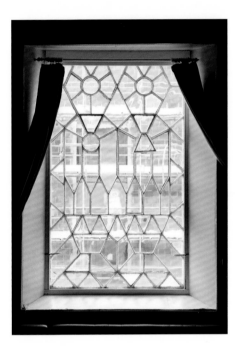

Fig 174
The striking use of glazing bars to create patterns in Egyptian-style buildings during the Regency may have been intended to echo 'Egyptian' elements elsewhere in their design. [DP130105]

to a committee room. Beyond these, two openings led to stairs on the right and a back hall on the left, with a further door on the left from the back hall to a keeper's room. The stairs led via two landings to the middle of the first floor. The original staircase has been removed to enlarge a modern bar area decorated in an Ancient Egyptian style and based around the old reading room, and the first floor is now reached by a staircase on the left side of the building, through what would have been the committee room.

The first floor was originally lined with bookcases between the window surrounds up to the level of the tops of the window openings. The cases had coved tops, with decorations echoing the solar discs outside, and other stylised circular motifs. At one end of the room was a fireplace flanked by crouching lions facing outwards with bookshelves above it. Tables were set into the wall and window alcoves and there was a larger table in the middle of the room. All of the fittings have now gone but enough architectural elements remain to see the outline of the original layout (Fig 175). The three battered window openings still have their coved cornices and are surrounded by a torus moulding. Inside this, above the two outside windows, is a frieze of stylised figures which may be intended as *uraei* but also look birdlike. At either end of the room, which still retains its open plan, are battered false doorways with the same torus mouldings, cornice and frieze as the side windows on the front wall. The wall opposite the windows has two doorways similar to those on the end walls. One is still a false doorway but that on the left has been opened to lead through to a rear extension, not part of the original building, which houses toilets on this floor and was probably created at the same time that the original staircase was taken out and the new one put in. Also on the wall opposite the windows is the door that led to the original landing and stairs. This is lower than the other doorways and now leads to a storage cupboard. Its door is decorated with two large carved motifs with four spear-like shapes at their base, which are suggestively

Egyptian, but like the frieze motifs cannot be specifically identified with any symbols.

The front of the building originally had full-length railings with alternating lotus flower and bud or spearhead capitals, joined by twisted bars. Almost all of these have been removed, but the remains of the base of one section can be seen to the left of the door. The railings flanking the three steps up to the entrance remain and show the original form of the capitals. A wrought-iron structure resembling a pergola stands at the bottom of the steps and originally had a large lantern in the centre of its arch.

The Civil and Military Library was closed in 1865 and its books transferred to the Devonport Mechanics' Institute. At some point the building was taken over by the Odd Fellows friendly society, and 'Odd Fellows Hall' can still be seen above the first-floor windows. It is now the Ker Street Social Club. The exterior is easily visible from the street but the interior is not accessible to the general public.

Fig 175
Unlike a number of other buildings in the Egyptian style, Foulston continued the theme on the interior of the Civil and Military Library, although in a fairly restrained style.
[DP130102]

The Egyptian House

A surprising number of the Egyptian-style buildings created in the late Georgian era were built in the West Country. Although the style was only at the height of fashion for a relatively brief period, its popularity would probably have lasted longer outside the capital and it was used for civic buildings in the expanding towns of the region, such as Foulston's Civil and Military Library at Devonport (see p 229), and St Bartholemew's catacombs at Exeter (see p 242). The Egyptian style has always lent itself to commercial applications, however, and one of the most spectacular buildings in this part of the country is the Egyptian House in Penzance, built around 1834–7 to house the mineral collection and dealership of John Lavin.

In 1834 Lavin bought, for £396, what were originally two modest 18th century cottages. He extended them upwards, but more importantly added an extraordinary stucco and Coade stone façade. Like a miniature version of the now lost Egyptian Hall in Piccadilly, it leaps out at passers-by as they round a bend in narrow Chapel Street; three storeys of battered pylon shapes, cornices and columns (Fig 176). The Egyptian Hall in London (see Fig 13) opened in 1812 and had been built to display the private museum of William Bullock. This contained what were referred to as Natural and Artificial Curiosities, by which was meant things like anthropological material from Captain Cook's voyages in the South Seas, natural history specimens, arms and armour, and oddities including a rice paste model of the Death of Voltaire, and later the coach used on campaign by Napoleon Bonaparte. This eclectic mix was typical of the 18th and early 19th centuries and Bullock, who advertised himself as a silversmith and jeweller, was also a manufacturer of bronze figures, vases and other decorative items,

and dealt in antique and modern works of art. His museum was a commercial venture, which could claim to educate and inform but was also intended to entertain and act as a showroom, in the same way that no museum is now complete without its gift shop.

Lavin sold stationery, including maps and guides, and this side of the business was later carried on by his son in the Egyptian House with the addition of printing and bookbinding – but the most important part of Lavin senior's business was dealing in minerals and fossils. At this time, Cornwall still had a thriving mining industry, extracting tin, copper and even gold, and exported its

6 Chapel Street, Penzance TR18 4AJ

Fig 176
This view of the Egyptian House shows the underlying structure of the original building. [DP114988]

expertise all over the world. The growth of industry and the development of inorganic chemistry had increased demand for raw materials, making geology economically as well as scientifically important, and fossil collecting was not only popular, but increasingly important to the study of geology and biology. Lavin would probably have maintained a collection of prime specimens for display, and dealt in rarities for collectors, and he provided ready-made mineral collections and associated literature in various sizes and at varying prices, from the shop and also by mail order.

In isolation, the choice of the Ancient Egyptian style for a mineral shop in Penzance seems strange, but seen in context, Lavin's choice is a logical one for an ambitious businessman. The Egyptian House was clearly inspired by the Egyptian Hall in London. It has the same stepped window openings on the ground floor, the same papyrus bundle columns flanking the entrance, the same pylon shapes on the first floor, with the stepped central window

opening and flanking figures, even the central mouldings breaking into the upper cornices. The only significant differences are those resulting from the reduced scale of Lavin's building, for instance smaller female terms replacing the the Portland stone caryatids of the Egyptian Hall representing Isis and Osiris, changes to the pattern of the glazing bars, and the small second-floor windows that have been added (Fig 177). William Bullock sold his ethnological and natural history collection in 1819, and thereafter concentrated on exhibitions, but at the time the Egyptian House was built the Hall was still a highly visible and successful venue. A smaller version of it would have brought some of the glamour of the metropolis to Penzance, and attracted the attention of visitors from London. Nearer home, the extensive mineral collection of Sir John St Aubyn, who lived at St Michael's Mount, across the bay from Penzance, had been sold after his death in 1834, the same year that Lavin began work on the Egyptian House, and a substantial part of the former St Aubyn collection had gone to the

Fig 177
The upper storeys of the Egyptian House show its debt to the original Egyptian Hall in London, and demonstrate how the façade allowed a battered effect to be achieved on a terraced building with perpendicular walls. [DP114990]

Egyptian-style Civil and Military Library built in 1823 by John Foulston in Devonport (see p 229).

The architect responsible for the Egyptian House will probably never be identified for certain as no record of their involvement seems to have survived. It is unlikely, although not impossible, that John Lavin himself designed it but there is no evidence for this. Peter Frederick Robinson, who designed the Egyptian Hall, has also been suggested and at first this seems plausible as the Egyptian House is so obviously based on his London building. However, in a reasonably well-documented career, there is no evidence for his involvement with the Egyptian House, although it was built before Robinson fled to France in 1840 to avoid his creditors. The name of John Foulston has also been suggested, since he built the Civil and Military Library at Devonport, which also has similarities to the Egyptian Hall. Foulston's *The Public Buildings Erected in the West of England, as Designed by J. F.*, which describes the Library, makes no mention of the Egyptian House, although it was published in 1838. If he also designed the Egyptian House this may have been too late to be included in his book, but the Library is plainer than the Egyptian Hall, and there is nothing in Foulston's record as an architect, or the rather scholarly tone of his book, to suggest the flashy commercial style of the Egyptian House. One other name that has been suggested is that of Philip Sambell. He is best known for a number of buildings which have been attributed to him in Truro, such as the church of St John in Lemon Street and the Royal Institution of Cornwall and adjacent Baptist chapel. He is believed to have written on Egyptian architecture for the Royal Institution of Cornwall and was active at least until the late 1840s. Intriguingly, he was deaf and without speech, and 72 Holloway Street, Exeter (see p 238), built around 1826, has Egyptianising features,

and seems to have housed the West of England Institution, founded in that year as a school for deaf and dumb children. Its architect is unknown, but Sambell would be an appropriate candidate. Again, however, there is no firm evidence for his involvement with the Egyptian House, and the Egyptian-style features of the Exeter building are minimal and in a very plain style.

The Egyptian House itself originally had granite walls, a slate roof and brick chimneys. A brick and stucco façade was added to the front. Like the shopfront at Fore Street in Hertford (see p 249) it is not actually battered, but the cavetto cornice at the top forms a parapet concealing the roof behind and the banded torus moulding below it extends outwards to the base of the building, creating a battered pylon profile. Like the Hertford building, it has distinctive decorated blank cartouches and vertical banding on the cornice.

The windows themselves are rectangular but the architraves have been battered. The upper, second-storey windows are sash windows with plain surrounds and the polygonal glazing bars shared by this building, the Egyptian Hall and Foulston's library. On the first floor the windows are larger and more elaborate. The pylon form of the whole front is repeated on the side windows, with a decorated cavetto cornice and torus moulding. Below this the window has its own small decorated cornice. In the centre, the window is stepped, with a rectangular fanlight above the level of the side windows. Above this is a decorated cornice, topped by the royal coat of arms of William IV, which help date the building's completion to no later than 1837 when Victoria acceded to the throne. The deeply moulded royal coat of arms overlap a cornice decorated in the same style as the roof cornice and a banded torus moulding which runs down to the window architrave.

Above the window cornice a stepped panel supports another deep moulding, almost in the round, of an eagle perched on a pile of rocks and flapping its wings. Inside the stepped architrave of the central window, there are small side windows separated from the main window by two female terms. The cornices of the side windows on this floor, and the lower cornice of the central window, are decorated with motifs resembling winged solar discs flanked by *uraei*, but these have become stylised into abstract floral elements, with swags running to the outside of the cornice. The polygonal glazing bars are more elaborate than those on the smaller second-storey windows, especially in the centre.

Below the first-floor windows, a full-width cornice runs between the torus mouldings on the outside and is slightly stepped in places to match the ground floor of the building below. The cornice is decorated with a winged solar disc over the doorway, flanked by vulture heads, and by pairs of the decorated blank cartouches on the other cornices. Below the cornice, the side windows have battered sides and a stepped top, and the system of glazing bars is more elaborate than on the storeys above, reflecting the greater size of the windows. In the centre, a deep porch is flanked by

papyrus bud pillars with especially elaborate bases representing the stem sheaths which protect the emerging papyrus bud. Three half-glazed doors with large diamond-pattern glazing bars run off the porch, on each side to shop premises, and in the middle to the backyard and upper floors of the house (Fig 178).

In debating the identity of the architect of the Egyptian House, it is easy to focus on the similarities between this and other early 19th century buildings in the Egyptian style, particularly the Egyptian Hall. Equally interesting, though, are the differences between them – often quite subtle. If the same architect was designing more than one Egyptian-style building, you would expect to find that even though larger features of the design were changed, elements of the decoration would tend to repeat and form a sort of signature (see, for example, the work of Thomas Wallis on the GEC Factory at Witton, p 256). It is, after all, such diagnostic features that allow us to recognise or identify the work of artists and architects. Things like the decorated blank cartouches and the banding on the torus moulding however, are slightly different in all the buildings that use them. The first-floor cornices of the original Egyptian Hall were decorated with clearly Egyptian winged solar

Fig 178
The stepped form of the windows on the ground floor of the Egyptian House, shared with the Egyptian Hall in Piccadilly, may ultimately be derived from elements in the designs of Piranesi (see Fig 31).
[DP114992]

discs and *uraei*, and the moulded relief in the centre had two sphinxes facing outward and flanking a solar disc with a scarab superimposed. On the Egyptian House, these elements have not been simplified, but changed completely, and where the stepped panel at the top of the façade on the Egyptian Hall was blank, the Egyptian House has an eagle which is not even remotely Egyptian in style. All this suggests that no two Egyptian-style buildings of this period were built by the same architect but that each was built by a different architect using common design sources – particularly those showing the late temples of Upper Egypt. Later architects would borrow from earlier buildings with idiosyncratic variations in various elements depending on the architect's familiarity, or lack of it, with Ancient Egyptian styles and symbols, their faithfulness in adhering to their design sources, and their own personal taste.

After Lavin's death, his family continued to own the Egyptian House until 1910 but after being used for a time by his son Edward, it was let out to a variety of tenants. It was at one time divided vertically into two shops below and two flats above, each with their own staircase. It passed through a variety of owners before being sold in 1968 by the last of them, the Cornish Stone Company, to the Landmark

Trust. By this point, the building had badly deteriorated. There were problems with the roof, structural issues with the side walls bowing away from the front wall, and decoration on the façade was coming loose. It was riddled with woodworm and had dry rot in the basement and ground floor. A comprehensive rebuilding programme converted it internally into three flats, each running the full width of the building, with the original two shops and cellars below. The front was repaired and repainted based on research into surviving layers of paint and contemporary coloured illustrations of other Egyptian-style buildings of the same period. The ground-floor shop windows had been replaced with plate glass by 1859 but the mortices of the glazing bars survived and from these, the windows of Foulston's library and illustrations of the Egyptian Hall it was possible to reconstruct the pattern they now have.[176]

Rescued from possible collapse and demolition, the Egyptian House continues to decorate Penzance – an extravagant architectural rarity surprising visitors like one of the exotic blooms which the mild climate of Cornwall allows to flourish there. The ground floor is occupied by shops but the remainder of the property is Landmark Trust apartments.

144 Fore Street

Around 1830, the façade of this house, originally 17th century, was remodelled to add a segmented bay window on the first floor and a square bay on the second. A coved cornice joined these to the original front.[177] It was described by the architectural historian Nikolaus Pevsner as having 'Egyptianesque features',[178] and although the decoration on the cornice is not Egyptian, the cast-iron column in the

doorway has elements which suggest lotus pillars on its upper part, and the shopfront itself is slightly battered (Fig 179). Although it does not look particularly Egyptian it may well have been seen at the time as being in this style. An 1840 book by Nathaniel Whittock, illustrating examples of shopfronts in London as a style guide, showed (plate XII) a chemist shop in Great Russell Street, near the British Museum, describing it as a

Exeter
EX4 3AN

Fig 179
Despite being built after 42 Fore Street in Hertford (see p 249) and before the Egyptian House in Penzance (see p 233), both of which were also commercial buildings and have elaborate Egyptian features, the remodelled exterior of 144 Fore Street in Exeter has minimal Egyptian features, confined to the ground floor.
[© Mr Ian Wright LRPS. Source English Heritage, IoE089097]

'very elegant specimen of the Egyptian Style', and also commented that if a 'draper or tailor chose this style of architecture, it might be made very showy and attractive, by employing a judicious decorative painter'.[179] The illustration shows a shop whose only Egyptian features seem to be a torus moulding above the windows with 'barber's pole' diagonal banding, and pilasters either side of the entrance which are generally Classical in style, including a simple incised decoration on the front with a simple Greek Key motif at the top, but which are battered. Like the façade of 72 Holloway Street it seems that the inclusion of a single Egyptian element, particularly battering or a cavetto cornice, was enough to qualify a building as 'Egyptian'. The interior of the building is not accessible to the public.

72 Holloway Street

Exeter
EX2 4JD

This is one of a group of varied early to mid-19th century buildings and may be

Fig 180
The windows of 72 Holloway Street show a mixture of Classical and Egyptian elements.
[DP114985]

the former home of the West of England Institution, founded in 1826 as a school for deaf and dumb children. *White's Devonshire Directory* of 1850, in its section on Exeter charities, describes this as occupying 'a handsome building in the Egyptian style, pleasantly situated on the south side of Topsham road'.

At first sight, the building (Fig 180) lacks any obviously Egyptian features. It has three storeys with a triangular pediment at roof level and similar pediments over the first-floor windows. The inset doorway is rectangular but all the windows are slightly battered and although they do not have cavetto cornices, the extension of the window frame at the top suggests the classic pylon outline. If this is the building referred to in the *Directory*, it suggests that at this period such elements of battering were enough to qualify a building as being in the Egyptian style. The interior of the building is not accessible to the public.

Kingston Lacy

The Bankes Obelisk

The Rosetta Stone has become the iconic key to the translation of hieroglyphs but the lesser known obelisk at Kingston Lacy was also of critical importance in the race to unlock the secrets of Ancient Egypt (see pp 76–82). The Bankes Obelisk, named after William John Bankes, the wealthy traveller and pioneer Egyptologist who brought it back to England, was originally set up as one of a pair by the Greek ruler of Egypt, Ptolemy IX, who ruled between 116 and 81 BC, in front of a new pylon he had built at the Temple of Isis on the island of Philae, in Upper Egypt. Although the Ptolemies were Macedonian Greeks, descendants of one of the generals of Alexander the Great, they ruled Egypt as pharaohs and the four faces of each obelisk were decorated with conventional inscriptions honouring Ptolemy IX and his queen, Cleopatra, and dedicating the obelisks to Isis.

In 1815, Bankes was travelling up the Nile and stopped at Philae where he examined the remains of the temple. Both obelisks had fallen by this time but one was still virtually intact, and also had a buried base with a Greek inscription which Bankes uncovered. He was an accomplished Greek scholar, who had already noted in another Graeco-Roman temple (at Diospolis Parva, modern Hiw) that the name of Cleopatra in a Greek inscription preceded that of Ptolemy, indicating that she was the ruling monarch. He found that this was also reflected in the order of figures carved on the temple walls, confirming that some of the figures represented monarchs and not priests or gods. By this time, a number of scholars had reached the conclusion that the oval rings now known as cartouches contained royal names, and Bankes was able to match a name in hieroglyphs, previously translated by the English polymath Thomas Young as

that of Ptolemy, to a cartouche over a male figure. Bankes knew that the inscription on the base of the obelisk at Philae mentioned Cleopatra and found other Greek inscriptions at Philae mentioning this name. He appreciated that the obelisk, like the Rosetta Stone, had inscriptions in both hieroglyphs and Greek, and that correspondences between them could potentially provide crucial insights into the nature of the hieroglyphic script.

Unable to transport the obelisk himself because of the lack of suitable equipment, Bankes had to wait until he made another trip to Egypt in 1818 when he enlisted the help of Giovanni Belzoni – the former strongman and theatrical performer who had travelled to Egypt to unsuccessfully promote a new design of water wheel, and gone on to transport the colossal statue and torso of Ramesses II from Thebes to England for Henry Salt, the British Consul General. The obelisk at Philae was about 22ft high, and weighed about 6 tons. Belzoni's initial attempt to load it onto a boat failed when the jetty that had been built for him collapsed and the obelisk was nearly lost in the turbulent river. A second attempt proved more successful and the obelisk was transported to Alexandria and from there aboard HM Naval Transport *Dispatch* to Deptford in London, but not until September 1821. In London the obelisk and other antiquities which had been sent back for Bankes' father Henry, a Trustee of the British Museum, were admired by the Duke of Wellington. It was most probably at the suggestion, and with the assistance of the Duke of Wellington, that the obelisk was transported from London to Kingston Lacy in Dorset on a converted gun carriage. Even now the journey is a long one and what it must have been like on the roads of those days is difficult to imagine. The obelisk had

Wimborne Minster
BH21 4EA

arrived at Kingston Lacy, the Bankes family seat, by August 1822 and was joined by its pedestal in the spring of 1823. However, although the Duke of Wellington laid the foundation stone for the pedestal in April 1827, it was not to be until October 1830 that the pedestal was completed and the obelisk finally erected in its new home.

Bankes had copied the Greek inscription on the base of the obelisk in 1815 and when the pedestal was being cleaned, two more Greek inscriptions were discovered on it, painted rather than inscribed. Unlike the hieroglyphs they were not exalted religious formulae and royal titles, but like the inscription on the Rosetta Stone rather bureaucratic legal texts intended as a public record. The first is a complaint to Ptolemy, Cleopatra his sister and Cleopatra his wife, that a succession of royal officials, military, police, inspectors, their scribes, guards and other servants had been descending on the Temple of Isis and expecting the priests to maintain them during their stay. Pleading poverty, the priests humbly supplicated their rulers to command that this practice should cease, to confirm their decision in writing, and to allow the priests to record the decision in an inscription so that the problem would not recur in the future. The second text was a copy of the letter they received from the king, his wife and his sister granting their request, and the third a copy of a letter sent to the royal relative Lochus, *Stragegos* or Governor of Upper Egypt, asking him to see that their decision was implemented. In 1821 Bankes had published a set of engravings showing the hieroglyphic and first Greek inscription on the obelisk and also an impression of how it would look when set up at Kingston Lacy. A simple pencil annotation by Bankes on some copies of these engravings was to lead to a protracted and bad-tempered dispute which still echoes in some quarters to this day.

The hieroglyphic form of the name Ptolemy had already been deduced from the Rosetta Stone, set up in the reign of Ptolemy V. The Philae obelisk was important not only because it was inscribed in two languages, Egyptian and Greek, but because the Greek text contained the name of Cleopatra and it was likely that this also occurred in the hieroglyphic inscription, as it does. On the assumption that the hieroglyphs used to spell out the queen's name were largely phonetic, this would allow sound values to be assigned to more hieroglyphs. This proved to be the case, and along with the identification of the names of Alexander the Great and the Ptolemaic Queen Berenice, allowed most of the hieroglyphs with alphabetic values to be deduced. The identification of Cleopatra's name was not, however, a simple matter of identifying the cartouche that didn't contain the name of Ptolemy as being that of Cleopatra. There were six cartouches on the obelisk, two giving the birth name of Ptolemy transcribed into hieroglyphs, three giving his Egyptian throne name and a religious title, and one with the name of Cleopatra. In the Greek texts, however, the name of Ptolemy occurs only once and the name of Cleopatra twice. There are other complications, resulting from the viciously incestuous politics of the later Ptolemies. We now number the monarchs but this system tends to assume a stable system of succession, which was far from the case, and there are disputes over whether some actually ruled at all. The titles of monarchs, such as *Soter* or Saviour, were used by more than one ruler so they tended to have nicknames. That of the Ptolemy usually numbered IX was *Lathyros*, Grass Pea or Chick Pea. He ruled at least twice, being displaced for a while by his brother Alexander, usually numbered as Ptolemy X. Ptolemy *Lathyros* ruled initially with his mother, Cleopatra III, then with his sister, and wife, Cleopatra IV, then another sister, Cleopatra V Selene. Some sources give him a third, unrelated wife and he may also have married his daughter by his first wife, Cleopatra Berenice, who eventually succeeded him. Fortunately, while this makes it tricky to be sure who are the two Cleopatras, wife and sister, referred to in the Greek text, it does not affect the reading of the hieroglyphic name.

Examining the texts on the obelisk and its base, Bankes was able to identify the name of Cleopatra in one of the cartouches and communicated this information to Henry Salt and Thomas Young. Bankes also annotated in pencil, according to Salt, 'many' copies of the lithographs of the obelisk and its texts, with the name of Cleopatra, indicating that it was contained in one of the cartouches. When Jean-François Champollion (see p 80) also claimed to have identified this name in hieroglyphs, Bankes and his supporters claimed that it was as a result of seeing Bankes' annotation.[180] Champollion always denied that this was the case. He may well have seen the lithographs

of the obelisk, as material was widely circulated between European scholars, but it is likely that they only acted as confirmation of conclusions he had already reached from studying another text on papyrus. He soon used inscriptions on the temple of Abu Simbel to read the names of Egyptian rulers, allowing him not only to prove that alphabetic hieroglyphs were not just used to write the names of foreign rulers, but that a number of different hieroglyphs could make the same sound, and that some of them were read as two or three syllables. From that point onward, while he may have failed to acknowledge the debt he owed to others, his own achievements cannot be denied.

The obelisk now stands on a simple three-tier plinth not far from the house at Kingston Lacy, on the south lawn (Fig 181). Bronze plaques on the plinth give information on the Greek and hieroglyphic inscriptions, the role of Bankes and Belzoni in transporting it from Egypt, and of Bankes

Fig 181
Despite its modest size, the Bankes Obelisk was of crucial importance in the decipherment of hieroglyphs (see p 80). [CC52/00162]

in bringing the granite plinth from a site in Nubia, and the repair of the obelisk using granite from the ruins of the Roman city of Leptis Magna in modern Libya, donated by George IV. The Greek inscription is on the south side, and can be located by the bronze plaque describing its contents. It has suffered badly from the effects of weathering and even in 1914, when the Egyptologist Wallis Budge inspected it, he commented that 'in a few years' time many portions of its inscriptions will be illegible'. Not far away is a section of the second obelisk from Philae, also brought back by Bankes, and the 19th Dynasty granite

sarcophagus of Amenope, King's Scribe and Chief Steward of Amun. The sarcophagus was found in 1821 by the Greek excavator and collector Giovanni d'Athanasi and given to Bankes by Henry Salt. Around a hundred Ancient Egyptian antiquities from Bankes' collection are on display in the former billiards room of the house, including the lithographs which caused so much argument, and a rotating display of material from the mass of drawings, watercolours and notes that he made during his travels but failed to publish. The house and grounds are a National Trust property and open to the public.

St Bartholomew's catacombs

St Bartholomew's Cemetery, Exe Street, Exeter EX4 3HA

In late Georgian England, a rising population, especially in cities (Exeter's population rose 60 per cent between 1801 and 1831), was putting intolerable pressure on the traditional practice of burial in the graveyards of parish churches. Following a cholera epidemic in Exeter in 1832 which killed over 400 people it was decided to build a new cemetery in Bartholomew Street. This was constructed between 1835 and 1837 to the designs of Thomas Whitaker and was the first publicly funded cemetery in England, rather than one run by a joint stock company, paid for by rates raised by the city's Improvement Commissioners.

The cemetery was built on quite steeply sloping ground beneath the city walls and its key feature was a series of catacombs at its summit (Fig 182). Whitaker chose a severe, almost stark Egyptian style, making it the first cemetery in England to have buildings in this style. (Highgate did not start accepting burials until 1839.) The catacomb entrances were constructed in local stone ashlar as a series of four pylons with battered fronts and sides. Those on the outside have a

plain doorway, with a small plain rectangular opening above it and a simple torus moulding around the edge of the pylon. Inside these pylons were two more, much wider, with three section entrances divided by two plain square pillars in granite, with a granite lintel above. A torus moulding ran along each side of the entrance and above the lintel and over the moulding was a plain cavetto cornice. Another torus moulding ran round the edge of the pylon. Between the two larger pylons is a simple central buttress. The catacomb entrances have plain barred gates.

Sadly, the cemetery was plagued with problems from the beginning. The sloping ground caused the initial foundations to fail and the cost rose from an initial estimate of £2,300 to a final cost of £6,000. A persistent problem in the 19th century was the resistance of the Anglican church to burying Nonconformists in consecrated ground, and equally the wish of Nonconformists to have their own burial grounds. Even though many of the new cemeteries tried to be non-denominational, or at least open to both Anglicans and Nonconformists, they still tended to be divided into consecrated and non-consecrated sections, and Exeter was no exception. In this case the division was marked by a wall, allegedly at the insistence of the Bishop of Exeter. An initial eight catacombs were extended to 20, more than doubling the initial capacity of 1,400 burials, but eventually only 11 people were buried in them. This may have been due to the fact that burial in them was more expensive than in the rest of the cemetery, and for those that could afford it, lacked a suitably impressive monument. The more successful catacombs at Kensal Green (see p 184) tended to be used by declining members of the upper classes who could not afford monuments, or those without surviving family who could not rely on their monuments being maintained after their death.

The cemetery was virtually closed in the 1870s, although a few burials continued until 1946, and has been turned into a landscaped park which is open to the public.

Fig 182
St Bartholomew's Cemetery, Exeter. One of the larger central sections of the catacombs, showing three distinctive features of the Egyptian style: battered sides, torus mouldings, and a cavetto cornice.
[© Mr Terence Harper. Source English Heritage, IoE088856]

Stourhead House

Thomas Chippendale Egyptian furniture

For those wanting to use the Ancient Egyptian style when it was at its most fashionable, it was not always possible, or desirable, to create entire new buildings or to remodel interiors in the style, and furniture and furnishings provided an alternative. Sometimes, as with Thomas Hope's London residence at Duchess Street (see p 204) and the Egyptian Dining Room at Goodwood (see p 215), both were done, with interior decoration and fixtures like chimneybreasts in the style, but also furniture and decorative items like lamps and candelabras. At Stourhead, the Egyptian was introduced into a Classically inspired interior through elements in a set of library furniture, designed by Thomas Chippendale the Younger.

Sir Richard Colt Hoare, who inherited Stourhead from his grand-uncle Henry Hoare II, came from a prominent banking family, but retired from the business. After extensive travels in Europe following the death of his wife, he was forced to return to England in 1791 by the outbreak of the French Revolutionary War, and in 1800 added a picture gallery to the south end of the east front of Stourhead and a library to the northern end. Between 1795 and 1820, he employed Thomas Chippendale the Younger to supply furniture and furnishings and as a result the house contains the largest known collection of documented furniture supplied by Chippendale's workshops. Although his name is now a byword for furniture, Chippendale was much more than just a cabinetmaker.

Stourton,
Warminster
BA12 6QD

243

Like his father, he provided a wide-ranging house furnishing service. This could include not only designing and manufacturing furniture, but repairing, hiring, storing and transporting it, supplying marble, wallpaper, carpets, blinds, hardware, and upholstery from seats and loose covers to bed hangings and curtains. Despite this versatility, Chippendale was made bankrupt in 1804 and the long-running commissions from Colt Hoare were important for the survival of his business.

Sir Richard was a collector, patron of artists and antiquarian, being a member of the Society of Antiquaries. His library was not merely decorative, as after donating many works on Italian topography and history to the British Museum, he built up another extensive collection of material on the history and topography of the British Isles and, in collaboration with others, produced important works on the ancient and modern history of Wiltshire. In 1804, he

commissioned Chippendale to produce a set of furniture for the new library, and by June of that year pieces were being delivered. Not all of them had Egyptian decoration, but they included a square mahogany table with Egyptian heads at the top of the legs, and in 1805 the magnificent 'Philosophers' table in mahogany with ebony banding (Fig 183).[181] This is similar in shape to a large double pedestal desk, with drawers in the pedestal concealed by panelled cupboard doors, but the top and pedestal extend at each end, supported by two tapering columns with Egyptian-style heads, stylised drapery and human feet. There are drawers all round the top, although three on one side are dummies. The 'pedestal' sections are each framed by four tapering pilasters resembling terms, two on each side, and similar to those on the ends, but these are decorated with the heads of Greek philosophers and have fluted mouldings rather than the stylised drapery, although they also have human feet

Fig 183
In this photograph of the 'Philosophers' table at Stourhead, the Egyptian-style supports can be seen on the end to the left.
[Hugh Kelly]

at their bases. Later that year, eight cane-seated armchairs, also in mahogany, were added, with Egyptian heads at the top of the front legs under the arms, and in December two matching chairs without arms.

Chippendale was probably the first British cabinetmaker to use Egyptian motifs. They had been used in French furniture since the late 1790s, drawing on works like Bernard de Montfaucon's *L'Antiquité Expliquée*, the seven-volume *Recueil d'antiquités égyptiennes, étrusques, grecques, gauloises* of Anne-Claude-Philippe de Caylus, and Giovanni Battista Piranesi's *Diverse Maniere d'adornare i Cammini* (see pp 47–9). Even during the period of the French Revolutionary and Napoleonic Wars, French taste was highly influential, particularly with the support of the Prince Regent, later to become George IV. Chippendale is believed to have gone to Paris in the early 19th century, and to have sketched contemporary French furniture while there. The library furniture he produced for Stourhead is typical of the Egyptiana of this period. It uses isolated Egyptian motifs rather than, as happened later with furniture like the Liberty Egyptian pieces (see p 55), basing the furniture on genuine Ancient Egyptian models. Also, the style of the Egyptian heads is typical of the way that elements like these were interpreted by artists unfamiliar with the conventions of Ancient Egyptian art. Stourhead House is a National Trust property and open to the public.

The Wellington Monument

The first Duke of Wellington, Arthur Wellesley, took his title in 1809 from the small town of the same name in Somerset, although he only visited it once, in 1819, and his victory at Waterloo is commemorated at Wellington by a towering monument on the Blackdown Hills. Designed in 1817, it was the first major commission of the local architect Thomas Lee, but the project was to be dogged by problems from the start. The monument had been suggested by William Ayshford Sanford, a local landowner who lived at nearby Nynehead House, and after £1,450 had been raised by public subscription to construct the monument, a competition was held to select a design. Lee's winning entry envisaged a 95ft-high pillar topped with a cast-iron statue of the Iron Duke on its summit and with three cottages in its base for veterans of the Napoleonic Wars, but the actual structure became much higher. It was built of local stone on the highest point of the local landscape that was part of the duke's estates. Building started in 1817, but a year later only 47ft of the monument had been built, and in 1820 a further appeal for £500 to continue the project had to be launched. Nine years later, in 1829, the monument had reached 121ft tall but an estimated £2,000 was still needed to complete it and the project was left incomplete. The situation was made even worse when lightning struck the monument in 1846 badly damaging it. In 1852 the Duke of Wellington died and a fresh appeal for funds was launched to complete the structure as a memorial to him. The Taunton architect C E Giles was hired but a survey revealed that leaving the unfinished monument exposed to the elements had meant that by this time much of the original mortar had been washed out. Within a year, the monument's height had been raised to 170ft, with stairs inside and a viewing chamber at its top (Fig 184). The underlying structural problems had still not been addressed, however, and in 1890 more work had to be carried out. The Wellington

Wellington
TA21 9PA

the battle placed around the monument, but this was finally reduced to four and these were to be removed for scrap during the Second World War. In 1985 a single cannon of appropriate vintage and origin was donated by the local rotary club.

The final monument has sometimes been described as an obelisk but it is actually triangular, rather than having four sides like a true obelisk, and it has been claimed that it was intended to resemble a bayonet. Inside, a staircase led up to a viewing platform with small circular windows. The Duke of Wellington had little, if any connection with Egypt, but British victories over the French in Egypt during the Napoleonic Wars may have been the inspiration for Egyptianising features added by Charles Giles in 1853–4. Giles created a three-sided base with slightly stepped plinth and massive battered corner pilasters, a cavetto cornice with vertical banding and a plain torus moulding, and a winged solar disc over the doorway to the stairs inside.[182]

The obelisk was taken over by a charitable trust in 1893, and in 1933 passed to the National Trust, with 12½ acres of surrounding land. Surveys in 2005 and 2008 revealed cracks in the monument due to flexing from wind pressure, and fears that stones from the facing might fall led to it being closed to the public and fenced off, although it is still easily visible. At the time of writing a plan for repair is being costed.

Monument was finally finished in 1892, at its final height of 175ft, but without the statue of the duke or the cottages at its base. The original plans had included 24 cannons from

East of England

Blickling Park

The pyramid is an iconic Egyptian form but it is ironic that although pyramidal mausoleums have been built in England, their main inspiration was Roman. Caius Epulo Cestius, a Plebeian Tribune in Ancient Rome who had visited Egypt and died around 12 BC, was buried in a steeply sloping pyramidal mausoleum. Because this was eventually used to form part of new fortifications around the city, it survived intact into modern times and would have been seen by many travellers, particularly those on the Grand Tour in the 18th century, and by architectural students who travelled to Rome to study its Classical remains. It was illustrated by Giovanni Battista Piranesi (see Fig 20), whose designs for Egyptian-style interiors were so influential in the late 18th century and its pitch, far steeper than that of most actual Ancient Egyptian pyramids, became a model for those built in Europe up until the 19th century.[183]

In 1794, the architect Joseph Bonomi, father of the draughtsman and Egyptologist Joseph Bonomi Jnr, built a mausoleum, probably inspired by the Cestius pyramid, for the remains of John Hobart, the 2nd Earl of Buckinghamshire (Fig 185). It was erected in the grounds of Blickling Hall and took the form of a limestone pyramid with a doorway in the centre of the east side, a memorial panel on the opposite side and two square window openings in the other

sides, all likewise in the centre of their respective sides. All are cut into the sides of the pyramid. The doorway has a simple stone door case or architrave and stepped entablature. On top of the entablature is a heraldic achievement, showing the arms of the earldom, and below this the Latin motto 'AVCTOR PRETIOSA FACET' (approximately, 'The giver makes it precious'). The memorial panel, with an architrave and entablature similar to the door, has an inscription recording that the monument was erected to the earl, and the burial of other family members, and has a small stone bull above the entablature. The two-barred window openings have moulded stone architraves. The iron railings surrounding the pyramid were a later addition. Inside, the mausoleum has a domed vault with eight arched recesses. Three of these link to the doorway and windows, the remaining five contain sarcophagi and monuments mounted on the walls. An earlier design for the monument had an even more steeply pitched pyramid with a square rusticated stone base and a flight of steps leading up to the entrance.[184] Another example of this style of monument can be found at Brightling (see p 208).

The Blickling Estate is a National Trust property and the gardens are open to the public.

Blickling
NR11 6NF

Fig 185
The Cestius pyramid in Rome does not appear to have originally been built with an entrance, although it was later broken into. However, the 18th-century pyramids built as monuments or landscape architecture, for which it is assumed to be the model, usually had a pedimented doorway of the sort seen here on the Hobart mausoleum in Blickling Park. [BB93/09310]

42 Fore Street

Hertford
SG14 1BY

There is a certain irony in the fact that despite the debates, designs and scholarship of architects, some of the most dramatic examples of the Egyptian style in England were essentially created by the whim of fashion and the generous application of stucco by an anonymous architect. Like the Egyptian House in Penzance (see p 233), 42 Fore Street was a commercial property, and basically a fairly standard building of its time, transformed by the addition of an exotic façade (Fig 186) some time in the early 1820s.[185] Given the comparative ease with which this could be done, it is also quite remarkable that these buildings remained intact and were not remodelled when fashions changed again.

At the top of the building, a cavetto cornice was added to conceal the slate roof behind. The cornice was decorated with vertical bands, interspersed with motifs resembling crowned cartouches resting on the *nbw* or 'gold' hieroglyph. (The cartouche containing the royal name could be shown on the 'gold' sign; see for instance a limestone lintel of Amenemhat III in the British Museum, EA 1072.) The cornice flares out at either end to occupy the whole width of the building, but the torus moulding at its base, with the traditional Egyptian design of horizontal and diagonal banding, extends outwards down the sides of the building to create a battered profile. Below the cornice, symmetrically placed recessed windows on the first and second floors have been given gently battered architraves (compare the windows on the building to its left). The upper windows are without decoration, those on the first floor have cavetto cornices with winged solar discs, and plain torus mouldings under these.

On the ground floor, there is a full width cavetto cornice above the shopfront. The cornice flares out over the neighbouring building on its left but is cut short by a corbel on the building to its right. The cornice is decorated with a large winged solar disc in its centre. On each side of this are two of the cartouche-like motifs used on the roof cornice, with low barred rectangular panels between them. The ends are completed with vertical banding, again repeating the pattern of the roof cornice. Below the cornice is a fairly plain timber shopfront, in which the display windows have been given a battered profile, and the pairs of slim pilasters that flank each of them tapered downwards to make room for this. The pilasters have quite elaborate foliated capitals, but these are not in an Egyptian style. The doorway is inset, with a plain two-leaf door, three-quarter glazed with a fanlight above. Originally, the display windows would have had glazing bars and small panes but these were removed, probably in the late 19th century, and replaced with plate glass. Below the windows are metal grilles with a pattern of vertical bars and the motifs used on the cornices. Here, the 'crown' element is made up of an oval base with three wedge or fan-like elements above it. The cartouche has two diagonal bars running across it, for functional reasons, while the base element has the same shape as on the cornices. The interior is without Egyptian features, and at the time of writing was occupied by a restaurant. In the 1980s, the façade was coloured to recreate something like its original appearance.

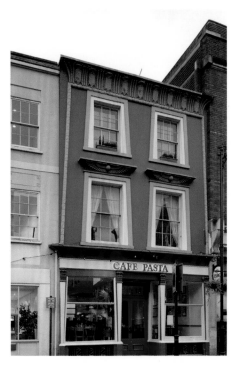

Fig 186
The Egyptian theme was comprehensively applied to the façade of 42 Fore Street, Hertford, from cornice to pavement. [BB007033]

This building predates the Egyptian House in Penzance and may have influenced it, as the decorative elements on the roof cornice there are almost identical, except that the cartouches have a border and the crowning element more closely resembles a rayed sun. This in turn suggests that both drew on a common design source, which may have been plates in Vivant Denon's *Voyages*. There is no single image in Denon which matches these decorated cartouches, but plates illustrate similar ones from Philae (plate 56 no. 8, and plate 83) and Tentyris/Dendera (plate 57). The elements can be seen more clearly on the cornice of the offices of Marshall's Mill in Leeds (see p 265), which is based on the portico of the Temple of Horus at Edfu, but they also occur on a number of Egyptian temples, such as those illustrated by Denon, built during the Ptolemaic period, when it was ruled by monarchs of Greek descent, and extended under Roman rule.

East Midlands

Freemasons' Hall

Main Ridge West,
Boston
PE21 6QQ

The idea that Freemasonry had its roots in Ancient Egypt has not been able to withstand modern historical scholarship but in the 19th and early 20th centuries it enjoyed a degree of popularity in Masonic circles. Although they were never common, a number of Masonic temples in England had Egyptian decoration, including now vanished ones in London at the Horseshoe Hotel in Tottenham Court Road, Café Verrey in Regent Street and one at the Great Eastern Hotel near Liverpool Street Station which survives as a gymnasium in the basement. The most impressive example of this exotic style, however, and the only one with an Egyptian exterior, is outside London and was created for the Lodge of Harmony in Boston between 1860 and 1863.

It has been suggested that the building was designed by Joseph Bonomi Jnr,[186] but it is now credited to the London architect George Hackford,[187] although it seems to have been mainly inspired by one man, Cabourn Pocklington. Little is known of him, although it seems reasonable to assume that he was the father of Henry Cabourn Pocklington, the physicist and mathematician, but he was a dedicated Freemason and in 1892 the lodge celebrated both his golden wedding and his fortieth year as a Freemason. In the 18th and early 19th centuries, Masonic lodges usually met in public buildings, often inns and taverns, and it was not until the 19th century

that it became common for dedicated Masonic buildings to be built and used. The Lodge of Harmony had been founded in 1806 when it took over the warrant of a dormant lodge in Northampton. In 1856 it celebrated its jubilee with a banquet, with Pocklington as Worshipful Master of the lodge. Not long after this, a committee was established to look into the construction of a new, purpose-built Masonic hall at Main Ridge, and it was 'Bro. Pocklington who was foremost in urging the committee in 1859 to consider adopting a style… that would endorse the Lectures which teach that "our usages and customs were derived from the Ancient Egyptians".'[188]

The committee duly agreed and capital for construction was raised through the issue of 60 £5 shares for a building with an entrance hall, kitchen and banquet room on the ground floor, and the robing room, Tyler's anteroom and temple itself on the floor above, reached by a spiral staircase. The foundation stone was laid on 20 April 1860 but the decoration of the building was not finished for three years, although the lodge rooms were in use before this. On 28 May 1863 the building was dedicated by the Provincial Grand Master, William Beauclerk, 10th Duke of St Albans.

The new building was described in an 1894 history of Freemasonry in Lincolnshire by William Dixon as a 'reproduction of the

Temple of Dandour, in Nubia' and as being 'pure Egyptian'.[189] Apart from the fact that the size and style of this particular temple meant that its proportions could be fairly easily adapted to those required by the new building, the choice is said to have been influenced by pictures of the temple that had been published in 1860. (J S Curl has suggested that the inspiration for it was one of the plates in Vivant Denon's *Voyages*.) The side and rear walls are of red brick, and the roof slated but the façade, built of Gault clay bricks and ashlar, or dressed stone, has battered sides edged by stone torus mouldings and a carved stone cavetto cornice, with a small parapet set back above it. In the centre of the portico two palm columns are topped by square abaci and a stone entablature or lintel. Inset in the portico is the actual doorway, which is battered and with an ashlar surround (Fig 187).

The temple on which the building is based, Dendur, originally stood about 77km south of Aswan, but although the Boston hall resembles Dendur it is not a direct copy. The temple, dating from the period of Roman government of Egypt, is now in the Metropolitan Museum of Art in New York having been given by the Egyptian government in 1963 in recognition of American help in saving the monuments of Nubia from being submerged when the new Aswan dam was built. It is in two parts, a pylon gateway with cavetto cornice and winged solar disc flanked by *uraei*, and beyond a small courtyard a columned *pronaos* or portico with two pillars, screen walls (only one of which survives) linking the main façade to the pillars, and a doorway to an inner hall and sanctuary. The Boston Freemasons' Hall has combined the portico and gateway, and changed the style of the columns from the quite elaborate Late Period style of the originals to a much more classically Egyptian palm column, with dates as well as leaves.

A large winged solar disc is carved on the cornice and another above the inner door. The entablature, abaci and columns are carved with hieroglyphic inscriptions, which were composed by Cabourn Pocklington. (The actual carving was carried out by Abraham Kent, a member of the lodge who was appropriately also an operative stonemason.) In 1894, Dixon's history of Lincolnshire Freemasonry translated them as follows:

In the 22nd year of the reign of Her Majesty, the Royal Daughter, Victoria Lady most gracious, this Hall was erected; May it be prosperous [on the entablature and abaci]: Zetland was Ruler of the Mysteries [on the upper left column] and St. Albans Ruler of the District [upper right column] when this building was dedicated to the God of Truth, who lives for ever [lower left column], in the year 1863, 5th month and 28th day [lower right column].[190]

Fig 187
The façade of Freemasons' Hall, showing how it slopes inwards at the front and from the side (battering), and the conventional design of the rest of the building. [DP103991]

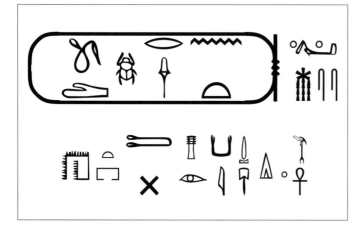

Fig 188 (above)
In the actual hieroglyphic inscription on the lintel and column abaci, the first glyph is reversed, the second is upside down, and the bird in the cartouche is a Griffon Vulture (*Gyps fulvus*) rather than the Egyptian Vulture (*Neophron percnopterus*), which would affect the reading of Victoria's name. These errors have been corrected here and the inscription shown as a single line.
[Mark Rudolph]

Fig 189 (below)
Rather than using genuine Ancient Egyptian words and phrases, much of this inscription seems to have been written phonetically, and a number of the signs would now be given different sound values. The arm with flail used to write 'ruler' is used in the same way for inscriptions at Crystal Palace (Fig 105) and Hartwell House (Fig 167).
[Mark Rudolph]

There are problems with the first part of this, however. Victoria acceded to the throne in 1837 and was crowned in 1838. This would date the building to either 1859 or 1860 and of these the latter is more likely. Curl, and others who have presumably taken their date from him, give the translation as 'In the Twenty-Third year'. The hieroglyphic numerals on the entablature actually refer to the *twenty-fourth* year of her reign, thus dating it to 1861/2 (Fig 188). The rest of the inscription, on the pillars, refers to Thomas Dundas, 2nd Earl of Zetland, who was Grand Master of the United Grand Lodge of England between 1844 and 1870, and hence head of English Freemasonry at the time the Hall was built, and William Beauclerk, 10th Duke of St Albans, and Provincial Grand Master at the time it was dedicated (Figs 189 and 190). On the basis of the main inscription on the lintel, and the writing of a number of signs there and in the column inscriptions, it is likely that Pocklington based his text on the inscriptions in the Egyptian Court at the Crystal Palace (see p 148).

In addition to the main inscriptions the columns are also decorated with leaf patterns at their base, a frieze of *ankh* and *was* hieroglyphs, read as 'Life' and 'Dominion', below the first band of the hieroglyphic inscription, a frieze of five-pointed stars and one 'Maltese' cross in a circle between this and the second band of inscription, and incised horizontal banding separating the various elements. The hieroglyphic frieze closely resembles one found on door jambs in Egyptian temples, and known as the 'Shadow of the Door', marking where the leaves of the door rested when it was open (see Fig 161). Ancient Egyptian palm columns did not represent the tree itself but a number of branches from it lashed to a column, or together to form a primitive column. The 'U'-shaped elements with lines inside them below the capitals therefore represent the ends of palm branches, and the banding above the rope lashing these to the column. On the lintel of the doorway is an inscription in Greek 'ΓΝΩΘΙ ΣΕΑΥΤΟΝ' (*Gnosi* or *Gnothi Seauton*) which translates as 'Know Thyself', an aphorism said to have been inscribed on the forecourt of the Temple of Apollo at Delphi, and the motto of the lodge.

Upstairs, the temple itself is 40ft long and 20ft across and proportionately high so as to form a symbolically significant double cube. As well as the normal items which would be expected, there are several unusual symbols which continue the Egyptian theme. On the wall above the Master's chair is a hand holding a cross, emerging from an equilateral triangle surrounded by rays of light. Over the entrance doorway at the other end of the temple is a winged solar disc, again surrounded by rays of light, and below it a scarab beetle (Fig 191). On the north wall is a lotus resting on a triangle and encircled by a serpent, again surrounded by rays of light (Fig 192), and on the ceiling a solar disc combined with another equilateral triangle.

All the Egyptian elements were seen as being related to the principles and precepts of Freemasonry, and Dixon's book noted that 'Their connection with and application to Freemasonry are of exceeding interest to the intelligent craftsman.'[191] he went on to remark that 'A visit to the hall under the guidance of Bro. Pocklington is a source of great pleasure. Few have studied this division of Masonry more or have a better grasp of the subject than he.'[192]

Although he may have composed the hieroglyphic inscriptions and proposed the style of the building's exterior, Pocklington was not the only lodge member with an interest in Ancient Egypt. Dr Walter Clegg, commemorated by a plaque in the temple as the author of the lyrics of two pieces often used to open and close meetings of Masonic lodges, gave an account of the symbolism of the decorations in the temple when it was formally opened. He described the symbol of the hand with the cross as coming from 'the Temple of Edfon [Edfu]' and as representing the Master's hand holding the Key of Light and Knowledge. The symbol of the lotus was meant to represent different stages of growth while the serpent represented Eternity. The solar disc and triangle on the ceiling stood for the True God and was described as a common symbol in Egyptian temples, while the scarab beetle was said to be copied from examples at Karnac [sic] and to signify Industry, Patience and Secrecy.[193]

However, while the front of the building is a fairly accurate copy of its Ancient

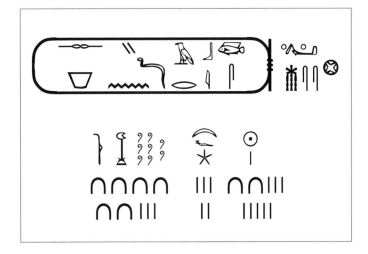

Egyptian model, the symbols in the temple are less accurate stylistically. This may reflect the fact that their designer used outdated Egyptological sources, but given the interpretations placed on them by Clegg probably reflects a desire to stress their relevance to Masonic teachings, and the supposed origins of the Craft in Ancient Egypt. From an Egyptological point of view, the hand holding the cross most closely resembles images from the Amarna period

Fig 190 (above)
The name in the cartouche seems to have been written phonetically, with one sign per sound, and the title is repeated from the other column with the addition of a sign used in the writing of Ancient Egyptian placenames. The writing of the date follows the form in genuine hieroglyphic inscriptions, although the writing of 'month' (above the five strokes) is faulty.
[Mark Rudolph]

Fig 191
While the decoration above the door at one end of the temple, by which it is entered, resembles an Ancient Egyptian winged solar disc flanked by cobras, the disc is actually a terrestrial globe, and the outlines of Africa and several other areas can clearly be made out.
[DP103989]

Fig 192
The decoration on the north wall of the temple represents a lotus plant resting on a triangle or pyramid, which can just be seen behind it, surrounded by an *ouroboros* serpent swallowing its tail (see p 264), with rays of glory emerging from the whole. Lotus flowers are shown in four stages, representing infancy, youth, maturity, and old age.
[DP103984]

of Ancient Egypt when rays coming from the Aten, or solar disc, were shown ending with hands and those pointing to members of the royal family ended in *ankhs*, symbols of life. Without a more specific reference it is difficult to link it with the later Temple of Horus at Edfu. The lotus was a solar symbol in Ancient Egypt and connected with creation myths, and a serpent (probably representing the deity Mehen) can be shown surrounding the pharaoh whilst swallowing its own tail in a form resembling the ring-shaped *shen* symbol, symbolising both eternity and protection. Solar images are not so much common as ubiquitous in Egyptian temples, but despite the pyramids, triangles are not common in Egyptian art. The scarab beetle is a solar symbol, and associated with the god Khepri, but its associations are with creation and coming into existence rather than those cited by Clegg, which more closely resemble the speculations of Hermetic philosophers made before the translation of hieroglyphs. At one point one of the ceilings in the building (most likely that of the temple itself) was painted to resemble a starry sky like the ceilings of Egyptian temples and tombs.

The Hall was altered at some time in the 20th century to extend it into the building next door and create a lounge and bar area, but the original features survived more or less intact, although some of the carving on the front columns is beginning to weather badly. Inside, the ground floor is plain and without Egyptian features but the main temple still has its Egyptian decoration. All the doorways have simple cavetto cornices decorated with ornate solar discs with a scarab beetle in their centre, except that on the north wall, which has had its solar disc removed and replaced by a fire exit sign. The two doorways on the east wall lead to cupboards. The ceiling is decorated with gold stars but these are likely to be modern, although they may have replaced original ones.

This is not only a striking building and one whose use of the Egyptian style is generally well-informed, but also one which acts as a reminder of the powerful influence that Ancient Egypt has had on speculative Freemasonry. The exterior can easily be viewed from the street but the interior is not accessible to the public.

West Midlands

Biddulph Grange Gardens

In 1840 the horticulturalist and botanist James Bateman and his wife Maria moved to Biddulph Grange, and began turning the 15 acres of gardens into the extraordinary creation that it is today. With the help of the painter Edward Cooke, Bateman laid out a series of themed and connected areas, each separate and hidden from one another.[194]

One of the areas was an Egyptian Court in which two pairs of sphinxes on triple plinths flank a pathway leading to a pylon-shaped doorway with a cavetto cornice above. On a panel on the cornice is carved a winged solar disc flanked by *uraei*. The disc itself is gilded, the wings are painted red and the *uraei* blue. Through the doorway a dim passageway lit through a red glass window leads to a statue of the god Thoth in baboon form. A junction in this small building allows a visitor to exit to (or enter from) other sections of the garden, with that side of the building designed to match the theme of the particular section. Most of what appears to be the building, seen from the entrance to the Egyptian Court, is actually clipped yew hedges trimmed into stubby obelisk or block shapes, and with a pyramid above the doorway (Fig 193).

Cooke, best known as a marine painter, had visited Egypt, but it was the sculptor Benjamin Waterhouse Hawkins, who also modelled the life-sized dinosaur figures in the grounds of the Crystal Palace, who created the sphinxes and other animals for Biddulph between 1859 and 1862.[195] The sphinxes, carved from local millstone grit, are quite blocky and stylised but clearly intended to be Egyptian. They have royal cartouches carved on their 'forearms', which may have been readable at one time but are now too worn to be legible.

Obelisks and sphinxes have been used to decorate gardens since at least the 18th century and there are examples at Chiswick House and Buscot Park. The grounds or gardens of other houses featured pyramids, of the steeply pitched Classical style, either as actual mausoleums as in the case of Blickling Park in Norfolk (see p 247), or as eye-catchers, like the now destroyed pyramid by Vanbrugh in the grounds of Stowe House. The Egyptian Court at Biddulph, however, is unusual for the fact that its Egyptian theme is so consistent and self-contained.

Bateman left Biddulph for London in 1869, and after a period of neglect and decline the gardens were acquired by the National Trust in 1988 and have subsequently been restored to Bateman's original designs.

Biddulph
ST8 7SD

Fig 193
The Egyptian Court at Biddulph Grange before its replanting as part of the restoration of the gardens. [BB93/24643]

The Egyptian Court represented Biddulph Grange on one of a series of four postage stamps depicting British Gardens in 1983, and was replanted around 1994. Biddulph Grange and its gardens are open to the public.

GEC Witton Factory

Dulverton Road,
Birmingham
B6 7JJ

Between the two World Wars, there was an interesting and important development in the use of the Egyptian style in England. In the 19th and early 20th centuries, the most popular use of the style, by far, had been for monuments and of these the overwhelming majority had been in cemeteries. There had been a number of commercial buildings; the Egyptian House in Penzance (see p 233), Fore Street Hertford (see p 249) and Fore Street Exeter (see p 237) and some public and religious; the Civil and Military Library Devonport (see p 229), Masonic Halls at Warwick (see p 261) and Boston

(see p 250) and the Old Synagogue in Canterbury (see p 222), but only three which could clearly be identified as industrial. Two of these were associated with waterworks, the Maidstone Waterworks building at East Farleigh (see p 209) and the valve house at Widdop Reservoir (see p 280). The other was Marshall's Mill in Leeds (see p 265). By contrast, between the two World Wars the primary use of the Egyptian style was in public, commercial and industrial buildings. These included cinemas and offices, but four were factories; the W H Smith works in Stamford Street (see p 195), Greater London House (see p 152), the GEC Factory at Witton, and the Hoover Factory (see p 174), and of these two were the work of one man, the architect Thomas Wallis.

Between 1918 and 1922, Wallis Gilbert and Partners (which had only been founded in 1916) built three extensions to the existing factory complex of the General Electric Company Ltd (GEC) at Witton. GEC had been founded in 1886 as a London-based wholesaler of electrical goods. It moved to Manchester in 1889 and began manufacturing, and then in 1900 set up a new factory at Witton. By 1902 the site covered 45 acres and during the First World War plans were made to double factory space. Of seven major projects three went to Wallis Gilbert. These were for the machine shop extension (1918–20), the switchgear works (1919–21) and the general administration building (1919–21), which was also to house drawing offices.[196] Wallis had set up his new practice to collaborate on the design of factories with

Trussed Concrete Steel (Truscon), the British outpost of an American company formed to promote a system of concrete reinforcement developed and patented by the Kahn brothers. As heavy manufacturing industry declined in Britain, many of Wallis's buildings were at least partly demolished or changed use and most of what remains is the decorated fronts of the factories, but when built they were conceived as a unified design. Like the new Arcadia Works of Carreras in London (see p 152), the extensions to the GEC works incorporated numerous improvements in factory design either resulting from the extensive use of reinforced concrete, or aimed at increasing amenities for the workforce. There was widespread use of natural light, a system to filter, heat and circulate air, and heating by hot-water pipes that passed under lockers to dry clothes. The machine shop extension used some Egyptian-style elements, notably pylon-shaped doorways with battered sides, but it was the general administration building that showed the strongest Egyptian influence (Fig 194).

Fig 194
The elaborate entrance of the GEC Factory, with its battered sides and Egyptian decoration, dominates the approach to the works, and is one of the most important elements helping to establish the company image.
[DP139063]

This was the first large office block that had been built by the practice and it showed many of the features which were to become typical of Wallis's work. The front elevation was long (over 200ft) and low, with a central entrance tower, two main storeys and an attic storey, and subtle corner towers. The entrance dominated the end of a short road leading off Electric Avenue. His later Firestone Factory in London shared this layout but lacked the central entrance tower, and in his Hoover Factory the attic storey has gone and the two-storey layout is less marked, although the corner towers are still there and more strongly emphasised. The Witton administration building was 'E' shaped, wrapping around an existing central stores, and internally was dominated by corridors that ran along its length. If the machine shop extension and switchgear works were designed with function in mind to allow an efficient manufacturing process, one important role of the administration building was to assert the company's identity.

Interestingly, Egyptian elements do not seem to have been Wallis's first choice. Initial designs for the central tower and entrance featured Roman elements, particularly fasces-shaped columns either side of the door. The Classical theme continued over the doorway in a pediment with a roundel which featured the head of a female figure representing Electricity. In the built version, a number of changes were made. The head of Electricity was replaced by a circular window, and above this was added the serpent-twined staff or caduceus of Mercury or Hermes, both deities being messengers of the gods, and which symbolically still represented the electricity which was at the heart of the company's products. In the initial design, the company identity had also been explicitly referred to in other parts of the building, as on the corner towers where the GEC initials and its magnet logo were once placed, and again over the inner doors.

A number of other changes were made to the building both before and after it was built, and it is difficult to establish from surviving records what was done when. Between the pilasters there were originally panels with moulded plaster medallions emphasising the division between the two storeys inside, nailhead motifs on the columns of the frontal column capitals were replaced by tasselled discs, and there were also large single tassels at the base of the pilasters to repeat those on the capitals. A decorative element above the entrance was also removed at some point.

Despite the presence of Neoclassical motifs, the battered shape of the Portland stone entrance already suggested an Egyptian influence, and the central tower and entrance as it survives today has papyrus columns, and in the reveal over the doorway itself Wallis added an unmistakably Egyptian winged solar disc flanked by *uraei*. The roundel in the pediment is now blank, but the winged staff survived and the wings expand to fill the interior of the pediment (Fig 195). The decoration of the building included elements which were to become typical of Wallis, particularly the use of nailhead motifs and tassels. On the entrance, nailhead motifs and plain discs are combined with ridged or barred elements, again in a way that Wallis would go on to use in other designs. Here, the long sides and barring suggest the *nemes* headcloth worn by pharaohs and Egyptian gods, and other buildings by Wallis also used this device of an opening or disc element framed on three sides. Elsewhere, the overlapping wheel designs to either side of the doorway may refer to the company's products, and the design on the capitals of the pilasters along the front resembles a meander, often known as a Greek Key, but can also be seen as a stylised alternating wave pattern, again alluding to the company's core focus.

Fig 195 (far left)
The final version of the entrance of the GEC Factory, with elongated papyrus capital pilasters, and a winged solar disc over the doorway.
[DP139065]

Fig 196 (left)
The entrance lobby repeats many of the elements from the front of the buildings, especially in the ridged and tasselled decoration of the pilaster capitals.
[BB96/10624]

Inside the building, in the lobby or entrance hall, the same elements of tassels, nailheads, discs and banding are again used (Fig 196). Ridged pilasters are decorated at the top with moulded plaster capitals where a tasselled disc is framed on three sides by barred elements echoing those on the entrance, and at their bases by tasselled nailheads. Bars and plain discs decorate a border linking the pilasters, and the lift entrance is framed by a simple barred frame with squares and inset plain discs at the corners. On the first floor, above the lobby, is a meeting or reception room (Fig 197). This is decorated with walnut panelling highlighted with ebony. The banded framing and nailhead elements are used around doors and at the top of a bookcase, while the inset wall panels are battered. The ceiling features winged flaming torches, probably in plaster painted to imitate bronze (Fig 198).

By the 1980s, the site had become run down and was partially leased. Some buildings were demolished and lack of maintenance caused damage to others. Eventually, the buildings to the rear of the administration building were replaced with a modern warehouse, but fortunately the front elevation was preserved and restored. This is one of Thomas Wallis's most interesting buildings because it shows him using recognisably Classical and Egyptian elements, together with other more stylised motifs that were to become distinctive in his work. Here the different elements can still be distinguished. In later buildings, such as the Hoover Factory, they are thoroughly digested into the modernised Neoclassical style that was his signature. However, knowing that the Egyptian style was an influence in the early stages of his factory design, it can be argued that it is still present in the later designs. The simple coloured decoration at the base of the Hoover Factory echoes the Egyptian use of colour, and his fondness for long, low buildings with simple shapes and columned fronts suggests the influence of buildings like the Mortuary Temple of Hatshepsut at Deir el-Bahri.

The exterior of the building can be seen from Dulverton Road but the interior is not accessible to the public.

Fig 197
The panelling in the reception room is slightly battered around the doorways, and employs the same ridged and banded elements used throughout the building. [BB96/10627]

Fig 198
The wings on the torches are similar to those used on winged solar discs by the Ancient Egyptians, but the torches are solidly Classical. This mixture, together with Wallis's signature decorative elements, is typical of his 'Fancy' factories. [BB96/10630]

3 High Street

At a casual glance, there is nothing particularly Egyptian about this handsome two-storey red-brick building with its dormer windowed attic, constructed around 1700, but a closer look at its elaborate carved timber door case reveals some unexpected features (Fig 199).

The door case has pillars either side of the door with a lintel above, and over this a semicircular pediment. The pillars have three shallow bands of decoration, the bottom suggesting the leaves or stem sheaths that decorate the bottom of Ancient Egyptian papyrus columns, and the middle resembling *mw*, the Egyptian hieroglyph for water. Intriguingly, the third and uppermost band is a repeating pattern of diamonds within double-lined horizontal borders, which is a simpler version of the pattern found on the ceiling moulding of the Egyptian Hall at Stowe (*see* p 214). Above these bands, intricate floral capitals include elements resembling lotus flowers, but the cross-hatched and swagged tops are not at all Egyptian, although the plants sprouting from them may also be intended to represent lotuses. The lintel, which extends at the sides to support the deep pediment above, has a simple frieze of rosettes at its base and above this a cavetto cornice with a frieze of lotus flowers in rounded arches. The interior of the pediment has another frieze of larger lotus flowers, without the arches, and above this a simple frieze of triangles. In the centre of the pediment is a keystone carved with a triangle surrounded by a double circle carved with eight symbols.

These symbols link the building to its use by the Shakespeare Lodge of Mark Master Masons. Mark Masonry is a 'side' or linked order of Freemasonry, that is one where a candidate must already have become a Master Mason. In Mark Masonry, the

allegory around which the ritual dramas used to teach its principles is based is that of the masons working on the building of Solomon's Temple and its keystone, and the marks they made on stones to denote their own work. Initiates to the Mark Degree choose their own mason's mark and wear a members' 'jewel' (like a medal) consisting of the keystone. On the obverse of the stone is an equilateral triangle surrounded by a double circle containing Hebrew characters, as on the door case, and on the reverse a double triangle featuring the letters HTWSSTKS, standing for 'Hiram The

Warwick
CV34 4AP

Fig 199
The elaborate decoration of the door case of 3 High Street, Warwick is heavily symbolic and would have been intended to indicate the function of the building at the time it was added. [DP139062]

Widow's Son Sent To King Solomon', and referring to a biblical passage in II Chronicles on which the Mark ritual is based. The meanings of the Hebrew letters and the biblical passage are revealed during the Mark Degree ceremony. The tympanum, or window area, of the pediment, used to have a stained-glass window reading 'Shakespeare Lodge ... founded 1791', but although Mark Masonry was worked sporadically in the latter half of the 18th century and first half of the 19th, it was not until 1856 that the Grand Lodge of Mark Master Masons was founded as an independent grand lodge. The Provincial Mark Grand Lodge of Warwickshire and Staffordshire was formed in 1876 and in 1880 the Shakespeare Lodge of Mark Master Masons No. 40 was warranted to meet in Warwick. As Lord Brooke, the 5th Earl of Warwick was Mark Provincial Grand Master of Warwickshire and Staffordshire between 1882 and 1886. The building at 3 High Street was used from 1806 as the estate office for the earls of Warwick, and occupied by their land agent. The door case was carved in 1892 by a local craftsman called Kendall, who used timber reclaimed from a recently demolished windmill at Birdingbury, and indicates that the building was in use by the Shakespeare Lodge, and probably by Craft Masons as well, by this date. A contemporary report in the *Warwick Advertiser* noted that

> ...the decorative details of the design are an ideal of a possible resemblance to the character of the ornamentation of King Solomon's Temple so far as may be imagined from the scriptural description thereof, and their significance will be readily understood by those who have been initiated into the mysteries of freemasonry... .

This helps to understand why the decoration on the door case is not fully Egyptian. By the time it was created, the use of the Egyptian style in architecture tended to be archaeologically correct, as in Freemasons' Hall at Boston in Lincolnshire (see p 250), but the inspiration of this piece comes primarily from the biblical narrative that is central to Freemasonry, and not from the belief that the Craft had its roots in Ancient Egypt. For example, II Chronicles, chap 3 v 16 (King James version) tells how Solomon created the two pillars named Jachin and Boaz that stood before the Temple, 'And he made chains, as in the oracle, and put them on the heads of the pillars; and made an hundred pomegranates, and put them on the chains.' Looking closely at the door case, it can be seen that the swagging on the column capitals is in fact made up of pomegranates and the links of a chain can be glimpsed behind the uppermost row. The Egyptian elements in the decoration can also be explained by another biblical passage in the Book of Kings, which records how Solomon took as his wife the daughter of a pharaoh of Egypt.

The interior of the building is not accessible to the public but the door case can be viewed from the street.

Yorkshire and The Humber

General Cemetery and Montague House

In 1836, only a year after Egyptian-style catacombs were built in Exeter (*see* p 242), Sheffield got its own cemetery, and it was also one with Egyptian features. The population of the city trebled between 1801 and 1851, and like many cities at this time it suffered severely during the worldwide cholera epidemic of 1832. One of the leading campaigners for a new cemetery was Thomas Asline Ward, master cutler of the city and founder of the Sheffield Literary and Philosophical Society. In 1834 the General Cemetery Company was founded, many of its supporters being Nonconformists. A nine-acre site was purchased, chosen to be near the new western suburbs and prosperous middle-class areas of the city. A competition to design the new cemetery was won by Samuel Worth, who was assisted in the layout of the grounds by Robert Marnock, who would later design and become curator of the Royal Botanical Society's gardens in Regent's Park in London. It was one of the first of the new garden cemeteries, inspired by Père Lachaise in Paris, and influenced John Claudius Loudon's 1843 work *On the Laying Out, Planting, and Managing of Cemeteries*, which was to become a key text for those promoting cemetery reform. The cemetery was built on a site sloping down toward the Porter Brook. Sandstone for the cemetery buildings was quarried out of the hillside, and the resulting space was filled again and used for vaults. Two sets of catacombs were created by the main gatehouse and entrance on Cemetery Avenue, which now joins Eccleshall Road, but these were no more popular than others of their kind, and few were ever occupied.[197]

Most of the cemetery buildings are in a plain Greek Revival style, but several, designed by Samuel Worth, have Egyptian-style features. At the southern entrance to the cemetery are the offices of the General Cemetery Company, built in sandstone ashlar and known as Montague House. These are in a plain, almost severe, Greek Revival style with a simple portico framed by two Doric columns. The windows are in a simple Egyptian style, slightly inset in battered openings with plain mouldings and cavetto cornices.

Nearby is the Egyptian Gate, a pedestrian entrance opening onto Cemetery Road, which was restored in the 1990s (Fig 200). It is a battered archway, with bevelled inner edges and angled top on the inside. A plain torus moulding runs round the edges of the arch and it has a flared cavetto cornice with vertical banding and winged solar disc

Cemetery Road, Sheffield S11 8FS

Fig 200
The Egyptian Gate, built as a pedestrian entrance to the General Cemetery, shows the eclectic mix of Classical and Ancient Egyptian motifs often found in 19th-century cemeteries. In 1843, A W Pugin was to strongly criticise the use of pagan symbols in Christian cemeteries (see p 38).
[DP092861]

above it. Although the winged disc is clearly recognisable as an Egyptian symbol from its context, the wings are partly in the round and their shape owes more to European artistic models than the Egyptian, where the wings are normally flat and almost rectangular. To either side of the gateway itself, flanking walls just below the level of the cornice with large plain torus mouldings along their top lead to square pillars joining the gate to the cemetery wall. The outer face of the pillars is carved to suggest a battered shape.

The actual gates are Graeco-Roman in style rather than Egyptian. Some of the bars are stylised fasces, there are geometric designs at the base of the gate, the outer bars have capitals made up of bulbs, spheres and fluted cones, and the inner bars have capitals with inverted triangles topped with more

of the fluted cones. In the centre of each gate is the figure of a serpent swallowing its own tail. The *ouroboros*, a Greek name meaning 'tail swallower', is an ancient symbol associated with concepts of rebirth. It is probably used here in a general symbolic sense, alluding to the Christian concept of resurrection, rather than as a specific reference to its symbolism in alchemy or Gnostic and Hermetic philosophy. The symbol of a serpent swallowing its tail is found in Ancient Egypt, for example the serpent god Mehen is shown in this way protectively encircling the pharaoh on one of the shrines in the tomb of Tutankhamun, but it is not common.

There seem to have been plans for two paths leading from the company offices to Egyptian gates, but only one was built. The Nonconformist chapel was built downhill and north-west of the Egyptian Gate. It is in the Greek Revival style, with a triangular pediment and a portico with four Doric columns. It has an entrance and windows with battered sides but the architraves and cornices of these are in Classical rather than Egyptian style.

Within a few years of opening, the cemetery had to reduce its charges and with them the dividends it paid to its investors, and largely survived on pauper burials for which it was paid five shillings apiece – although there was another cholera epidemic in 1849. A new Anglican chapel in fashionable neo-Gothic style and a further consecrated area for Anglican burials were added in the 1850s. The same story of gradual decline familiar from other joint stock cemeteries followed. The catacombs were rebuilt to create concrete vaults when space became limited but even in the 1950s plots were still being sold in perpetuity. Income fell and costs increased, including the need to repair war damage. The cemetery was eventually offered for sale to the City

Council, which, however, was not willing to assume responsibility for it. In 1963, a developer took a majority shareholding in the General Cemetery Company and plans were put forward to clear the site for housing. Fortunately, planning permission was withheld and in the 1970s the City Council took on the site. The decision was taken to maintain the original site but after photography and recording of monuments the Anglican extension was cleared and thousands of gravestones removed. The last burial was in 1978. The original cemetery was designated a Conservation Area in 1986 and the Friends of the General Cemetery were established in 1989. The Conservation Area has now been extended and the cemetery is a Grade II listed Park.

The Egyptian-style buildings in the Sheffield General Cemetery show the same use of simple battered windows and doors in otherwise conventional buildings as the building in Holloway Street in Exeter (see p 238); even in the most Egyptian structure, the gateway, Egyptian elements are mixed with features in the Classical tradition. In such buildings, lacking the exuberance of the early and more commercial applications of the Egyptian style but not as archaeologically accurate as buildings that began to be built in the 1840s, like the gate lodges of Abney Park (see p 88) and Marshall's Mill (see below), the principle at work seems to be that the use of Egyptian elements is enough to suggest the values associated with Ancient Egypt without having to make the building fully in the Egyptian style.

The cemetery is open to the public. The office building is not, but can be clearly seen from the street.

Marshall's Mill

In Benjamin Disraeli's 1845 novel *Sybil, or The Two Nations*, he describes the establishment of a Mr Trafford – 'a factory which was now one of the marvels of the district; one might almost say, of the country: a single room, spreading over nearly two acres, and holding more than two thousand work-people'.[198]

This was not a product of Disraeli's imagination but based on a real building – a gigantic flax mill with a grassed roof on which sheep used to graze and a front like an Ancient Egyptian temple. Marshall's Mill, now known as Temple Mill, is a unique building and one of the most spectacular uses of the Ancient Egyptian style anywhere outside Egypt.

In 1836, the prosperous linen-thread spinning company Marshall and Co was looking to expand into cloth manufacture and began to make plans for a new mill, counting house and warehouse in its main base of Leeds. Integrated production of both yarn and cloth would allow the company to reduce costs and compete in export markets with other firms using power looms to produce cloth. The senior member of the Marshall family at this time was John Marshall, but his sons were beginning to take over from him and one of them, James Garth Marshall, took the lead in the planning of the new site. By May 1838 he had two clear alternatives. One was a design for conventional multi-storey buildings, a seven-storey warehouse and six-storey mill, produced by Peter Fairbairn, a Leeds architect and brother of the Scottish civil engineer William (later Sir William) Fairbairn. This would have been built on the site of a demolished mill north of Water Street in Leeds. The other proposal was for an

Marshall Street,
Leeds
LS11 9YJ

innovative single-storey complex to be built at the south end of Marshall Street. (Only one other mill of this sort had previously been built, at Deanston near Stirling in Scotland, and its creator had recommended the design to James Marshall.) After carefully comparing the two proposals, including having a model measuring 6ft high and 24ft square made so that the effect of lighting could be simulated, James Marshall concluded that the single-storey mill (Fig 201) could be built for £24,300, over £4,000 cheaper than the six-storey mill. (The actual cost was higher, at £27,443, but still just cheaper than the alternative by Marshall's calculations.) He wrote to advise his father accordingly and it was decided to go ahead with the single-storey design.[199]

The most striking feature of the new mill and offices, apart from their single-storey layout, was the Ancient Egyptian style chosen for the façade, and this has led to their design being variously and sometimes incorrectly attributed. They have been credited to the artist David Roberts, the Egyptologist and sculptor Joseph Bonomi Jnr,[200] and to his architect brother Ignatius[201] A name less often mentioned is that of James Combe, but it seems almost certain that the original design of the building was Combe's, based on the Deanston mill. The Leeds mill was in operation by June 1840 with a simple Egyptian façade on Marshall Street, but the more elaborate Egyptian façade for the attached 'counting house' or office was not built until two years later. It was to be based on the Temple of Horus at Edfu and David Roberts, who had sketched the temple in 1838–9, was consulted by J G Marshall, and lent him drawings. Roberts also introduced Bonomi to Combe, who wanted to research details of the temple's columns, and Bonomi himself later produced detailed designs for the façade of the office building. There is currently no evidence that Ignatius Bonomi was involved at any stage.

Fig 201
This view of Marshall's Mill shows how strongly it contrasted with traditional multi-storey mill buildings, and resembles the designs of later Egyptian-influenced commercial buildings such as Thomas Wallis's GEC Factory in Birmingham and Greater London House in London (see Figs 194 and 112). [BB89/01688]

Sheep may (sometimes) safely graze

In May 1842, Combe was elected as an Associate of the Institution of Civil Engineers, and on his application form it was stated that this was 'because he is engineer and draughtsman at the works of Messrs Marshall and Co'.[202] He was proposed by John Farey Jnr, a senior consulting engineer, and his application was supported by J G Marshall (who had been elected an Associate himself in 1838), William Fairbairn, and George Leather, another senior civil engineer. Just under a week after his election, Combe presented a paper to the Institution, describing the new mill.[203] Although it briefly mentioned the building's 'ornamental stone front', later also described as a 'cut stone front', the paper concentrated on the unusual construction of the mill. It had been based on the single-storey mill built by James Smith at Deanston in Scotland, but was several times larger. (Smith was present at the meeting and spoke about his mill.)

Marshall's Mill was 396ft long and 216ft wide, built, except for its carved stone front, of brick on a cast-iron frame, with 21ft-high hollow cast-iron pillars and 66 groined brick arches, each spanning 36ft, supporting a flat roof with 60 conical skylights nearly 14ft in diameter and 10 high, each with a ventilator at its apex, one at the centre of each arch. The arches were roughly plastered, and over this was spread a covering of coal tar and lime to form a waterproof barrier. This was then covered by 8in of earth and Smith commented that at his mill frost had only penetrated a similar roof to a depth of 1½in when it had penetrated the ground to 12 elsewhere. The insulating effect of the roof was important in a flax-spinning mill where temperature and humidity needed to be controlled to keep the fibres workable, particularly now that machines, rather than hand spinning, were being used. The enormous room was used for drawing, roving, spinning, including hot-water spinning, and doubling and reeling yarn and thread, 'the dusty operations of dividing and heckling being confined to the old mill'.[204]

The new mill was featured in a contemporary article on the flax spinning industry, where the writer, Charles Tomlinson, who had clearly visited it, noted:

> If the [mill and its cellar] are calculated to delight and instruct the observer, a visit to the roof will certainly create the liveliest admiration. On ascending a flight of steps within the room, we come out, not upon an ordinary flat roof, but into a grass field, from the surface of which rises a number of what, at first sight, appear to be green-houses … but on approaching them the whirling machinery below shows them to be the skylights already noticed … to prevent this [the tar and lime covering] from cracking, a layer of earth, eight inches thick, was placed upon it, and sown with grass, which flourishes so well that sheep are occasionally sent up to feed upon it.[205]

The roof and its sheep seem to have been accessible to visitors (Fig 202). Oral tradition records that one of the sheep fell through a skylight, killing a worker below, and the incident is said to have been witnessed as a boy by one Keith Johnson, whose father and grandfather worked at the mill.[206] Gratings on the roof covered the tops of the hollow cast iron pillars inside, which acted as drainpipes.

A huge vaulted cellar with brick pillars extended under the building, housing not only the shafts conveying power from a pair of massive steam engines to the spinning and weaving machinery, but gas and water pipes, joiners' shops and warehouses, and a system of steam chests, fans and flues, driven by a small steam engine, through which air could be heated and humidified to the

THE ROOF OF MARSHALL'S ONE-STORIED FLAX MILL.

desired degree and circulated throughout
the mill above. The single storey, single
room design not only made it easier to
achieve and maintain the ideal temperature
and humidity, but also simplified the
arrangements for powering machinery, made
maintenance and repairs easier, allowed a
logical arrangement of work and facilitated
supervision of the workforce.

The workplaces of the Industrial Revolution,
often described in William Blake's phrase
as 'dark Satanic mills', earned themselves a
dreadful reputation which was in many cases
justified, but by the standards of the day the
Marshall family were enlightened employers.
Combe's paper to the Institution of Civil
Engineers spoke of 'the excellent ventilation
which is so desirable for the health of
the workpeople' and Tomlinson's article
rhapsodised that 'the lightness and airiness,
warmth and ventilation, of this room are

beyond all praise'.[207] He went on to note
the provision in the cellars under the mill of
baths: cold for free, hot for one penny – 'the
operatives are entitled to the use of them
on exhibiting a ticket of good conduct from
the overlooker'.[208]

In Disraeli's novel, there can be no doubt
that Trafford's model mill is based on
Marshall's Mill, as Disraeli mentions that its
'roof of groined arches, lighted by ventilating
domes at the height of eighteen feet, was
supported by hollow cast-iron columns,
through which the drainage of the roof was
effected'.[209] He contrasts the conditions
there with other mills and factories, where
ceilings were lower, and the multi-storey
layout meant that ventilation was poor and
the 'heat and effluvia' from lower storeys
rose to those above. He also noted what
we would now refer to as the health and
safety and welfare benefits of the design:

The physical advantages of thus carrying on the whole work in one chamber are great: in the improved health of the people, the security against dangerous accidents for women and youths and the reduced fatigue resulting from not having to ascend and descend and carry materials to the higher rooms. But the moral advantages resulting from superior inspection and general observation are not less important: the child works under the eye of the parent, the parent under that of the superior workman; the inspector or employer at a glance can behold all.[210]

The main mill building was almost complete by June 1840 when its opening was marked by a Temperance Tea for its workforce of 2,600. By December, the steam engines used to power the looms and other machines and the machines themselves had been installed, and the mill began production.[211]

Egyptian by design

The choice of an Egyptian design seems to have been made from the start as the cast-iron columns inside have palm leaf capitals, those in the basement have simple open papyrus capitals, and some of the engaged columns with palm capitals on the façade formed part of the structure of the building and were not simply decorative.[212] Also in the Egyptian style was the massive 240 horsepower double beam engine (technically a pair of coupled steam engines each of '120 horses power'[213]), built by Benjamin Hick at the Soho Iron Works in Bolton. Hick had been apprenticed to Matthew Murray at the Round Foundry in Leeds, across the road from Marshall's old mills, and Murray in turn had worked for Marshalls for 12 years. It was probably this connection which in 1840 secured the order for the new beam engine for Hick, who had founded his firm in 1833.

The engine had twin cylinders 4ft 6in in diameter, with a 5ft stroke, driving a crankshaft via overhead beams. These beams had been a feature of steam engines since their first practical industrial application in the early 18th century, and although they were no longer necessary, their use saved floor space at the cost of increased height. Operating at a leisurely 19 revolutions per minute the crankshaft drove a toothed flywheel, and from there power was taken off via spur and bevel gears to drive the shafts that ran under the mill. The original engine was broken up around 1890, but it had been sufficiently impressive for a one-tenth scale model of it to be made for the Great Exhibition in Hyde Park in 1851, and it was also described and illustrated in the 1856 *Imperial Cyclopaedia of Machinery*. The model still survives and shows the Egyptian decoration that was incorporated to match the theme of the mill (Fig 203). The main cylinders are fluted and the entablature supporting the beams has a pylon form with banded torus mouldings on its edges, and a cavetto cornice with vertical banding. The column leading to the governor is also fluted and banded, with a palm capital at its top, and the rotating vane linked to the speed governor is in the form of a winged solar disc. Some idea of the engine's size can be gathered from the fact that the winged disc vane was 7ft 6in from tip to tip. Steam and exhaust passages were built into the pylon framework. The bedplates of the original engine were supported on masonry, but in the model this was removed to show the inner workings and palm capital columns substituted.

The Egyptian decoration inside the mill paled into insignificance when set against its exterior, but both raise the question of why the Marshalls chose to build a mill in the Egyptian style. The link between Ancient Egypt and flax, the raw material for linen, was an easy one to make (although

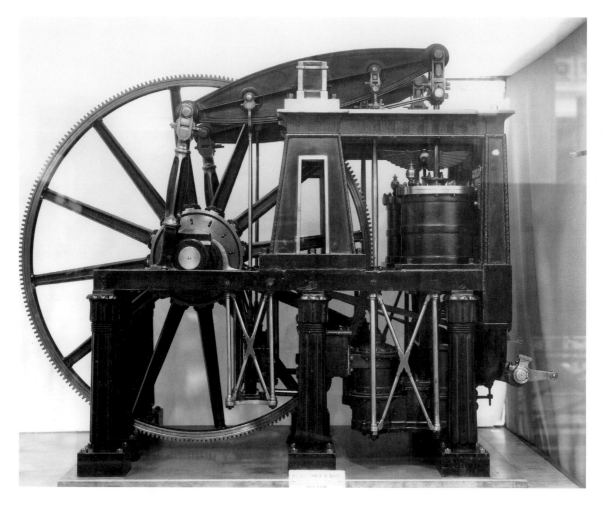

Fig 203
The one-tenth scale model of the beam engine in Marshall's Mill made for the 1851 Great Exhibition. A person of average height would have come about halfway up one of the pillars at the base.
[© Science Museum/ Science and Society]

it had not been until 1834 that James Thomson had conclusively demonstrated that mummy bandages were made of linen, and not cotton as some authorities had still maintained), but this in itself would probably not have been enough. A more convincing explanation is the influence of the Leeds Philosophical and Literary Society, whose founder-president from 1821 until 1826 was John Marshall, James Garth Marshall's father. Like many such 19th-century societies, it covered a wide range of topics, including Egyptology, and in 1823 was given three mummies purchased for it by the local banker John Blayds. One of them, that of Nesyamun, was unrolled in 1824 and

an account of the unrolling published in 1828. That account was written by William Osburn, an antiquarian and historian and secretary to the Society, who was later to publish several books on Egypt and the Bible, a two-volume *Monumental History of Egypt*, and to visit Egypt in 1847–8. For its time, the examination was both thorough and scientific. Osburn's account shows him to have been familiar with the work on hieroglyphs of both Thomas Young and Jean-François Champollion, and he declared himself in his account of the unrolling to be a follower of Champollion's system 'being entirely convinced of the correctness of the principle upon which it is founded'.[214] As will be seen, Osburn was involved with the design of the mill and may have championed an Egyptian style for it in the first place.

A temple of trade

Some time after the main mill itself had been completed work began on the attached offices. These were also to be in an Egyptian style with an elaborate façade modelled on the Temple of Horus at Edfu. The original design for this has been credited to David Roberts, who is said to have been commissioned by Marshall to prepare designs,[215] or alternatively to have been called in as an adviser to assist Combe,[216] but it now seems clear that he was only marginally involved. The first evidence of Roberts' involvement with the project is a letter which he wrote to Bonomi on 23 July 1842. In it, Roberts explains that:

> Mr Marshall of Leeds, some years ago erected a building in the Egyptian style of architecture … in addition to this he is now about to raise a second … The one which he is now about to erect is a copy of that of Edfou. The drawings for which I have lent him. I daresay you will say what the devil have I to do with all this? – nothing further than this, that his architect or builder Mr Combe, thinks there are casts of the freeze [sic] and capitals, in the Architects Institute, if not at the British Museum. Now as I know no man so likely to afford him information on such a subject as yourself – I intend taking the liberty of introducing him to you for that purpose. In order that you may understand a little about the subject I herewith inclose you a letter which I have just recd. If you would have the kindness to add to this favor by putting into the Egyptian form of characters the two names (Marshall) & (Victoria) I mean of course in the way of business, I as well as he will feel obliged.

Mr Combe is to be in London tomorrow for the purpose stated – where he will visit the British Museum. If you can procure him admissions to draw at either place you will be doing me a favour – as I have no further interest than a desire to see the thing done correctly – rather than some abortion which they may fancy an Egyptian Temple … PS Perhaps you will add one more to all the other favours I have asked in giving Mr Marshall some insight into what he asks in the concluding part of this letter.[217]

A few days later, probably on 29 July, Roberts wrote again to Bonomi:

> Many thanks my dear Sir, the bearer Mr Combe will show you the details I had made for him of Edfou – I fear nothing less than a model of the capitals will make him understand it – do you know anyone who could do it? Of course should you undertake it or the other things such as the cartouches – make your charge in the normal way… .[218]

From this, we can infer a number of things with a fair degree of confidence. From the tone of Roberts' first letter it seems clear that he had had no involvement with the design of the original mill building and that he was contacted for advice in mid-1842 by J G Marshall, who had already decided to base the design of the new office building on the Temple of Horus at Edfu. Roberts, who had left England for Egypt and the Holy Land in August 1838, was the first independent professional British artist, as opposed to those employed by patrons, to travel throughout the area. When he returned in July 1839 it was with, as he put it in his journal, enough material to last him for the rest of his life, nearly 300 sketches, three sketch books and a panorama of Cairo. Over the next 10 years these would be turned into numerous oil paintings and, with the assistance of Louis Haghe, the series of 247 coloured lithographs for which he is now best remembered.

Marshall, and his father, could have seen pictures of the Temple of Edfu in Denon's *Voyages* (see p 15), but these would not have been detailed enough for masons and sculptors to work from, especially if they were not familiar with the Egyptian style. (Later, in a letter to Robert Hay, for whom he had worked as an artist in Egypt, Bonomi was to complain that 'there is nothing in the French work to be depended on'[219].) It also seems clear that Combe was still responsible for the design and that Roberts was simply making available to him some of his sketches of the temple, or copies of elements from them. He refers to lending drawings, which was not likely to be the case if he were preparing original material, while by contrast he is careful to emphasise that the work he is suggesting that Bonomi might undertake would be chargeable. The letters also suggest that Combe travelled to London to collect the drawings from Roberts and to discuss the material with him. However,

the Egyptian elements of the mill itself had been relatively simple, consisting of plain cavetto cornices and screen walls, and palm capital columns with even simpler papyrus capitals on the columns in the basement level. The office building was to feature decorated cornices, winged solar discs and much more elaborate column capitals (Fig 204). Combe, as his work on the mill had shown, was certainly a competent, even innovative designer of industrial buildings, but Roberts' comments suggest that he was having difficulty coming to grips with the very different style of architecture which was called for by the offices.

Bonomi, on the other hand, had originally trained as a sculptor, and had spent a number of years between 1824 and 1834 in Egypt, working as an artist and draughtsman for the wealthy traveller Robert Hay and others. On 3 August 1842, J G Marshall wrote to Bonomi (Fig 205), thanking him for 'the coloured sketch of the elevation of our proposed Egyptian building which at the request of our common friend Mr Roberts you were kind enough to

Fig 204
The columns on the new office building had 'composite' capitals, often found in late period Egyptian temples and probably intended to represent bunched floral offerings.
[BB87/01712]

send me.'[220] He also thanks Bonomi for unspecified information given to Combe, and goes on to say:

> It would certainly be desirable, as you suggest, to make this, which I hope will be a tolerably complete sample of Egyptian architecture, an example of the best and purest type;- & the more simple & ancient style is moreover more pleasing, & more suitable than the more recent, & highly ornamented.[221]

Having seen the surviving monuments of Ancient Egypt for himself, Bonomi knew that they had been brightly painted and had reflected this in his coloured drawing of the new building. Marshall confessed that, 'To an English eye the painting of the exterior walls appears a very bold step; I hardly know whether we shall screw our courage up to that. – However that may easily be added at any time.'[222]

He then went on to the 'principal object' of his letter – to find out if Bonomi was willing, and whether his other commitments would allow him, to carry out the detailed design of the façade, providing 'such drawings and models as would enable a working mason with the assistance of Mr Combe to execute the work correctly'. This would involve preparing a detailed elevation or architectural plan of the front and working scale drawings of the carvings. An alternative that had been suggested in discussions involving Combe was to make half-scale models of the column capitals from which masons could carve the full-size versions. Marshall was keen that Bonomi should agree to accept the commission:

> As we are now preparing to put down the foundations & it is of some importance to the convenience & arrangement of our works to complete the building, as early as we can, time is an important element,

Fig 205
A pencil portrait of Joseph Bonomi Jnr, probably made around 1845, when he married Jessie, daughter of the painter John Martin. [By kind permission of Mrs Virginia de Cosson and Yvonne Neville-Rolfe]

and I should be glad to know how soon, in the event of your undertaking the work, we could have drawings & models to keep the men at work upon.[223]

Bonomi, who two years before had drafted a short hieroglyphic inscription for the entrance lodges at Abney Park Cemetery (see p 89) had obviously commented on the proposed inscription for the new building mentioned in David Roberts' letter, and Marshall had written that, 'You would also, I infer, furnish the hieroglyphics for the inscription:- that you suggest appears a very suitable one; giving the date & usual titles and name of the Sovereign, & of the builders.'[224] This would have been similar to other 19th-century hieroglyphic inscriptions, such as those on the Crystal Palace Egyptian Court (see p 148), the Egyptian Seat at Hartwell House (see p 221) and Freemasons' Hall at Boston (see pp 251–3). In fact, Bonomi did not compose the inscription and it was done by William Osburn, who wrote to him on 16 August 'I have an application to write hieroglyphic inscriptions for Mr Marshall's mill. I am now at work upon them. They have adopted your suggestions, I hope colours and everything.'[225] Osburn prepared

273

the inscription, and gave it to Marshall, who sent it to Bonomi, but in the end, the offices were without colour or inscriptions.

Marshall also suggested in his letter, perhaps implying that it would lead to more work for Bonomi, that the mill 'may lead to further applications of the Egyptian architecture in this country'. In fact, the only other Egyptian building designed by Bonomi was the very modest Egyptian Seat at the country home of Dr John Lee (see p 219). However, Bonomi's work on the Marshall's Mill did allow him to successfully apply in 1861 for the post of curator of Sir John Soane's Museum in London, the holder of which had to be an architect. One of his references came from J G Marshall, who wrote to Bonomi stating 'That when I was consulting Mr David Roberts respecting the elevation of the Egyptian Façade of our works in Holbeck, he recommended us to apply to you for the drawings in full detail… '.[226]

Bonomi was certainly keen to accept the commission, as on 4 August, the day after Marshall had written, and the same day that Bonomi would have received his letter, he wrote to Robert Hay asking for his help. While working for Hay in Egypt, Bonomi had helped to make detailed records and casts of the surviving monuments. He now needed access to these materials, particularly measurements that had been made, in order to execute the commission for Marshall, and hoped to secure Hay's cooperation by stressing the archaeological accuracy of the design for the new offices. Bonomi knew that there was suitable material taken from the Temple of Isis at Philae and so it seems that rather than referring to Marshall's original conception of a design modelled on the Temple of Edfu, which might have allowed Hay to make the excuse that he did not have the required material, Bonomi says instead that it will be based on Philae:

There is a man at Leeds who proposes to build a portico to a large cotton [sic] mill after the fashion of the portico of the Temple of Philae and has written to me to make him out working drawings which I cannot do without the measurements and without your assistance I cannot have them. I ask this favour the more willingly because I know you would be sorry to see any more buildings in the Egyptian style such as we have already and such as this mill will assuredly be from the design [Combe's?] I have seen unless you will favour me with a tracing from the capital of the col[umn] near the entrance and the one beyond it. If it be drawn out to scale I could do with the measurements, if not I should beg to have this addition.[227]

Hay wrote back two days later, on 6 August, promising to send the requested tracing. (He did not share Disraeli's positive view of the Marshalls and their new mill, commenting that if withholding the tracings could prevent the mill being built he would do, as there were already too many, in his opinion, of these 'slavery prisons'.[228]) Subsequent correspondence between them clarified the specific columns at Philae that Bonomi needed details of and shows that the original intention was to follow the style of the Ancient Egyptian original and to have three different column capitals, the most elaborate in the centre, the least on the outside, repeated on either side of the entrance. In the final building only two types of capital were used, although Bonomi seems to have intended to base the design of the third on more material supplied by Hay from another temple.[229]

On 20 August Marshall wrote to Bonomi again noting that the hieroglyphic inscription had been received by Marshall from Osburn, and anxiously enquiring about progress by Bonomi on models of the column capitals.

The foundations of the façade were nearly dug, stone had been ordered according to the dimensions in Bonomi's drawing, many of the stones were ready to lay, and suitable lifting tackle had been purchased from a firm of railway contractors. (Marshall also commented, as Osburn had in his letter to Bonomi four days earlier, on the recent 'Chartist holiday insurrection' in the area, 'which however is now happily subsiding'.[230])

Bonomi was unable to see the mill project through to completion because less than two weeks later, after a meeting at the British Museum with the Prussian Crown Prince, the Prussian ambassador and the Egyptologist Richard Lepsius, he was invited to accompany Lepsius on the great Prussian archaeological expedition to Egypt and left only two days later. This caught everyone by surprise, including Marshall, although he seems, from the fact that he later gave Bonomi a reference, to have accepted it with good grace. When Bonomi left for Egypt, he passed on the remaining work on the mill to the architect George Alexander to complete, saying in a letter to Hay, written from the Oriental Steam Packet boat on his way to Egypt, that Alexander had 'been in Egypt and is therefore a very proper person to conduct the whole affair'.[231] Bonomi left his affairs in the hands of his friend, the Revd F O Ward, who wrote to him in early September. Ward itemised the correspondence that had arrived for Bonomi, including a letter from Hay 'enclosing a drawing of an Egyptian column – forwarded along with Roberts' drawing to Alexander'. Ward also notes that Marshall has contacted him to be put in touch with Alexander 'to the end that the drawings may be continued'.[232] On 8 September, Hay addressed an indignant letter to Ward, saying that

…as you will have observed in my note to him with the capitals, that they were only intended for his [Bonomi's] use, may I beg you will have the kindness to return them to me – & not hand them over to Mr Alexander, a gentleman with whom I am not in the slightest degree acquainted.[233]

From Ward's letter it seems likely that although the drawings would eventually have been returned to Hay, that they had already gone to Alexander, who was able to make enough use of them and whatever material he had been left by Bonomi, to successfully complete the façade – although in the end there was to be no colour and no hieroglyphic inscription. This could have been because Alexander lacked Bonomi's detailed experience of Ancient Egyptian architecture and inscriptions, but it is equally probable that Marshall, already anxious about progress and probably with an eye on cost as well, decided to abandon these elements.

The mills – today, yesterday, and tomorrow

Today, seen from the street outside, the mill and offices make an imposing group, of the same height and both with columned fronts. The appearance is deceptive, however. Not only is the mill building much wider but it goes back even further, and seen from the rear the offices appear tiny in comparison. The front elevation of the mill building consists of a battered single storey with a plain cavetto cornice and plain torus moulding beneath this, the moulding continued down the edges of the building. Along the front of the building is an unbroken run of 18 engaged palm capital columns or pilasters, joined by screen walls about one third the height of the building, and with small paned wooden windows in rectangular openings between the pilasters. The actual entrance to the mill was via the north side where the building makes a return. Here, a flight of six curved steps leads up to a double door. Beyond the entrance, the mill and the office block are joined by a short section of the building which continues some distance back, and used to be the engine house of the mill.

The office block has a similar layout to the mill, of battered sides, cornice, mouldings, columns and screen walls and windows, but the decoration is more elaborate and the windows are narrower and set deeper back (Fig 206). The cavetto cornice is decorated with the same elements of vertical lines and elaborate blank cartouches which can also be seen on the cornices of buildings like 42 Fore Street in Hertford (see p 249) and the Egyptian House in Penzance (see p 235). In this case, however, the element above alternate cartouches can be recognised as a solar disc flanked by ostrich feathers. (This is a form used to crown Egyptian gods, and can be seen in representations of the hybrid deity Ptah-Sokar-Osiris.) The remaining

cartouches on the cornice have above them motifs resembling short dumbbells. Under all the cartouches are shallow dish or bowl shapes with bases, probably a version of the *nbw* or 'gold' hieroglyph (Fig 207). Similar elements can be found on the cornice of the Temple of Horus at Edfu, and also that of Hathor at Dendera.

In the centre of the office block cornice is a large winged solar disc flanked by *uraei*. A second winged disc, also with *uraei*, sits on the entablature under the torus moulding that runs beneath the cornice. Unlike the plain torus moulding on the mill itself, this has the classic horizontal and diagonal bands often found on such mouldings on Ancient Egyptian buildings. The office windows are set further back, meaning that the six columns are more rounded, and form a sort of *pronaos*. The columns also have more elaborate composite papyrus capitals, typical of late Egyptian temples built in the Graeco-Roman period, and bases decorated with leaf motifs. The screen walls are also more elaborate, with friezes on their tops of stylised *uraei* crowned with solar discs, and small flared cavetto cornices with winged solar discs and *uraei* under the friezes.

The space between the middle columns is wider to accommodate a doorway slightly higher than the screen walls. This doorway is rectangular, but a cavetto cornice with vertical banding and winged solar disc with *uraei* flares out to its edges, and the plain torus moulding which runs under the cornice and down the sides of the doorway is slightly battered, to give the overall impression of a pylon form. The door itself is plain, of panelled wood whose two leaves. Inside, a flight of stairs whose cast iron railings have capitals in an Egyptian floral style leads up from a small hall. A chimney once stood at the back of the mill, and was described as looking like Cleopatra's Needle – 'the lofty chimney, which towers above the whole, closely resembles the

Fig 206
This view of the offices, taken after the closure of Marshall's flax-spinning business, shows the three winged solar discs, decorated screen walls, elaborate column capitals and decorated cornice. [AA59/02943]

celebrated Cleopatra's needle, whose name it bears, and is a conspicuous landmark to the stranger approaching Mr Marshall's factory from a distance'.[234]

An 1849 painting of the mill and office, by W R Robinson, shows a plain four-sided chimney behind the office.[235] It cracked in 1852 and was demolished and replaced by a conventional brick chimney.[236] There is a small gatelodge adjoining the office block, which has battered sides, and a plain cavetto cornice and torus moulding.

Despite the influence of material from the Temple of Philae, the office block closely resembles, but is not an exact copy of, part of the Temple of Horus at Edfu. This is one of the best preserved Ancient Egyptian temples but is also from the late period of Ancient Egyptian history, being built between approximately 237 and 57 BC by the Ptolemies, Greek rulers of Egypt. It preserved the classic form of the Egyptian temple, in which beyond the twin towers of the pylon gateway, a semi-public court with columns around its outside, the peristyle court, led to the temple proper. The design of the office block at Marshall's Mill is based on the portico at the rear of the peristyle court leading to the first hall of the temple. Although about three times the size of the mill offices, the original temple has the same number of columns, and the screen walls with their frieze and the entrance doorway, but the columns at Edfu are in pairs, the outside having composite palm capitals, the middle palm capitals and the remaining pair composite papyrus capitals. On the office building, all the columns have composite papyrus capitals with the middle column on either side being different to the other two. (The façade of the mill itself was more constrained by the interior layout of the building, so its design is much simpler, and the columns all have the simpler palm capitals.) At the time Roberts and Bonomi

travelled in Egypt, many of the temples were still partly buried in sand, which meant that at Edfu the screen walls were almost completely covered. This, and the huge cost that would have been involved, meant that the mill buildings did not reproduce the elaborate carvings that covered the walls of genuine Egyptian temples.

The construction of this great mill 'five times larger than Westminster Hall, and seven times larger than Exeter Hall, London'[237] represented the peak of Marshall's achievements. However, it was actually smaller than originally envisaged by James Marshall and never achieved its full potential, particularly in the production of cloth, rather than yarn or thread. The entrepreneurial drive of the early generations was lost and Marshall's closed in 1886, less than 50 years later. The mill became the clothing factory of James Rhodes & Co, later the offices and warehouse of Kay & Co, the catalogue and mail order firm, and after the takeover of Kay by GUS housed Reality, the GUS transport fleet operation, until 2004 when it was acquired by a property management company. In December 2008, part of the front of the Grade I listed mill collapsed, raising fears for its structural integrity. At the time of writing, it is being restored as part of the creation of the new Holbeck Urban Village area. Unique for its scale, Marshall's Mill was also a landmark in the introduction of archaeologically correct Egyptian elements in modern buildings. It also shares with buildings such as Greater London House (see p 152), the GEC Factory at Witton (see p 256) and the Hoover Factory (see p 174) the marriage of innovative industrial design with Ancient Egyptian architecture.

The interiors of the buildings are undergoing restoration at the time of writing, and are not accessible to the public, but the outside of both buildings can be seen from the road.

Fig 207
The hieroglyph for *nbw* or 'gold' represents a collar of gold with hanging ends and beads hanging from its lower edge. The metal, regarded as divine and imperishable, had solar symbolism, and connotations of the afterlife.
[Mark Rudolph]

Undercliffe Cemetery

127 Undercliffe
Lane,
Bradford
BD3 0QD

The mausoleum of Alfred Illingworth

It was wool rather than the more Egyptian linen that was the foundation of the Illingworth fortune. Daniel Illingworth created the family worsted spinning business and was succeeded by his sons Alfred and Henry, who built Whetley Mills, one of the largest in Bradford. Alfred Illingworth (1827–1907) was Member of Parliament first for Knaresborough, between 1868 and 1874, then for Bradford West between 1880 and 1895. A radical Liberal of the Manchester free trade school, he was a member of the Peace Campaign and opposed many of Britain's military campaigns.[238] He was against British intervention in Egypt, and although he seems to have had few leisure interests and did not, unlike other industrialists like the tea magnate Frederick Horniman, collect Egyptian antiquities or sponsor excavations in Egypt, his political

interest in the country may have been the inspiration for his choice of an Egyptian-style monument.

His grey granite mausoleum is prominently situated in the central avenue of Undercliffe Cemetery (Fig 208). It has been described as a 'mastaba', a style of tomb typical of the Old Kingdom in Ancient Egypt, where the superstructure usually contains a funerary chapel and the burial chamber is underground.[239] Mastaba tombs, however, get their name from the Arabic for a mud-brick bench and are low and relatively plain rectangular structures with battered sides. The Illingworth mausoleum is more elaborate. Basically rectangular in plan, battered corner pilasters give it the classic Egyptian profile. The sides are inset and perpendicular, which gives room for 10 palm capital columns, three on each side

Fig 208
The strongly Egyptian style of the Illingworth mausoleum contrasts with the largely Gothic and Classical style chosen for other monuments in Undercliffe Cemetery.
[DP116904]

and two at the front and back. A banded torus moulding runs along the edges of the corners and below the cavetto cornice and flat roof.

The back of the monument may at one time have had a bronze panel as its centre is filled with a different colour stone slab, but like the bronze door with Egyptian decoration which once graced the front, this would have been stolen during the years when the cemetery was neglected. At the front, the mausoleum has a central doorway with battered sides and torus mouldings, with the name 'Illingworth' across the lintel in large capital letters and a winged solar disc flanked by *uraei* on a cavetto cornice above this. The doorway is flanked by two palm capital columns, and above them and the door's cornice the pattern is repeated again. A plain lintel joins the battered corner pilasters, and above this is another cavetto cornice with a winged solar disc flanked by *uraei*.

The base of the mausoleum is extended to the front in line with the pillars and on these projections is a pair of sphinxes. Their design is unusual, particularly their prominent ears, manes and false beards, but they resemble fairly closely genuine examples from the Middle Kingdom, for example those of Amenemhat III of the 12th Dynasty, and they may have been based on one in the British Museum (Fig 209). Like the doors, the sphinxes were also the target of thieves but this time the attempt was abandoned and they are now secured to their bases. Between the sphinxes a short flight of three steps leads up to the doorway of the mausoleum. The interior now holds small urns and loose decorative elements from around the cemetery. It may once have held the ashes of Alfred Illingworth and his wife Margaret, who died 12 years after him, but the description of the monument as a 'mastaba' suggests that their ashes may be in a vault under it. The mausoleum is

Fig 209
Egyptian Sculpture Gallery at the British Museum, showing a cast of a sphinx, probably originally from the reign of the Middle Kingdom pharaoh Amenemhat III and set up at Bubastis in the Delta, moved by several later pharaohs, and finally set up by Psusennes I in the Delta city of Tanis. The distinctive ears and mane or *nemes* suggest that it was the inspiration for those on the Illingworth mausoleum.
[BB76/03208]

surrounded by a stone kerb with stubby obelisks at intervals. At one point, as the remains of fixtures show, these would have been joined by a chain, possibly of bronze. The designer and builder of the mausoleum are currently unknown, although the now demolished cemetery chapels were built by the local firm of Lockwood and Mawson.

The cemetery itself was designed by William Gay, and opened in 1854. The Bradford Cemetery Company, which ran it, went into liquidation in 1976 and the site was disposed of by the liquidator two years later to a property developer for £5. Following this, there was widespread destruction of buildings and removal of grave surrounds, as well as casual vandalism and theft of valuable fittings such as the mausoleum doors. The Friends of Undercliffe Cemetery were formed and a restoration programme agreed. In 1984 the site was compulsorily purchased and became a conservation area. The Friends disbanded and were succeeded by the Undercliffe Cemetery Charity, which now has responsibility for the cemetery. The cemetery is open to the public.

The Valve House

Widdop Reservoir,
Ridehalgh Lane
HX7 7AT

Probably the most isolated Egyptian-style building in England is the small valve house on the south-east corner of Widdop Reservoir, on the moors in Calderdale between Hebden Bridge and Burnley. It is a plain square building of large ashlar blocks with battered sides and corner pilasters. The doorway has monolithic door jambs and lintel, and there are similar window openings on the other three sides. A stepped cornice above a plain frieze forms a low parapet, and the roof is flat and sealed with bitumen. Pipes lead from the back of the building down into the reservoir itself (Fig 210).

Figure 210
This small valve house at Widdop Reservoir is probably the most isolated Egyptian-style building in England, and in a setting far removed from the sandy desert of the Suez Canal. [© Richard Sweetnam. Source English Heritage, IoE424093]

The valve house was built as part of the reservoir designed and constructed between 1872 and 1878 by the Halifax born civil engineer John Frederic La Trobe Bateman, whose 50-year career saw him involved in water supply projects throughout the British Isles, especially that to provide water for Manchester, which laid the foundations for the modern system. In 1869, at the invitation of Ismail Pasha, the khedive of Egypt, Bateman attended the opening of the Suez Canal as the representative of the Royal Society. On his return, Bateman wrote a report of his visit, which was published in the *Proceedings* of the Society.[240] The visit must also have inspired him to use an Egyptian style for the valve house. The civilisation of Ancient Egypt was so intimately linked to the River Nile that the association between Egypt and water is a n easy one to make, and this is one of several buildings to use the style (*see* pp 193 and 209).

The valve house is easily visible and can be walked to, but the interior is not accessible to the public.

North West

Anfield Cemetery

236 Priory Road,
Liverpool
L4 2SL

McLennan monument

In the centre quadrant of Anfield Cemetery
is the handsome black granite monument
of the Scottish-born Alexander McLennan
CE [Civil Engineer], of Bonavista House,
Seaforth, who died in 1893, aged 69, and
of his wife Isabella, who died three years
later (Fig 211).

The monument itself can be described as
a *naos*, or shrine-style Egyptian design, as
it is fairly tall, symmetrical, and has inset
openings on each side resembling the false
doors of Ancient Egyptian tombs. At each
corner are battered pilasters, giving the
whole structure the characteristic Egyptian
profile. Like a number of other Egyptian-
style monuments built to cope with the
English climate it has a pitched roof, in this
case formed by a raised superstructure
with a cavetto cornice, a series of simple
mouldings above this, and then a shallow
pyramidion. Below the cavetto cornice
proper on the monument itself is a border
of hexagons with an abstract four-petalled
floral motif inside them. On the front of the
monument, the face between the pilasters
is engraved in low relief, with a large winged
solar disc flanked by *uraei* at the top. Below
this is a double border of five-pointed stars
set in circles, with the stars reversed in the

lower border. Between these two borders
is another with an abstract design which
may be floral given other decoration on
the monument. Below these three borders,
to either side, are stylised papyrus plants.
The inner 'false door' opening has a top
border of inverted lotus flowers above the
dedicatory inscription. Given the shape of
the monument, it is likely that it contains
cremated remains. (*See also* the Hughes
monument at Brookwood, p 202.)

The man commemorated by it appears
to have had no connection with Egypt.
He was a marine engineer and eventually
became the first Chief Engineer of
Isambard Kingdom Brunel's SS *Great
Western*, the first steamship purpose built
for Atlantic crossings, and superintended
the construction of its huge iron-hulled
successor the SS *Great Eastern*. In 1859,
aged about 35, he was Chief Engineer on
the *Great Eastern* at the time of her maiden
voyage. Later, he became a consulting
engineer and a shareholder in the Heliades
Steamship Co.[241]

The City of Liverpool Cemetery in Walton
Road, Anfield, was designed by T D Barry
in 1860 and the grounds were laid out
by Edward Kemp (1817–91) a student of
Joseph Paxton. It is open to the public.

Fig 211
The McLennan mausoleum in Anfield Cemetery is unusual for the amount of fine engraved decoration used on it. This type of machine engraving would have been suitable for reproducing hieroglyphic inscriptions, but these were apparently never used on funerary monuments.
[DP109980]

Gillow mausoleum

The Gillow family were one of the leading British cabinetmaking firms of the 18th and 19th centuries, with premises in London and Lancaster. By the time of the third Robert Gillow they had become wealthy and married into the gentry and at some time around 1817–20 he built a house at Clifton Hill, near Forton in Lancashire. The family was Roman Catholic and had supported

the construction of a chapel, opened in 1818 and built on land given by John Dalton whose family home was the nearby Thurnham Hall, so it was not surprising that the Gillow mausoleum was built near the new chapel and can now be found outside the church of SS Thomas and Elizabeth which replaced it. What was unusual was the style in which it was built.

SS Thomas and Elizabeth RC Church, Thurnham LA2 0DT

The Gillow mausoleum has been described by the architectural historian J S Curl as being in a 'remarkably severe Neoclassical Egyptianising style'.[242] It is a substantial monument, built in local sandstone ashlar, the size of which can be judged by the fact that inside it contains 24 loculi, or recesses to hold coffins. It is rectangular, with battered corner pilasters but perpendicular sides. At the top of the walls a plain torus moulding runs below an undecorated cavetto cornice. Above the cornice is a stone roof with a stepped pediment at either end and with Maltese crosses at the centre of the pediment on both ends. At one end, facing the church lychgate, is a simple doorway with a small plain torus moulding around it and a small and unflared cavetto cornice above. Two small carved stone markers, possibly grave markers, stand one either side of the doorway, but do not have any Egyptian decoration. At the other end of the mausoleum is a matching, but blind, doorway (Fig 212). On the side of the mausoleum

facing away from the church, a square section central pilaster is flanked by a small rectangular blind window on each side. The side of the monument facing the church has four Egyptian-style columns, equally spaced between the corner pilasters, with square abaci above them. The column capitals are decorated with a simpler version of the sort of mixed plant motifs found on composite capital columns in the late, Graeco-Roman, temples of Upper Egypt, and the rest of the mausoleum columns are decorated with closely spaced horizontal banding and vertical fluting. There are four horizontal bands above the vertical fluting, and below a section of three horizontal bands, and then one of two (Fig 213). The style of the capital resembles one shown in Vivant Denon's *Voyages* (plate 44 no. 2), which was often cited as a source of designs for Egyptian style architecture. Denon's plate shows 12 column capitals but not their shafts, and the shafts on the Gillow mausoleum were probably devised by its architect.

Fig 212
The Gillow mausoleum, seen from the rear, and showing the blind doorway. Only the side facing the church is decorated with columns.
[DP136915]

Fig 213
The multiple groups of bands and fluting on the columns of the Gillow mausoleum are not typically Egyptian, but the capitals resemble those found in temples from the Graeco-Roman era in Egypt, such as the Temple of Isis at Philae, when their decoration tended to become more elaborate.
[DP136920]

The designer and architect of the mausoleum are not known for certain. Most sources give the third Robert Gillow (1764–1838) as the designer and this seems probable. Joseph Bonomi Jnr has been suggested but this is unlikely to have been the case. After studying at the Royal Academy, he went to Rome in 1823 to continue his studies, and went from there to Egypt where he remained until returning via Palestine and Syria in 1834. His known architectural works, such as Marshall's Mill in Leeds (see p 266) and the Egyptian Seat at Hartwell House (see p 219) were designed after the burials in the Gillow mausoleum, and their style, as would be expected from Bonomi's extensive experience in Egypt, was archaeologically correct. Robert Gillow is not known to have had an active interest in Ancient Egypt, but his work

as a cabinetmaker would have equipped him with the necessary skills to design the mausoleum, and the style of the columns would not look out of place on furniture of the period.

Various dates for construction have been suggested and a date between 1812 and 1830, and probably toward the later end of this range, seems most probable. Richard Gillow, Robert's father, died in 1811, and was buried in the churchyard of the Priory Church of St Mary in Lancaster. Had the mausoleum been built by then, it seems certain that he would have been buried in it. Inside the Gillow mausoleum, only four of the loculi are occupied. Although some parts of the inscriptions are badly weathered, the burials recorded are of Robert Gillow on 11 July 1838 and his wife Anna, whose date of death was 6 January 1841. Both are given as 'of Clifton Hill'. Another is of Sarah Agnes Keene, date of death given as 6 September 1830, at Clifton Hill, aged 23. The final inscription is one of the most worn but seems to commemorate Francis, son of Francis O'Byrne, born 1841, died 1842. This would seem to indicate that the earliest burial was that of Sarah Keene, possibly a married granddaughter, with Robert and Anna following eight to 11 years later, and Francis, who must have died in infancy, in 1842. This would make a date of around 1830 for the mausoleum the most plausible, although it is just possible that some of the burials were originally in a church vault

and were later moved to the mausoleum. However, the mausoleum was built after the first chapel on the site, but before the current church, of SS Thomas and Elizabeth, which was consecrated in 1848. The original chapel, the first Catholic church in North Lancashire to be built since the Reformation (although there was a church in Lancaster in a converted building) was apparently a very small building, and would probably not have had a vault. Clifton Hill incorporated a small chapel, but again was highly unlikely to have had a vault.

The churchyard is open to the public but the interior of the mausoleum is not.

Pyramid Cinema

22 Washway Road,
Sale
M33 7QY

The Pyramid was one of the last Egyptian-style cinemas to be built in England, but is unusual both in having an Egyptian exterior and interior and in having survived relatively intact when so many others have been lost.

It was designed, as the Pyramid Theatre, for John Buckley by Joseph Gomersall and his chief assistant architect Leonard Speak, of the Manchester firm of architects Drury and Gomersall, and built in 1933 at a cost of £70,000 to seat 1,940. The two rows of shops flanking the cinema were also built at the same time, and reflecting the rise in car ownership at this period, it had a large car park at the rear. On the first floor was the Pyramid Café, advertised as a 'rendezvous for discerning folk' and open from noon to 10 pm. Initially, objections to the new cinema were raised, especially from other nearby cinemas, but the support for it was shown by public meetings and a petition with over 18,000 signatures and it eventually opened on Saturday 24 February 1934.[243]

Externally it relies, like a number of other Egyptian-style cinemas, on a series of

columns to establish the style. In this case, four engaged columns with simple palm capitals are set above the canopied entrance to create a portico effect, with windows between them and a screen wall with an abstract floral design at the level of the column capitals. On either side of the building, simple pylon shapes with very slight battering extend from the front, topped by cavetto cornices with abstract floral friezes. Below the cornices, at the same level as the central windows, are narrow inset window openings with the same pattern of glazing bars and cornices with vertical banding supported by corbels at their tops. At the base of each pylon is a set of double doors with a moulding over them resembling an abstract winged solar disc. The name of the cinema was originally displayed right across the front in huge inset letters, above the columns and between the pylons at the level of their cornices. Above the name was a clock, which broke into the line of a simple moulded frieze that ran along the parapet at roof level (Fig 214). The shape of the frieze can be seen as an abstract version of the frieze of rearing cobras which decorated

Fig 214
The original façade of
the Pyramid Cinema,
with its prominent name
and the clock face above
it. Despite the theatre's
name, there seems to
have been no attempt to
echo the pyramid form
in its design.
[Reproduced with kind
permission of Trafford
Local Studies]

the screen walls of late Egyptian temples.
The combination of the cinema's name, the
columns, the pylon shapes and the cavetto
cornices are enough together to suggest
the Egyptian style, but the stylised nature of
many of the elements reflects the cinema's
relatively late date, and the increasing
influence of Art Deco in which Egyptian
elements were assimilated with those from
a number of other cultures.

Inside, the dominant theme of the
decoration is floral motifs, often fairly
abstract, but suggesting lotus and papyrus
forms, or the bundled floral offerings which
can be seen in Ancient Egyptian tomb
decoration. The proscenium arch has a
moulded plaster surround with a vulture
with outstretched wings in its centre, holding
stemmed floral motifs in its claws. (The

vulture represented the goddess Nekhbet,
the patron of Upper Egypt.) The rest of the
arch is decorated with a floral frieze and
there are giant floral mouldings running
vertically beside it. Similar shapes are used
in the large grilles on either side of the
auditorium. (That on the left is false, the one
on the right was originally built to connect
to chambers for the theatre organ, although
these were not used, and other chambers
were constructed under the stage.) An
elaborate frieze running above the level
of the doors in the auditorium has floral
elements suggesting the plants of marsh
scenes in Egyptian tombs, and at intervals
panels, also with floral elements, and the
almost circular form of the vulture goddess
with outstretched wings and claws, holding
the *shen* hieroglyph (Fig 215) symbolising
both eternity and protection which is found

Fig 215
The *shen* hieroglyph
represents a loop of
knotted rope, which
because it had no end
and could encircle, was
used to symbolise both
eternity and protection.
Deities shown in a
funerary context
could hold the sign,
symbolically granting
eternal protection
to the pharaoh.
[Mark Rudolph]

in Egyptian jewellery. Above the vulture on these panels are lotus flowers and a winged solar disc flanked by *uraei*. The triangular mirrored wall lights in the auditorium are modern replacements for simpler originals. The cinema foyer had a coffered ceiling and both it and the flooring reflected the same lotus motifs. The plasterwork in the auditorium is now all painted brown but may originally have been in different colours.

The Egyptian theme of the cinema was evoked in many ways. The centre pages of the programme for the opening week (Fig 216) were framed, like a proscenium arch, by a border of unreadable but reasonably recognisable hieroglyphs. At the corners were lotus-like floral motifs and in the

middle a large winged solar disc. At the base of each side of the border were pyramids and the name of the cinema in the same font that was used on the façade of the building. Extending across the bottom of both pages was a line drawing of the cinema and the shops flanking it, and behind them the head and torso of a dramatically lit Ancient Egyptian man wearing a *nemes* headcloth and with arms outstretched – presumably to indicate the wonders of the programmes set out to either side. The Pyramid was a theatre, rather than just a cinema, so as well as showing films, newsreels and cartoons, it could also mount stage productions. On offer during the first week were the Gaumont film *My Lips Betray*, a 'Ruritanian Musical Romance',

Fig 216
The souvenir programme for the opening week of the Pyramid. A banner outside the theatre on opening night in 1934 claimed that 'Only the best is good enough for Sale', and the Egyptian style was clearly seen as having connotations of splendour and luxury. [Reproduced with kind permission of Trafford Local Studies]

the Pyramid Orchestra (augmented for the occasion by the Lido Orchestra) and the theatre's organ, as well as variety acts supported by the Pyramid Girl Dancers. The theatre organ was a twin console 'Christie' Unit organ, built by Hill, Norman and Beard. One console was in the orchestra pit, the other on stage. The pit console was fixed but that on stage could be moved to any position required. Other cinema organs had decorative casework but this one had a possibly unique Egyptian-style one with pharaonic heads on either side, lotus columns, and a winged music stand (see Fig 28). The casework could be switched between consoles as required. Often at the keyboard was Reginald Liversidge, the first resident organist (Fig 217). (After a last broadcast on BBC Radio Manchester in 1972, the organ was removed the following year by the Lancastrian Theatre Organ Trust, installed for a while at the Blue Coat School in Oldham, and it and its unique casework are now back in storage looking for a

new home.) Although the cinema's phone number when it opened was SALe 2247, it seems that when a new phone exchange was later opened, the prefix for local numbers changed to PYR after the cinema. Rather confusingly, as there is not a sphinx in sight at the Pyramid, a 1930s ad featured the cinema's name with the central 'A' extended to create a pyramid shape and the slogan 'The Riddle is Solved'.

Bought in 1941 by the Rank Organisation, then owners of the Odeon name, the Pyramid later became an Odeon, although the name itself was not changed until 1945. Attempts were made to have the building listed in the 1970s, but 1973 correspondence with the Department of the Environment preserved in local history archives reveals that at that time it was considered 'not of sufficient interest to merit inclusion in the statutory list'. It was sold again in 1981 and reopened as part of the Tatton group, eventually returned to

Fig 217
The Pyramid's resident organist, Reginald Liversidge, whose signature tune, appropriately enough, was *The Desert Song*. [Reproduced with kind permission of Trafford Local Studies]

Rank and finally closed as a cinema in 1984. Bought by the local council for £200,000, it was nearly demolished for office or retail properties but saved after a local campaign. In 1987 it was listed Grade II for internal and external features, although the clock and its original name had been lost from the façade. It was converted to a nightclub and conference suite, and at the time of writing has been converted to a fitness centre (Fig 218).

The strains of *The Desert Song* may no longer swell through the auditorium, and the Pyramid was never pyramid shaped, but its survival as one of the most complete Egyptian-style cinemas is surely cause for celebration. The interior is not accessible to the general public, but the exterior can be easily seen from the road.

Fig 218
The Pyramid in 2011, the cinema has lost its name and clock, but the Egyptian style façade is still otherwise intact. [DP109992]

Architectural glossary

This is not a comprehensive list of architectural terms but a brief explanation of those used in this book. More information can be found in any good dictionary of architecture, and one of these, along with several specialist titles on Ancient Egyptian architecture, can be found in the bibliography.

Abacus (Singular, plural abaci) The flat slab, usually square, on top of the capital of a column.

Acroteria (Plural, single acroterion) Architectural ornaments placed on plinths at the apex or outer corners of the pediments of buildings, usually those in the Classical style.

Architrave A moulded frame surrounding a door or window. More strictly a beam or lintel resting on columns.

Ashlar Smoothed and squared blocks of masonry, as opposed to rubble or rough quarried stone. In Freemasonry, small rough and smoothed (or 'Perfect') ashlars can be placed in a lodge to symbolise Apprentice and Master Masons.

Batter A sloping face on the wall of a building. Ancient Egyptian buildings of stone or mud brick were probably originally built in this way to ensure their stability. The form became typical of Ancient Egyptian temples and was retained even for those built in Greek and Roman times. Door and window openings can also be described as 'battered' when they slope outwards at the sides.

Blocking course In Classical architecture, a plain course of stone above the cornice, or a similar course at the base of the building.

Capital The ornamental head of a column or pillar. Those on Ancient Egyptian columns are normally of plant form, and separated from the shaft of the column by horizontal bands. In some columns these bands must have originally represented rope tying together bundles of palm fronds or papyrus, or tying them around a wooden column, and the earliest Egyptian columns were found in tents or structures made from reed matting. Common types of Ancient Egyptian capitals are papyrus bundle and bud, open papyrus, lotus, palm, and in later temples composite, or mixed plant form, which may represent bunched floral offerings.

Caryatid A sculptured figure, in Classical architecture female, used as a column to support an Entablature.

Cavetto cornice A cornice is a projecting horizontal moulding on the top of a building or wall. A cavetto cornice is a concave, quarter round moulding, also known from its French name as a Gorge (literally 'throat') cornice. One of the most distinctive features of Ancient Egyptian architecture, in use from the Old Kingdom. They may have originally derived from the characteristic shape of palm fronds arranged in a row along the top of a wall, or protruding from the top of a wall made from palm branches and mud plaster. Some are plain, but many have vertical banding suggesting their origin in these palm fronds.

Chest tombs Box-shaped stone monuments above graves. They can be in a variety of styles, such as Gothic or Classical.

Coade stone A ceramic based artificial stone developed in the late 18th century by Eleanor Coade and manufactured for about 70 years until about 1837. It was used for busts, statues and architectural ornaments, often elaborate ones. Many were stock patterns, but bespoke pieces were also created. It was cheaper than stone, and immensely durable, resisting the effects of frost, rain, sun and smoke.

Colonnade A general term for a long row of columns or pillars. These are often in a single row, although they can be more than one row deep, and attached to a building, forming a covered walkway behind. Where they form part of the entrance they are known as a portico, and when they are round the outside of a courtyard they are known as a peristyle colonnade.

Corbel A projecting support for part of the building above, such as a balcony or windowsill.

Column A circular support in a building often tapering slightly upwards. In Ancient Egypt, the originals of many types of column would have been made of wood, or bundled plant stems, and these were later reproduced in stone. The commonest types of Egyptian columns were papyrus bud, papyrus bundle, open papyrus, lotus, and palm. Papyrus and lotus columns were associated with Lower Egypt, but the lotus column could also be found in domestic architecture. In the Late Period of Ancient Egypt, and particularly in Graeco-Roman times, columns found in Egyptian temples often had plain unfluted shafts, but their capitals took on elaborate forms, known as composite capitals, which combined a number of plant forms in a single capital. (These are not the same as composite capitals in Graeco-Roman architecture.)

Cornice A projecting moulding along the top of a building.

Dado In modern architecture, the lower part of a wall, often marked by a moulding running at about waist height, known as the dado rail.

Dentil moulding One made up of a series of small square blocks (literally 'tooth' shaped), sometimes extended into rectangles, often under the cornice of a building. Originally the projecting ends of rafters.

Engaged columns Ones attached to, or appearing to be sunk into a wall. Pilasters are shallower, and do not extend outward so far.

Entablature In Classical architecture, the horizontal part of the building above its columns, but beneath its pediment. Normally divided into three parts: architrave, frieze and cornice.

Façade One side, normally the front, of a building. Also used to describe a new exterior applied to an existing building.

Façadism The superficial use of design elements on the front of a building.

Faience Ancient Egyptian decorative items with a ceramic body and a glazed surface, usually bright blue or green, though other colours were also used. Early Egyptologists gave it this name because of its resemblance to European faience, or tin-glazed earthenware, now more commonly referred to as majolica. The term 'faience' is also commonly used nowadays to refer to glazed architectural terracotta used to decorate buildings.

Fasces The bundle of rods, usually with a protruding axe blade, bound together with leather strips, and carried in procession as the symbol of authority of Roman magistrates and other officials. More generally a symbol of the power of the state. They symbolised the power of magistrates to inflict corporal and capital punishment. As architectural decoration, they would invoke Classical architecture in general, Roman architecture in particular, and suggest imperial power.

Finials Ornaments on the tops, ends, or corners of buildings.

Foliated With architectural ornaments in the shape of a leaf, or carved with leaf patterns.

Frieze A flat, usually decorated band on the entablature of a building below the cornice, or a decorated band on a wall.

Gault brick A type of brick made from a clay that produces a light brick, ranging in colour from almost white to shades of yellow.

Hypostyle hall A hall with a flat ceiling supported by many columns. In Ancient Egyptian temples, these symbolised the marshes from which the primeval mound of creation rose, and the columns almost always have columns or capitals with plant forms, particularly papyrus.

Ledger A stone slab covering a grave, often inscribed or otherwise decorated. Some can be stepped or curved. An angled ledger is described as 'gabled'.

Lintel A horizontal beam running between two columns or pillars, or bridging an opening such as a window or door.

Mausoleum A large and elaborate monument above a grave, or enclosing a burial chamber. Named after the monument of Mausolus, ruler of Caria, now modern Anatolia, under the Persian Empire, whose tomb was one of the Seven Wonders of the Ancient World.

Nailhead A small pyramid shaped ornament. They can occur singly or in bands.

Naos A Greek word, from the inner chamber of a temple housing the cult statue of a god. From this, extended in Egyptology to refer to a type of freestanding shrine with doors, used to contain the statue of a god. Usually rectangular and upright, with a square base, and made of stone or wood, with wooden doors. They often have a cornice with a frieze of *uraei*, and a low pyramidal roof, symbolising the primal mound which rose out of the waters of chaos at the time of creation in Egyptian myth.

Obelisk A tall narrow four-sided stone architectural ornament, square in section, which tapers towards its top, and whose top forms a small pyramid or pyramidion. In Ancient Egypt these were normally set up in pairs either side of temple gateways and entrances, and were monolithic, that is made from a single piece of stone. They were also carved with hieroglyphic inscriptions, and often gilded, particularly the pyramidions.

Pedestal The base supporting a column, statue, flagpole or other upright structure, including obelisks. The Ancient Egyptians did not erect their obelisks on pedestals, but in Graeco-Roman times this became the custom, and it was copied when the obelisk was introduced into European architecture.

Pediment In Classical architecture, the part of a wall, often triangular between the edges of a sloping roof, and above the entablature. Pediments can also be segmental, or made up of a segment of a circle. Other architectural elements which have a similar form can be described as pedimented.

Peristyle court An open courtyard, surrounded by columns or pillars supporting an architrave and roofed with stone slabs, and forming a colonnade. The name comes from the Greek, and literally means a court with columns around its edges. In Ancient Egyptian temples, these may have been semi-public areas, particularly during festivals and other important ceremonial occasions.

Pilasters A shallow column or pillar, often rectangular, used to decorate a wall, or at the corners of a building.

Pitch Normally the slope of a roof, here used to refer to the angle of the sides of a pyramid.

Plinth A projection at the bottom of a wall or pedestal of a statue or column, also used loosely for the whole support of a column or statue.

Portico An open or semi-enclosed entrance or porch to a building, often with columns and a pediment. Originally used for temples in Greece and Rome, their use in secular buildings was popularised by the Renaissance architect Andrea Palladio. The columns can project in front of the building, or be aligned with its wall.

Pronaos A pillared hall in front of the main body of a temple or shrine, with a partly or wholly open front. A distinctive feature particularly of Late Egyptian temples where the space between columns is often half filled with a screen wall.

Proscenium A large frame or arch surrounding a stage or cinema screen, or the space between this and the audience.

Pylon From the Greek word meaning a large entrance gateway or a building of which a gateway forms a part. Technically the pylon on an Egyptian temple includes both the towers on either side and the gateway between them, but in practice the towers are also referred to individually as pylons. The towers have battered sides and cavetto cornices, and are about twice as high as the gateway between them. From the New Kingdom onwards, the fronts of the towers were grooved to allow large flagpoles to be secured to them. Colossal statues of pharaohs and pairs of obelisks often stood in front of the pylons of temples.

Rustication The use of large masonry blocks, with deep joints between them, and often with a rough or heavily textured surface. Usually found on the lower parts of walls.

Scagliola A technique of creating imitation marble, hard or semi-precious stone, used for columns, statues and other architectural items. It was especially popular in the 17th and 18th centuries.

Segmental pediment *See* pediment.

Solar disc The disc of the sun is one of the most common images in Ancient Egyptian art, and is often shown flanked by wings and pairs of the *uraeus* serpent. It could symbolise the god Re as the noonday sun, the 'Eye' of Re or Horus, or the passage of the sun through the day and night.

Stele (singular, plural stelae) Usually a slab of stone, but sometimes of wood, with an inscription, relief or painting. In Egyptology these are often of a funerary nature, but they can also be commemorative, record offerings or act as boundary markers. They can be rock cut, and the false doors in Ancient Egyptian tombs are a type of stele, but many are rectangular round-topped slabs, and a form of statue where a figure is shown holding or offering a stele is known as stelophorous, literally 'bearing a stele'.

Stucco A type of hard plasterwork, often used on exterior walls, but also for interiors. It can be moulded or carved to produce a decorative finish.

Terazzo A type of flooring made from marble chips mixed with cement or set in a layer of cement, and then polished and sealed. Metal strips can be used to create areas of different colours and patterns.

Term An architectural ornament consisting of a head or torso which continues as a tapering four-sided pillar. They were employed in furniture as supports for tables and chairs, and as elements of candleholders.

Torus moulding A semicircular convex moulding. Frequently used on the vertical and horizontal edges of Ancient Egyptian buildings. Torus mouldings can be plain, but often have a pattern of alternating horizontal and diagonal banding, which probably originated in the binding used to lash together bundles of reeds in archaic buildings made of matting, reed, or papyrus bundles and wooden poles.

Uraeus (Singular, plural *uraei*) A Greek word, possibly from the Ancient Egyptian *iaret* 'she who rears up' referring to the rearing cobra with open hood. It often had a protective function, and could spit fire at the enemies of the pharaoh. It was sometimes seen as the Eye of Re, and pairs of *uraei* often flank the solar disc, with or without wings. It could also be an emblem of the goddess Wadjyt, patron of Lower Egypt.

Glossary of gods and goddesses

Around 1,500 Ancient Egyptian deities are known by name, and they came in a seemingly infinite variety of forms, human, animal and hybrid, but only a tiny sample of them, mainly the more important, are mentioned in this book. A common occurrence in Egyptian religion was syncretism, when the attributes and sometimes names of deities were combined, and, particularly in later periods of Egyptian history, it can be difficult to clearly identify them. For example, a number of goddesses could be depicted as cows, and several deities could be shown as lion-headed. (*See* Wilkinson's book, *Complete Gods and Goddesses* for further details).

Fig 219
Anubis in human form, holding the *was* sceptre, symbolising power or dominion, and carrying the *ankh* hieroglyph, meaning 'life'.

Anubis The god associated with cemeteries and mummification, said to have mummified Osiris, and normally depicted as a jackal or desert dog, or sometimes with a human body, and very rarely as entirely human. The god in jackal form is often shown crouched on a shrine or chest. Priests taking part in funeral ceremonies would wear a jackal mask, symbolising the role of the god (Fig 219). Anubis is often mentioned in early tomb inscriptions intended to ensure a constant supply of offerings for the spirit of the deceased, and also took part in the ceremony in the afterlife where the heart of the deceased was weighed against the feather of truth.

Bastet Cat goddess and daughter of the sun god Ra. Originally depicted as a lioness, and as a royal protector, with many similarities to the lion goddess Sakhmet. Bastet was worshipped, especially in the later period of Ancient Egyptian history, at her cult centre at Bubastis in the north-east Delta, and thousands of cats were mummified as offerings to the goddess.

Hathor A daughter of the sun god Ra, often associated with love and music, and regarded as the divine mother of the pharaoh. Hathor was also associated with foreign lands and was usually depicted as a woman with cow's ears (as on the columns of her temple at Dendera), a cow, or a woman with a wig and headdress featuring horns and a sun disc (Fig 220). She also had funerary aspects, and was invoked in childbirth and as a healing deity.

Isis The sister and wife of Osiris and mother of Horus, often almost interchangeable with Hathor in her human form. Isis is usually represented in human form, and can be identified by the hieroglyph on her head which stands for 'throne'. Isis collected the dismembered body of Osiris, and revived him to conceive Horus (Fig 221). One of her titles was *Weret Hekau*, 'She Who is Great of Magic', and she was a goddess of healing. During the period of Greek and Roman rule of Egypt, the worship of Isis spread across the Western world and elements of it were absorbed into Christianity, particularly in the cult of the Virgin Mary.

Khnum The ram-headed god of the Nile Cataracts, worshipped at Elephantine near Aswan, Khnum was also described as a potter who fashioned men, and was thus a creator god as well as one associated with the life-giving Nile flood, which he was believed to control.

Nefertem God of the blue lotus blossom, usually shown as a man with a headdress shaped like a lotus flower. Sometimes considered to be the son of Ptah and Sekhmet. In some versions of Ancient Egyptian creation myths, the sun was said to have risen

Heryshef A primeval fertility god, shown as a ram or man with a ram's head. His cult centre was in Middle Egypt and he was associated with both Ra and Osiris.

Horus A sky god, depicted as a falcon or a man with a falcon's head and known from the earliest periods of Egyptian history, Horus was the embodiment of kingship and protector of the pharaoh. Another form of Horus, as the son of Isis, was shown as a child with the sidelock of hair worn by children and sucking his finger. He was also, as the son of Osiris, the avenger of his father after his murder by Seth, and the successor of Osiris as king. As a sky god, the left eye of Horus represented the moon, and as the *wedjat* was a popular amulet. Horus was also merged with Ra to become Ra-Horakhty (Ra-Horus of the Horizon).

from a lotus flower, and so Nefertem was linked with the sun god Ra. This also reflected the way the flower opens in the morning and closes at night. In Ancient Egyptian tomb paintings, guests at banquets are often shown smelling blue lotus flowers and there has been speculation that it was used medicinally and even, dissolved in wine, as a recreational narcotic and aphrodisiac. Although these theories are controversial, the plant was definitely associated with fertility, sexuality and rebirth.

Neith A creator goddess known from the earliest periods of Egyptian history, whose cult centre was at Sais in the Nile Delta. She could be seen as the mother of Sobek and wife of Seth, and was one of the four guardian goddesses depicted on coffins. She is usually shown as a woman wearing the red crown of Lower Egypt. Her symbol was a shield and crossed arrows, and one of the hieroglyphs with which her name was written represents two bows bound together in a bow case.

Nut The sky goddess, and in one version of the creation myth the daughter of Shu, god of air and sunlight, and Tefnut, the goddess of moisture. The sister and wife of Geb, the earth god, and mother of Osiris, Seth, Isis and Nephthys. Often shown in human form in royal tombs, temple ceilings, and on the lids of coffins, swallowing the sun at night and giving birth to it the following morning. Her depiction on the lids of coffins symbolised her protection of the deceased.

Fig 222
Known from the earliest periods of Ancient Egyptian history, the God Sah could be shown sailing across the night sky in a papyrus boat.

Osiris Originally Osiris was probably a fertility god, associated with the germination of seeds underground, but he grew to become one of the most important and widely worshipped Ancient Egyptian gods, symbolising death and resurrection as well as fertility. He was usually shown as a mummified man, with hands or arms emerging from the bandages and holding the emblems of kingship, the crook and the flail, and wearing the white crown of Upper Egypt flanked by two long plumes. His skin could be white like the bandages, black like the soil of Egypt or green like vegetation. He absorbed the attributes of many other gods as his cult spread throughout Egypt. This was later reflected by the legend that he had been killed by his brother Seth, and that after Osiris's wife Isis had magically revived him and conceived their son Horus, Seth dismembered the body of Osiris and scattered the pieces. Isis searched for them and buried them where she found them. The most important cult centre for Osiris was at Abydos where his head was supposed to have been buried. The dead king became identified with Osiris and the living with Horus. Osiris became the ruler of the Underworld and later it was common for any deceased person to be identified with Osiris.

Ra-Horakhty A combination of the sun god Ra and Horus 'of the Horizon', that is the East, where the sun rose. The pharaoh was said to be born as Horakhty.

Sah The personification of the constellation which we know as Orion (Fig 222). It rose in the night sky immediately before Sirius, which was used by the Ancient Egyptians for calculations related to their calendar. Sirius was represented by the goddess Sopdet (also known as Sothis), and it was easy for Sah and Sopdet to be identified as manifestations of Osiris and Isis.

Seth God of the desert, storms, chaos, violence and confusion, but also the patron deity of several pharaohs of the Ramesside dynasty. He could take the form of an animal of unknown species, with a snout like an anteater, upright ears with square tips and a forked tail, or as a human with the head of this beast. Known from the earliest periods of Egyptian history, he had an important role as a balancing force in the Ancient Egyptian concept of the cosmos, and it was only in later periods that he came to be seen almost wholly negatively.

Sobek A crocodile god mainly worshipped in Upper Egypt, where he shared a temple with Horus at Kom Ombo, and in the Fayum. Shown as a crocodile or a man with a crocodile's head, often with a headdress of a horned solar disc flanked by feathers. The worship of this god probably had an element of propitiation, intended to avert the danger of real crocodiles, but Sobek was also symbolic of the power of the pharaoh.

Thoth The god of writing and knowledge, usually shown as a man with the head of an ibis, holding the pen and palette of a scribe, but also as an ibis or baboon. A lunar deity, he is often shown with a headdress made of the crescent and full moons. The god of scribes, Thoth was 'Lord of the Sacred Words', or hieroglyphs, scribe of the gods, and Recorder of the underworld, registering the results of the tribunal which weighed the heart of the deceased in the scales of Truth. He was also responsible for recording the passing of time and assigning long reigns to pharaohs, and was closely associated with the calendar. The goddess of writing, Seshat, was sometimes described as the sister or wife of Thoth, but a little-known goddess called Nehemetawy is also named as his wife.

Uraeus The rearing cobra, which together with the vulture formed the two symbols of kingship on the crown of the pharaoh, is known as the *uraeus*, a word which comes from the Greek for 'serpent', but may have originally come from an Egyptian word meaning 'she who rears up' (Fig 223). The *uraeus* was identified as Wadjet, 'the green one', a cobra goddess of Lower Egypt, and the vulture as Nekhbet, the patron goddess of Upper Egypt (Fig 224). As protector of the pharaoh, the *uraeus* could spit fire at his enemies, particularly in wartime.

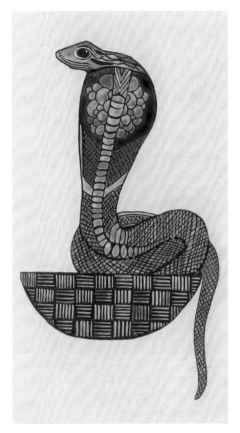

Fig 223
The basket hieroglyph below the cobra is read as *neb/nebet* (lord or lady), and Wadjet and Nekhbet, shown together in this way, identified the 'Two Ladies' name of the king, part of his royal titles.

Fig 224
The link between Wadjet and Nekhbet, as patron goddesses of Upper and Lower Egypt and protectors of the pharaoh, could be emphasised by showing Wadjet as a serpent-headed vulture.

297

Notes

Understanding Egypt in England

1   Smith 1998, 27
2   Ibid, 29–30; Wildung 1997, 7
3   Wildung 1997, 9–10
4   Lloyd and Müller 1986, 117–18
5   Clayton 1982, 8
6   Wilkinson 2000, 149–51, 201–2, 204–7, 209–10 and 213–15
7   McKenzie 2007, 35, 125
8   Davies 1987, 11
9   McKenzie 2007, 33, 35
10 Ibid, 35, 140, 141
11 Clayton 1982, 8, 9
12 Habachi 1978, 109
13 Curl 1994, 17–24; Wildung 1997, 226
14 Curl 1994, 18–19, 28–9
15 Ibid, 29
16 Clayton 1982, 9
17 Vitruvius (De architectura, VI III, 8–9) referred to a type of basilical hall as 'Egyptian' in contrast to 'Corinthian'. See McKenzie 2007, 34–5 for the suggestion that this may refer to an architectural form developed in Ptolemaic Egypt.
18 Colvin 2008, 147–52
19 Although usually described as a billiard room, it has been suggested that it might have been intended for Masonic use. See Curl 2011 for the use of Egyptian elements in Masonic contexts.
20 Colvin 2008, 762–4
21 Denon 1802, 305–6
22 Denon 1802, xvi
23 Sonnini 1799, 156
24 Colvin 2008, 826–9
25 Elmes 1829, 301
26 Colvin 2008, 388–90
27 Ibid, 904–12
28 Ibid, 802–3
29 Ibid, 376–7
30 Foulston 1838, address
31 Colvin 2008, 1049–51
32 Conner 1983, 87
33 Colvin 2008, 167
34 Brown 1841, 280–82
35 Colvin 2008, 141–3
36 Ibid, 1062
37 Quoted in Halls 1834, 303
38 Soane 2000, lecture 1, 36
39 Ibid
40 Ibid, 36–7
41 Ibid, 3, 7
42 The Builder 119 July 1920, 93
43 Dickens 2000, 12, 110
44 Walker 1839, 149–87
45 Loudon 1843, 13
46 Ibid, 13
47 Pugin 1843, 5
48 Ibid, 5
49 Curl 1994, 182
50 Clapham and Lambeth News 27 Jun 1930
51 Picture House 14/15 Spring 1990 (publication of the Cinema Theatre Association).
52 Shand 1930, 19
53 Clapham and Lambeth News 27 Jun 1930
54 Ibid
55 Luxor Cinema planning prospectus nd London Borough of Richmond upon Thames Local Studies Collection.
56 Courtesy of the Society of Antiquaries of London. I am grateful to Dr Dilwyn Knox of University College London for the transliteration and translation, but any errors of interpretation are mine.
57 Tatham 1799, preface
58 Ibid
59 Ibid
60 De Bellaigue 1997, 189–90
61 Collard 1985, 82, 211, 215
62 Kelly 2004, 83
63 I am also grateful to Dr Dilwyn Knox for alerting me to the shape of traditional Italian chimneys, and the influence these may have had on Piranesi's designs.
64 Hope 1807, 51
65 Kelly 2004, 91–4
66 De Bellaigue 1997, 190

67 Collard 1985, 215–20
68 Wilkinson, J G 1854, preface
69 Reid 2002, 100–1
70 Dawson 1995, 329–31
71 Hamill & Mollier 2003, 207–8

72 Library and Museum of Freemasonry – paper presented to Quatuor Coronati Lodge (24 Jun 1939) by Lewis Edwards.
73 Adams 1895, preface, xi–xii
74 *The Gentleman's Magazine* Apr 1827, 324

Finding Egypt in England

1 Cambridge University Library ADD 9389/2/B, 24 Mar 1840
2 Quoted in Meller 2008, 72
3 V&A Museum 1982: *The Sèvres Egyptian service 1810–12*, 18
4 Truman 1982, footnote 18, 10
5 Ibid, footnote 23, 16–17
6 *Architects' Journal* 4 Sept 1929, 345–7
7 *The Builder* 10 June 1921, 740
8 *The Architect & Building News* 27 Sept 1929, 384–5
9 *The Architects' Journal* 4 Sept 1929, 345
10 National Archives. WORK 38/146 & WORK 16/45
11 Ibid
12 Ibid
13 Ibid
14 Ibid
15 Ibid
16 Ibid
17 Ibid
18 Ibid
19 Ibid
20 Habachi 1978, 164–76
21 Wilson 1802, 218–9 and footnote 219
22 *Fraser's Magazine* **33** Jan–Jun 1846, 95 ('Titmarsh's Tour through Turkeydom')
23 *All The Year Round* 1859 **1**, 562
24 V&A Museum: Archives MA/2/C
25 Ibid
26 MacGregor 1869, 69
27 Wilde 1839, 5
28 Ibid, 6
29 Noakes 1962, 12–13
30 Alexander 1879, 13–14
31 Ibid, 15
32 Ibid, 16

33 Ibid, 25
34 Ibid, 29
35 British Museum Archives, AES Av 70074
36 Ibid
37 Demetrio 1878, 7
38 Reprinted in *The Times* 24 May 1877
39 *Newcastle Daily Chronicle* 1 Feb 1878
40 Alexander 1879, 90
41 *The Times* 12 Mar 1878, 4
42 *The Times* 1 Feb 1878, 10
43 *The Times* 27 Sept 1877, 6
44 *Hansard* **235** 25 Jun 1877, 190
45 Alexander 1879, 64
46 *Hansard* **237** 31 Jan 1878, 724
47 *The Times* 8 Sept 1911, 2
48 Alexander 1879, *vii*
49 *The Times* 3 Oct 1877, 5
50 *The Times* 11 Feb 1878, 8
51 *The Times* 23 Jan 1878, 8
52 *The Times* 27 Sept 1877, 6
53 *The Times* 19 Sept 1877, 6
54 *The Times* 3 Oct 1877, 5
55 *The Times* 6 Oct 1877, 11
56 *The Builder* **463** 20 Dec 1851, 798
57 Ibid
58 *The Times* 1 Feb 1878, 10
59 Wilson 1877, preface
60 Sinclair 1878, 12
61 *The Times* 1 Feb 1878, 10
62 *The Times* 31 Jan 1878, 5
63 London Metropolitan Archives Q/CN
64 Egypt was still technically under Turkish rule.
65 Sinclair 1878, 11
66 *The Times* 23 Aug 1878, 5

67 *The Times* 31 Oct 1878, 5

68 The citation for Wilson's knighthood mentioned his presidency of the Royal College of Surgeons, and other medical achievements, but not his role in bringing the Needle to England. However, it was widely believed that the latter was a factor. I am grateful to Dr Ian Pearce for this information. *The Times* (10 Oct 1878, 9) had suggested that both Wilson and Dixon deserved honours.

69 *The Times* 31 Oct 1878, 5

70 *The Times* 31 Oct 1878, 5

71 London Metropolitan Archives Q/CN

72 *The Times* 31 Oct 1878, 5

73 *The Times* 31 Jan 1882, 11

74 *The Times* 2 Sept 1878, 4

75 *The Times* 17 Feb 1879, 6

76 Ibid

77 *The Times* 23 Aug 1878, 5

78 *The Times* 13 Sept 1878, 7 & 9

79 For example, *Punch* 9 Feb 1878, where the khedive is described as 'this leech of old Nile', and as 'robbing his own till'.

80 *The Times* 1 Feb 1878, 10

81 *Hansard* **238** 7 Mar 1878, 826 (House of Lords)

82 *The Times* 12 Mar 1878, 4

83 Also known as Browning's Colourless Preservative. Believed to be a preparation of Dammar resin (used as a varnish) and wax in petroleum spirit. *See* Teutonico & Fidler 2001, 163 and footnote 1.

84 Ball 1978, 32

85 Teutonico & Fidler 2001, 160

86 *The Times* 10 Nov 1877, 9

87 Sketchley 1878, 105

88 Quoted in full in Ryan 2007, 99

89 Williams 1878

90 *The Times* 27 Sept 1877, 6

91 Phillips 1862, 9

92 Ibid, 5

93 Ibid, 8

94 Colvin 2008, 1107–1121

95 Phillips 1862, 6

96 V&A Museum Archives MA/2/C, 9 Nov 1852

97 *The Times* 11 Nov 1852, 3

98 *Illustrated London News* 2 Apr 1853, 242

99 V&A Museum Archives MA/2/C, July 1865

100 V&A Museum Archives MA/2/C, 3 Nov 1865 (?)

101 Jones 1854, 3

102 Ibid, 8

103 Ibid, 26

104 *Crystal Palace Matters* **10**, 7–12

105 *New Crystal Palace Matters*, Summer 1994 issue **5**, 25

106 *Illustrated London News* 22 July 1854, 70

107 *Transactions of the Ancient Monument Society* **40** 1996, 1–15

108 *St Pancras Chronicle* 9 Nov 1928, 6–10

109 Ibid

110 Ibid

111 Ibid

112 William Mitchell, pers comm

113 *Architects' Journal* 21 Nov 1928, 736–40

114 Op cit

115 Cherry and Pevsner 1998, 385

116 Old Humphrey *c* 1843, 323

117 Meller 2008, 187–92

118 *Public Archaeology* 2006, 5, 42–50

119 Jencks 1991, 78

120 *Architects' Journal* Jun 1998, 5

121 Ibid

122 Jencks 1991, 80

123 *Building Design* 1 July 1988 **892**, 1

124 Skinner 1997, 76–8, where she notes that the GEC contract was completed prior to the publicity generated by the discovery of Tutankhamun's tomb and cannot therefore be attributed to that influence.

125 *Notes and Queries* 16 Mar 1929

126 Saxon 1978, 371 and Meller 2008, 235, where the 'decoration' of the monument is credited to John Cusworth. *See also* http://www.britishlistedbuildings.co.uk/en-203836-tomb-of-andrew-ducrow-kensington (accessed 26 March 2012).

127 Urwin 1997, 4–8

128 Carter 1972, 112

129 *Wandsworth Borough News* 16 Sept 1910, 'Deaths'

130 *Hamilton Journal-News* 3 & 10 Mar 2004

131 W H Smith archives and *The Burlington Magazine*, **30** Jan–Jun 1917, 82–3

132 Meller 2008, 339–43

133 Curl 1993, 288–9

134 Curl 1994, 19 & plate 11

135 *Oxford DNB* – Hope, Thomas (1769–1831)

136 Conner 1983, 47

137 Hope 1807, 27

138 *Oxford DNB* – Fuller, John (1757–1834)

139 Institution of Civil Engineers – Obituary, Minutes **117** 1894, 381–2

140 'the late Marquess of Buckingham, whose taste and skill in designing can only be equalled by the other distinguished talents [he] so eminently possessed'. Soane 2000, 213

141 Stowe 1817, 37–8

142 Ibid

143 Conner 1983, 52–3

144 Buckinghamshire County Museum 1983, cat. no. 98

145 Stowe 1817, 37–8

146 Colvin 1991, plate 306

147 I am grateful to Hettie Dix, Restoration Project Researcher for the Stowe House Preservation Trust, for information on the progress of restoration.

148 Baird 2007, 55, 148

149 Jacques 1822, 21–2

150 De Bellaigue 1997, 190

151 Baird 2007, 148

152 Ibid

153 Ibid, 150

154 Smyth 1851–64, 156

155 Ibid, addenda, plate 1

156 Dawson 1995, 241; *Oxford DNB* – Lee, John (1783–1866)

157 Dawson 1995, 45–6; *Oxford DNB* – Birch, Samuel (1813–85)

158 *Transactions of the Society of Biblical Archaeology* 1878 **6**, 573

159 Dawson 1995, 53; *Oxford DNB* – Bonomi, Joseph (1796–1878)

160 Carrott 1978, 35; Smyth 1851–64, 156 and 222

161 Hope 1893, 5

162 Conner 1983, 91

163 I am grateful to Carol Andrews for her advice on translation of the inscription, particularly the reading of the Ancient Egyptian titles.

164 Smyth 1851–64, 41

165 Kadish 2006, 63–4

166 Cohn-Sherbock 1984, 19

167 Kadish 2006, 64

168 *Jewish Chronicle* 15 Nov 1889

169 Quoted in Cohn-Sherbock 1984, 11

170 Wilkinson 1994, 104–125

171 Wilkinson 1992, 135

172 Foulston 1838, address

173 Ibid

174 Ibid

175 Carrott 1978, 46. Notes to chap 2 no. 70, notes the use of the 'sun disc with drooping wings, a later Ptolemaic element found at Edfou, among others'– as one of the 'noteworthy' similarities of the decorative details of a number of Egyptianising buildings including Ker Street and the Egyptian House in Penzance.

176 Lennox-Boyd, Charlotte – Egyptian House Album, Landmark Trust, kept in property.

177 Parker 2001, 183–204

178 Cherry and Pevsner 2004, 423

179 Whittock 1840, plate XII

180 Usick 2002, 79

181 I am grateful to Judith Goodison for permission to use this photograph, and to draw on her article in *Furniture History* on Chippendale's work at Stourhead.

182 Curl 1994, 192–3

183 Humbert & Price 2003, 26

184 Meadows 1988, 24–5

185 Pevsner 1977, 190, where the date is given as 1825

186 Curl 1994, 197

187 Hackford is credited as the architect in material on the history of the building provided by the Lodge of Harmony, and on a plaque erected by the Boston Preservation Trust.

188 Cryer 1989, 12

189 Dixon 1894, 207

190 Ibid

191 Ibid

192 Ibid

193 Cryer 1989, 15

194 *Oxford DNB* – Bateman, James (1812–97)

195 Ibid – Hawkins, Benjamin Waterhouse (1807–94)

196 Skinner 1997, 67–79

197 Horton 2001, 15, 17

198 Disraeli 1845 109

199 Rimmer 1960, 201–7

200 Conner 1983, 89; Curl 1994, 170

201 Carrott 1978, 35 and note 71. *See also* Bonser, *Architectural Review* CXXVII **758** 1960, 280–2 and Wood, G Bernard 'Egyptian Temple Architecture in Leeds', *Country Life* CXXVIII **3326** 1 Dec 1960, 1, 363–5

202 Institution of Civil Engineers archives

203 Institution of Civil Engineers: *Abstract of Minutes of the Proceedings* May 10 1842, 142

204 Tomlinson 1866, 122

205 Ibid, 124

206 *See also* Bonser, *Architectural Review* CXXVII **758** 1960, 281

207 Tomlinson 1866, 123

208 Ibid, 124

209 Disraeli 1845, chap 8, 109

210 Ibid

211 Rimmer 1960, 203

212 Throssell 2011, fig 153 and caption

213 Johnson 1852–6, plate XX

214 Osburn 1828, 9

215 Conner 1983, 89

216 Curl 1994, 170

217 Throssell 2011, 256–7. I am extremely grateful to Eric Throssell for bringing to my attention this material in a private archive.

218 Throssell 2011, 257

219 Throssell 2011, 64

220 Cambridge University Library ADD 9389/2/M/15, J G Marshall 3 Aug 1842

221 Ibid

222 Ibid

223 Ibid

224 Ibid

225 Cambridge University Library ADD 9389/2/O/3–8, W Osburn 16 Aug 1842

226 Cambridge University Library ADD 9389/2/M/16, 30 Jan 1861

227 British Library, Additional MS 38094 fol 166

228 Throssell 2011, 261

229 Throssell 2011, 263–6

230 Cambridge University Library ADD 9389/2/M/16

231 British Library, Additional MS 38094 fol 176

232 Cambridge University Library ADD 9389/2/W/6

233 Cambridge University Library ADD 9389/2/H/152

234 Tomlinson 1866, 124–5

235 Leeds Library Services SPQ 942/75T396

236 Rimmer 1960, 203

237 Tomlinson 1866, 122

238 *Oxford DNB* – Illingworth, Alfred (1827–1907)

239 Clark 2004, 6

240 *Oxford DNB* – Bateman, John Frederic La Trobe (1810–89)

241 *Liverpool Mercury* 20 Jan 1893; *Manchester Times* 3 Feb 1893, genealogical forums

242 Curl 1994, 178

243 Rendell 1988, 37–45

Bibliography

Adams, W M 1895 *The House of the Hidden Places. A Clue to the Creed of Early Egypt, from Egyptian Sources.* London: John Murray

Adkins, L & R 2000 *The Keys of Egypt: The Race to Read the Hieroglyphs.* London: Harper Collins

Alexander, J E 1879 *Cleopatra's Needle: The Obelisk of Alexandria; its Acquisition and Removal to England Described.* London: Chatto & Windus

Architects' Journal 21 Nov 1928 (Greater London House); 4 Sept 1929 (Britannia House); June 1988 'Pollarding Architecture', 5; Astragal column 'Manqué business', 6 (Warwick Road)

Arnold, D 2003 *The Encyclopaedia of Ancient Egyptian Architecture.* London: I B Tauris

Ball, A 1978 *Cleopatra's Needle: The Story of 100 Years in London.* Havant: K Mason

Baird, R 2007 *Goodwood: Art and Architecture, Sport and Family.* London: Frances Lincoln

Barnes, R 2004 *The Obelisk: A Monumental Feature in Britain.* Kirstead: Frontier

Bevington, M 2002 *Stowe House,* rev edn. London: Paul Holberton

British Museum Archives: AES Av 700 (Cleopatra's Needle)

Brown, R 1841 *Domestic Architecture: Containing a History of the Science, and the Principles of Designing Public Buildings, Private Dwelling-houses … With Observations on Rural Residences … and Instructions on the Art of Laying out and Embellishing Grounds.* London: George Virtue

Buckinghamshire County Museum 1983 *Drawings of Stowe by John Claude Nattes in the Buckinghamshire County Museum.* Buckingham: Buckinghamshire County Museum

Budge, Sir E A T W 1926 *Cleopatra's Needles.* London: Religious Tract Society

Butler, R 1982 'Le Sphinx de Tanis'. *Crystal Palace Matters* **10** 7–11. London: Crystal Palace Foundation

Cambridge University Library, Bonomi correspondence: ADD 9389/2/B 44–152 (Samuel Birch to Bonomi), ADD 9389/2/M (J G Marshall to Bonomi), ADD 9389/2/O (William Osburn to Bonomi), ADD 9389/2/W (Frederick Oldfield Ward to Bonomi)

Carrott, R G 1978 *The Egyptian Revival: Its Sources, Monuments, and Meaning, 1808–1858.* Berkeley; London: University of California Press

Carter, H 1972 *The Tomb of Tutankhamen.* London: Sphere Books

Cherry, B and Pevsner, N 1998 *Buildings of England: London: 4, North.* London: Penguin

Cherry, B and Pevsner, N 2004 *Buildings of England: Devon.* London: Yale University Press

Clayton, P 1982 *The Rediscovery of Egypt.* London: Thames and Hudson

Clear, G 1949 *The Story of W H Smith & Son.* Privately printed

Clark, C 2004 *In Loving Memory: The Story of Undercliffe Cemetery.* Stroud: Sutton

Cohn-Sherbok, D 1984 *The Jews of Canterbury 1760–1931.* Canterbury: Yorick

Collard, F 1985 *Regency Furniture.* Woodbridge: Antique Collectors' Club

Colvin, H 1991 *Architecture and the After-life.* New Haven; London: Yale University Press

Colvin, H 2008 *A Biographical Dictionary of British Architects 1600–1840.* New Haven; London: Yale University Press

Conner, P, ed c 1983 *The Inspiration of Egypt: Its Influence on British Artists, Travellers and Designers, 1700–1900: An Exhibition held at Brighton Museum, 7 May–17 July 1983, and at Manchester City Art Gallery, 4th August–17 September 1983.* Brighton: Brighton Borough Council

Croad, S 1996 'Changing perceptions – a temple to tobacco in Camden Town'. *Transactions of the Ancient Monument Society* **40** 1–15

Crystal Palace Matters **10** Summer 1982 and *New Crystal Palace Matters* **5** Summer 1994: The Journal of the Crystal Palace Foundation. London

Culbertson, J & Randall T 1991 *Permanent Londoners: An Illustrated Guide to the Cemeteries of London.* London: Robson Books

Cryer, N B 1989 *Masonic Halls of England (Midlands)*. Shepperton: Lewis Masonic

Curl, J S 1993 *A Celebration of Death: An Introduction to Some of the Buildings, Monuments, and Settings of Funerary Architecture in the Western European Tradition*, 2nd rev edn. London: B T Batsford

Curl, J S c 1994 *Egyptomania: The Egyptian Revival: A Recurring Theme in the History of Taste*. Manchester and New York: Manchester University Press

Curl, J S 2005 *The Egyptian Revival: Ancient Egypt as the Inspiration for Design Motifs in the West*, new edn. Abingdon: Routledge

Curl, J S 2006 *A Dictionary of Architecture and Landscape Architecture*. Oxford: Oxford University Press

Curl, J S 2011 *Freemasonry and the Enlightenment: Architecture, Symbols and Influences*. London: Historical Publications

Davies, W V 1987 *Egyptian Hieroglyphs*. London: British Museum

Dawson, W R c 1995 *Who Was Who in Egyptology*, 3rd rev edn by Bierbrier, M L. London: Egypt Exploration Society

De Bellaigue, G 1997 'The Vulliamys' chimney-pieces'. *Furniture History* **XXXIII** 188–99

Demetrio, G di 1878 'Cleopatra's Needle, letter … to the "Times."' Translated from the French original (Alexandria)

Denon, D V 1802 *Voyage dans la Basse et la Haute Égypte pendant les Campagnes du Général Bonaparte*, 2 vol. Paris

Dickens, C 2000 *The Uncommercial Traveller and Other Papers, 1859–70* vol 4 of *The Dent Uniform Edition of Dickens' Journalism* edited by Slater, M and Drew, J. London: Dent

Disraeli, B 1845 *Sybil; or, The Two Nations*. London: Henry Colburn

Dixon, W 1894 *A History of Freemasonry in Lincolnshire*. Lincoln: James Williamson

Draper, C nd *Islington's Cinemas and Film Studios*. London: Islington Libraries

Elmes, J 1829 *Metropolitan Improvements: Or London in the Nineteenth Century*. London: Jones

Elwall, Robert 1990 'The dream lands of Julian Leathart'. *Picture House* (annual journal of the Cinema Theatres Association)

Foulston, J 1838 *The Public Buildings Erected in the West of England, as Designed by J. F. With description of the Plates*. London

Goodison J 2005 'Thomas Chippendale the Younger at Stourhead'. *Furniture History* **XLI** 57–60

Habachi, L 1978 *The Obelisks of Egypt: Skyscrapers of the Past*. London: Dent

Halls, J J 1834 *The Life and Correspondence of Henry Salt, … Late Consul General in Egypt*. London: Richard Bentley

Hamill, J-M & Mollier, P 2003 'Rebuilding the Sanctuaries of Memphis: Egypt in Masonic Iconography and architecture' in Humbert and Price 2003

Hayward, R A 1978 *Cleopatra's Needles*. Buxton: Moorland Publishing Company

Hitchmough, W 1992 *Hoover Factory: Wallis Gilbert and Partners: London 1931–1938*. London: Phaidon

Hope, T 1807 *Household Furniture and Interior Decoration Executed from Designs by Thomas Hope* (facsim edn with preface by Musgrove C, Alec Tiranti 1970)

Hope, R C 1893 *The Legendary Lore of the Holy Wells of England: Including Rivers, Lakes, Fountains and Springs. Copiously illustrated*, etc. London: Elliot Stock

Horton, J c 2001 *Remote and Undisturbed: A Brief History of the Sheffield General Cemetery*. Sheffield: Friends of the General Cemetery

Humbert, J-M and Price, C (eds) 2003 *Imhotep Today: Egyptianising architecture*. London: UCL Press

The Illustrated London News. London: Illustrated London News & Sketch Ltd

Institution of Civil Engineers: Minutes of the Proceedings

Iversen, E 1972 *Obelisks in Exile*. Copenhagen: G E C Gad

Jacques, D 1822 *A Visit to Goodwood, the Seat of the Duke of Richmond. With an Appendix Descriptive of an Ancient Painting*. Chichester: L P

Jencks, C 1991 'The carnival: Grotesque and redeemable' in Papadakis, A C (ed) *Architectural Design: Post-Modern Triumphs in London*. London: Academy Editions

Johnson, W 1852–6 *The Imperial Cyclopædia of Machinery, being a Series of Plans, Sections and Elevations of Stationary, Marine and Locomotive Engines, Spinning Machinery, etc. With Descriptive Letterpress, an Essay on the Steam Engine, and a History of the Railways of Great Britain by W. J.* Glasgow; Edinburgh; London

Jones, O 1854 *Description of the Egyptian Court Erected in the Crystal Palace … With an Historical Notice of the Monuments of Egypt; by Samuel Sharpe, Esq*. London: Crystal Palace Library

Jones, O 1856 *The Grammar of Ornament ... Illustrated by Examples from Various Styles of Ornament. One Hundred ... Plates, Drawn on Stone by F. Bedford, and Printed in Colours by Day and Son*. London: Day & Co

Kadish, S 2006 *Jewish Heritage in England: An Architectural Guide*. Swindon: English Heritage

Kelly, D St L 2004 'The Egyptian revival: A reassessment of Baron Denon's influence on Thomas Hope'. *Furniture History* **XL** 83–98

Lennox-Boyd, C nd *House Album for the Egyptian House, Penzance*. The Landmark Trust

Lloyd, S and Müller, H 1986 *Ancient Architecture*. London: Faber

Loudon, J C 1843 *On the Laying out, Planting, and Managing of Cemeteries and on the Improvement of Churchyards*. (facsim edn Ivelet Books 1981)

MacGregor, J 1869 *The Rob Roy on the Jordan, Nile, Red Sea, & Gennesareth, etc*. London: John Murray

Mallett, L 1988 'Deconstruction hits Homebase'. *Building Design* **892**

Mayes, S 2003 *The Great Belzoni: The Circus Strongman who Discovered Egypt's Treasures*. London: Tauris Parke

McKenzie, J 2007 *The Architecture of Alexandria and Egypt 300BC–AD700*. New Haven; London: Yale University Press

Meadows, P 1988 *Joseph Bonomi Architect: 1739–1808*. London: Royal Institute of British Architects

Meller, H c 2008 *London Cemeteries: An Illustrated Guide & Gazetteer*, 4 edn. Stroud: History Press

Montserrat, D 2000 *Akhenaten: History, Fantasy, and Ancient Egypt*. London. Routledge

Morris, B 1989 *Liberty Design, 1874–1914*. London: Pyramid

National Archives: WORK 38/146 & WORK 16/45 (Kilmorey mausoleum)

National Library of Scotland, Manuscripts Division: David Roberts correspondence (Acc 11760)

Noakes, A 1962 *Cleopatra's Needles*. London: H F & G Witherby

Old Humphrey c 1843 *Old Humphrey's Walks in London and its Neighbourhood*. London: Religious Tract Society

Osburn, W 1828 *An Account of an Egyptian Mummy Presented to the Museum of the Leeds Philosophical and Literary Society, by J. Blayds Esq. With an Appendix Containing the Chemical and Anatomical Details of the Examination of the Body; by E. S. George, T. P. Teale and R. Hey*. Leeds

Oxford Dictionary of National Biography

Parker, R 2001 'Archaeological Recording of a 17th-century House at 144 Fore Street, Exeter'. *Devon Archaeological Society, Proceedings* **59**, 183–204

Pevsner, N 1977 *Buildings of England: Hertfordshire*. Harmondsworth: Penguin

Phillips, S, 1862 *Guide to the Crystal Palace and its Park and Gardens: A Newly Arranged and Entirely Revised Edition*. Sydenham: Robert K Burt, Crystal Palace printing office

Pugin, A W N 1843 *An Apology for the Revival of Christian Architecture in England*. London: John Weale

Reid, D M c 2002 *Whose Pharaohs?: Archaeology, Museums, and Egyptian National Identity from Napoleon to World War I*. Berkeley, London: University of California Press

Rendell, D 1998 *Cinemas of Trafford*. Altrincham: D Rendell

Rimmer, W G 1960 *Marshalls of Leeds. Flax-spinners, 1788–1886*. Cambridge: University Press

Ryan, D P (ed) 2007 *A Shattered Visage Lies ... Nineteenth Century Poetry Inspired by Ancient Egypt*. Bolton: Rutherford Press

Saint Pancras Chronicle 9 Nov 1928

Saxon, A H 1978 *The Life and art of Andrew Ducrow & the Romantic Age of the English Circus*. Hamden: Archon Books

Seeley, J see Stowe

Shand, P M 1930 *Modern Theatres and Cinemas*. London: Batsford

Sinclair, W M 1878 *Cleopatra's Needle. A Sermon, etc. [on John iii 16]*. London

Sketchley, A 1878 *Mrs. Brown on Cleopatra's Needle*. London

Skinner, J S 1997 *Form and Fancy. Factories and Factory Buildings by Wallis, Gilbert & Partners, 1916–1939*. Liverpool: Liverpool University Press

Smith, W S 1998 *The Art and Architecture of Ancient Egypt*, rev edn. New Haven; London: Yale University Press

Smyth, W H 1851–64 *Ædes Hartwellianæ, or Notices of the Mansion of Hartwell*. London: Privately printed

Soane, J 2000 *Sir John Soane: The Royal Academy Lectures*, edited and with an introduction by David Watkin, rev & abridged edn. Cambridge: Cambridge University Press

Society of Biblical Archæology 1872–93 *Transactions of the Society of Biblical Archæology*. London: Longmans, Green, Reader, and Dyer

Solé, R & Valbelle, D 2001 *The Rosetta Stone*. London: Profile

Sonnini de Manoncourt, C N S 1799 *Voyages dans la Haute et Basse Égypte, fait par ordre de l'ancien Gouvernement. (Travels in Upper and Lower Egypt). Illustrated with Forty engravings … Translated from the French by H. Hunter*. London

Stowe 1817 *A Description of the House and Gardens of the … Marquis of Buckingham*. Buckingham: J Seeley

Tatham, C H 1799 *Etchings, Representing the Best Examples of Ancient Ornamental Architecture; Drawn from the Originals in Rome, and other Parts of Italy, During the Years 1794, 1795, and 1796*. London: T Gardiner

Taylor, J R 'In the wake of Tutankhamun'. *Art & Artists* **200** May 1983–10

Teutonico J & Fidler J eds 2001 *Monuments and the millennium*, proceedings of a joint conference organised by English Heritage and the United Kingdom Institute for Conservation. London: James & James.

The Architect and Building News Sept 1929 (Britannia House)

Throssell, E 2011 *Joseph Bonomi: The Egyptianised Enigmas, Hartwell, Buckinghamshire*. Aylesbury: Long Gallery Press

Titmarsh, M A (Thackeray, W M) 1846 *Notes of a Journey from Cornhill to Grand Cairo*. (Reprinted 1991, Heathfield: Cockbird Press.)

Tomlinson, C 1866 *The Useful Arts and Manufactures of Great Britain. First [and] Second Series New Edition Revised*. London: Society for Promoting Christian Knowledge

Truman, C 1982 *The Sèvres Egyptian Service 1810–12*. London: V&A Museum

Ucko P J, Quirke S & Price C 2006 'The Earls Court Homebase car park façade'. *Public Archaeology* **5** 42–50

Urwin, A C B 1997 'The Second Earl of Kilmorey and his Mausoleum in St Margarets'. *Borough of Twickenham Local Historical Society* Paper **75** (October)

Usick, P 2002 *Adventures in Egypt and Nubia: The Travels of William John Bankes (1786–1855)*. London: British Museum Press

Victoria and Albert Museum: Archives MA/2/C (Cleopatra's Needle)

Walker, G A 1839 *Gatherings from Grave-yards: Particularly those of London. With a Concise History of the Modes of Interment Among Different Nations … and a Detail of … Results Produced by the … Custom of Inhuming the Dead in the Midst of the Living*. London: Nottingham

Whittock, N 1840 *On the Construction and Decoration of the Shop Fronts of London, Illustrated with … Coloured Representation … By N. W. Forming an Appendix to the Decorative Painter and Glazier's Guide, by the Same Author*. London

Wilde, W R A 1839 *Proposal Relative to the Nelson Testimonial*. Dublin: William Curry, Jun and Company

Wildung, D 1997 *Egypt from Prehistory to the Romans*. Koln: Taschen

Wilkinson, J G 1854 *Popular Account of the Ancient Egyptians: Rev. and abr. fr.: Manners and Customs of the ancient Egyptians. (Facsim edn Studio Editions 1990)* London

Wilkinson, R H 1992 *Reading Egyptian Art: A Hieroglyphic Guide to Ancient Egyptian Painting and Sculpture*. London: Thames and Hudson

Wilkinson, R H 1994 *Symbol & Magic in Egyptian Art*. London: Thames and Hudson

Wilkinson, R H 2000 *The Complete Temples of Ancient Egypt*. London: Thames and Hudson

Wilkinson, R H 2003 *The Complete Gods and Goddesses of Ancient Egypt*. London: Thames & Hudson

Williams, C 1878 *Cleopatra's Needle … . Comic song, written, composed and sung by C Williams*. London: C Sheard

Wilson, E. 1877 *Cleopatra's Needle: With Brief Notes on Egypt and Egyptian obelisks*. London: Brain

Wilson, P 2004 *Sacred Signs: Hieroglyphs: A Very Short Introduction*. Oxford: Oxford University Press

Wilson, R T 1802 *History of the British Expedition to Egypt*. London: L P

Wolff, A 2003 *How Many Miles to Babylon?: European Travels and Adventures in Egypt, 1300–1600*. Liverpool: Liverpool University Press

Acknowledgements

Sir Isaac Newton once famously wrote to Robert Hooke that if he, Newton, had 'seen a little further, it is only by standing on the shoulders of giants'. That may have been true for him, but I have come to feel that anyone writing a book like this crowd surfs on the outstretched arms of other contemporary scholars. It would not have been possible without the generous help of many people, from all walks of life. I have done my best to thank them all, but if I have overlooked anyone they have my sincere apologies as well as my sincere gratitude.

Special thanks to the staff of the British Library, and the staffs of Local Studies and Local History libraries and archives throughout London and elsewhere in England. Special thanks also for their comments on the manuscript to John Taylor at the Department of Ancient Egypt and Sudan at the British Museum, Professor David Watkin at the University of Cambridge and the English Heritage referees. As always, any remaining errors are the responsibility of the author. I must also record my appreciation for the photographers including Alun Bull, Steve Cole, Nigel Corrie, James O Davies, Bob Skingle and Peter Williams, who took the original photos for this book, my copy editor Sue Kelleher, designer Andrea Rollinson and indexer Ann Hudson, for turning a manuscript into a book, and last, but by no means least, Robin Taylor for liking the idea in the first place, the publications board at English Heritage for agreeing with him, and my project managers, René Rodgers and Jess Ward, for their enthusiasm, patience and when necessary professional rigour.

Thanks also to Mark Rudolph for hieroglyphic typesetting, using HieroTeX by Serge Rosmorduc, Brian Austen, Furniture History Society, and Judith Goodison for allowing the use of a photo from her article in *Furniture History* on Thomas Chippendale at Stourhead, Carol Morgan, Archivist at the Institution of Civil Engineers, Marta Leskard, Kirsten Strachan, Jonathan Hobbs, Rory Cook and Graham Wheeldon at the Science Museum, Sue Jenkins at the Bank of England Museum for providing its historical price conversion table, Keith Bonnick at the Cuming Museum for making me aware of the marmalade jar, Helen Dorey, Susan Palmer and colleagues at the Sir John Soane Museum, Lynn Miller, Museum Information Officer at the Wedgwood Museum, for a copy of her article on Egyptian influenced Wedgwood, the late Dick East, for his original copy of the London Encyclopaedia and the loan of other material, John Hamill and colleagues, especially Martin Cherry, at the United Grand Lodge of England and Library and Museum of Freemasonry, Richard Lunn, who co-authored the chapter on 'Egyptianising Architecture' in *Imhotep Today*, Brian Parsons, editor of the *Funeral Service Journal* and the 4th edition of Hugh Meller's *London Cemeteries*, for assistance with matters monumental, The Excellent Scribe, Vivien Raisman, for help with readings of hieroglyphic texts, Patricia Spencer, Chris Naunton, Roo Mitcheson, Andrew Bednarski and everyone else at the Egypt Exploration Society, Shirley Lancaster and Roger Jee at Museum Books for allowing me to use some of their images, Dr Peter Meadows at Cambridge University Library, Dr Iain Brown at the National Library of Scotland, and John Packer for assistance with Joseph Bonomi Jnr's correspondence, Dr Dilwyn Knox, Reader in Renaissance Studies at University College London for translating a passage from Piranesi's correspondence, Sue Swatridge at the Lytham Archives Centre and Andrew Walmsley for information on the Lytham Palace Cinema.

In London: the late Mrs Jean Pateman MBE and Pavel of the Friends of Highgate Cemetery. At Abney Park, Lisa Hook and colleagues, Abney Park Visitors Centre, Abney Park Cemetery Trust, and Friends of Abney Park, and Ron Kuhns, a fellow student of The Excellent Scribe, for drawing Abney Park Cemetery to my attention in the first place. Terry Oldrey and Tony Green of Thames Water for access to the Temple of Storms. Gail Collingburn, Archivist, W H Smith for assistance with information on the Stamford Street printing works. Melvyn Harrison, Chairman, The Crystal

Palace Foundation. At West Norwood Cemetery, Jillian Dudman and Colin Fenn of Friends of West Norwood Cemetery and colleagues, especially Eddie the groundsman, without whom I might have missed David Roberts' daughter. William Mitchell at Harrods, for first-hand accounts. For information on Reliance Arcade, Brixton, Fiona Price, Lambeth Archives, Alan Piper, Brixton Society, Camilla Goddard, and Lynn Pearson of the Tile Society for first alerting me to Reliance Arcade. Matthew Shaw at Brompton Cemetery, Arthur Tait and Robert Stephenson of the Friends of Brompton Cemetery, Janet Smith of the Wandsworth Historical Society and Peter Tutt and Keith Bailey for information on Alexander Gordon. For help with Putney Vale Cemetery, Janet Smith and Keith Bailey, Wandsworth Historical Society, and Bridget and colleagues at the cemetery itself. Mark De Novellis, Curator of Exhibitions and Collection at the Orleans House Gallery, London Borough of Richmond upon Thames, for access to the Kilmorey mausoleum. Stephen Lovegroves and Kathy Powers at Apsley House. Ian and Barbara Pollard for their generous help, including information on the Sainsbury's Homebase and Ramesses II project in Warwick Road, his early involvement in Harrod's Egyptian Hall, and for comments on the draft text on those locations. Katherine Griffis-Greenberg, who co-authored the chapter on 'Egyptianising Architecture' in *Imhotep Today*, including the section on Greater London House, and Eleanor van Heyningen, who was studying for an MA at the Institute of Archaeology in June 1999, and generously shared contacts for information on the Carreras and Hoover buildings. At Kensal Green Cemetery, Signe Hoffos and Henry Vivian-Neale of the Friends of Kensal Green Cemetery and colleagues, including Lynne McLaren and John the groundsman for help in locating graves. Bernard Stringer at OC&C Strategy Consultants for information on Britannia House. Tom Burke and colleagues at Westminster City Council for information on work on Cleopatra's Needle since its erection, and Cathie Bryan for information on the Needle sphinxes and Embankment benches.

Outside London: Birmingham: Steven Smythe at PTS for assistance visiting the former GEC Factory. Biddulph Grange Gardens: Paul Baker. Leeds: Helen Skilbeck, Leeds Library Service, Lynda Kitching, Friends of Beckett Street Cemetery, Peter Hirschmann and Susan Wrathmell of the Victorian Society, West Yorkshire Group, Professor Anthony North, Leeds Philosophical and Literary Society, and Geoffrey Forster, the Leeds Library. Anfield: Martin Doherty, Cemeteries Manager Liverpool City Council, Mick Macilwee of John Moores University Liverpool, Roger Hull, Liverpool Record Office, Charlie Rogan at Scottie Press, Steve at Friends of Anfield Cemetery and Janette Byers, Ronald Mummery and Peter Craig of the bootlehistory forum for information on Alexander McLennan. Sale: Lee, at the LA Fitness Centre, Margaret, at Trafford Local Studies Library and George Cogswell, for help with images of the Pyramid Cinema, and Don Hyde of the Lancashire Theatre Organs Trust. Sheffield: Hilary McAra, Sheffield General Cemetery Trust. Thurnham: John Regan, Paul Thompson (Lancashire Museums), Dr Andrew White and Stephen Sartin for assistance with the mausoleum. Warwick: James Mackay and Christine Hodgetts of the Warwick Society, Peter Wellings, Warwickshire Freemasons Information Officer, and Derek Maudlin. Aylesbury: Eric Throssle, for generously sharing the results of his research into Bonomi's architectural work, particularly correspondence held in a private archive. Canterbury: John Armitage and Peter Henderson at the King's School. Goodwood House: James Peill, Curator. Stowe: Ruth Peters and Hettie Dix. Brookwood Cemetery: Mr Guney of the London Necropolis Company and John Clarke. Boston: John Warwick, Provincial Grand Secretary, and Chris Bradley. Buscot Park: David Freeman. Sphinx Hill: The owners. Devonport: Mandi Leaves at the Ker St Social Club. Exeter: John Allan, Exeter City Council Project Manager. Kingston Lacy: Freda Gibson-Poole and Rob Gray, House and Collections Manager. Stourhead: Emily Blanshard, Collections Manager.

Index

Page numbers in **bold** refer to illustrations or captions. Buildings are indexed under places and peers are indexed by title.